Oliver Goldsmith, Christopher Smart, Samuel Jenkins Johnson, Wil Harrison

The World Displayed

Vol. 2

Oliver Goldsmith, Christopher Smart, Samuel Jenkins Johnson, Wil Harrison

The World Displayed
Vol. 2

ISBN/EAN: 9783337346218

Printed in Europe, USA, Canada, Australia, Japan

Cover: Foto ©Thomas Meinert / pixelio.de

More available books at **www.hansebooks.com**

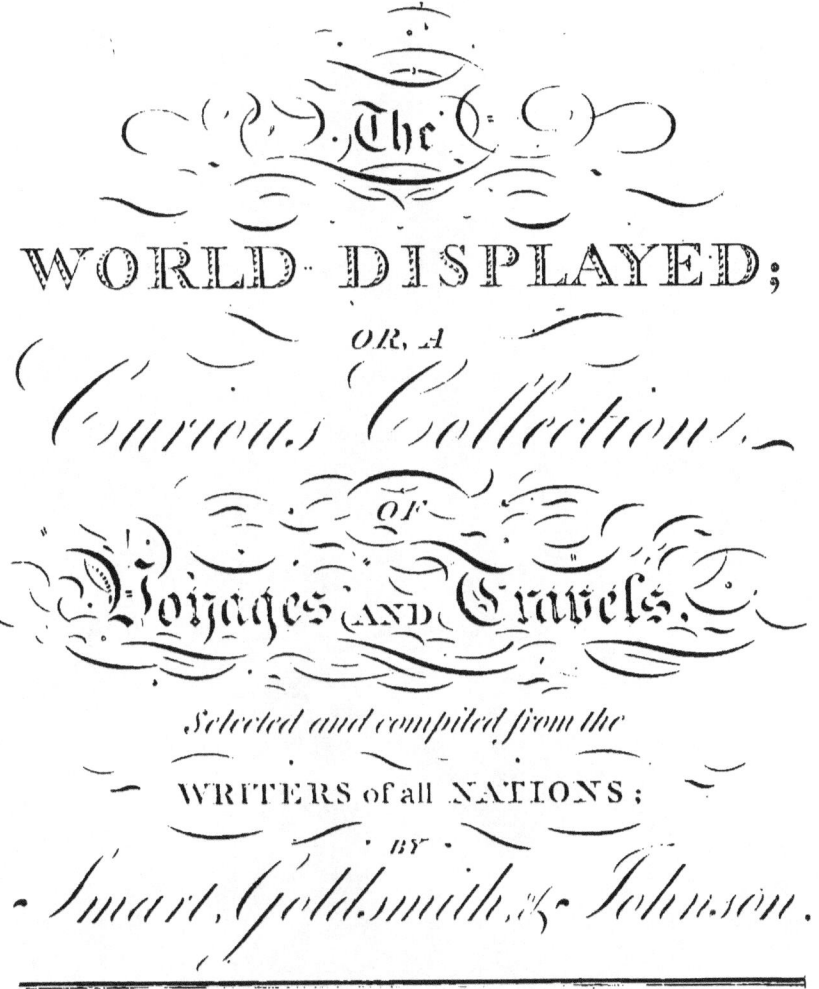

The
WORLD DISPLAYED;
OR, A
Curious Collection
OF
Voyages AND Travels.

Selected and compiled from the
WRITERS of all NATIONS;
BY
Smart, Goldsmith, & Johnson.

FIRST AMERICAN EDITION.
Corrected & Enlarged.
IN EIGHT VOLUMES.
VOL II.

Philadelphia.

Publish'd by Dobelbower, Key, and Simpson. 1795.
W. Harrison Sen.r Sculp.t

CONTENTS OF THE SECOND VOLUME.

The Settlement of Brasil, by the Portuguese, 1

Discoveries of the English in America, - 78

Discoveries and Settlements of the French in America, - - - - - - - 264

Discoveries and Settlements of the Dutch in America, - - - - - - - 302

Discoveries of the Danes in America, - 318

The Voyage of Sir Francis Drake, round the World, - - - - - - - - 321

The Voyage of Schovten and Le Maire, round the World, - - - - - 345

The Voyage of Captain William Dampier, round the World. - - - - - 375

DIRECTIONS FOR PLACING THE PLATES IN VOLUME II.

	Page
Brazilians and their houses to face	5
Admiral Lichthart, &c.	44
Ten Canoes of Indians, &c.	112
Venables attacks Jamaica,	203
Beavers building their huts,	322
Admiral Drake seizes the Silver,	332
The English coming to their boat, &c.	383

THE
SETTLEMENT OF BRASIL,
BY
THE PORTUGUESE,
AND ITS SEVERAL REVOLUTIONS.

CHAPTER I.

The difcovery of Brafil by Don Pedro Alvarez de Cabral. The fmall advantages at firft expected from it. Some account of the country, and its ancient inhabitants, and the manner in which it was firft fettled by the Portuguefe.

IN the fecond voyage of the Portuguefe to the Indies in 1500, De Cabral, after paffing the Cape de Verde iflands, ftood fo far out to fea with a view of avoiding the calms, common on the coaft of Africa, that on the 24th of April he obferved an unknown country on the weft; but the fea running high, he was obliged to fail along the coaft as far as 15 degrees fouth latitude; where finding a good haven, he gave it the name of Porto Seguro, or the Safe Port; and the country itfelf he called the Land of the Holy Ghoft; but this name was afterwards changed to that of Brasil, from its abounding with Brasil wood, which had been so called in Europe about 300 years before this country was discovered.

Cabral sent some people on shore to examine this new country, and they reporting that it was well watered, extremely fertile, full of fruit trees, and inhabited by a mild and gentle people, he resolved to suffer his men to refresh themselves on shore. On his landing he found the place exactly agreed with the description that had been given of it, and that the peaceful natives were so far from offering any insult to the Portuguese, that they received them with more kindness than they had reason to expect. As De Cabral had some condemned criminals on board, whose sentence had been changed from that of death to transportation, he left two of these fellows in the country, to learn the language, to make farther discoveries, and to acquire the best knowledge they were able, of this unknown land and its inhabitants. Being sensible that this discovery was of great importance, he resolved to lose no time in sending an account of it to the king of Portugal, and therefore immediately dispatched one of his vessels back to Lisbon, with some persons on board, on whose fidelity he could depend, together with one of the natives, in order to his being instructed in the Portuguese language. He also set up a stone cross as a monument of his having been there, and of his having taken possession of the country in behalf of the king of Portugal; which was the more necessary, as Columbus was then on his third voyage, making such discoveries as amazed all Europe.

In consequence of this advice, the king of Portugal sent several persons to make discoveries of the coast, who soon found that this was part of the continent of that new world discovered by Columbus;

upon which great disputes arose between the two crowns, about the extent and boundaries of this country discovered by the Portuguese; but it was at last settled, that from the river of Maranon to the river of Plate should be yielded to the king of Portugal.

Affairs in the beginning went on very slowly: the first Portuguese inhabitants were sufficiently sensible that the soil was fertile, the air temperate, and the country well watered; but they could report no more. Brasil appeared a pleasant, fruitful, and well situated country, capable indeed of furnishing abundance of the necessaries of life, though it was imagined to be destitute of gold and silver.

Upon these reports, the ministry did not desert the country, though they contented themselves with transporting thither from time to time those villains whose crimes brought them under the censure of the law; which not only gave the Portuguese a mean opinion of the colony, but proved an effectual method of corrupting the poor Indians.

Indeed neither these discoverers nor the court of Portugal, could from any distinct idea of the importance of so vast a country, which, according to its present boundaries, may be reckoned 2000 miles from north to south, and 1000 from east to west; though the Portuguese even to this time have scarce any where penetrated 500 miles. As the northern parts of the country lie near the equator, they are subject to great rains and variable winds, particularly about the months of March and September, when they are frequently disturbed with hurricanes and tempests, which lay the country under water.

The middle part of Brasil from $5°$. of south latitude to the tropic, has the winds and seasons directly the reverse of those in other parts of the world, within the same latitudes; for in them the dry season comes on when the sun advances to the northward, and the wet season begins when the sun returns to the southward; but here the wet season begins in April, when the south-east wind sets in, with violent tornadoes, thunder and lightning; and in September, when the wind shifts to east-north-east, it brings with it a clear sky and fair weather. There is no country between the tropics where the heats are more tolerable, or the air more healthful, it being constantly refreshed with breezes from the sea, and cooled by the lakes and rivers which annually overflow their banks; and in the inland part of the country, the winds from the mountains are still cooler than those that blow from the ocean.

That part of Brasil which lies more to the south, and without the tropic of Capricorn, is in all respects one of the finest countries in the known world; but here the Portuguese dominions are narrow, they being confined by the Spanish territories and the river Plate.

The Indians differ very little in stature or complexion from the Portuguese themselves; but much exceed them in strength and vigour. Some lived in villages, and others moved about according to their humours. These villages consisted only of three or four very large houses; in each of which a whole family or tribe lived together, under the authority of the eldest parent. They procured subsistence by fowling and fishing, and made up the rest of their diet with the fruits of the earth; but though they had no luxurious plenty, yet, in so fertile a country, they were in no great danger of want. They were, however, continually at war with each other; but for what cause is not easily determined, unless we should admit what some old writers affirm, that they made these wars

The Brasilians & their Houses

chiefly that they might kill and eat each other, esteeming human flesh the greatest dainty. But perhaps the testimony of those, who own themselves guilty of extirpating thousands of these poor creatures, to whom they could have no quarrel worthy of rational beings, ought not to be of much weight; since men are apt to calumniate and misrepresent those they have injured; as if by aggravating their vices, they could justify, or at least palliate, their own. And besides, as none of the late travellers observe any sign of their ever being cannibals, they ought to be vindicated from so cruel an aspersion.

The Portuguese and Dutch writers give the name of Tapuyers to the native inhabitants of the north part of Brasil, and that of Tupinambies or Tupanamboys to those who dwell in the south of Brasil; but divide these again into several petty nations, who speak different languages, though their manners and customs are much the same.

The Tapuyers are pretty tall, and as they live almost under the equator, are of a dark copper colour, their hair which is black, hanging over their shoulders; but they have no beards nor hair on any part of their bodies, and go naked, the men only inclosing their nudities in a case, and the women concealing theirs with leaves; the men also wear a cap or coronet of feathers. Their ornaments are glittering stones, hanging to their lips and nostrils, and bracelets of feathers upon their arms; some of them paint their bodies of various colours; while others rubbing themselves with gums, stick beautiful feathers upon their skins, which at a distance make them look more like fowls than human creatures.

The Tupinambies who inhabit the south of Brasil, are of a moderate stature, and not of so dark a complexion as their northern neighbours, who live nearer the line. They are indeed neither of them so dark as the Africans in the same latitude, for there were no negroes in America, till they were transported thither by the Portuguese and Spaniards. The Tupinambies, however, resemble the Africans in their flat noses, which being esteemed a beauty, are made so by art in their infancy. They have also black lank hair upon their heads; but, like the Tapuyers, have no hair on their bodies and faces, and, like them, paint their bodies.

The general food of the Brasilians is the cassavi or mandioka root dried to powder, of which they make cakes like our sea-biscuits. This flour they also carry with them on journeys, and it being infused in water, serves them both as meat and drink; they do not appear to have had any corn till the Europeans carried it thither. They also feed on other roots, fruit and herbs; on wild-fowl, the venison they take in hunting, and on fish, and with every thing eat a great deal of pepper. They generally drink spring-water, of which they are said to have the best and the greatest variety in the world; yet they have other kinds of liquors made of the fruits pressed and infused, or of honey, with which they sometimes get very drunk, sitting whole days and nights over their cups.

Before the arrival of the Portuguese, they were masters of the art of spinning, weaving, and building their houses, and of forming their arms, which consisted of bows, arrows, lances and darts; and they had some knowledge of the virtues of several herbs and drugs, which they frequently administered with success to the sick.

Hunting, fowling and fishing were then rather their business than amusement, these being absolutely necessary for the support of their families, in a country where they had no tame cattle or corn;

drinking, dancing and singing were more properly their diversions, which they practised on their days of rejoicing for a victory, or on the birth of their children. They are at present great smokers and take the strongest tobacco; their pipes are a hollow reed or cane, and the bowl is a large nutshell that almost holds an handful of tobacco.

In short, they are a tractable and ingenious people, ready to learn any art or science the Portuguese will teach them, and taking nothing so kindly of the priests as the instructing of their children; whence the Jesuits have made many converts; and those who live under the Portuguese, generally conform to their customs in eating, drinking, and cloathing. They are but little inclined to labour, from their not being infected with avirice: for their desires are but few, and those easily gratified. Their greatest vice is their thirst of revenge.

To return to the steps by which the Portuguese settlements in Brasil became at length so considerable.—The crown had at first recourse to the making extensive grants to such as were inclined to settle there, or had the power of sending others; whence some of the richest and most powerful of the nobility had districts given them equal in extent to Portugal itself. This was at first attended with little inconvenience, since the king might without expence, give to others what he never actually possessed. This step was the more necessary, as the whole attention both of the ministers and nobility was taken up with the East-Indies, where the latter found means to repair their fortunes by obtaining governments, by which they soon acquired vast estates; while those who were contented to try their fortunes in this new colony, found that the natives were resolved not to bear the yoke of slavery, and grew desperate at every attempt to bring them into subjection.

The fertility of the country, however, made some amends for these inconveniencies, by drawing abundance of people from other parts of America to settle there, where they erected a new kind of government, dictated by necessity, in which every master of a family was both a planter and a soldier. He laid out as much land as himself and his family could cultivate, and daily performed his military exercises to enable himself to defend his property; and hence every district had the title of captainship; which they still retain, though the state of affairs is absolutely changed.

By this means the colony grew apace, and in fifty years time spread over a large tract of country, and erected many good towns, the principal of which were Tamacara, Fernambuca, Ilheos, Porto Segura, and St. Vincent, each of which was surrounded by a populous and well cultivated territory.

The flourishing state of Brasil soon began to awaken the attention of the court; king John III. became concerned at the grants made by his predecessors, and therefore in the year 1549, ungenerously revoked all those made to the original proprietors. The same year he made Thomas de Sousa governor-general of Brasil, who setting sail with a fleet of six men of war, carried with him many officers, civil and military, with a considerable body of soldiers, and six fathers of the new order of Jesuits, who were to convert the Indians. He had also a new plan of power adjusted according to the views of the court, and was directed to build a new town in the bay of All Saints.

De Sousa, soon after his arrival at Brasil, began to enter upon the execution of what he was ordered to perform. He made war upon the natives, built the town of St. Salvador, and erected monasteries for the Jesuits.

What De Sauſa could not finiſh, was completed by Edward Acoſto, his ſucceſſor, in whoſe time the number of towns and of the inhabitants was doubled; he was alſo obliged to ſtrengthen the towns, by erecting better fortifications than thoſe with which they had been hitherto ſurrounded. He therefore demoliſhed the old fortifications, which were of earth, and raiſing others of brick and ſtone, furniſhed them with artillery, the neceſſity of which was ſoon juſtified by experience.

CHAPTER II.

Attempts made by the French to ſettle a colony in Braſil by the Sieur de Villegagnon, capt. Riffaut, and M. Rivardier, without ſucceſs.

At this time the affairs of France being in the greateſt confuſion, and the diſputes between thoſe of the church of Rome and the Calviniſts being carried to the utmoſt height, many of the moſt active and induſtrious people were deſirous of leaving their native ſoil, and ſeeking an eaſier and more contented ſtate in diſtant climates. Among theſe was Nicholas Durant, lord of Villegagnon, knight of Malta, and vice-admiral of Britany, who being treated ill at Nantz, ſuddenly reſolved to leave the kingdom, and carry a colony into ſome diſtant part of the world, and hearing ſome account of Braſil, he drew up a ſcheme for fixing a ſettlement in that country. This he preſented to Gaſpar de Coligny, admiral of France, deſiring his aſſiſtance towards fitting out a ſquadron for that purpoſe.

The admiral was diſtinguiſhed for his abilities and virtues, and, being a very zealous proteſtant, readily promiſed to give him all the encouragement he could deſire, in hopes of ſettling a proteſtant colony; that, in caſe the affairs of his friends ſhould be totally ruined in France, they might have a place to which they might retire out of the reach of their enemies. De Villegagnon, readily undertaking to put this in execution, the admiral made ſuch a repreſentation of the affair to king Henry II. that he had leave to fit out three large veſſels, with a ſufficient number of ſeamen and adventurers on board; and in May 1555, this ſmall ſquadron ſailed from Havre de Grace for Braſil, where, after a tedious and troubleſome voyage they arrived in November.

This colony landed upon a rock, which they found uninhabitable; but marching farther within land, fixed upon a very commodious ſpot of ground almoſt under the tropic of Capricorn, where they erected a convenient fortreſs for their ſecurity both againſt the natives and the Portugueſe, which they called fort Coligny. From this place the Sieur de Villegagnon ſent the admiral a long account of his proceedings and ſituation; deſcribed the country and its inhabitants, and obſerved that it was extremely practicable to make that both a uſeful and thriving colony; but remarked that ſuch as were ſent to him muſt not expect the delicacies of Europe, that their bread was made of a certain root ground to powder, that they had no wine, much fiſh, and ſome veniſon; and that thoſe who could live contentedly upon ſuch proviſions, might find a ſecure retreat at his fort in Braſil.

This letter the admiral communicated to the famous reformer John Calvin of Geneva, who prevailed on a dozen zealous proteſtants of that city, to engage in the deſign of improving this new ſettlement. Du Pont, a man of fenfe, with a good character, was put at the head of this affair, and with him were joined two minifters, Peter Richer who had been formerly a Carmelite, and William Chartier; thefe fetting out together from Geneva, waited upon the admiral at Chatillon, who gave them a kind reception; and by his affiftance, joined to their own intereft, they foon got together 300 men, who embarked at Honfleur on board three veffels, in November 1556, and arrived at fort Coligny on the 7th of March 1557, where they werereceived with great joy.

Things, however, did not long continue in this fituation; for the Sieur de Villegagnon, who had pretended to be a rigid calvinift, foon fhewed, that he had only worn a mafk. This produced a quarrel between him and the minifter Richer, in which the difputes rofe fo high, that he drove the latter and all his adherents out of the colony; upon whch they failed up the Rio Janeiro, and eftablifhed themfelves upon its banks; where having ftaid about eight months, they returned to France, where they reprefented the Sieur de Villegagnon, in the blackeft colours, as an hyprocrite and an impoftor: at which the admiral, finding that this affair was not likely to be of any advantage to the proteftant caufe, refolved to give himfelf no farther concern about it.

The Sieur de Villegagnon being thus abandoned, took the beft meafures he could for the fecurity of the colony in his abfence, and then returned to France; where he endeavoured to raife a belief of his being a zealous calvinift, and publifhed an apology for his own conduct, in which he painted the minifters in as bad a light as they had placed him; but findnig this produced no good, he retired to a commandery of his own order, and fpent the remainder of his days in writing againft the protestants. In the mean time the Portuguese laid hold of this opportunity to rid themselves of their new neighbours; and the next year Emanuel Sa, governor of Brasil, cut off the French that were left behind, and demolished their fort.

It is observable, that during the short time the French were possessed of this settlement, they made a greater progress in trade, and established a more friendly correspondence with the natives, than the Portuguese had been able to do in about fifty years. This indeed was owing to a very odd accident. About twenty years before, a ship from Normandy having been lost upon that coast, some of the men got un shore, where being well received by the natives they married among them, and exactly conformed to their manners, and these men were of great service to the colony.

The Portuguese now for some time quietly enjoyed their settlements, till at length one captain Riffaut, who had been cruizing on the Spaniards, touched at the island of Maragnan, on the coast of Brasil, contracted so great an intimacy with the Indian chief of the island, that he invited him to bring a sufficient number of his countrymen to fix a settlement there, promising to give him all the assistance in his power. This offer the French captain readily embraced, and at his return to France, found means, by his credit and interest, to equip three ships so effectually, that there was great reason to expect extraordinary success; but his men mutinying before he reached the island, and the largest of his ships running upon the coast as soon as he got to it, by which means she was lost, he was obliged to return to France; but some of his people, among whom was M. de Vaux, chose to stay with the natives, who made them extremely welcome: This young gentleman was remarkably brisk and active; he liked the climate, and continued there some time. His behaviour to the Brasilians was very engaging, and he in many respects proved so useful to them, that they made the same applications to him, as the Indian chief had done to captain Riffaut, which at last engaged him to think seriously upon the subject, and to return home by the first opportunity.

On M. de Vaux's arriving in France, he applied to king Henry IV. to whom he represented the vast advantages that would flow from such an establishment; upon which that prince who had the good of his subjects at heart, and was unwilling to place too great a confidence on the credit of a young adventurer, sent a small vessel, under the command of M. Rivardier, a person of great merit, upon whose report he could depend, who took M. de Vaux with him, and after remaining six months in Brasil, returned to France, from whence he made several voyages back, before the government could come to any resolution about settling a colony. Preparations were, however, at length actually made for sending a strong squadron thither, when a stop was put to them by the murder of Henry IV. But M. Rivardier was so fond of the place, and so fully persuaded that a settlement there would immediately turn to account, that he embarked his whole private fortune, and engaged several of his friends to do so too; by which means he equipt three stout vessels, and engaged about 300 men to go to Brasil, with whom he embarked at Cancale, on the coast of Britany, and in July following arrived at the island of Maragnan.

He there erected a fortress on the summit of a hill near the best port in the island, between two fine rivers that washed both sides of the mountain, and ran from thence into the sea. Upon the bastions of this fort he mounted twenty-two pieces of cannon; and every thing seemed to promise all the success that could be desired, when, about two years after their first arrival, a strong squadron, sent by Don Jerom de Albuquerque, the Portuguese governor of Brasil, appearing before the bay, soon forced them to surrender, and, according to his orders, the place was instantly demolished; which cured the French of all farther thoughts of settling in that country.

CHAPTER III.

The Dutch make themselves masters of Brasil; but are driven out by the united force of Spain and Portugal. The Dutch, however, being resolved to make a fresh attempt, send a large fleet under the command of Admiral Lank, with a body of land forces commanded by General Wardenbourgh. The latter takes the city of Olinda, and all the coasts to the south; while Admiral Lank takes an island called the Sandy Receif. Admiral Pater being afterwards sent from Holland with a large fleet, the Dutch oblige the Portuguese to raise the siege of Olinda; and this brave admiral, with only six ships, engages the Portuguese fleet of forty-five, and comes off with great honour.

IN the year 1581, the crown of Portugal devolving on the head of Philip the II. king of Spain, he not only became possessed of all the rich countries in America discovered by the Spaniards, but of Brasil, and all the Portuguese settlements in the East-Indies. These he left to his successors, together with the war he had carried on against the Seven United Provinces, who had shaken off their dependence on the crown of Spain, and formed themselves into a Republic, which, by attending to trade, made the most rapid progress. This new Republic, by forming an Eaſt-India company obtained ſuch prodigious advantage, that, in 1624, they were induced to ſet up alſo a Weſt-India company, which from its firſt inſtitution proved fatal to the Portugueſe.

The Dutch being now ſenſible of the ſtate of Braſil, and the ſmall reſiſtance they were like to meet with in caſe they made a deſcent on the coaſt, which was no leſs than 1200 leagues in extent, equipped a ſquadron under the command of James Wilikens, which entering the bay of All Saints, the Portugueſe were ſo frightened, that, inſtead of providing for their defence, they immediately uſed all poſſible methods to carry off and ſecure their effects.

The Dutch obſerving the conſternation into which they had thrown the enemy, inſtantly landed, and without much difficulty made themſelves maſters of St. Salvador, the capital of Braſil. Don Diego de Mendoza, the Portugueſe governor, not having the courage to defend the place, fled; but Michael Texeira, the archbiſhop, who was of one of the beſt families in Portugal, notwithſtanding his being in years, ſummoned all the clergy and monks about him, and repreſenting the neceſſity they were under of laying aſide their clerical capacities, prevailed on them to take up arms; and though deſerted by the governor, the ſoldiers and the inhabitants, they for ſome time made a very gallant defence, and at laſt retreated to a neighbouring town; where, after acting the part of ſoldiers, they turned pioneers, and, under the conduct of the archbiſhop, fortified the place, and gave the enemy as much trouble as if they had been the moſt regular troops in the world.

By the taking of this town, the Dutch not only acquired an immenſe plunder, but became maſters of the largeſt and beſt peopled diſtrict in the whole country, and seemed in a fair way of making, in a short time, a complete conquest of the whole colony; which they would probably have done, had it not been for the heroic archbishop, who assumed the title of captain general, an office which he said came to him from Heaven, in the legible characters of public necessity.

The news of this misfortune no sooner reached Portugal, than it threw both the city of Lisbon and the whole kingdom into confusion, which was increased by the suspicions of the nobility, that the Spanish ministry were not much displeased at this event, as it would lessen the wealth and power of the grandees of Portugal, who had the greatest part of their estates in Brasil. However, king Philip IV. in whose reign this happened, shewed that these suspicions were but ill founded. He immediately sent orders to Portugal to equip a fleet for the recovery of St. Salvador, and at the same time wrote a letter with his own hand to the nobility, desiring their assistance on this occasion.

This revived the spirits of the nation, and the Portuguese lords exerted themselves so effectually, that in three months time they had a fleet of twenty-six sail ready to put to sea; but though the Spaniards did not make equal dispatch, yet, in February 1626, their fleet joined that of Portugal, and they set sail, under the command of Don Frederic de Toledo Osorio, marquis of Valduesa, with 1500 men on board.

In the mean time, the Dutch being in possession of St. Salvador and the adjacent country, began very rashly to extend themselves on every side, either from contempt of the Portuguese, or an extravagant thirst of plunder. The heroic archbishop, however, soon convinced them of their mistake: he had now assembled 1500 men, and with these not only cut off most of their parties, but at last forcing them to take shelter in the town, blocked them up, and reduced them to great distress; which he had no sooner done, than he resigned the command first to Nunez Marino, and afterwards to Don Francis de Mauro, declaring that his own commission expired with that necessity, which had forced him to take it up.

Things were in this situation, when the united fleets of Spain and Portugal arrived in the bay of All Saints. Don Emanuel de Menessez immediately landed 4000 men, and joined the army before St. Salvador. The Dutch governor was, however, resolved to defend it to the last extremity; but the garrison mutinying, forced him to surrender on the 20th of April; when the Spanish and Portuguese commanders, supposing that the war was at an end, and that the Dutch, like the French, would be afraid of making any new attempts upon Brasil, returned home with the fleets in triumph.

They were however greatly mistaken, for the rich plunder of St. Salvador, which had been brought by admiral Wiliken's into Holland, made the Dutch desirous of engaging in other expeditions of the same kind, and encouraged the West-India company to think of making another expedition. They accordingly fitted out a strong fleet of 46 men of war, commanded by admiral Lonk, with a considerable body of land forces on board, under gen. Wardenbourg, which setting sail, arrived in sight of Fernambuca on the 3d of February 1630, and gen. Wardenbourg landing with near 3000 men on the 15th of the same month, marched directly towards the city of Olinda, which he found covered by three forts, with a numerous garrison in each; he however attacked and carried them all, but not without a vigorous resistance; and this success so frightened the inhabitants of the city, that they immediately surrendered, though the natives, who had turned Chriftians, fhewed great fpirit, and behaved on this. and on every other occafion, with the utmoft courage and fidelity.

While general Wardenburg was thus employed on fhore, Admiral Lonk was no lefs active by fea; and as the Portuguefe had no confiderable naval force to oppofe him, he, in a very fhort time, reduced all the coaft to the fouth of Olinda, fecuring and fortifying every place that fell into his hands; it being refolved, to obtain fuch a footing in the country, as would enable the Dutch to keep their ground againft the whole force of Portugal.

With this view Admiral Lonk refolved at all events, to make himfelf mafter of a very ftrong poft, that feemed the fitteft for his purpofe, and of which it is neceffary that we fhould give our readers fome account.

The whole coaft of Brafil is bordered by a thick and flat ridge of rocks, which is in fome places twenty, and in others thirty yards broad; and were it not for feveral breaks and paffages in this rocky inclofure, it would be impoffible to approach the fhore. In particular, there is a very large paffage towards the north of Olinda; but the ridge of rocks appears again almoft before the city, and the inhabitants pafs to it in boats at high water. This part of the ridge is called by the Portuguefe Reciffo, and by the Dutch the Receif. On the north point is a very narrow open paffage for the fhips to approach the fhore; and between this ridge of rocks and the continent, is a fandy ifland about a league in length called the Sandy Recief Upon this ifland, which is in 8° 26 fouth latitude, was a good caftle, called Fort St. George, well provided with artillery, and efteemed impregnable, and of this the Dutch admiral made himfelf mafter, when having ftrengthened the Stony Receif, he made this the chief feat of commerce, and afterwards it became one of the moſt confiderable places in Braſil.

The Portugueſe and Spaniards were exceſſively alarmed at the news of this ſecond attempt upon Braſil, and at the Dutch having conquered the Captainſhip of Fernambuca; they therefore reſolved to ſend thither immediately a force ſufficient to drive them out, and effectually to ſecure the country to themſelves for the future; but the diſaffection of the Portugueſe to the Spaniſh government, divided and perplexed their meaſures ſo, that they were a long time in fitting out a fleet; during which the Dutch were employed in fortifying themſelves, in extending their conqueſts, and in taking all the neceſſary precautions for their defence; wherein they proceeded with the utmoſt induſtry and vigilance.

The Dutch fleet no ſooner returned from Braſil, than admiral Pater was ſent thither with a much ſtronger force, in order to make a conqueſt of the whole country. He arrived in ſight of the coaſt of Fernambuca on the 1ſt of May 1631, where finding the city of Olinda cloſely blocked up by a numerous army, commanded by Albuquerque, the famous Portugueſe general, who had landed 400 men under the command of an experienced officer, to take a view of the enemy's works, in order to form a juſt judgment of the beſt manner of beginning the attack; but the Dutch garriſon ſeeing his fleet come to an anchor, and the troops landed, made ſo vigorous a ſally on the beſiegers, as forced them to retire from before the city with conſiderable loſs. Admiral Pater now enabled his countrymen to extend their conqueſts very conſiderably, particularly towards the ſouth, intending to attack the city of St. Salvador both by ſea and land; but was prevented by his receiving intelligence that the Spaniards and Portugueſe had ſent a ſtrong fleet, which was actually at fea, in order to undertake the relief of Brafil.

This fleet confifted of about thirty ſhips, commanded by admiral D'Oquendo, who failed from Spain in a very indifferent condition: but at the Canaries was joined by fifteen more, and near the Cape de Verd iſlands received ſuch an acceſſion of force, as made D'Oquendo's fleet confiſt of fifty-four large ſhips. The Dutch admiral had but fixteen, but being jealous of the honour of his country, boldly refolved to fight under this amazing difadvantage, and was even determined to meet the enemy, which he accordingly did in 6°, ſouth latitude: but as ſoon as they appeared in fight, and the Dutch fleet ſaw how unequal the difpute was like to prove, ten of the captains bore away, and left the admiral only fix ſhips to fight an enemy that had almoſt ten times his number; and though he had two flags under him, theſe, to their immortal honour, were two of thoſe who had joined him, ſo that there were three admirals to fix ſhips. The battle was long and bloody, for many of the Portugueſe ſhips were funk; and it is evident, that if the other ten ſhips had ſtaid, victory would have declared for the Dutch; but at laſt admiral Thys in the Prince William was funk, and foon after, a ball unhappily falling into the Dutch admiral's powder room, the ſhip was blown up, and that brave man loſt. Upon this the four Dutch ſhips that remained, retired; but did it with ſuch courage and addreſs, that they not only fafely arrived at Olinda, but carried off a Portugueſe man of war they had taken, and indeed, it may be fafely affirmed, there never was a more glorious action.

When admiral D'Oquendo arrived on the coaſt, he was fatisfied with fending refreſhments and reinforcements to the army under Albuquerque, but made no attempt againſt the city of Olinda; the great lofs he had fuffered in the battle, which amounted in the whole to no lefs than thirteen fail taken and funk, made him leave things in a ftate little better than that in which he found them. He therefore, after repairing his fhips, fet fail for Lifbon, in the month of October, but in his paffage had the misfortune to meet with four Dutch men of war well manned, who bravely refolved to attack him, though he had ftill forty fail, and moft of them large fhips.

In this engagement D'Oquendo loft the captain of his own fhip, with twenty-two other captains; his vice-admiral, three men of war, two frigates, and about 700 private men; after which he returned home, with the wretched remains of his unfortunate fleet; but the blame fell entirely upon the minifters, who, in fpite of his remonftrances, had obliged him to fail with fhips half equipped and half manned.

As this misfortune could not be remedied, the minifters expreffed their willingnefs to do all in their power in order to repair it, and therefore gave orders for providing a larger fleet, better equipped and manned, to fail under the command of Don Frederic de Toledo, who had acquired great reputation. But notwithftanding all their endeavours nothing could be done that feafon, and therefore it was deferred to the next fpring; when it was refolved to fend fuch a force, as fhould put an end to the war at once; but as it is much eafier to lay fine fchemes in the cabinet, than to carry them into execution, fo, notwithftanding this celebrated admiral actually proceeded on his voyage with a very large fleet, every way well provided, he returned to Portugal without doing any thing of importance.

CHAPTER IV.

The furprifing fuccefs of the Dutch againft the united forces of Spain and Portugal, induces the directors of the Weft-India company to fend count Maurice of Naffau, as governor of Brafil, who, by his wife conduct, and prudent adminiftration, fecures and fettles the beft part of the country.

MEAN while the Dutch taking advantage of thefe delays, made a furprifing progrefs, and, in the fpace of feven years, reduced under their dominions the captainfhips of Fernambuca; Tamaraca, Paraiba and Rio Grande. In fhort, they had fuch aftonifhing fuccefs againft the Spaniards in this and other parts of America, that from the time of their Weft-India company's being erected, in 1624, to the year 1637, they deftroyed and took from them in money and merchandize, to the value of forty-five millions of florins, or four millions and a half fterling; and of 800 fhips fitted out againft them by the crown of Spain, they deftroyed or took 547.

By this fuccefs the directors of the Weft India company were induced to put themfelves upon a level with the Eaft India company, and were refolved to place at the head of their affairs, a perfon whofe credit and power would add ftrength to their own. With this view they pitched upon count John Maurice of Naffau, a near relation to the Prince of Orange, who had diftinguifhed himfelf in the fervice of the States with great applaufe.

This nobleman, readily accepting the propofal, was declared governor of Brafil and South-America; and that he might enter upon his office in a manner fuitable to his quality and character, the company refolved to fit out a fleet of thirty-two large fhips, with 2700 land forces; but the count being impatient to be gone, failed before they were ready, on the 25th of October 1636, with only four fhips, and 350 foldiers on board. With this fmall fquadron he arrived on the coaft of Brafil, on the 23d of January 1637, with Adrian Vander Duffen, who had joined him near the ifland of Madeira, and was foon followed by other captains.

Count Maurice took the field with two confiderable bodies of troops, one of which confifted of 300 men; with thefe he refolved to attack the Portuguefe army; and the other of 600 was to be employed in various expeditions, in order to divide and diftract the enemy, who had a large body of forces in the field, under the command of the count de Benjola, an officer of great bravery and experience, who affembled the bulk of his army at Porto Cavallo. Thither count Maurice marched, and after a very obftinate refiftance, the Portuguefe were defeated, and at length forced in their camp, notwithftanding its being ftrongly intrenched. The count de Benjola then retired with the remains of his troops, under the cannon of the citadel of Povacaon, from whence he retreated on the approach of the Dutch, who befieged and took that fortrefs, in which was a garrifon of 600 men.

Count Maurice next took the town of Openeda on the river St. Francis; built a citadel there, and another at the mouth of the river, by which he effectually covered his new conqueft. Then returning to Olinda, he fettled the civil and military government; and fitted out two fleets; one under the command of admiral Lichchart, who had orders to attack the fouth coaft of Brafil; and the other commanded by commodore Hanſkins, who was deſtined to a ſervice of ſtill greater importance, which was fixing themſelves on the oppoſite ſhore of Africa. For this purpoſe it was reſolved to attack the caſtle of St. George de la Mina on the coaſt of Guinea, in the poſſeſſion of the Portugueſe; for the Dutch having a ſtrong ſettlement in that neighbourhood, the governor ſent to adviſe count Maurice, that this was the proper time for carrying this important project into execution. Commodore Hanſkins joined the Dutch governor on the 25th of July, when attacking the caſtle, which was one of the ſtrongeſt in that part of the world, they, after a regular ſiege, obliged the Portugueſe to ſurrender. After this ſucceſs, commodore Hanſkins returned to Olinda, where he was received by count Maurice with all the marks of honour and reſpect, that the performance of ſo important a ſervice deſerved.

The campaign in 1638 was equally glorious for the Dutch, for the count de Banjola having aſſembled a numerous army to defend the captainſhip of Segerippa, count Maurice attacked and defeated him, took the capital, and reduced the whole province. This great ſucceſs induced the natives of Siarra, one of the northern captainſhips, to declare for the Dutch, and to offer, upon the promiſe of being reſtored to the enjoyment of their freedom, to aſſiſt them againſt the Portugueſe, when a body of troops being ſent to join them, they reduced that whole diſtrict.

Count Maurice now reſolved to attack St. Salvador in the bay of All Saints, which was conſidered as the capital of all Braſil: for this purpoſe he embarked all the troops he could aſſemble at Olinda, and landed them in the bay of All Saints, in hopes of ſurpriſing the Portugueſe. The count de Banjola, who was in the neighbourhood with a small body of regular troops, immediately threw himself into the place, though the governor was his avowed enemy, and count Maurice expected that the differences which subsisted between them, would facilitate his taking the city. Indeed, the Portuguese governor at first disputed the command with the count de Banjola; but that nobleman told him, that their quarrels would only serve to ruin them; whereas, if they agreed, each of them might become as great as he could wish. To which the governor answered, " Sir, I perceive you are " a wiser man than I, and nobody shall obey your " orders more punctually."

Count Maurice without much resistance made himself master of the strong fort of Albert, of that of St. Bartholomew, and the famous castle of St. Philip. Encouraged by this success he erected two batteries, in order to attack fort Roses, which covered the city on one side, and a horn-work, that was its principal strength on the other. Between these lay a piece of ground, covered with shrubs and bushes, where count de Banjola advised the governor to post himself with 400 men, while he made a sally. This scheme had the desired effect, for the Dutch, after an obstinate dispute, endeavouring to retire through that piece of ground, were attacked in their rear, and lost four officers of distinction, their principal engineer, and 300 of their best men; upon which count Maurice abandoned the castle he had taken, and raised the siege with some precipitation.

On count Maurice's return from this fruitless expedition, he with the utmost diligence applied himself to the establishment of good order and perfect discipline in all parts of his government; fortifying the frontier places, reviewing his troops in person, appointing experienced officers to command them, and giving the utmost encouragement to such of the natives as shewed an inclination to assist him, or to live peaceably under the protection of the Dutch; by which means he prevented the enemy from taking advantage of their late success.

Mean while the Spanish government having received an exact account of the state of affairs of Brasil, resolved to send a fleet and army sufficient to put an end to the war at once, by obliging the Dutch to abandon all their conquests. This fleet consisted of twenty six galleons double manned, twenty large men of war, and 5000 regular troops, under the command of Don Fernandez count de las Torres, who set sail in the autumn of 1639, and received considerable reinforcements in his passage; but having the misfortune to be detained by calms on the coast of Africa, the plague broke out in his crouded ships, and swept away above 3000 men, before he reached All Saints Bay; and the remainder of his troops were in so bad a condition, that he was obliged to put them into quarters of refreshment; while the Dutch were waiting with great impatience for the succours which soon after arrived from Holland.

The count de las Torres, however, put to sea in January 1640, with a fleet of ninety-three sail great and small, with 12,000 men on board: While count Maurice assembled forty-one men of war, and waited for the Portuguese within four miles of the port of Olinda This last fleet was commanded, under his excellency, by William Leos, a Dutch admiral of great bravery. On the 12th of the same month, the fleets met and engaged near the island of Tamaraca, and fought from one in the afternoon till it was night. In this engagement the Dutch lost their brave admiral Leos, but only three other men. The next day he was replaced by James Huyghens, who engaging the Spanish fleet a second time, obtained great advantages. The following day he attacked them a third time with ſtill greater ſucceſs, on the coaſt of Paraib, but the greateſt victory was on the fourth day, when the Portugueſe ſuffered exceſſively, and were at laſt driven upon the ſhoals on the coaſt, where many periſhed by ſhipwreck, and more by hunger and thirſt. Thoſe who eſcaped endeavoured to return to Spain; but great diſputes ariſing among the commanders, they ſeparated; by which means only two men of war and four galleons arrived ſafe in the ports of Spain, and even theſe with much difficulty eſcaped a Dutch fleet, that was ſteering for Braſil.

Mean while the Portugueſe being informed that count Maurice had embarked his whole ſtrength on board his fleet, fell upon the Dutch ſettlements and took ſeveral places; but a check was ſoon put to them by Hanſkins at the head of a body of planters; and ſoon after admiral Lichthart and commodore Cornelius Jol, arriving with great reinforcements from Holland, the former was immediately ſent by count Maurice into the Bay of All Saints, where he deſtroyed the country with the utmoſt barbarity, while commodore Jol acted the ſame part in the country near the river St. Lawrence.

The count de Montalvan, the Portugueſe viceroy of Braſil, immediately ſent deputies to repreſent the cruelty of this behaviour, and to deſire that the proceedings of war might be regulated, in order to prevent for the future ſuch horrid ſcenes of murder and devaſtation. As count Maurice had with reluctance given theſe orders, agreeably to the company's inſtructions, he very gladly embraced this opportunity of giving way to his own inclinations, and offered to ſend commiſſaries immediately to St. Salvador, to ſettle a provincial treaty with the viceroy: but the departure of these deputies was stopped by the arrival of two gentlemen of diſtinction, from the count de Montalvan, who informed count Maurice of the amazing revolution that had happened in Portugal, which would probably have a great effect on the ſtate of affairs, as the war in Braſil had not hitherto been carried on by the Dutch againſt the Portugueſe nation, but againſt the Portugueſe as ſubjects of Spain.

This revolution, which was one of the moſt ſudden and ſuccefsful in the world, happened in December 1640; when John duke of Braganza, ſeated himſelf on the throne of his anceſtors, and took the title of John IV. by which means he became poſſeſſed of the whole dominions of Portugal, except the little town of Ceuta in Africa. Count Maurice ſoon receiving an exact relation of the whole affair, and foreſeeing that it would be attended either with a peace or truce, between the ſtates-general and the new king, reſolved to exert himſelf with the utmoſt expedition; he therefore made himſelf entirely maſter of the captainſhip of Segerippa, which had been recovered by the Portugueſe; reduced the iſland of Laonda on the coaſt of Congo, and that of St. Thomas, which lies directly under the equinoctial; and in purſuance of his inſtructions which repreſented the captainſhip of Maragnan as a healthy country, abounding with ſugar, cotton, tobacco, ginger, and other valuable commodities, he diſpatched admiral Lichthart and commodore Hanſkins, with ſix men of war and ſix frigates, with which they ſoon reduced the iſland of Maragnan and the town of St. Lewis, whereupon the reſt of the diſtricts ſubmitted without reſiſtance; ſo that at the end of the year 1641, the Dutch were in poſſeſſion of ſeven of the fourteen captainſhips into which Braſil was divided.

King John the IV. soon sent an ambassador to the Hague to represent to the states general, the reasonableness of owning his title, and the advantages they should mutually receive from keeping up a good correspondence. The Dutch readily owned his title; but thinking themselves gainers by the war, and too strong for Portugal unsupported by Spain, they deferred as long as possible the conclusion of the treaty. However, on the 13th of June, 1641, they signed a league offensive and defensive with that crown, in relation to the dominions of both states in Europe, and a truce for ten years in the East and West-Indies. However, on complaints being afterwards made, that several places were taken from the Portuguese, after the publication of the truce, they refused to part with some of these; and though orders were given for delivering up others, these orders were drawn up in such a manner, that most of the Dutch governors refused to comply with them.

Upon these unjustifiable proceedings, the Portuguese viceroy, and the rest of that nation in Brasil, attempted to counteract the Dutch, by playing upon them their own politics. They magnified the wisdom of the Dutch government, pretended to confide in the promises made them, and took in good part all the excuses brought for their non-performance; by which means, they persuaded count Maurice and the directors of the West-India company, that the Dutch territories were effectually settled, and that they had nothing to fear in Brasil, either from the natives or the Portuguese; but these arts would probably have proved abortive, if the directors of the West-India company had not in a manner entered into the conspiracy themselves.

Finding that they were now possessed of what they had so long fought for, they sent repeated orders to count Maurice to take such measures as would increase their revenue, and, in particular, to send over vast quantities of sugar, and other valuable effects; with orders not to suffer such as were indebted to the company to pay in small sums, but to discharge their debts at once. Count Maurice observed, that the execution of these orders would be attended with many inconveniencies; that a long war had been carried on, and the country but lately reduced; that most of those who were in debt to the country, were Portuguese, who had settled in their territories, and had hitherto behaved well, and therefore ought to be kindly treated, and not driven to extremities: but the directors would not attend to his arguments. They knew that Brasil was very rich, and could see no reason why all that it produced should not be immediately shipped for Holland.

Other things also gave them great uneasiness. Opposite to the Receif was a commodious island, upon which the count caused a new town to be built and well fortified, chiefly out of the ruins of the city of Olinda. This town, to which he gave the name of Mauriceburgh, soon growing to a very considerable place, he united it to the Receif, which was become the centre of the Dutch commerce, by a stone bridge.

Though all this was done for the benefit of the Dutch inhabitants, and to secure the company's capital from danger, yet, as it cost 40,000l. they could not help grudging the expence. They were, however, most out of humour at the fine palace count Maurice built for himself. This magnificent edifice was erected in the most commodious part of the town, and in the midst of gardens elegantly laid out, and planted with cocoas of various sorts, citrons, lemons, pomegranates, figs and other fruit trees. The palace was so contrived as to command a moſt admirable proſpect, both by sea and land: before its front was a battery of marble, riſing gradually from the river ſide, upon which were mounted ten pieces of large cannon. Count Maurice had alſo a magnificent villa at ſome diſtance in the country, ſurrounded by fine gardens, adorned with curious fiſh-ponds, and encompaſſed with ſtrong walls; the whole being ſo diſpoſed, as to anſwer at once, the views of pleaſure, and the defence of the city, which it covered on that ſide as a fort. He alſo laid out parks and meadows, within the fortifications, which, while properly managed, produced every thing neceſſary for the ſubſiſtence of the garriſon, and were in every reſpect equally commodious and beautiful.

Thus count Maurice employed thoſe treaſures which were the fruits of his many victories and extenſive conqueſts, and which a perſon of leſs generoſity would have tranſported to Holland, as his own private fortune. But theſe marks of public ſpirit, which ought to have extinguiſhed, nouriſhed that envy which had been conceived againſt him; and while he was labouring to extend and ſecure the company's power in Braſil, the directors of that company in Holland employed themſelves in cenſuring his conduct, and in magnifying his extravagance in expending ſuch vaſt ſums, while the colony produced ſo little to the company's ſtock. They therefore formed the deſign of recalling him, as the only means of making the colony produce ſuch a revenue, as would be proportionable to the expectations of the company.

CHAPTER V.

Count Maurice of Naſſau forms a ſcheme for erecting a Dutch empire in America, equal, if not ſuperior, to that of the Spaniards. General Brewer's expedition to Chili, and its miſcarriage, occaſioned by the ill conduct of the Dutch, and the count's being recalled.

MEAN while the count, who was one of the beſt patriots, and moſt able politicians Holland ever produced, formed the ſcheme of raiſing ſuch an empire at once in America, as, had it been ſteadily purſued, would have defied the rage of all their enemies. He plainly ſaw, that the Dutch eſtabliſhment in Braſil, as fair and flouriſhing as it ſeemed, under his wiſe and glorious adminiſtration, would ſink to nothing, if not ſupported by new acquiſitions.

Being therefore informed, that the inhabitants of Chili, which lies on the back of Braſil on the South Seas, had driven out the Spaniards, he conceived the deſign of fixing a Dutch colony there, which he thought might be eaſily done, under the plauſible pretence of aſſiſting the natives againſt their late imperious lords the Spaniards.

This deſign he communicated to the ſtates-general, and ſhewed them the utility of it, by obſerving, that it would give them the poſſeſſion of a large, fertile and agreeable country, abounding with all the neceſſaries of life, and with the richeſt gold mines in the world; that it would humble the Spaniards, and open a trade to the South Seas; and laſtly, that it would firmly cement the circle of their commerce, as the flaves procured by their fettlements in Africa, would be taken off by that colony, and by Brafil.

The States approving of this propofal, appointed captain Henry Brewer, who had ferved with reputation in the Eaft-Indies, to fail with a fquadron of five fhips, on board of which were 1800 men. This fquadron weighed from the Texel on the 6th of November, 1642, and arrived at Fernambuca on the coaft of Brafil on the 22d of December following; where, having confulted with count Maurice of Naffau, as general and commander in chief for the Dutch, in Brafil, he failed from Fernambuca on the 16th of January following, and on the 5th of March came in fight of the Streights Le Maire, where he caft anchor in the bay of Statefland; where having remained till the 25th, they failed round Cape Horn, and, after fuffering much by ftormy weather, and lofing the company of one of their fhips, he arrived with the other four on the coaft of Chili; then fteering along the coaft, they, on the 9th of May, came to an anchor in a bay of the South Sea, in 41° 36 fouth latitude, to which they gave the name of Brewer's Haven.

An officer with a company of foldiers being fent on fhore, they difcovered a great number of fheep, oxen, and horfes, and fome houfes; but the inhabitants were fled. They, however, fuppofed part of the country to be in the poffeffion of the Spaniards, from the large wooden croffes they faw fixed at the entrance of the houfes; and the next day going on fhore they obferved a party of Spanifh horfe, and fome cannon-fhot was fired at the boat.

On the 20th of May, a company of 50 foldiers being again fent on fhore, they difcovered the town of Carelmappa, and had a fmart engagement with a party of Spaniards, confifting of 90 men horfe and foot, whom they defeated; when, the

Spaniards abandoning the town, the Dutch took poſſeſſion of it, and remained there till the 25th, and then ſetting fire to the town, and killing the horſes they had taken in the engagement, they returned to their ſhips.

They afterwards ſteered to the town of Caſtro, on the iſland of Chilo, where arriving on the 6th of June, a conſiderable body of Spaniſh horſe and foot appeared on the coaſt; but the Dutch no ſooner landed ſome ſoldiers, than the inhabitants ſet fire to the town, and abandoned it, having before carried away every thing that was valuable.

Caſtro had been adorned with many magnificent buildings, and was pleaſantly ſituated on a hill. It was ſurrounded with fruitful orchards and gardens; the fields beyond it were well cultivated, and at this time the fruit remained on many of the trees, notwithſtanding its being winter. The Dutch took 100 ſheep and ſome hogs off the iſland and re-embarking on the 17th of June, returned to Brewer's Haven, from whence they propoſed to ſail to the river Baldivia; but the north wind blowing hard, they returned to Carelmappa, where landing a company of ſoldiers, they took three Spaniards priſoners, who informed them, that there were gold mines at Orſorno, and more at Baldivia; but that they had not been wrought of late, as the Indians had not been compelled to work in the mines ſince the general revolt in 1595.

They alſo learned from an old Spaniſh woman, they had taken, that before the above revolt, the Spaniards lived in great ſplendor at Orſorno, the meaneſt of them having at leaſt 300 vaſſals, who were compelled to pay their reſpective lords a certain weekly tribute in gold; but were uſed ſo cruelly by the Spaniards, that they aroſe as one man, and drove them from Orſorno, and other Spaniſh towns; and that the Spaniards poſſeſſed little more in that part of Chili, than Carelmappa and St. Michael de Calembuco. Since that time the Indians of Orforno, Baldivia, and five other towns, had, till lately, kept up a pretty good correfpondence with the Spaniards, but had fince taken up arms againft them.

The truth of this intelligence was confirmed by five Indians Caciques, who came on board, and affured the Dutch, that they were extremely glad at finding they were come to affift them againft their ancient enemies; to which, the Dutch anfwered, that they had brought arms to exchange with the natives of Orforno, Baldivia, and other places, for fuch merchandizes as Chili afforded, to enable them to carry on the war againft the Spaniards ; and that they were ready to affift them to the utmoft of their power.

To this the Chilefe replied, that they lived very uneafy under the Spanifh government of Carelmappa, and wanted to get to their friends at Orforno and Baldivia: but the Spaniards had poffeffed all the paffes, and the country was overflowed by the winter rains ; they therefore defired Mr. Brewer to take them to Baldivia in his fhips. To this he readily confented, and they returned on fhore to give their friends an account of what had paffed, and to make preparation for the voyage.

The next day more of the natives went on board, and one of them bringing the head of a Spaniard whom he had killed, they declared their refolution to fhake off the Spanifh yoke ; upon which Mr. Brewer made them a prefent of fome fpears, fwords and mufkets, with powder and ball ; in return for which, they fent him fome black cattle.

Thus far this expedition fucceeded perfectly well ; but Mr. Brewer, who alone was equal to the enterprize, dying on the 7th of Auguft, Captain

Hackerman, who succeeded him in the command, behaved with so little address, that he soon let the natives know the motives which had induced the Dutch to visit their coast, and created jealousies, which he afterwards found impossible to remove.

The late general was so confident of the success of the enterprize, that he had directed his countrymen to take his corpse with them, and bury it at Baldivia, which he had intended to fortify; and appointed the Chilese to rendezvous there and meet the fleet, not doubting of a general revolt in their favour. His great ambition was, to have a tomb erected in that place, to perpetuate the memory of his being the author of so great a good to his country.

But, to proceed, the Dutch, having taken 470 Chilese on board, who had furnished themselves with corn, cattle, and other provisions for the voyage, set sail for the river Baldivia on the 21st of August, and arrived there on the 24th.

The Dutch having sailed half a league up the river, observed three channels, and taking the middle one, had the misfortune to run a-ground, so that it was two or three days before they could get all their ships afloat. On their arrival at Baldivia, they only found the ruins of the ancient gates, which were very high and strong built; but the place was overrun with weeds and bushes. Here they found 3 or 400 Chilese horse and foot, armed with spears eighteen feet long, some of whom came on board to welcome them on their arrival. Mr. Hackerman then harangued them by an interpreter, and informed them that the Dutch were now in the possession of Brasil, which lay upon the same continent, and were in a condition to supply them with arms and ammunition. He promised to assist them in driving their enemies the Spaniards, out of the country, and defired them to enter with him into a league offenfive and defenfive. He alfo prefented them with letters from the prince of Orange, to the fame purpofe, which were interpreted to the Chilefe: for as neither the people of the Eaft or Weft-Indies had any notion of a republican form of government, the Dutch conftantly in all their negotiations with thofe diftant nations, pretended to be authorized by the prince of Orange, or fome fingle perfons, whom they infinuated was their monarch.

The Caciques replied, that they would confult their brethren of Orforno and Coneo, and then return to Baldivia; upon which the Dutch proceeded to land their foldiers, and the commander took a view of the ground, in order to erect a fort. The fame evening above 1000 Chilefe arrived from Orforno and Coneo to treat with the Dutch; and the next day Mr. Hackerman by his interpreter, made them another fpeech, in which he told them, that the chief motive of his voyage was to affift the Chilefe, the fame of whofe actions had reached as far as Holland; that the Dutch had been at war with the Spaniards for upwards of fourfcore years, like them, for the recovery of their liberties, which they had at laft obtained; and that, if the Chilefe would enter into a confederacy with them, they were ready to fupply them with cannon, fmall arms and ammunition, which they would exchange for the produce of the country. To this, the Caciques replied, that they were happy in meeting with a fupply of arms, from fo diftant a country as Holland, and that they would confider of what was propofed.

The Dutch then afked, if they could fupply them with provifions, upon which they readily promifed to bring them plenty of corn and cattle. After this they entered into a verbal alliance offenfive and defenfive againft the Spaniards; but the Chilefe abfolutely refufed to execute fome written articles, that were interpreted to them, alleging, that this was not cuftomary with them, and that they always confidered promifes as facred.

The Dutch then proceeded to build a fort at Baldivia; but when they propofed to exchange arms with the natives for their gold, the Caciques appeared alarmed, and jealous of their new allies, declaring that they had no gold mines, and that there was no fuch thing as gold in ufe among them; that they indeed remembered, that formerly they had been obliged to pay heavy taxes to the Spaniards in gold, on pain of lofing their ears and nofes, as many of them actually did, who could not procure as much as was expected; and this had given them fuch an abhorrence of that metal, that they could not bear to hear it named; that they were far from valuing it, as they found all ftrangers did, to whom it was the caufe of many mifchiefs from which they were free.

To this the Dutch commander replied, that he was not come to exact any thing of them, as the Spaniards had done, but was ready to pay for their gold with arms, or whatever merchandize they liked beft. At this, the Caciques immediately penetrating into his views, ftared at each other, without returning one word of anfwer. Upon this, he did not think fit to urge them any farther, though he was fenfible that there were very rich mines in that part of the country. He perceived that they were deeply alarmed, and filled with the fufpicion, that the Dutch for the fake of their gold, would treat them in the fame manner as the Spaniards had done. And therefore Mr. Hackerman being fenfible that he could not now expect much affiftance from the natives, and that it would be impoffible for him to maintain his ground, he difpatched a letter to Fernambuca, by one of his captains, whom he fent with two of his fhips, fending an account of the ftate of his affairs, and defiring a reinforcement. In the mean time, he continued to fortify the poft he had taken at Baldivia, where he hoped to defend himfelf, till the arrival of thefe fupplies.

This exprefs had not been difpatched a week, before the Dutch commander became fenfible of his miftake, and that whatever mifunderftanding there might be between the Chilefe and the Spaniards, the former were as much afraid of the Dutch, as of their ancient enemies, and would probably join with the Spaniards to expel them out of the country; for at his next conference with the Caciques they let him know, that he muft expect no provifions from them; and even endeavoured to terrify him, by reporting that the Spaniards were affembling their forces by fea and land, to drive the Dutch from Baldivia. Soon after which he demolifhed his new erected fortification, and having re-embarked his people, fet fail for Brafil on the 28th of October 1643; he doubled Cape Horn, and, after being only two months in the voyage, arrived on the 28th of December, at Fernambuca in Brafil.

In the mean time, the Dutch Weft-India company had carried their parfimonious fcheme into execution, and the count being as weary of their management, as they were of his, he, on the 11th of May, 1644, quitted the government, which he had held eight years, and being gone when the above fleet returned to Brafil, thofe on board were no longer at a lofs for the reafon of their not being fupported in time, as with great juftice they expected, and as the importance of the enterprize deferved.

CHAPTER VI.

The Dutch West-India company being now resolved to proceed in the most frugal manner, strip the country of the troops employed in its defence; and send new governors, who lessen the expences of the country, and encrease their immediate profits; but neglect the fortifications, and oppress the Portuguese under their subjection; upon which they take up arms for the recovery of their liberties, and, after a long war, drive out the Dutch.

THE count returned to Europe with a fleet of thirteen large ships, and near 3000 soldiers on board, and, agreeable to the instructions he had received, and to the new scheme of frugal government, he left only eighteen companies for the defence of the Dutch settlements.

The illustrious persons who were the successors of the great count Maurice of Nassau, one of the ablest, bravest, and most worthy men of that family, so famous for producing heroes, were chiefly Mr. Hamel, a merchant of Amsterdam, Mr. de Basis, a goldsmith of Haerlem, and Mr. Bullestraat, a carpenter of Middleburgh; men of good sense, and great fidelity to the company; but they had narrow minds, and not the least idea of the art of government. They forced the Portuguese who lived under them, to pay what they owed the company in a short time, by such methods as made them lose their hearts for ever. They sent to Holland the produce of the very lands count Maurice had assigned for maintaining the fortifications, which they suffered to run to ruin. They granted licences upon very easy terms to the soldiers to return home; which leſſened the expence of the army, and the very next year ſent a greater quantity of ſugar to Holland, than had ever been ſent in one year before; but all theſe applauded meaſures tended ſolely to the deſtruction of the ſettlement, and to deprive the Dutch of this invaluable acquiſition.

Don Antonio Tellez de Silva, who was at this time the Portugueſe viceroy, was a man of the greateſt wiſdom and abilities, and at the ſame time had every other qualification of a good governor. This gentleman was no ſooner informed that count Maurice had carried with him two thirds of the force of Braſil, than he inſinuated to the Portugueſe ſubject to the Dutch, that they were only labouring for ſtrangers, while they might be maſters of all they now farmed at an exorbitant rent, if their king was but reſtored to his juſt rights. Theſe ſuggeſtions had great weight; but the whole affair, of recovering Braſil, was undertaken by Juan Fernandez Viera, a very extraordinary perſon, who was originally a butcher's boy, and was afterwards page to one of the magiſtrates of Olinda, while it was in the poſſeſſion of the Portugueſe. He afterwards became a kind of factor to the Dutch, had four ſugar plantations of his own, beſides being intruſted with the management of many more, and, by his induſtry and art, he grew extremely rich.

This perſon having laid the ſcheme of the conſpiracy, ſent it over to Portugal by one who was ignorant of the deſign; after which, he ſent a relation of his to court, with a letter recommending him to the king, who granted him a troop of horſe: upon which he acted there as agent for the conſpirators.

As Viera foreſaw, that this would reach the ears of the Dutch, he went directly to the council, owned what he had done, and offered to give security for his good behaviour; when two of the richest Portuguese in the Dutch territories, who were as deep in the conspiracy as himself, became bound for him. For as he owed the chief persons in the administration upwards of 200,000 florins, they thought it adviseable not to ruin him; and by this contrivance he effectually secured his liberty, that he might be able to carry on his great design, in which he was assisted by Antonio Cavalcante and Amador Aragousa, who were equally deep in the management of the Dutch affairs, and determined, like him, to contribute all in their power to the ruin of those who trusted them.

This plot was proposed to be put in execution on the 24th of June 1645, when one of Antonio Cavalcante's daughters was to be married, and a great entertainment given at Viera's house, to which most of the officers and principal persons in the company's service were invited, where they would doubtless have been seized, if not murdered, if the design had not been discovered the very evening before it was to have been executed; but, at this instant a ship arriving from Amsterdam, brought letters from the directors of the West-India company, containing an account that the minister from the states-general at the court of Portugal, had discovered that a great conspiracy was carrying on in Brasil, and that they would do well to enquire what supplies had been lately sent from Lisbon to the Portuguese in that country. This enquiry produced such discoveries, as filled the Dutch with a consternation that gave Viera and his associates time to escape into the neighbouring woods, where they immediately took up arms.

Viera now assumed the character of general and commander in chief, and being assisted by colonel Diaz with a few Portuguese troops, and colonel

Cameron at the head of a numerous body of Brafilians, he fixed his head-quarters at Pojug, a town between the Receif and Cape St. Auguftine; fo that, to the misfortune of the Dutch, this unexpected war broke out in the very heart of their dominions. Antonio Cavalcante at the fame time raifed another part of the country; and Amador Aragoufa, at the head of a flying party, was employed in burning and deftroying all the Dutch plantations without mercy.

The council feeing themfelves in this dreadful fituation, affembled all the troops they were able, and publifhed a proclamation, promifing to pardon all who would fubmit and return to their duty, except Viera, Cavalcante, and Aragoufa. They gave the command of a few ill-provided troops they got together, to colonel Huys, to whom they gave the title of General, and, in fhort, fent two captains to the Viceroy at the bay of All Saints, to complain of this infraction of the truce, which had ftill four years to come.

The Viceroy received thefe captains with great civility, and anfwered with much prudence, that he was anfwerable for the conduct of the inhabitants of the part of Brafil fubject to the crown of Portugal; and if they had broke the truce, he would have given the Dutch what fatisfaction they could defire; but if the Portuguefe fettled in the Dutch dominions, had been induced by oppreffion to take up arms, he could not help it, and it was very unjuft to blame him for it.

This was the anfwer he gave in public; but in a private converfation with capt. Hoogftrate, one of the gentlemen fent on this negociation, he not only drew him over to his intereft, but prevailed on him to deliver up the important poft of St. Auguftine, of which he was governor.

In the mean time general Huys attacking colonel Cameron, had the misfortune to be defeated with the lofs of 100 men. Soon after the Portuguefe admiral Salvador Correa de Bonavides appeared with a numerous fleet on the coaft; upon which admiral Lichthart, though he had but five men of war, offered him battle; but this the Portuguefe commander refufed, under the pretence of his having no orders to act againft the Dutch, and that he was only to land a body of men in his mafter's dominions; which he had no fooner done, than thofe men, without ceremony, entered the Dutch territories, and made themfelves mafters of all the places that fell in their way. Upon this the council fent orders to general Huys to make a retreat; but he ftaying for an officer whom he had fent to bring feveral ladies and rich effects out of the country, had the misfortune to be furrounded by the Portuguefe, who, after beating him, took him and his men prifoners.

Orders were now fent to admiral Lichthart to attack the Portuguefe fhips whenever he had an opportunity, and upon this occafion, he gave a frefh proof of his courage and admirable conduct; for with four fhips, a frigate and a bark, he attacked a Portuguefe fleet of feventeen fail, took three of the largeft fhips, together with the admiral, burnt and funk almoft all the reft, and killed 700 men.

This fuccefs began to revive the hopes of the council, when they received the unexpected news, that Hoogftrate had treacheroufly delivered up the poft of St. Auguftine. For this bafe action he received the fum of 18,000 florins, which he employed in raifing a regiment of 650 Brafilians, of whom he was made colonel by the Portuguefe, and appearing at the head of this body againft his countrymen, behaved with refolution and fidelity in the fervice of Portugal.

Admiral Lichthart, with 4 Ships, a Frigate, & a Bark attacks the Portuguez Fleet of 17 Sail.

The great fuperiority of the Portuguefe now enabled them to make quick difpatch in moft of their expeditions, and in a little time they became mafters of almoft all the ftrong places in the captainfhip of Fernambuca. At length, they blocked up the Receif, the only ftrong place the Dutch had left.

When the news of thefe proceedings reached Holland, the people were extremely irritated, and though the Portuguefe ambaffador endeavoured to perfuade the ftates-general that his moft faithful majefty had no concern in what had happened at Brafil, the Dutch fitted out a fleet of fifty two men of war, under the command of M. Blankert, admiral of Zealand, who was declared admiral of Brafil, Guinea, and Angola; and with him they fent colonel Schuppen and colonel Henderfon, who had acquired great reputation in the fervice of count Maurice. Thus was an open war begun between Holland and Portugal.

But hardly any fleet ever met with fo many unfortunate accidents, and fo many delays; for within two days after they failed from the Texel, they were forced to anchor in the Downs; where they loft two fhips in a ftorm; they failed again, and were forced into the Ifle of Wight, where the firft fight they faw was the wreck of a large Dutch merchantman from Brafil, with a cargo of immenfe value, which was entirely loft, and out of 300 perfons, only thirty faved: in the port of St. Helen's they remained wind-bound feven weeks, and at laft met with a ftorm, on their putting again to fea, by which they fuffered extremely. By thefe and many other accidents, they were fo long delayed, that they did not arrive at the Receif till the garrifon was reduced to the utmoft extremity, and was on the point of furrendering. However, by the help of thefe reinforcements, the war was ftill continued, and fome fmall advantages obtained.

But in the beginning of the year 1647, the Portuguese again blocked up the Receif, where the whole force of the Dutch confifted of only 1800 men, who, however, made a gallant defence ; but at length fallying out with all their ftrength to attack the enemy in the field, they were overpowered by numbers, and entirely defeated with the lofs of 1100 foldiers, moft of their officers, and all the artillery and ammunition they had carried with them. This hindered them from making any more fallies ; but at the fame time enabled them to make a longer defence, as they had now provifions for feven months, which would otherwife have lafted but three.

The progrefs of the Portuguefe became now fo great, that nothing feemed capable of preventing the entire ruin of the Dutch affairs in that part of the world. This produced a kind of national defpair, which haftened the ruin that was but too plainly forefeen. The province of Zealand recalled admiral Blankert, with whom came moft of the officers they had fent with him. The difficulties they had met with in their paffage thither, were repeated on their return: fo that the admiral died before the fleet arrived in Holland, as did feveral of his officers almoft as foon as they came on fhore : but the Sieur Shuk, who had been fent by the governors of Brafil, furviving, gave the States fuch an affecting account of the pofture of affairs in that country, that they refolved to make a great effort for the prefervation of fo valuable an acquifition, and gave orders for fitting out a fleet of fifty large men of war, and for embarking 6000 regular troops, the command of which was given to admiral Witte-Wittezen, who was then efteemed the ableft officer in the Dutch fervice, and it was alfo refolved to fend after him an additional fupply of between 5 or 6000 men more. The admiral failed towards the end of the year 1650, and after suffering much by storms and tempests in the passage, at length arrived on the coast of Fernambuca; but instead of a colony, the admiral found a mere hospital of sick, maimed, and infirm people: and instead of those fortresses which he was to have relieved, church-yards, filled with the bodies of those who had before been sent on the same errand. For the Portuguese, Brasilians, and Negroes living on the natural produce of the country, where healthy and strong; while the Dutch pent up in their forts, were obliged to subsist entirely on the provisions sent them from Europe; by which means they grew pale, wan and feeble, and died in great numbers. The affecting sights the admiral saw there, made him resolve, notwithstanding the orders he had received, to return home without delay; this he accordingly did, leaving things in a much worse condition than he found them; for which he was afterwards called to an account by the States, though he soon justified himself to their satisfaction.

In short, the Dutch still continued to meet with ill success, and towards the conclusion of the year 1653, the Portuguese, who now publicly assisted Viera, sent a fleet of sixteen large men of war to attack the Receif by sea, and to blow up part of its fortifications: which terrified the garrison that they absolutely refused to fight. The next year, the Dutch surrendered every thing they possessed in Brasil, and in 1655 they returned to Holland.

It is impossible to conceive the uproar that this raised in the country, or the heat and fury with which the people demanded justice against general Sigismund Schuppen, who had commanded in chief for many years, and was governor of the Receif when it surrendered. The states, to secure him and his officers from their resentment, sent them to prifon, and granted the only favour he afked, which was his being allowed to make a public defence. In this, he fo clearly laid open his own long and faithful fervices, recapitulated all the fucceffes they had under the adminiftration of count Maurice, and gave fo true and affecting a picture of the miferies, and misfortunes he himfelf and his men had fuffered fince he went laft thither, that the people wept and his judges acquitted him.

To conclude this fubject: when count Maurice, after refiding eight years in Brafil, quitted the government, he left them feven captainfhips, one city, thirty great towns, forty-five regular fortreffes, ninety fail of good fhips, 3000 regular troops, 20,000 Dutch of all ages and fexes, 60,000 negroes, and above twice as many Brafilians. At that time the colony annually yielded 25,000 chefts of fugar; and a carpenter, cooper, or fmith could earn five or fix guilders a day, and live very comfortably upon one. But the above avaricious and parfimonious management, occafioned not only the lofs of this invaluable colony; but the expending of millions upon it, for ten years together: and after the deftruction of feveral thoufands from time to time fent thither, there returned to Holland in 1655, no more than between fix and feven hundred perfons, none of whom were worth a groat.

CHAPTER VII.

A description of the present state of the several captainships or provinces of Brasil, and their produce; the manner of making clayed sugar, and an account of the Brasil tree; the principal cities and towns of each province, and the discovery of gold and diamonds in that country.

SINCE this time the Portuguese have remained in the quiet possession of all this vast country; but suffer no ships to trade thither besides their own. The whole trade of the five northern captainships, Paria, Maragnan, Siara, Rio Grande, and Paraiba, are carried on at the last mentioned port, which is situated on a river of the same name, at about five leagues distance from the sea. Paraiba is a fine populous town, and seven or eight ships of 250 tons burden each, are annually sent thither from Lisbon and Oporto. Their lading chiefly consists of sugar, more of which has been cultivated in the northern captainships than in the south, especially since the discovery of the gold mines, which have rendered the southern inhabitants more negligent about the improvement of their lands.

The sugar of Brasil was the first sent to Europe, the Portuguese having set up their works in this country about the year 1580. Their trade in this commodity soon became extremely great, and their being so long in possession of it, has made them more careful in the management of sugar, than any other nation; and even at this time the clayed sugars of Brasil, are finer and whiter than ours; though the manner of preparing it is extremely easy.

When their fugar is put into pots, and is funk two or three inches below the brim by draining out the molaffes, they fcrape off a thin hard cruft that is found on the top of the fugar, and then pour in their mixture for refining it, which is nothing more than a fine foft white clay, beat and mixed with water, till it is of the confiftence of cream; with this they fill up the pot or pan, and in ten or twelve days, the white water paffes quite through, whitening all the fugar, while the thick body of the clay lodges at top, and is eafily taken off with a knife.

They alfo bring from Paraiba, notwithftanding its being the leaft frequented port in Brafil, dying woods, feveral forts of drugs, and other valuable commodities, and it is generally allowed that thefe northern captainfhips are the beft peopled, and the inhabitants in very eafy circumftances, though no mines have yet been wrought in thefe parts.

Next to Paraiba is Tamaraca, the trade whereof is carried on at the city of Olinda, which was rebuilt by the Portuguefe, after its being demolifhed by count Maurice. It is feated on the fide of a hill near the fea, but this fituation renders the ftreets very uneven and incommodious. The port is alfo narrow, and the entrance into it extremely difficult, yet fhips continually refort thither from the other parts of Brafil and the Canaries, as well as the annual fleet from Lifbon, which generally confifts of about thirty fail, efcorted by a man of war. Thefe fhips are chiefly loaded here with fugar and Brafil wood, which laft is fuppofed to be the beft of its kind in the world.

Of this wood there are different forts; as the Brafil of Japan, that of Lamon, that of St. Martha, and Braziletto from Jamaica and the Leeward Iflands; but the very beft is produced in this country, and the beft there is at Fernambuca.

The Brafil tree generally grows in dry barren places, and among rocks; it is thick and large, and the timber is ufually crooked and knotty. It bears flowers of a moft beautiful bright red, that have a very fragrant fmell, which, inftead of hurting, ftrengthens and cherifhes the brain. Though the tree is very large, it is covered with fo thick a bark, that when the Brafilians have taken it off, a tree as bulky as a man's body is left no thicker than the calf of his leg. The wood is very hard, dry, and heavy; it crackles much in the fire, and fcarce raifes any fmoak. That is efteemed the beft which is the foundeft, thickeft, and hardeft. It ought alfo upon fplitting to turn from a pale to a deep red, and upon chewing the chips, the beft fort yields a fweet tafte, fomewhat like fugar. This wood is put to various ufes, by the turners, and takes a very good polifh; but it is principally ufed in dying, in which it yields a very fine bright red.

The next captainfhip, is that called by the Portuguefe the Bay of Bahia, or the Bay of All Saints: it is about twelve leagues over, but in feveral places is fcarce navigable on account of the fand banks and fhoals. In this bay there are feveral fmall iflands, on which the Portuguefe have a tobacco and fugar plantations, and they have alfo very good fifheries on the coaft of thefe iflands, and on the banks. At the entrance of the bay is the city of St. Salvador, which lies in 14° fouth latitude, and is at prefent the centre of the Portuguefe trade in this part of the world. It has a very fine port, which might be rendered ftill more commodious if art and induftry gave a little affiftance to nature.

The city of St. Salvador, which is at prefent the feat of an archbifhop, is divided into the upper and lower. The upper town is feated on the summit of a mountain. The houses are large and pretty convenient, but the inequality of the ground on which they stand, renders the streets very disagreeable. In the middle of the town is the great square, the four sides of which are taken up with the viceroy's palace, the town-house, the mint, and other public buildings, built of stone brought from Portugal. The Jesuits college is by far the largest and finest edifice in the city, particularly the Sacristy, which is lined throughout with the most beautiful tortoise-shell, wrought and fixed together in the most elegant manner, so that nothing can be conceived more agreeable to the eye. There are several very fine churches, as that of the Benedictine-Abbey, which rivals that lately possessed by the Jesuits; but the cathedral, which, at a distance, seems the noblest structure, upon being nearly examined, appears neither neat nor regular. However, in richness of gilding, it surpasses all the other churches. Among the convents in this capital, is a remarkable one of the order of St. Clare, and another for such young girls as are exposed and abandoned by their parents. It is surprizing to see how these foundlings are considered in this country; the king adopts them all, and the ladies of the first quality frequently take them home, when at a proper age, and breed them up as their own.

The lower town, wherein all the merchants and people of business reside, is situated at the foot of the hill, which is excessively steep, though not very high, and is a place of the greatest hurry and trade. There are here a royal arsenal, the king's warehouses and magazines, which are large, well filled, and kept in excellent order. There is also a fine yard for building of ships, which is of considerable advantage. These ships are not only built at an easier rate, but are more serviceable than others, the timber being excellent in its kind, from its having the peculiar advantage of the worms being unable to penetrate it.

With refpect to the fortifications of the city, there is a large fquare fort, and below it a fmaller, with ten large pieces of cannon. Thefe two fortreffes command the mouth of the bay. They have a new fort called St. Peter's Caftle, which is alfo very ftrong; and in the middle of the harbour is a large fortrefs. At the point of Montferat they have a fmall but ftrong fort, with twelve pieces of heavy cannon. Between Montferat and the city is a fine citadel, which is a regular fquare admirably fortified, and well furnifhed with brafs cannon, and the arfenal is flanked by two ftrong baftions that command the whole fort. There are yet two other fortreffes to be mentioned; one between St. Antonio and the city, where they make their gun-powder; and the other the powder-houfe, which lies on the other fide of the city, and commands a large artificial lake, made by the Dutch, by which the city of St. Salvador is covered on one fide, as it is by the fea on the other.

The fleet fent annually hither from Lifbon, confifts of about thirty fhips, efcorted by two men of war, which ufually fail about March, and in this bay the whole Brafil fleet generally affemble, in order to return together to Europe. From this port they bring home gold, amethyfts, diamonds, and the beft tobacco in Brafil, which is much efteemed; indigo, fugar, balfam of capivi, ipecacuanha, pereira brava, cinnamon, long pepper, ginger, woods for dying, and fome for inlaying, ambergris, and other rich drugs and perfumes. They alfo export raw hides, train oil, and whalefins.

All the reft of the captainfhips lie farther to the fouth, and carry on their trade by the Rio Janeiro, so called from its being discovered in January 1550, and is at present one of the most considerable rivers in the world. Its banks are as beautiful as can be imagined, the climate is fine, and the soil is extremely fertile, producing sugar, indigo, tobacco and cotton, in very great perfection, and European corn has been found to grow there with very little trouble. But this, and all other improvements have been discouraged on account of the gold mines that have been discovered in this and the neighbouring captainships of St. Vincent; though independently of these mines, this may be considered as the richest part of Brasil. The Portuguese settled here are very different in their manners from those in the bay of All Saints, for they are active and industrious, and suffer the Indians who live among them to enjoy as much freedom as themselves.

The city of St. Sebastian, the capital of this country, is very commodiously situated on the west side of the river about two leagues from the sea, and in the 23° south latitude. This city, which is very well fortified, is the seat of a Portuguese governor, and is a bishop's see, suffragan to the archbishop of St. Salvador.

There are also several other considerable towns on the Rio Janeiro, all of which carry on a considerable trade, as appears from the number of ships annually sent thither from Portugal. These consist of between twenty and thirty vessels of 500 tons each, usually escorted by two men of war. The commodities brought from thence are generally the same as those exported from St. Salvador; besides these, gold and diamonds are found in this province.

With respect to the gold and diamonds of Brasil, minerals, which mankind hold in the greatest esteem, and exert their utmost art and industry in acquiring; the former was firſt found in the mountains near the city of Rio Janeiro. The manner, however, in which this diſcovery was made, is differently related; but the moſt common account is, that the Indians on the back of the Portugueſe ſettlements were obſerved to make uſe of this metal for their fiſh-hooks; and enquiry being made of their manner of procuring it, it appeared that conſiderable quantities of it were annually waſhed from the mountains, and left among the gravel and ſand that remained in the valleys, after the running off, or evaporation of the water.

This diſcovery being made, confiderable quantities of gold were imported from Braſil to Europe, and the annual imports have been continually augmented by the diſcovery of places in other provinces, where it is to be found in as great plenty as at firſt about Rio Janeiro; and it is even ſaid, that a ſlender vein of this metal runs through the whole country at about twenty-four feet from the ſurface, but is too thin and poor to anſwer the expence of digging. However, gold is always to be collected when the rivers or rains have had any courſe for a confiderable time, and therefore the being able to divert a ſtream from its channel, is eſteemed an infallible ſource of gain.

The employment of ſearching the bottoms of rivers and torrents, and waſhing the gold from the dirt and ſand, is principally performed by ſlaves, who are chiefly negroes, of whom the Portugueſe have great numbers kept for that purpoſe. By a very ſingular regulation, each of theſe ſlaves are obliged to furniſh their maſter every day with the eighth part of an ounce of gold; and if by their induſtry or good fortune, they collect a larger quantity, the ſurplus is confidered as their own property, and they are allowed to diſpoſe of it as they think fit; by which means ſome negroes, who have fallen upon rich wafhing places, have, it is said, purchafed flaves of their own, and lived in great fplendor. Their original mafter having no other demand upon them than the daily fupply of an eighth of an ounce, which amounts to about nine fhillings fterling; the Portuguefe ounce being fomewhat lighter than our troy ounce.

The annual return of gold to Lifbon may be computed from the amount of the king's fifth, which, one year with another, is eftimated at 150 arroves of thirty-two pounds Portuguefe weight each, which at 4l. the troy ounce, is near 300,000l. fterling; and therefore the capital, whereof this is the fifth, is about a million and a half fterling. To which if we add the gold exchanged with the Spaniards for filver, and what is privately brought to Europe, without paying the duty, which may amount to half a million more, the annual produce of the Brafilian gold muft be about two millions fterling. An immenfe fum to be found in a country that a few years ago was not known to produce a fingle grain.

It is but about thirty years fince the firft diamonds were brought from this country into Europe. Thefe valuable ftones are, like the gold, found in the beds of rivers and torrents; but not fo univerfally. They were frequently perceived in wafhing the gold, before they were known to be of any value, and were confequently thrown away with the fand and gravel; and numbers of large ftones, that would have enriched the poffeffors, have paffed unregarded through the hands of feveral perfons now living. However, at length a perfon acquainted with the appearance of rough diamonds, imagined that thefe pebbles were of the fame kind; but it was difficult to perfuade the inhabitants that what they had been fo long accuftomed to defpife could be of fuch immenfe value and in this interval, it is faid that a governor procured a confiderable number of thefe ftones, under the pretence of ufing them as counters to play at cards. But the moft fkilful jewellers in Europe being confulted, they declared that thefe ftones were true diamonds, and that many of them were not inferior, either in luftre or any other quality, to thofe of the Eaft-Indies. Upon this, many of the Portuguefe in the neighbourhood of the places where they had been firft obferved, began to fearch for them with great affiduity, and as large rocks of chryftal were found in feveral of the mountains, where the ftream flowed which wafhed down the diamonds, they flattered themfelves with the hopes of difcovering diamonds of a prodigious bulk But the king of Portugal being told that this would debafe their value, ruin the Europeans who had in their poffeffion a great quantity of Indian diamonds, and render the difcovery of no importance, his majefty thought proper to reftrain the fearch after them; for which purpofe he erected a diamond company with an exclufive charter, which, in confideration of a fum annually paid to the king, has the property of all the diamonds found in Brafil; but to prevent their reducing their value by collecting too large quantities of them, they are not allowed to employ above 800 flaves in fearching for thefe jewels. To prevent interlopers in this trade, a large town in the neighbourhood of the place where the diamonds are found, and a confiderable diftrict round it, have been depopulated, and the inhabitants removed to another part of the country.

Southward from the captainfhip of Rio Janeiro lies the captainfhip of St. Vincent, which is fuppofed to be the richeft country in Brafil, and perhaps in all South-America. It is bounded on the north by the captainfhip of Rio Janeiro; on the east by the ocean; on the south by the new captainship, or that styled Del Rey; and on the west by the mountain of La Plata, and the countries inhabited by various savage nations, extending from 22° to 27° south latitude. It is in length from north to south, about 300 miles, and in breadth from east to west, in some places, near 180; though, for the greatest part, it is not above half that breadth.

The town of St. Vincent is situated in a very fine bay of the Atlantic ocean, and is well fortified. A little to the north-west lies the town of Santos, which some consider as the capital of the province, and it has as fine a port as any in the West Indies, it being capable of holding the largest ships, and of being fortified in such a manner as to resist any force that could be brought against it.

The only captainship to the southward of St. Vincent, is Del Rey, which extends from 28 to 34° 30 south latitude, and is about 400 miles in length, but not above 100 broad in any part of it. Though this country is pleasant and fertile, it was entirely neglected by the Portuguese, till the discovery of the mines of St. Vincent put them upon planting it, and erecting several forts on the north side of the river La Plata. But though this country is as capable of improvement as any in Brasil, yet, as it has not been inhabited so long as the other captainships, it is far from being thoroughly peopled, and there are only a few villages upon the sea-coast, and some fortresses on the river La Plata.

The chief advantage drawn from this province by the Portuguese, is a kind of smuggling trade carried on with the Spaniards, whom they furnish with rum and tobacco of their own growth, and with cloths, silks, linen, and brandy from Europe.

CHAPTER VIII.

An account of a people in Brasil called Paulists, with a description of the manners of the inhabitants in general.

THE important discoveries mentioned in the last chapter, occasioned new laws, new governments, and new regulations to be established in many parts of the country; which renders it necessary for us here to go back a little, in order to take notice of a set of people named Paulists, who had erected themselves into an independent state, and whom it soon became proper to reduce.

It being suggested to the Portuguese ministry, about the year 1685, that the climate at the bay of All Saints would frustrate whatever endeavours might be used to render the people active and industrious, and that a settlement at the northern and southern extremities of Brasil would render the country of much greater advantage to the crown of Portugal, than it had hitherto been; this occasioned, on the one hand, the establishment of forts and settlements towards the river of the Amazons, and on the other, the improvement of a new colony at Santos, which was then but small.

Most of the persons made choice of for this purpose, were Mestizes, the offspring of such of the Portuguese as had married Brasilian women; and the persons entrusted with the government of these new planters, were priests and monks; but they were sent expressly from Portugal, and care was taken that they should be fit for the purpose. The captain-general of Brasil, and all the officers in the southern captainships, had orders to treat these people kindly, and to give them no disturbance.

It soon appeared that this plan was wisely concerted; for the people multiplied prodigiously, and soon became in very easy circumstances. This drew a number of adventurers thither, among whom were Spaniards as well as Portuguese, free negroes, mulattoes, and all the different mixtures that are to be met with in Brasil down to the Carabocas, who are the offspring of Brasilian savages by negro women; there were also monks as well as laymen, soldiers, mechanics, broken planters, and, in short, all those sort of men who are ready to go any where, or to do any thing to get a living.

As these were a very different sort of men from those of the new colony, it was impossible for them to dwell together; for the former were the quietest and most simple, and the latter the most turbulent people in the world. These adventurers therefore looked out for a new settlement, and at a small distance found one of the properest places upon earth for their reception. This was the thick and vast forest of Parnabaccaba, which overspread all the mountains at the back of this captainship, and in this forest none but wild beasts had hitherto taken up their dwelling They soon cleared a part of this wilderness for their habitation, wherein they established not only a new town, which they named San Paulo, but a new republic, in which they lived after the manner they liked best.

This was at first overlooked; for the country was judged of no great value, and the adjacent captainships were pleased at getting rid of those who resorted thither. However, in the space of a very few years they were too strong to be dealt with; for receiving all sorts of people, they quickly increased from two or three hundred to as many thoufaud men, and being a bold, hardy, enterprifing and daring people, the governors knew not how to deal with them. In the firft place, they took care to fortify the avenues to their territory, which were naturally ftrong; and they feldom ventured abroad, but in bodies of fourfcore or a hundred men; and in fuch parties they frequently traverfed the whole extent of Brafil.

This new and extraordinary commonwealth, were denominated Paulifts, from the city where they lived; they barely acknowledged the fovereignty of the crown of Portugal, without fubmitting to its jurifdiction; and as the tyranny of the governors of Brafil, and the oppreffion of the Spanifh governors in the adjacent provinces furnifhed this new ftate with abundance of members, it at laft became very difficult to gain admittance among them.

They obliged fuch as prefented themfelves upon their frontiers, which they were not allowed to enter, to fubmit to a very ftrict examination, that they might know whether they were fit for their community, and not fpies, or perfons who intended to betray them; upon the bare fufpicion of which they made no fcruple of beating out their brains; but if upon this examination, they judged they might prove ufeful members, they obliged them to bring in two flaves for their fupport; affigning them a dwelling and plantation, by which they commenced Paulifts, and were to continue fo to the end of their lives, for any attempt to defert was punifhed with death without mercy. They made no exception of country or complexion; a favage was as welcome to them as an European, and every man after his admiffion, was at liberty to lead what kind of life he liked beft, provided he did not difturb the peace of fociety.

These people rejecting and despising the mandates of the court of Portugal, were often engaged in a state of hostility with the Portuguese; but, the mountains surrounding their country, and the difficulty of clearing the few passages, that opened into it, generally put it in their power to make their own terms; but as gold was found to abound in this province, the last king of Portugal, (during whose reign the discoveries of Brasilian gold and diamonds were begun and completed) thought it incumbent on him to reduce this province, which now became of great consequence, to the same subjection and obedience with the rest of the country; which he was at last so happy as to effect, and the city of St. Paul is now considered as the centre of the Portuguese mines.

Having thus run through the several captainships, and mentioned the produce and commodities of each, it will not be improper to take some notice of the government and the people in general.

The viceroy has two councils in which he presides, one of criminal and the other of civil affairs; but justice goes on very slowly, and there is not perhaps a country upon earth where so much paper is blotted by the lawyers, before any final judgment is obtained.

There is perhaps no part of the world, China and Japan excepted, where there is so much trouble in getting on shore, or so much difficulty in knowing how to act when a person is landed. The difficulties commodore Anson met with in this respect, will be mentioned in the account we shall hereafter lay before our readers of his voyage round the world. To give a just idea of the manner of their proceeding, it will not be unentertaining if we here present a short abstract from an account of a voyage to Brasil, by a French gentleman, published in the year 1717.

When they came within a league of the city of St. Salvador, they were reftrained from proceeding any farther by a gun fired from a little fort: upon which they came to an anchor, and fent their fupercargo afhore in the boat. He was a very fenfible man, and had withal a great deal of gravity, a quality of all others the moft neceffary, for one who has any bufinefs to tranfact with the Portuguefe.

As foon as he landed, he was conducted to an audience of the Viceroy, who received him with great ftate, and yet fhewed him as much civility as he could expect. He told his Excellency, that he came on behalf of three French fhips homeward bound from the Eaft-Indies, that were greatly diftreffed, and had no hopes of performing their voyage without his protection and relief. The Viceroy, after continuing for fome moments filent, replied, he was very forry for their misfortune, becaufe his mafter's orders were very precife againft admitting any foreign veffels into the port, and that the King had given him directions to feize and confifcate without diftinction, whatever foreign fhips entered their harbour, unlefs it plainly appeared, that they were unable to keep the fea; but that he would allow them twenty-four hours to confider, whether they would come and anchor under the guns of the fort, in order to be examined, or put to fea without receiving any relief at all; adding, that if the cafe was as he reprefented it, care fhould be taken to affift and fupply him: but that the French would do well to remember that the Portuguefe were not to be impofed upon.

As the fhips were really in a very bad condition; they had no reafon to fear any examinations, they therefore on the return of the fupercargo came to an anchor under the fort, and the next day the

Judge came on board, attended by feveral fecretaries and other officers, all of them people of great gravity, who examined every thing with all the nicety and ftrictnefs of an inquifition. They called for their journals, queftioned their pilots, mariners, and even cabbinboys, whether they had not formed the defign of touching at Brafil before they were in fuch diftrefs. They all anfwered in the negative; but ftill they had fo little hopes, that every one in the fhip who had it in his power, made them fome prefent or other, which they received indeed, but fcarce gave them thanks. At laft, however, they took their leave, and fent fome carpenters on board, to whom the Captains made fuch application, that they reported that the leaks were fo dangerous, that the crews were afraid of finking before they could get out of the fhips.

This report was no fooner made, than they had leave to go on fhore, and take lodgings where they thought fit in the city; but with ftrict caution not to attempt any kind of trade on pain of forfeiting both the fhips and cargoes. The officers put on board, at firft talking the fame language, but feeing the impreffion it made, and that the French continued very exact in that particular, they on the third day told them, that this was all a farce; that the Judges themfelves confidered it in that light, and that as they underftood by their prefents that they were a good fort of people, every night boats would come off with all forts of merchandize, and that they would take care the French fhould run no rifk either in buying or felling. The boats came accordingly, and though the French were at firft a little fufpicious, yet in a week's time, they and the Portuguefe perfectly underftood each other, and trade went on brifkly every night, as foon as it was dark.

The French now imagined, that they should find no difficulty in procuring carpenters, and other workmen, if they paid them good wages; but they were miftaken; for none of the people durft take their mony till they had leave; which was not to be obtained, but by dint of prefents; thefe however being properly beftowed, the carpenters came on board and began to work: for it is literally true, that in Brafil, money will do every thing, and that nothing is to be done there without it. They ftaid there four months, and found few honeft men except the Viceroy.

But to proceed: the inhabitants may be divided into three forts; planters, factors, and mariners. The former purchafe as many flaves as they can employ in their fugar and tobacco works, &c. and when the Lifbon fleet comes, fend away their commodities, and receive an equivalent in European goods and manufactures, by the next year's fleet. The factors keep magazines of all forts of goods that come from Portugal, with which they purchafe fugar, tobacco, and gold, of fuch planters as want an immediate fupply of European goods, and cannot wait for the next year's fleet. As for the mariners, their chief bufinefs confifts in their making frequent trips to Guinea to purchafe flaves. This trade is very confiderable. Thofe from the Bay of All Saints ufually bring over about 20,000 Negroes every year, and there is fcarce a Portuguefe here, who has not at leaft a dozen black flaves in his fervice. The people are fond of fhew and magnificence, of rich clothes, jewels, and a large train of fervants, and to enjoy thefe, are very fparing in the expences of their tables. They have however fome feafts; but thefe bring after them a long train of fafts: for every man has his guardian faint, upon whofe anniverfary, he fpends beft part of his annual revenue; and feldom has a good dinner afterwards, except at his neighbour's upon the like occafion.

The inland Brafilians of both fexes ftill go entirely naked; but near the fhore they put on different forts of coverings, fome wearing only fhirts of linen or calico, and others drefs after the European manner. The wives always follow their hufbands to war; but while the man carries nothing but his arms, the woman fupplies the place of fumpter horfe, and is loaded with fuch provifions as are thought neceffary, with a child or children, and a hammock, which at night they hang on trees, or faften to poles, making a defence from the rain with palm-tree leaves. Thefe hammocks are the chief part of their furniture, and are made of cotton, and formed like net-work, fix or feven feet long and four broad: but the Tapoyers make theirs twelve or fourteen feet long, fo as to contain four and fometimes fix perfons; their cans, cups or mugs, are made of callabafhes, fome of which hold thirty quarts. The poorer fort ufe knives of ftone, while the others purchafe theirs of the Europeans.

When at home, the hufband generally goes abroad in the morning with his bow and arrows, to kill birds or beafts, or goes to fifh, while the wife either employs her time in working at a plantation, or attends the hufband to bring home his game.

The Brafilian women are extremely fruitful, and have fuch eafy labours, that a woman immediately after her delivery, goes to the next river, where fhe purifies herfelf by bathing; and there are fome writers who ridiculoufly pretend, that the hufband goes to bed, and for the firft twenty-four hours is nurfed with all the care and ceremony ufed with refpect to a lying-in woman among Europeans. When a woman has conceived, fhe abstains from her husband till after her delivery; nor is it usual for her to cohabit with him while she gives suck. The mothers lament the death of their children with loud lamentations for three or four days; and when friends have been long parted, they meet with open arms, tears, and all possible marks of affection.

They reckon up their age by laying by a chesnut for every year, beginning the computation of their years with the rising of a star called Taku, or the rain star. Royalty is distinguished by the hair being cut in a particular form, and by the length of the thumb nails, which latter is an ornament entirely appropriated to the kings; but Nieuhoff observes, that the princes of the blood are allowed long nails on their fingers; but not on their thumbs.

The inland Brasilians have some knowledge of a Supreme Being, whom they call Tuba, which signifies somewhat most excellent; and the thunder they style Tubakununga, which may be interpreted, a noise made by the Supreme Excellency. They have a confused knowledge of the general deluge, and believe that the whole race of mankind were extirpated by it, except one man and his sister; which latter was pregnant before it happened, and that these by degrees repeopled the world. With respect to a state of future existence, they believe that the soul does not die with the body, but is translated to some pleasant vales beyond the mountains, where they are to enjoy great pleasures, and spend their time in dancing and singing. These are those who have distinguished themselves by performing great actions in defence of their country, &c. but such as have been idle, are supposed to be tortured by evil spirits, whom they call by different names, and of whom they are excessively afraid; and though they pay them no religious worship, yet they sometimes endeavour to appeafe their wrath, by certain prefents faftened to ftakes, which they fet in the ground. They have priefts among them, who are ufed as prophetic inftructors, and are carefully confulted in all material tranfactions, efpecially thofe of war: and there are people among the Brafilians called Potiguaras, accounted fo well fkilled in forcery, as to be able to kill their enemies by their enchantments.

CHAPTER IX.

An account of the vegetables, beafts, birds, and reptiles, found in Brafil.

In defcribing the produce of this country, we fhall begin with the vegetables, and firft mention the mandioca root, to which the Brafilians are indebted for a great part of their fubfiftence; for being dried, powdered, and afterwards baked in the manner of bread, it ferves for the common food of the inhabitants of a great part of America. This root fomewhat refembles a parfnip, and is about two or three feet in length, and of the thicknefs of a man's arm.—It has one peculiar quality, which is, that eaten frefh, it proves a mortal poifon to the human fpecies; but roafted it is not attended with the leaft ill confequence; and though all kinds of beafts will eat and grow fat upon it, yet its juice proves pernicious to them as well as to man.

The nara is alfo very remarkable; it refembles the fempervivum; but its leaves are not fo thick, and are full of prickles. In the middle grows a fruit like a pine-apple, which in taſte reſembles a melon, but is much more delicious, and has a very fragrant ſmell. The juice is eſteemed good for the ſtone. This fruit is ſo very plentiful, that the Indians fatten their hogs with it; and, except ſome ſmall quantities that are uſed for ſweetmeats, they have no other way for the common ſpending of them, but carrying them to ſea, where thoſe who are ſea-ſick receive great benefit from them.

The pacoba, alſo called Adam's fig-tree, is very large; the ſtalks are ſoft and ſpungy, and the leaves very long, ſmooth, and ſoft like velvet; theſe are ſo cool and refreſhing, that people ſick of fevers have them applied to their bodies to abate the violent heat of the diſtemper, and give them eaſe. The fruit grows in cluſters like figs at every foot diſtance upon the main ſtalk, and one cluſter frequently contains two hundred. The fruit being gathered, and laid to ripen, becomes yellow; it then acquires a pleaſant taſte, and is not only grateful to the palate, but eſteemed medicinal, particularly in fevers and ſpitting of blood.

The pocaire is a ſhrub ten or twelve feet high, and has a ſtem much thicker than a man's thigh, and yet ſo tender, that it may be cut aſunder with a ſword at one ſtroke. The leaves reſemble thoſe of water-ſorrel; they are generally ſix feet long, and very broad, but are extremely thin, and have only one ſtrong middle rib to hold them together; on which account they are ſo torn by the winds blowing them about, that they hang in rags, and theſe ſhrubs at a diſtance appear as if ſtuck with feathers. The fruit, which has the name of Poco, is as long as a man's hands, and both in colour and ſhape, are like a cucumber. In taſte they reſemble a fig, though they are much more delicate.

There are here also great plenty of ananas, or pine-apples, which when ripe, are here of a gold colour, and discover themselves to those that walk in the woods, or the places where they grow, by their fine scent. In taste they excel our richest preserved fruits; and the liquor drawn from them, is not inferior to Malmsey wine.

Some authors mention a tree, which, if their accounts be true, is one of the most extraordinary in the world; it has very broad spreading branches, and grows wild in the woods. The thick branches of these trees have large holes, sometimes as long as a man's arm, full of a clear well-tasted water, which when emptied fill again, and in this state continue winter and summer; so that a whole troop of weary travellers may refresh themselves under one of these trees; repose in the cool shade, and at the same time quench their thirst. The want of water being commonly one of the greatest inconveniencies that can be suffered by those who travel the inland parts of the country, it seems as if Providence had kindly provided this remedy, by disposing it up and down in such quantities, and in a manner not exposed to the uncertainties that attend springs and rivulets.

The country produces various sorts of palm-trees, and other fruits, and also mulberries and dewberries; woods of various colours, and some which produce very fragrant scents; in particular the mastic, which, with the rest of the odoriferous plants and shrubs, perfume the woods in the most agreeable manner.

The timbo, is a plant that springs up like a string, and rises up to the top of the highest mulberry-trees, to which it sometimes grows close like ivy. They are exceeding strong and tough, and even those as big as a man's leg, may be wound and twisted about without breaking. But the bark is an infallible poifon to the fifh, and being thrown into the water, leaves hardly any of them alive.

The bombafine cotton fhrubs, are found in great numbers in this country: they grow to an indifferent height, and the fruit when ripe, divides itfelf into four parts, each of which yields the cotton in flocks of the bignefs of a little ball; and in the midft of thefe flocks are black feeds, clofely preffed together.

The mangaba-tree is an evergreen, and bears fruit twice a year: its flowers are like thofe of the jeffamine, and fmells as well: the fruit, which is as big as an apricot, is yellow, fpotted with black, and has feveral kernels within; thefe are eaten as well as the fruit itfelf, and are wholefome, well-tafted, and lie exceeding light on the ftomach.

The araca is a fort of fmall pear, or at leaft it more nearly refembles that than any other fruit: it is of a red, yellow, or green colour; for there are of all thefe kinds in Brafil, and they are extremely beautiful. This fruit is very pleafant, and is admired by thofe who love but a fmall tafte of the four.

The tree jabaticaba, is remarkable for its being entirely befet with fruit, from the very root to the topmoft bough. This fruit is of the fize of a large lemon, it has a four tafte, and the Indians make a good wine of it.

The cabueriba is a very large tree, and affords excellent timber for ftrength and fervice; but what renders it moft valuable is the balm it affords, which, like that of Gilead, heals all green wounds. This is obtained by making an incifion in the bark, through which the balm diftils into a veffel fet to receive it. Both the balm and the tree itfelf have a very fragrant fmell.

The cupayba is a ftraight and tall tree, remarkable for its yielding when cut, a great deal of oil, which ferves both for lamps and the curing of wounds.

This country alfo produces many other trees and fhrubs different from thofe of Europe, and among the reft, of the Brafil-tree, of which we have given a defcription in a former chapter.

As to the beafts, the tapirouffon fomewhat refembles a cow in its fhape and fize, though in other refpects it differs very much from it; it has long fhaggy hair of a reddifh colour, no horns, a very fhort neck and tail, long hanging ears, flender legs, and a whole hoof: but though it has very fharp teeth, it never makes ufe of them againft man or beaft. The natives fometimes catch them in traps, and at others pierce them with arrows, not fo much for the fake of the flefh, (though that is good, and not much unlike beef) as for the hide, which when dry, is in a manner impenetrable.

The cuati is as grey as a badger, to which it has fome refemblance. Its claws and fnout are very long, and by the help of the former it climbs the trees like a monkey. Thefe animals are fo ravenous that there is no creature which is not an overmatch for them, that efcapes being devoured by them; though they chiefly live upon fnakes, birds, and their eggs.

The biarataca is like a ferret, but confiderably larger, and has a remarkable crofs of white and grey along the back; this creature alfo makes great havock among the birds and their eggs; but though it has neither fharp teeth nor long claws, yet it is as able to preferve itfelf from its purfuer, as any other beaft of prey; for nature has given it the power of making fuch an intolerable ftink upon thefe occafions, that both the men and dogs are almoft poifoned with it, and obliged to put an end to the chafe.

The apes and monkeys are very numerous in this country, and are of feveral colours. Thefe are efteemed pretty good food.

The wild boars are of feveral forts, as are alfo the leopards, tygers, and ounces: fome of thefe laft are black, others grey, and others fpotted. No beaft can be more furious. The boars will purfue a man to a tree, and ftay for him there; but the ounces will mount the trees and get up after him. There is nothing they meet can be fecure from their rage. They will affault whole troops of other animals at once, and break into the herds of fwine, deftroy the hen-houfes, and leave wafte and defolation wherever they come. The killing one of them is reckoned a very glorious action among the Indians, and he that is fo happy, has the honour of being efteemed and refpected ever after as a hero.

One of the moft extraordinary animals found in Brafil is the porcupine, called by the Brafilians Kuandu. It is about the fize of an ape; but inftead of hair is covered with fpikes of three or four fingers length, which this animal, when exafperated, darts forth, as the common porcupine does its quills, and that with fuch violence as to wound, and frequently to kill a man. Its eyes are round, ftaring, and as red as carbuncles; it has long whifkers like a cat, and its feet refemble thofe of an ape, only it has but four fingers, the place for the thumb being vacant. This creature ufually fleeps by day, and goes in fearch of prey by night. It is extremely fond of fowl, and climbs up trees, though flowly, in order to devour them. The flefh of this animal has no difagreeable tafte, and is eaten roafted by the inhabitants.

The armadilla, or fhield-hog, refembles our hogs in fize and fhape, but is covered with fcales like a fhield, which on the back has feven partitions, and between each of thefe appears a dark brown fkin. The head is very like that of other hogs, and has a fharp nofe with which it grubs up the earth: its eyes are fmall, and lie deep in the head: it has a fmall fharp tongue, and fhort ears coloured of a dark brown, without hair or fcales. This animal lives upon roots and all kinds of carrion, drinks a great deal, and is very fat. It is fond of marfhy places, but makes holes in which it fhelters itfelf under ground. Its flefh is much admired.

The Brafilian fluggard, fo called from the flownefs of his motion, it not being able to proceed a ftone's throw in many days, is about the fize of a fox. Its head is round, and its mouth, which bears a conftant foam, is little and round: its teeth are fmall and blunt: its nofe is black, high and fmooth; its eyes are fmall, black and heavy, and its body is covered with afh-coloured hair. It dwells upon trees, and lives upon their leaves, without ever tafting any drink; and is fo much afraid of rain, that upon its approach, it hides itfelf. Though the limbs of this animal are extremely weak, and feem in a manner disjointed, yet it will take fuch hold as is not eafily unloofed.

The tamandua, or ant-bear, thus named from its food, is of two forts, the great and the fmall. The former, which is about the bignefs of a middle fized hog, has a round head, a long fnout and no teeth. This animal catches ants by laying out its tongue, which Nieuhoff fays, is twenty-five and fometimes thirty inches long, upon a dunghill, till his prey fettle upon it, which they have no fooner done, than he draws them into his mouth, and fwallows them.

The fmall one is about the fize of a fox; on the four feet it has four crooked claws; and two broad black lifts run along its back. It is a very fierce creature: it grafps at every thing with its paw, and upon being ftruck with a ftick, it will fit upright, and take hold of it with its mouth. It fleeps all day, and at night goes in fearch of its prey: but when it drinks fome of the water fpouts through its noftrils.

The Senembi, or land crocodile, is very common in Brafil; but it feldom exceeds five feet in length. There are faid to be certain ftones in its head, which being given by two drams at a time, prove an infallible remedy for the gravel. It can live two or three months without food and afford flefh as white and as good as a rabbit.

Parrots are fome of the moft common birds of the country, for they fly together in large flocks and are killed by thoufands; notwithftanding which, they are fo numerous that thofe killed are not to be miffed: there are various forts of them, and all of them will talk with very little teaching except one fpecies. Their colours are very beautiful and fhining, and in many of them are moft admirably mixed. The breaft of fome is as red as fcarlet, and their bodies either yellow, green, or blue, but not without a little mixture of all thefe colours. Thefe never lay above two eggs at a time, and breed in the trunks of old trees, and about the rocks. Others, with all the former colours, have alfo a mixture of black and grey, and thefe breed in the houfes. Another fpecies is black, fprinkled with a little green, the eyes and beak are red, and the feet yellow. There is another fort whofe body is all green; it has a yellow cap and collar, the head is adorned with a fine tuft of blue feathers, and the tail red, yellow, and green. But the parrot called the Tuin, is fomething more fingular, if not for its colours, yet for its fize; for it is no bigger than a fparrow, and yet is always talking and finging after its manner;

and will skip into the bosom of the person who breeds it, and eat out of his mouth.

The Guiranheugeta is of the size of a goldfinch. Its back and wings are blue: its breast and belly yellow, and it has a diadem of the same coloured feathers upon its head. This is an admirable bird for the cage, for it has the notes of many other sorts of birds, and makes such a variety of changes and turnings in its singing, that it is a concert of itself.

In Brasil there is a kind of bats of the size of a crow: these have very sharp teeth and bite violenty. They build their nests in hollow trees and old walls.

There are here a kind of wild-geese, much like those in Europe, only somewhat larger, and their feathers vary more in colour; but though they are water-fowls they generally prove both fleshy and well-tasted.

The Barn-bird has a very odd appearance, it having a bill of an astonishing length, and a crown of green and white feathers upon its head; one half of which, as well as half the neck, has no feathers at all. It is about the size of a stork, and, when skinned and boiled, proves tolerable food.

The Bill-bird is about the size of a wood-pigeon, and has a saffron coloured crop about the neck, of three or four fingers in compass. Its bill, which is altogether as large as the whole body, is yellow without, and red within; and its feathers, which are yellow on the breast, and black on all the other parts, are tipped with red.

Brasil also produces many sorts of wild-fowl, that differ but very little from those of Europe. Among the small birds, the Brasilian humming-bird is the most singular; for though very small, it makes a loud noise, and is of so variable a hue, that turn it which way you please, it changes its colour. Some of the Brafilian women hang one of thefe at each ear, in the manner of a pendant.

Among the various forts of ferpents found here, is the rattle-fnake, alfo common in the Englifh fettlements; but the moft fingular is the Guaku or Liboya, a ferpent of a monftrous fize; fome of them being, according to Nieuhoff, twenty, and others even thirty feet long. It is extremely voracious, and will leap out of the hedges upon men or beafts. It is not, however, fo venomous as other ferpents, and the flefh is deemed tolerable food.

The Gekko is indeed of a moft venomous nature, and its bite proves mortal, unlefs the part wounded be immediately cut off, or burnt with a hot iron. The poifonous quality of this creature is particularly evinced, by the dreadful effects which proceed from an outward application of its urine, which, upon touching the fkin, caufes a blacknefs and gangrene. The Curcuma root, which we call Turmeric, is deemed by the Brafilians, the moft powerful remedy for this poifon.

There are lizards in Brafil four feet in length, which the negroes eat with fafety.

Scorpions here alfo grow to a very large fize, and their fting is venomous.

Among the fpiders, there is one fort of a remarkable large fize, generally found in dunghills, or the cavities of hollow trees, which weave webs like other fpiders; if provoked, they wound with a fting fo fmall, as to be fcarcely vifible, and yet fo venomous, that it raifes a bluifh fwelling, that is very painful, and even mortal, if not prevented by a timely antidote.

The *Discoveries of the English in America.*

CHAPTER I.

The discoveries made by the English during the reigns of king Henry VII. and VIII. containing the voyages of John Cabot, who first visited Newfoundland, and the island of St. John, and of Sebastian Cabot for the finding out a north-west passage, who first discovered the continent of America, and sailed along the coast as far as Florida, &c.

JOHN CABOT a citizen of Venice, who had been long settled at Bristol, sailed in an English ship, with a view of making discoveries, in 1494, while Christopher Columbus was performing his second voyage, and actually saw the coast of Newfoundland, to which he gave the name of Prima Vista or First Seen; and on the 24th of June landed in an island, which he called St John's, from his discovering it on the day of that saint. This island, which is in the bay now called St. Lawrence, appeared to be extremely barren; but the sea around it abounded in fish, and the natives, who wore the skins of bears for cloaths, were armed with bows and arrows, pikes and wooden clubs, darts and slings.

Upon this discovery, king Henry VII. granted a patent to John Cabot and his three sons, Lewis, Sebastian, and Sanchius, dated the 5th of March, 1495, with authority to sail with five ships upon discoveries to the east, west and north, allowing them the full properties of the countries they should discover, with this only reservation, that they should return to Bristol, and pay him the fifth part of the neat profits of the voyage, in consideration of which they were to have the exclusive right to the countries so discovered, and no other English subjects were to trade thither, without their licence. He had afterwards a new grant, by which he had leave to take ships out of any of the ports of England of the burden of 200 tons. John, however, dying before the squadron set sail, his son, Sebastian, made a proposal to the king, to discover a north-west passage to the Indies, and for that purpose had a ship manned and victualled at Bristol at the king's expence, and three or four other ships were fitted out by some of the merchants of that city.

With this squadron Sebastian set sail in May 1497, and on the eleventh of June got into the latitude of 67°. 30, where finding the sea still open, he imagined that he might have passed through into the Indian sea; but his crew mutinying, he was obliged to return into the latitude of 56°. and from thence he steered along the continent of America till he came into 38°. on the coast, which he expresly says, was afterwards called Florida, where provisions growing short, he steered back, and having touched at Newfoundland, returned to England.

This Sebastian Cabot was the first discoverer of the continent of America, which Columbus did not see till a year after, and the first who took a view of Florida, which was visited by Juan Ponce de Leon, in 1512, who gave it the name of Florida; took possession of it for the king of Spain, and usually passes for the first discoverer. This voyage gave great light to Ferdinand Magellan, and induced him confidently to affirm, that such a passage might be found by the south, which he happily effected twenty-two years after.

Sebaſtian Cabot after this entered into the Spaniſh ſervice, when he diſcovered the river Plata, and ſailed up it 360 miles. This occaſioned his being made grand pilot of Spain; but after reſiding for ſome time at Seville in that character, he returned to England, and was employed by king Henry VIII. in conjunction with Sir Thomas Pert, vice-admiral of England. Theſe gentlemen ſailed in 1516, with two ſhips of 250 tons, to the coaſt of Braſil, and afterwards viſited the Spaniſh iſlands of St. Domingo, and St. John Porto de Rico. In the laſt of theſe iſlands they traded, and paid for what they had, by giving in exchange veſſels made of pewter.

A war with Scotland put an end to any further diſcoveries during this reign. But at length Mr. Hore, a merchant of London, reſolved to attempt a ſettlement in Newfoundland, and to go thither himſelf. This gentleman receiving all the encouragement he could expect from king Henry VIII. many young gentleman of fortune and diſtinguiſhed rank, offered to ſhare both the expence and danger of the undertaking; Mr. Hore therefore fitted out two ſhips, which ſet ſail about the end of April 1536, with 120 men on board, including thirty perſons of character.

Within the ſpace of two months they arrived at Cape Breton, from whence they ſailed round a great part of Newfoundland to Penguin iſland, in the latitude of 50°. 40', where they found great plenty of the fowl from whence the iſland takes its name. They afterwards went on ſhore upon the eaſt ſide of Newfoundland, and had an accidental view of a boat-full of the natives of the iſland, whom they purſued both by ſea and land, but were not able to overtake them. They ſtaid here till their proviſions began to grow very ſhort, and being then afraid to truſt themſelves at ſea in ſuch a condition, delayed going on board, till they were in such distress that they actually eat one another; for some of them killed their companions privately in the woods, hid them, and then secretly roasted and eat their flesh, till this horrid practice coming to the knowledge of their commander, by a judicious and pathetic speech, brought them to resolve rather to live upon grass and weeds, than to subsist any longer by this detestable method.

Soon after a French ship well manned and victualled, put into the same harbour; of this the English, prompted by the irresistible calls of hunger, resolved to take advantage, and being weary of a country in which they had endured such miseries, waited for a fair opportunity, and then seizing the French ship, left their own, and sailed directly for the coast of England. They had a prosperous voyage, and arrived at St. Ives in Cornwall, about the end of October, so much altered, that their nearest relations did not know them.

Some months after the Frenchmen came to England to complain, that the English had run away with their ship, and that they should have perished with hunger, if they had not supported themselves by fishing. King Henry examined closely into the affair, and finding that extreme want was the sole cause of an action that could be no otherwise justified, he satisfied the French to the full extent of their demands, and pardoned his own subjects a crime which necessity had forced them to commit.

To these beginnings we owe the Newfoundland trade. That island is of a triangular figure, 350 miles in length from north to south, and 200 miles in breadth at the base from east to west, where broadest. On the north it is separated from the continent, by the narrow streights of Belleisle; on the west it ha the bay of St. Lawrence; on the south Cape Breton; and on the east the ocean. There is no country in the world better furnished with harbours, and it is abundantly supplied with fresh water. The climate in summer is very hot, and in winter so cold, that the snow lies upon the ground at least five months, notwithstanding its being situated in between 47 and 52 of north latitude, and consequently more to the south than England. It however produces filberts, strawberries, some kinds of cherries, and other hardy fruits. Corn and hay succeed but indifferently, yet it affords great plenty of venison, wild-fowl, and fish, so that with dry food in plenty from Europe, people may live there very comfortably even in winter, since the country produces fuel of several kinds in abundance. In short, notwithstanding the dreadful distresses of the above gentlemen who first attempted a settlement in this island, and notwithstanding the bleakness and barrenness of this inhospitable country, it soon became of the utmost consequence; for towards the close of queen Elizabeth's reign, there was annually employed upon its coast upwards of 200 fishing vessels, on board of which were above 8000 seamen.

Some time after Mr. William Hawkins, an officer in king Henry VIIIth's navy, made three prosperous voyages to Guinea, and from thence across the Atlantic ocean to Brasil, where having some dealings with the prince or chief of the Brasilians, he expressed a desire of seeing England; but at the same time shewed a suspicion of his not obtaining leave to return home. To remove this distrust, capt. Hawkins very readily offered to leave Mr. Martin Cockram, whom the Indians esteemed next to himself, as an hostage, and this offer was readily accepted.

This Brasilian chief he brought over, and presented to king Henry, who received and entertained him very kindly, and after a year's stay in England, generously dismissed him. But in his passage home, the Indian chief unhappily died, which gave all on board great concern, from an apprehension that Mr. Cockram would be either punished with death, or detained during life. Their fears were however ill founded; for the Brasilians hearing what they had to allege, readily concluded that it was far from being likely they would dare to return to their country if they had ill used their king, and that it was out of their power to preserve his life, if he was attacked by sickness. They therefore freely set Mr. Cockram at liberty, kindly entertained the men, and furnished the ship with a sufficient cargo for England. This encouraged other merchants to trade to those parts of Brasil that were not yet in the possession of the Portuguese.

CHAPTER II.

Capt. Drake's voyage to the isthmus of Darien, giving an account of what happened till his return to Plymouth.

IN the following reign, the people were unsuccessfully employed in discovering either a north-east or a north-west passage, in hopes of grasping the whole trade of the Indies, and by bending all their strength that way, neglected making those discoveries that might have been attended with success. But in the reign of queen Elizabeth, who made the naval power of this nation her peculiar care, discoveries were carried on with fresh vigour, and between the years 1562 and 1568, captain John Hawkins made three voyages to the West-

Indies, and in all but the laſt, had very great ſucceſs. In the year 1572, capt. Francis Drake alſo made his famous expedition into the Weſt-Indies.

This gentleman who had accompanied his kinſman Sir John Hawkins, in his laſt expedition, ſet ſail from Plymouth on the 24th of May 1572, in the Paſca of 70 tons burden, with the Swan of 250 tons, commanded by his brother John Drake. He had on board 73 men and boys, and had not only a good ſtock of ammunition and a year's proviſions, but had three pinnaces ſtowed on board, in pieces, that might, upon occaſion, be ſpeedily joined together. He made the Canary iſlands on the 2d of June and on the 29th paſſed between Guadaloupe and Dominica, on the ſouth ſide of which they came to an anchor, and finding ſeveral cottages formed of the boughs of palm-trees, but no ſign of inhabitants, he inferred that theſe were the occaſional reſidence of fiſhermen.

Having ſtaid here three days, he weighed anchor, and ſteering towards the main land of America, made Port Pheaſant, where he erected his pinnaces, and was ſoon after joined by James Rawſe, in a bark belonging to the Iſle of Wight, with 30 men, they being informed that he deſigned to ſurprize Nombre de Dios.

They left this place in company on the 22d of July, and three days after took two ſmall veſſels, from Nombre de Dios, laden with planks, by which they learned, that ſome ſoldiers were daily expected at that town from the governor of Panama, to protect the inhabitants from the Symerons, a people inhabiting the country between that place and Panama. Theſe were deſcended from thoſe, who flying from the cruelty of the Spaniards, about eighty years before, had by degrees formed themſelves into a nation.

Mr. Drake having treated thefe people civilly, fet them on fhore, judging it impoffible for them to convey any intelligence about him to the town, before his arrival, it being at a confiderable diftance by land; then taking 53 men with drums, trumpets, and warlike ftores, he left the reft of his company with their fhips, under the care of capt. Rawfe, in a fecure and fecret fituation, and proceeded in the pinnaces, keeping all day clofe under the fhore, and rowing hard at night, till he entered the harbour. He there got between the town and a fmall fhip juft arrived from Old Spain, which he forced to the other fide of the bay, to prevent her giving the alarm, and then landing without refiftance, marched up to the fort, where there was but one man, who fled to alarm the place. On the captain's entering it he found no more than fix brafs guns and a few culverins, which he difmounted.

Mr. Drake, then leaving a few of his men to keep poffeffion of the fort, and fome others to guard the pinnaces, marched to an high ground, where he divided the failors who accompanied him into two parties of fixteen men each. One under the command of John Oxenham, he ordered to enter the eaft end of the town, near the market-place, while he himfelf, with drums beating and colours flying, led the reft up the principal ftreets.

The inhabitants had drawn themfelves up near the governor's houfe, to cover the gate leading to Panama, in order to fecure a retreat; but were fo terrified at the fight of the Englifh, that after firing two or three times, they threw down their arms and fled with the utmoft precipitation. The alarm bell ftill continued ringing, but Mr. Drake, having ordered it to be filenced, marched towards the royal treafury, which was then immenfely rich; and the door of the ftore-houfe being in the confusion left open, saw a prodigious number of large silver bars, none of which the men were allowed to meddle with; but unhappily at this instant, a violent storm of thunder, lightning and rain, damaged their arms, and filled the men with apprehensions that their pinnaces were in danger. This threw them into confusion; however Mr. Drake boldly insisted upon their proceeding, and would doubtless have executed his design of plundering the treasury; but becoming faint through loss of blood, occasioned by a wound in his leg, which he had hitherto concealed, he was with much difficulty persuaded to have it dressed, and to be carried on board one of the pinnaces This obliged the rest to retire to their vessels, with the loss of one man.

They now proceeded to a small but plentiful island, about two leagues from the town, greatly mortified at leaving such immense wealth behind them. They there staid to refresh themselves, and then proceeded to their ships, which they reached on the first of August, when captain Rawse, having no hopes of their meeting with success, since they were now certainly discovered all along the coast, resolved to leave them.

Mr. Drake, having staid here six days, sailed for Carthagena, when he soon found, by the firing of the ordnance, and ringing of the bells, that he was discovered; he however seized an outward bound ship of 240 tons burden that lay in the road, and two smaller vessels, dispatched thither from Nombre de Dios, to give notice of his being on the coast: he however treated those on board with great civility, and set them on shore.

He now resolved to sink the Swan, and knowing that the sailors would oppose it, prevailed on the carpenter to bore three holes in her bottom, when the water pouring in, they removed her cargo, and then fet fire to her to prevent her falling into the enemy's hands.

This being done he appointed his brother to command his own fhip, and went himfelf on board one of the pinnaces. He foon found a convenient fertile fpot on the coaft of Darien, proper for erecting tents for his men, and preparing fuch warlike ftores as he moft wanted. They were here perfectly covered from view, and the veffel lay entirely concealed in a neighbouring creek, by which means he hoped to raife a belief, that he had entirely left the coaft.

Having ftaid here till the eighth of September, he told his brother to take care of the fhip, and, taking part of the men, proceeded with two pinnaces for the Rio Grande, keeping as much as poffible out of fight. He landed his men about two leagues to the weftward of Carthagena, where treating the Indians with great civility, they fupplied him with cattle and other frefh provifions; for which he gave them fome trifles in exchange. The next day he made the mouth of the river, where they had a terrible ftorm, and after that was over, the men were much peftered with mufketo's; but defended themfelves againft their attacks by rubbing their bodies with lemon-juice.

They found the channel of the Rio Grande twenty-three fathoms deep, and fo broad, that it required a very good eye to fee from fhore to fhore. They here faw feveral houfes, and a Spaniard beckoning to them, they made towards the land, when he finding that they were not his countrymen, as he had at firft imagined, betook himfelf to flight. They however landed, and found fome cheefe, white rufk, bacon, feveral forts of fweetmeats, and a confiderable quantity of fugar, out of which they fupplied their veffels, with as much as they wanted.

Mr. Drake now failed back to his brother, and by the way boarded several vessels in hopes of finding gold, but they happened to be laden only with provisions and other necessaries. Of these he took a great quantity, and disposed of it in an island in such a manner, that if any part of it should be surprized by the Spaniards, there would still be a sufficient supply left, in case he should stand in need of it. During his absence, his brother John had concluded a league of friendship with the Symerons, whom he promised to assist against the Spaniards, from whom they had taken a large quantity of gold and silver, and thrown it into the river; for as they set no value on that metal, they had no other motive for seizing it than that of exasperating their enemies.

As it was unusual for the Spaniards to bring down their treasures during the rainy season, which now approached, captain Drake resolved to cruize in those seas till the time of their setting out, during which he plundered a great number of ships, but unhappily his brother John was slain in gallantly boarding a frigate. Upon this he moored his ship, and resolved to appear no more till the Spanish treasurer was set out for Nombre de Dios. However while he thus lay by, several of his men died of calentures, among whom was his brother Joseph Drake.

The captain being at length informed by the Symerons that the treasurer was set out, he resolved, by their assistance, to march over land to Panama; these people not only consenting to serve him for guides, but to carry a large quantity of provisions; and when those failed, they agreed to supply him with more, by the help of their bows and arrows.

They set out on the 3d of February, 1573, being forty-eight in company, eighteen of whom were Englifh, who had nothing to incommode them but their arms. On the third day of their march they arrived at a town belonging to the Symerons, fituated on the fide of a hill, near a river, and encompaffed with an high mud wall. The inhabitants made a very neat appearance; their drefs differed but little from that of the Spaniards, and they received thefe ftrangers with great civility, and feemed to be in want of nothing, having all kinds of provifions in plenty.* This town was thirty-five leagues from Nombre de Dios, and fifty-five from Panama. It was conftantly guarded againft the Spaniards, and the natives having the moft implacable hatred againft that nation, they often furprized and cut them off in the woods.

The captain left this place after ftaying there only one night, and then marching ten days afcended a very high hill, where, from a tree pointed out to him by the Symerons, he beheld the north fea, which he had left on the one hand, and the fouth-fea on the other, and from that moment refolved, if poffible, to fail thither in an Englifh fhip.

Panama being now frequently in fight, he thought it prudent to keep his men as clofe together as poffible, and their fuccefs depending on their being concealed, they ftruck out of the common road and reached a grove in the road to Nombre de Dios, at a fmall diftance from Panama. Here capt. Drake fent a Symeron in difguife to act as fpy, who foon returned with intelligence that the treafurer of Lima was to fet out that very night with his family for Nombre de Dios, in order to embark for Spain, attended by fourteen mules, fome of which were laden with gold, others with filver, and one with valuable jewels; and that the fame night two caravans would pafs the fame way, with fifty mules in each, laden with provifions and a fmall quantity of filver. This intelligence was soon after confirmed by a centinel, whom they were so fortunate as to seize.

Upon receiving this intelligence, capt. Drake concealed himself with half his men fifty paces from the highway, while Mr. John Oxenham, and one of the Symeron chiefs, posted themselves with the other half on the opposite side. In this manner things were disposed, when one of the men who had drank too much, got up to see what approached, at the instant when the mules laden with provisions were passing by, though the captain had given strict orders that not the least notice should be taken of them, and this man being dressed in a white shirt, which was the mark of distinction worn by the English, was perceived by a Spaniard, who spread the alarm, so that the treasurer turned his baggage out of the road, and only the mules with provisions came forward, some of which they seized; but to their great mortification, got only about the quantity of two horse loads of silver.

Having staid to refresh themselves, they mounted the mules, and proceeded towards Santa Cruz, but set those beasts at liberty on their approaching the town. They were now met by a party of soldiers, who summoned them to surrender, and promised to give them very kind treatment. The English laughed at this proposal, and received the enemy's fire, which they so effectually returned, that they put them to flight, when briskly following the pursuit, they entered the town with them, the Symerons supporting them through the whole action with the greatest bravery.

Santa Cruz then consisted of about fifty neat houses, with a governor and other officers, with warehouses for receiving the Spanish goods which were brought thither from Nombre de Dios up the river Chagre, and from thence carried by mules to Panama. The captain here made an equal divifion of the plunder he found in the town, among his own men and the Symerons.

There were at that time at Santa Cruz three ladies, who came thither to lie in, the air being much better than at Nombre de Dios, to which city they belonged, and as it was Mr. Drake's conftant practice to behave upon all occafions with as much humanity and decorum as poffible, he was no fooner informed of their fituation, than he gave orders for their being particularly protected, and foon after vifited them himfelf, to prevent their entertaining any unjuft apprehenfions of his conduct

Though captain Drake was refolved to ftay fome time longer on the coaft, he now began to be uneafy for his fhip, from which he had been abfent above a fortnight. He therefore returned to it with all the expedition poffible, and to his great joy found every thing in as good order as he could defire.

The Symerons now propofed making an attack on the houfe of Pezoro an avaricious Spaniard deeply concerned in the mines, whofe income amounted to above 200l. a day, which he conftantly locked up in chefts. He lived near Verague, a town to the weft of Nombre de Dios, and one of the Symerons, who had been his flave and had fled from his tyranny, promifed to guide them to his treafures: but having only a fmall ftock of provifions remaining, the captain thought it more neceffary to obtain a frefh fupply, in order to preferve the health and vigour of his men; Mr. Oxenham was therefore ordered to proceed with one of the frigates towards Toulon, and to bring off all the provifions he could meet with, Mr. Drake refolved to ply off the Cabezas in hopes of becoming mafter of fome of the treafure barks that pafs and repafs, between Nicaragua and Veragua. Thus he wifely avoided the expedition againft Pezoro, which would have been extremely laborious, as his men muſt have marched through a confiderable tract of country.

Capt. Drake during this cruize feized only a fmall veſſel, in which was fome gold, and a Genoefe pilot, who informed him, that the Engliſh had every where fpread an univerſal terror; while Oxenham took but one frigate, wherein was about 200 cocks and hens, twenty-eight hogs, and a confiderable quantity of maize. But what was of more confequence, he learnt from the prifoners, that two galleys had been built at Nombre de Dios in order to ferve as a convoy to the Chagre fleet, the treafures of which now principally engroſſed Mr. Drake's attention.

While things were in this fituation, they were alarmed by obferving a fail bearing down upon them, which however proved to be only a French fhip of about eighty tons burden, the crew whereof were in great want of water, with which the captain ordered them to be fupplied; and they being informed of his defigns, offered to join him, which after fome deliberation was permitted.

The captain now leaving the two fhips in a fafe harbour, manned the frigate and two pinnaces, with fifteen Engliſh and Symerons, and twenty French, and with this force fteered to the Rio Francifco, where the water being fhallow, he left the frigate, with orders to lie clofe till the return of the pinnaces. In thefe he proceeded with his forces as far up the river Francifco as was thought convenient; and then landing, marched forward with great regularity and filence, guided by the Symerons, till they came within a mile of the high road, when they refreſhed themfelves, and took up their quarters.

The next day they were agreeably furprifed by the noife of the bells hung about the mules, they therefore fet out to attack them, and found three caravans near together, two of which confifted of seventy mules each, and one of fifty, all of them richly laden with gold and silver. They had a guard of forty-five soldiers, who fired on the approach of the English and French, and then retreated in order to call more assistance. By the above fire the French captain was wounded and one Symeron killed. The English and French now made the best use possible of their time, loaded themselves with as many wedges of gold and silver as they could carry, and having buried the rest in the sand, retreated towards the river, leaving behind them the French captain, who had fainted in the woods with the loss of blood, and a French sailor, who had overloaded himself with gold.

The next day they reached the Rio Francisco, where not finding the pinnaces, they began to fear they were lost; which appeared the more probable as seven Spanish pinnaces appeared hovering at a distance; but a sudden gust of wind attended with rain, obliged the Spaniards to sheer off.

Capt. Drake was much concerned at the apprehensions that if his pinnaces were taken, the poor men would be put to the torture to make them discover where his frigate and ships were; but being sensible that though this should really be the case, it would be some time before they could reach the ships, he assisted his men in making a raft, in order to attempt to get on board before the enemy. In this attempt he was accompanied only by one Englishman, two hardy Frenchmen, and a Symeron, who generously endeavoured to persuade him, in case his ships were destroyed, to live among those of his nation, who would do every thing in their power to serve him.

These having lashed the raft pretty securely, fixed a kind of rudder, and erected a sail made of a biscuit bag, they committed themselves to the mercy of the sea, sitting up to the waist, and sometimes up to the arm-pits in water, and after a fatiguing voyage of about fix hours, obferved the pinnaces lying behind a point where they had caft anchor.

Upon this joyful fight he ran the raft on the neareft fhore, and went to them by land, where after keeping them for fome time in fufpenfe, he informed them of his vaft fuccefs, and the lofs of their captain and a failor. He was now told, that the pinnaces were prevented from fteering up to Rio Francifco at the time appointed, by a hard gale of wind. They however made a fhift to reach that river at night, where they took in their comrades with the treafure, and then fteered directly for the frigate, and the fhips, which having come up with, the captain divided the gold and filver, to their mutual fatisfaction, equally between the Englifh and French.

A few days after, capt. Drake fent a detachment of twelve Englifh and fixteen Symerons, to bring away the reft of the treafure; but they could find only thirteen bars of filver and fome wedges of gold; for the reft had been difcovered and carried away, even the ground dug up for a mile round. They however brought this off, together with one of the Frenchmen, who, though he had been left behind, had the happinefs to efcape from the Spaniards.

The captain's thoughts were now bent on returning home, having therefore difmiffed the French fhip, he fteered to cape Cabezas, taking feveral Spanifh veffels laden with provifions by the way. At this laft place they ftaid feven days, and gave the Symerons all the iron work, of which they were extremely fond, and whatever elfe they chofe. Mr. Drake alfo made them feveral prefents of linen, and filks for their wives and female relations; and giving to one of them a very handfome cutlafs, was in return prefented with four wedges of gold; but he no fooner received them, than he threw them into the common stock, declaring that he thought it would be unjust not to share with those who had assisted in fitting him out, and had bought the cutlass, the price for which it was sold: A noble instance of disinterested integrity!

On their leaving these friendly people, they made some small prizes, and arriving at cape St. Anthony, took in a supply of turtle and their eggs, which were of great service during the rest of the voyage. Being soon after in want of water, there happily fell such a prodigious shower of rain as afforded them a sufficient quantity without their touching, as they intended, at Newfoundland: they therefore stretched over from Florida to the islands of Scilly, and came to an anchor in Plymouth harbour on the 9th of August, 1573, when the people being at church, and hearing the news of their arrival, instantly hurried out, and ran to the shore, to welcome him and his men on their happy return from this succefsful expedition.

CHAPTER III.

Sir Humphry Gilbert obtains a patent for settling the continent of North-America, discovered by John and Sebastian Cabot: Takes a formal possession of Newfoundland, but meets with many disasters, and is lost in his return.

CAPTAIN Drake's great succefs encouraged others to follow his example, and in a very short time the English privateers made various voyages into all parts of America, and soon pilots capable of navigating ships to any part of the known world became so numerous, that such projects were daily set on foot, as in the former age would have been thought impracticable; but in this were carried into execution at the expence of private perfons, without any affiftance from the crown, though they had all the countenance and encouragement they could defire: Among thefe, none was fo great a proof of maritime fkill, and fo honourable in every refpect to the nation, as the next expedition of capt. Francis Drake, in 1577, in which he failed round the globe, which voyage will be inferted among the moft remarkable of thofe excellent mariners who have alfo encompaffed the earth.

Some years after this voyage, Sir Humphry Gilbert, a gentleman of Devonfhire, reprefented to queen Elizabeth the expediency of fettling all thofe countries upon the continent of America, which had been formerly difcovered by Sebaftian Cabot, in order to prevent their falling into the hands of the French: Upon which her majefty granted him letters patent, to difcover, plant, fettle, and even to fortify and build caftles, in any of the northern countries, not then in the poffeffion of any chriftian prince.

Upon this encouragement this gentleman applied himfelf to his friends and relations, in order to form a fociety capable of carrying this defign into execution. In this he however met with many difficulties; notwithstanding which he put to fea, but his voyage proved very unfortunate, and was attended with the lofs of one of his beft fhips. After this fevere blow he fold his eftate, in order to furnifh the neceffary expences of another fquadron, in which feveral gentlemen of rank and fortune agreed to go with him in perfon.

This fquadron confifted of the following veffels; the Delight of 120 tons, in which went Sir Humphry himfelf; the bark Raleigh, fitted out by Mr. Walter Raleigh, of 200 tons; the Golden Hind, of forty tons; the Swallow, of forty tons; and the Squirrel, of ten tons; having on board in all 260 men, among whom were many shipwrights, masons, carpenters, smiths, miners and refiners.

It was resolved by the proprietors, that the fleet should sail to Newfoundland, and having taken in provisions there, proceed to the south, and not to pass by any river or bay worthy of notice, without examining it. On the 11th of June, 1583, this fleet set sail from Plymouth, but on the 13th the Raleigh, commanded by capt. Butler, left the fleet, under the pretence that the captain and his men were suddenly taken ill of a contagious disease. On the 30th of July they saw land in about the latitude of 51°, and from thence coasted along it to the south, and on the 3d of August entered St. John's harbour in Newfoundland, where they found the Squirrel, which had been separated from them, riding at anchor in the mouth of the harbour, having been refused entrance by the vessels that were fishing within it to the number of thirty-six sail, of all nations.

Sir Humphry now sending his boat to inform the masters of the fishing barks that he had a commission from the queen to take possession of those lands for the crown of England, they submitted to the levying a tax of provisions upon each ship, for supplying the wants of his squadron, and he entered the harbour.

The next day, Sir Humphry and his company were conducted on shore by the masters of the English fishing-vessels, and on the 5th, having caused a tent to be set up in the view of the ships in the harbour, and being attended by all under his command, he summoned the merchants and masters, both English and foreigners to be present at his taking a formal and solemn possession of those territories. These being assembled he caused his commission under the great seal of England, to be openly read before them, and to be interpreted to those who were strangers to the English tongue,

which being done, he declared that he took poffeffion of the harbour of St. John, and 200 leagues
every way, invefting her majefty with the title
and dignity thereof, and then had a turf of foil
delivered to him in token of taking poffeffion alfo
for himfelf, his heirs and affigns for ever.

Sir Humphry, after this formal manner of taking
poffeffion, had the country examined, and fome
pieces of ore brought to him, fome of which were
faid to be that of filver, and of this he had the
moft pofitive affurances from a Saxon miner in his
company. Having at length taken in a fupply of
provifions, he found himfelf obliged to proceed
on his difcoveries to the fouthward; for fome of
his men falling fick and dying, and others defert-
ing him, the number of his people was fo leffened,
as to oblige him to leave the Swallow behind.

Sir Humphry now went on board the Squirrel,
that fmall veffel being moft proper for difcovering
the coaft, on account of her being able to run
into every check, and on the 20th of Auguft,
failed from the harbour of St. John with three
fhips, the Delight, the Golden Hind and the
Squirrel. The next night they reached Cape
Race, which is twenty-five leagues diftant, and
from thence failed about eighty-feven leagues
towards Cape Breton.

On the 29th they had a violent ftorm, with rain,
and fo thick a mift that they could not fee a cable's
length before them; and early the next morning
they found themfelves in the midft of fhoals and
fands, upon which a fignal was given to the Delight to fteer to feaward; but it was too late, for
fhe immediately ftruck; and her ftern and hind-
quarter foon beat to pieces; however the Golden
Hind and the frigate bore away to the fouth, and
with much difficulty got clear of the fhoals.

In the Delight there unhappily perifhed Capt.
Maurice Brown with near 100 perfons: The Cap-

tain might indeed have probably faved his life, if he would have left the fhip immediately on her ftriking; but he would not be the firft in fetting an ill example. In the mean time fourteen perfons leaped into a fmall pinnace of a ton and a half burden, no bigger than a Thames boat. They for fome time looked out for the Captain, but not feeing him took in Mr. Clarke the mafter of the Delight, and one more. Being now fixteen in number, they cut the rope, and committed themfelves to the mercy of the waves, without any provifions, or a drop of frefh water, and nothing to work with but one oar. The boat feeming to be overloaded, one Edward Headly, thinking it was better for fome to perifh than all, propofed that four of the number might be thrown overboard to lighten the boat, and to caft lots in order to determine who fhould perifh; but he was over-ruled by Mr. Clarke, who, though it was propofed that he fhould be excepted from the number, perfuaded his comrades to fubmit their fafety to providence. The boat was driven fix days and nights before the wind; during which thefe poor wretches had no other fuftenance than their own urine, and fome weeds that fwam on the furface of the water. In this extremity of cold, wet, hunger and thirft, Headly, and one more perifhed on the fifth day; but the other fourteen lived till they were driven the feventh day on fhore on the coaft of Newfoundland; whence they failed in a French fhip to France, and before the end of the year returned to England.

Sir Humphry, difcouraged by thefe difafters, and his men being in want of neceffaries, propofed to return to England, having, in his opinion, made difcoveries fufficient to procure the affiftance neceffary for a new voyage in the fpring. His people when he made this propofal were at firft a little backward, but upon hearing his reafons, fubmitted; and according to his advice altered their courfe. On the 2d of September they paffed in fight of Cape Race, and had afterwards fuch bad weather with fuch high feas, that the people in the Hind frequently expected to fee thofe in the Squirrel fwallowed up, notwithftanding which, Sir Humphry could not be perfuaded to leave her. On the 9th, the ftorms and fwellings of the fea increafed, and he was again preffed to leave the frigate; but his anfwer was, We are as near to heaven at fea as by land. About midnight, the Squirrel being a head of the Golden Hind, her lights were at once extinguifhed, and it was fuppofed fhe funk that very inftant, for fhe was never heard of more.

The Golden Hind however arrived fafely at Falmouth on the 22d of September, after having loft only one man in this unfortunate expedition.

CHAPTER IV.

Sir Walter Raleigh gets the patent renewed for himfelf, and fends two barks, to make difcoveries to the fouth. The Englifh land in the ifland Wokoken, which is defcribed; and after a fuccefsful voyage return to England. Sir Richard Greenville forms two fettlements in Roenocke ifland, and Mr. White one; but owing to the want of fupplies and the annoyance from the Indians, are all obliged to remove.

AFTER Sir Humphry Gilbert's mifcarriage and lofs, the brave Sir Walter Raleigh, that unfortunate gentleman's half brother by the mother's fide, procured his patent to be renewed to himfelf, and making choice of two very able feaofficers, Captain Philip Amadas and Capt. Arthur Barlow, fitted out two fmall barks. Sir Walter had obferved, that all the attempts hitherto made had failed, by the adventurers purfuing their difcoveries from the north; he chofe therefore to proceed in another method, and confidering all the lands on the continent of America, from the laft fettlement of the Spaniards to 60 north, as lying within his grant, he refolved to fettle thofe firft, which lay neareft their fettlements.

The above two barks failed from the weft of England on the 27th of April, 1584, and, paffing the Canaries, fell in with the coaft of Florida, on the 2d of July and having failed 40 leagues along the fhore, came on the 13th to a river, where they caft anchor, landed, and took poffeffion of the country in right of the queen, and for the ufe of the proprietors.

This place they afterwards found to be the ifland of Wokoken, on the coaft of the country fince called Virginia, in 34° latitude. In this ifland they found deer, rabbits, hares, fowls, vines, cedars, pines, cyprefs, faffafras, and maftic-trees. They went to the tops of the hills that were neareft the fhore, from whence, though they were not high, they difcovered the fea on all fides, and found it to be an ifland of about 20 miles in length and fix in breadth.

It was the third day before they faw any of the natives, but then a little boat with three of them appeared; and one of them going on fhore, the Englifh rowed up to him, when he not only waited their coming, without any figns of fear, but readily went on board, where they gave him a fhirt and hat, with fome meat and wine, which he feemed to like. After he had with apparent fatisfaction narrowly viewed the barks with all that were in them, he went in his own boat to above a quarter of a mile's diftance, where he employed himfelf in fifhing, and in half an hour loaded his boat, as deep as it could fwim, and then returned to the point of land; where, to fhew his gratitude, he divided it into two parts, and making figns that he defigned it for the two barks, departed. After this, the natives from the continent, frequently repaired to their fhips, and exchanged feveral forts of fkins, white coral, and fome pearls, for toys made of tin, and other baubles of inconfiderable value.

The very next day after that in which they had feen the three Indians, feveral boats appeared in view, and in one of thefe was the king of the country's brother, attended by forty or fifty men, whofe features were tolerably agreeable. The prince made up to the Englifh, who gave him and four of his chiefs prefents of feveral toys, which he accepted very kindly; but took all himfelf, and let them know, that none there had a right to any thing but him. Two days after they let him fee their merchandize, of which nothing feemed to pleafe him more than a pewter difh, for which he gave twenty deer-fkins; and, making a hole in the rim, hung it over his neck for a breaft-plate, making figns that it would defend him againft the enemy's arrows. The next thing he bought was a copper kettle, for which he gave fifty fkins.

While he thought fit to traffic with them, none but fuch as like him wore plates of gold or copper on their heads, were allowed either to buy or fell; but as foon as they had done, every other Indian was allowed the fame liberty. They offered very good exchange for hatchets, axes, and knives, and would have given any thing for fwords; but the Englifh would not part with one.

The king's brother afterwards came frequently on board, and would eat, drink, and be merry with them; and once he brought his wife and children with him, who afterwards came frequently with only their followers. The Englifh often trufted him with goods upon his word, to bring the value at a certain time, which he never failed of doing. He had a strong inclination to have a suit of armour, and a sword which he saw in one of the ships; and would have left a large box of pearls in pawn for them, but they refused it, that he might not know they set a value upon them, till they could discover whence he got them.

The English learned from the natives, that their country which appeared extremely fertile, was called Wingandacoa, and their king named Wingina. When they went on shore they were entertained with extraordinary civility, and once in particular by the king's brother's wife, at a little village in Roenocke. She appeared to be a very modest woman, and wore a mantle of deer-skin lined with fur, with an apron of the same kind. She had a band of white coral on her forehead, and from her ears hung long bracelets of pearls, some of which were as large as peas. They were told of a great city, where the king resided, at the distance of six days journey on the continent, which however they did not see; for they made no long stay, nor proceeded any farther on discovery, going only to the neighbouring parts in their boats, and being satisfied with what they had seen, returned to England about the middle of September, pleased with their success in this short and prosperous voyage, and with the agreeable hopes of the future advantages that might be derived from it.

On their return, they represented the country so delightful, and so richly abounding with all the necessaries of life; the climate and air so temperate, and healthy; the woods and soil so charming and fertile, and every thing else so agreeable, that paradise itself seemed to be there in its utmost beauty. They gave particular accounts of the variety of excellent fruits they had found, some of which they had never seen before; and that there were grapes in great abundance; stately oaks, and other timber; red cedar, cypress, pines, and other ever-greens, and sweet woods, for tallness and largeness exceeding all they had ever heard described; wildfowl, deer, fish and other game, in such plenty and variety, that no epicure could desire more, than this new world seemed naturally to afford. To make it yet more desirable they reported, that the native Indians, who were then the only inhabitants, were so affable, kind, and good-natured; so innocent and unacquainted with all the arts of deceit, and so fond of the English, that they rather seemed ready to take any impression, than any ways to oppose their settling on the coast.

Queen Elizabeth, highly pleased with the representation given of this discovery, not only promised to grant all the assistance necessary for promoting and perfecting a settlement, but bestowed upon this delightful country the name of Virginia*; and it was not long before Sir Walter Raleigh resolved to fit out a more considerable fleet than had hitherto been employed in such undertakings. He was desirous of commanding in this expedition, but being jealous that his absence might be prejudicial to his interest at court, he committed the conduct of this second enterprize to his lieutenant Sir Richard Greenville, who, on the 8th of April, 1585, set sail from Plymouth, with seven ships fitted out by a company, of which himself and several gentlemen were members.

On the 26th of June he anchored at Wokoken, and in August following, began to plant on the island of Roenocke, five miles distant from the continent, where 180 men were landed under the command of Ralph Lane, who was made their

---

* This Virginia ought not to be confounded with the State now called by that name, for in those days it comprehended not only that State, but the whole country claimed by the crown of England, from the southern limits of Georgia, agreeable to the patents granted to Sir Humphry Gilbert, and his brother Sir Walter Raleigh.

governor, and capt. Philip Amadas, who was conſtituted admiral of the new colony, though it does not appear that he had ſo much as a bark left with him.

Sir Richard did not remain above three weeks longer in thoſe ſeas; for having made ſome diſcoveries to the ſouthward, and having traded with the Indians for pearls, ſkins, furs, and other commodities, he ſailed on the 25th of Auguſt, on his return to England, in which he took a very rich prize; ſo that this voyage appeared to the nation, as no leſs proſperous than the former, and the new Virginia company began to entertain very ſanguine hopes of their undertaking.

Let us now return to the firſt planters in Virginia, and give an account of what happened to the firſt colony the Engliſh eſtabliſhed there, or in any part of America. Sir Richard Greenville was no ſooner ſailed, than the people whom he left behind, applied themſelves with diligence to what had been recommended to them by Sir Walter Raleigh, which was diſcovering the continent, and with this view they travelled eighty miles ſouth, and 150 north from that part of the main, which was oppoſite to their iſland; but in theſe expeditions venturing indiſcreetly too high up the river, and too far into the country, the Indian governors grew jealous of them; began firſt to be weary of their company, and then to cut off ſuch of their ſtragglers as fell into their hands, and they even formed a plan for deſtroying all the reſt, but were happily prevented.

Mean while the company in England, were not ſo careful as they ought to have been in ſending them ſupplies of proviſions, and the Engliſh not underſtanding the nature of the climate, neglected to gather food in the proper ſeaſon, by which means they were reduced to great ſtraits. The natives never after kept faith with them, but watching all opportunities to cut them off, obliged them to be very cautious in landing on the continent, and prevented their having any supply from thence; they however endured every thing with incredible refolution, and extended their difcoveries near 100 miles along the coaft. The Indians they kept in awe, by threatening them with the return of their companions with a reinforcement of men; but no fhips coming from England all that winter, nor in the fpring following, nor even in the fummer, they defpaired of being able to fupport themfelves any longer. While the natives feeing them in a manner abandoned by their countrymen, began to look upon them with contempt, and the Englifh expected every day to be facrificed to their cruelty.

In this diftrefs, their chief employment was looking out to fea, in hopes of finding fome means of efcape, or of obtaining a recruit; but in Auguft, when they were almoft fpent with watching and hunger, they, to their great joy, difcovered fir Francis Drake's fleet returning from an expedition againft the Spaniards, in North-America, and this great man, having been commanded by the queen to vifit this plantation, and to fee what encouragement or affiftance they wanted, failed up directly to the ifland. Their firft petition was to grant them a fupply of men and provifions, with a fmall fhip or bark, that in cafe they fhould not be able to maintain themfelves where they were, they might embark in it for England.

Sir Francis having granted their requeft, they fet all hands to work, to fit the fhip he had given them, and to furnifh her with ftores fufficient for a long ftay; but a ftorm arifing, drove the veffel from her anchor to fea, by which fhe fuffered fo much, as rendered her unfit for their ufe. At this they were fo difcouraged, that though fir Francis offered them another fhip, they were afraid to ftay, and earneſtly intreated him to take them with him, which he did: and this put an end to the firſt ſettlement.

This misfortune was ſo far from being owing to ſir Walter Raleigh's negligence, that he had continually preſſed the company to reflect on the neceſſity of ſupporting the colony in time, and ſo ſolicitous was he to carry this point, that finding the fleet, which was preparing under the command of ſir Richard Greenville, went on but ſlowly, he propoſed, that the firſt ſhip that was completely manned and equipped, ſhould be ſent without ſtaying for the reſt; this was done: but when the veſſel, which was well ſtocked with proviſions, ammunition, and all manner of neceſſaries, arrived at the iſland of Roenocke, it was found deſerted, and therefore, after a ſhort ſtay, the people returned home.

In about a fortnight after, came ſir Richard Greenville with his ſquadron of three ſmall veſſels, and to his great diſappointment, found not a man in the iſland. He, however, reſolved to make another ſettlement, and therefore left behind him fifty men, with directions to build a fort for their own defence, and then furniſhing them with all neceſſaries for two years, returned to England, after giving them the ſtrongeſt aſſurance, that they ſhould be conſtantly and regularly ſupplied.

This colony was, however, more unfortunate than the firſt, for the Indians taking advantage of the ſmallneſs of their number, and the difficulties they had to ſtruggle with, attacked and cut them off, ſo that when Mr. White came thither, with three ſhips and conſiderable ſupplies, on the 22d of June, 1587, he found their fort demoliſhed, ſome huts they had erected near it deſtroyed, and not far from it the bones of a dead man. In all theſe revolutions, Manteo an Indian, who had been formerly carried over to England, from whence he safely returned, remained firm to the Englifh intereft, and from him Mr. White learned what was become of this colony.

The misfortunes which had attended thefe two fettlements, would certainly have difcouraged a man of lefs conftancy and fortitude than Mr. White; but he had a commiffion to be governor, and Sir Walter had ftrongly recommended his keeping poffeffion of the place. He therefore erected a new fort, and choofing eleven of the moft fenfible perfons he had brought along with him, conftituted a regular corporation, to which he gave the title of the Governor and Court of Affiftants of the city of Raleigh, in Virginia. On the 13th of Auguft, Manteo, the faithful Indian, was chriftened, and created by the Governor, Lord of Daffumonpeak, an Indian nation fo called, as a reward for his fidelity and fervice to the Englifh, and on the 18th of the fame month, was born the firft child that was the iffue of chriftian parents in that place. She was the daughter of Mr. Annias Dare, and after the name of the country, was named Virginia.

Good government and induftry foon rendered Mr. White and his men formidable to the Indians, who courted their friendfhip, and made leagues with the corporation, which they kept or broke, as they thought themfelves too weak or too ftrong for the Englifh, who, notwithftanding their feeming profperity, underwent the utmoft hardfhips, for want of receiving proper fupplies from Europe. Yet fo far were they from repenting of their undertaking, or defiring to return, that they difputed for the liberty of remaining at Roenocke, and obliged Mr. White their governor, to return to England, and folicit the company to fend them recruits of men and provifions.

Mr. White confented to negociate this affair, and leaving 150 men in the place, fet fail for England, where he arrived in fafety; but it was two years before he could obtain a grant of the neceffary fupplies. At laft, however, he had three fhips fitted out for him, with provifions and more men for the colony. On the 13th of Auguft he arrived at Cape Hattaras, and landing on the ifland Roenocke, found by letters cut on trees in large Roman characters, that the Englifh were removed. On feveral of thefe trees they found the letters C. R. O. and fearching farther on one of the palifadoes of the fort, found cut in large capital letters, the word Croatan, which is an ifland about twenty leagues to the fouth of Roenocke. On this advice, they embarked in order to fearch for the garrifon in that ifland, but they were fcarce all on board before a dreadful ftorm arofe which feparated the fhips, and lofing their anchors and cabals, they durft not venture in with the fhore. Upon which all of them fhifting for themfelves, failed back to England and Ireland.

This dreadful blow proved the ruin of the third fettlement, of which it does not appear that the company took any farther care, or made any new attempt for preferving the poffeffion of a country, the advantages whereof had been painted in fuch ftrong colours, to the crown of England: though a long time after they fent feveral fhips to vifit the coaft, and trade with the natives.*

---

* See Chap. VIII. and IX.

CHAPTER V.

Capt. Davis's voyages in search of a north-west passage, and the great discoveries made by him in North-America.

WHILE these proceedings were carrying on in the south, a design of attempting to discover a north-west passage was formed by some traders in the west of England, and the same project being set on foot at London, they both united, when capt. John Davis was appointed to conduct the enterprize, and to have under his command the Sunshine of London, a bark of fifty tons, with twenty-three persons on board; and the Moonshine of Dartmouth, a vessel of thirty-five tons, carrying nineteen persons. With this small force he sailed from the last mentioned port on the 7th of June, 1585, and on the 14th of the same month was forced into one of the Scilly islands, where being detained a fortnight, capt. Davis gave a proof of his activity and industry, by drawing a chart of those islands, which was at that time much wanted.

Capt. Davis with his two vessels, sailed from thence on the 28th, and continued his course to the north-west, till on the 19th of July, they came into a whirling tide, which set northwards, and sailing about half a league, into a very calm sea, they heard a prodigious roaring, as if it had been the beach of some shore, which was the more terrible, as the weather was so foggy that they could not see from one ship to the other, though they were at a small distance. Upon this, the Moonshine was ordered to sound, but not being able to find ground with a line of upwards of 300 fathoms, the captain, the master, and Mr. Jane, who wrote the account, went towards the beach to fee what it was, when they found it to be feveral iflands of ice broke lofe and floating in the fea; they got out upon thefe, and when they returned to their boat, carried feveral large pieces of ice with them, which melted into very good frefh water.

On the 20th the fog difperfing, they difcovered the land, which refembled a fugar-loaf, and made fo uncomfortable, or rather fo horrid an appearance, that capt. Davis called it the Land of Defolation. On the 21ft they were forced to bend their courfe to the fouth to clear themfelves of the ice, after which they ran along the fhore.

On the 24th the captain, to encourage the men, caufed their allowance to be increafed; but the weather was far from being very cold, for though it was pretty fharp when the wind blew from the fhore, it was very hot when it blew from the fea. On the 25th they bore away north-weft, and continued their courfe for four days; and on the 29th difcovered land in the latitude of 64°. 15'. with the fea quite free from ice, and the weather very temperate.

Upon viewing the coaft, they found many pleafant bays and commodious ports: they however, judged it not a continued land, but rather an Archipelago, and therefore refolved to go on fhore on one of the fmall iflands, in order to fearch for wood and water, and to gain a better knowledge of the country. But they had no fooner landed, than they found evident marks of the country's being inhabited, for there lay upon the ground a fmall fhoe, feveral pieces of leather fewed with finews, and a piece of fur like beaver.

They went next upon another ifland, where getting upon an high rock, they were feen by the people of the country, who inftantly fet up a moft hideous howling, which the Englifh perceiving, hallowed out to their companions to let them know

what had happened. Upon this, Capt. Bruton of
the Moonſhine came to their aſſiſtance with a good
number of his ſeamen. Soon after their arrival,
ten canoes full of the natives came from a neighbouring iſland, two of which advanced ſo near the
ſhore, that the Engliſh on land could eaſily talk
with them. The language of theſe people was
much in the throat, and their pronunciation harſh
and unpleaſant. One of them, however, ſeemed
inclined to come on ſhore, but firſt pointed to the
ſun, and then ſtruck his breaſt ſo hard that they
could hear the blow, upon which Mr. John Elias,
maſter of the Moonſhine, was appointed to treat
with him, and therefore going to the ſea ſide,
pointed to the ſun and ſtruck his breaſt, as the
ſavage had done, who at length ventured on ſhore,
and they threw him caps, ſtockings, gloves, and
ſuch other things as they thought would pleaſe
him; but the night drawing on they took their
leave on both ſides.

The next morning thirty-ſeven canoes rowing
by the ſhips, called to the Engliſh to go on ſhore,
but the latter being in no great haſte, one of the
Indians leaped upon land, and ran to the top of
a rock, where to ſhew his joy, he danced and beat
a drum. The Engliſh then manned their boats,
and went to them to the water ſide, where they
waited in their canoes; and after the formal ceremony of ſwearing by the ſun, the natives made no
ſcruple of truſting them, but on the contrary,
ſhewed all poſſible ſigns of kindneſs, and even of
politeneſs; for when the author offered to ſhake
hands with one of them, the Indian firſt took his
hand and kiſſed it. They readily parted with any
thing they were aſked for, and were content with
whatever was given them, ſhewing no ſigns of
greedineſs, and not the leaſt appearance of treachery. The Engliſh bought five of their canoes,
and ſeveral of their ſtockings and gowns, ſome of

Ten Canoes or Natives of an Island near the land of Desolation come & traffick with Capt.n Davis.

which were made of feal, and others of birds fkins, all of them well dreffed and neatly made, fo that it plainly appeared, they had fome trades among them. They had plenty of furs, and on their feeing that they pleafed the Englifh, informed them by figns, that they would go up into the country and bring them more; but the wind proving fair in the night, Capt. Davis fteered ftill farther to the north-weft; and on the 6th of Auguft entered a very fine road free from ice, in the latitude of 66°. 46. where they landed under a high mountain, the clefts of which fhone like gold.

Mr. Davis having here taken a view of every thing round him, began to think of beftowing names on the places he had difcovered: he therefore gave to the mountain the name of Mount Raleigh, the road where the fhip lay he called Totnefs road; the found at the foot of the mountain, Exeter found; the north foreland, Dyer's Cape; and the fouth foreland, Walfingham. They here difcovered four white bears of a prodigious fize, two of which they killed and brought on board, the fore paw of one of them meafuring fourteen inches. They faw a raven upon mount Raleigh, and at the bottom of the hill found fome fhrubs and flowers like primrofes: the coaft however was very mountainous, and entirely barren, affording neither wood nor grafs, nor fo much as earth; for the mountains were all ftone, and that the fineft our author had ever feen. The inland part of the country was probably fertile, fince the bears were very fat, and yet it appeared upon opening their ftomach, and upon viewing their dung, that they were not ravenous, but fed upon grafs.

On the 8th they weighed from mount Raleigh, and three days after came to the moft foutherly point of the land, which they called the Cape of God's Mercy, and here they were furprifed with a very thick fog, upon the breaking up of which they found themſelves in a ſtreight, that was in ſome places ſixty miles broad, and in others ninety; the weather was very fine and temperate, and the water of the ſame colour with that of the ocean, which filled them with hopes of finding a paſſage. They ſailed ſixty leagues through this ſtreight, and then diſcovered ſeveral iſlands in the midſt of it, by which they ſailed, one bark taking the north and the other the ſouth ſide, but the wind changing, and the weather growing foggy and foul, they were forced to lie by for five days in the paſſage, ſince called Davis's Streights.

On the 14th they went on ſhore, and ſaw evident marks of the country's being inhabited, for they found part of a ſtone wall, and an human ſkull. The next day they heard a great howling on the ſhore, which they ſuppoſed to be made by the wolves, and therefore landed in order to kill them; but inſtead of wolves they found only dogs, that came running to the boats, wagging their tails, and ſhewing other ſigns of joy, as it is uſual with thoſe animals at the ſight of men: there were twenty of them in all, and being of the ſize of maſtiffs, with ſhort ears and long buſhy tails, the ſeamen were afraid of them, and firing killed two, one of which had a leather collar: they alſo found two ſledges, one made of ſeveral boards, and the other of whale-bone. They likewiſe ſaw larks, ravens and partridges.

On the 17th they went on ſhore again, and in a place reſembling an oven, which was built with ſtones, they found a ſmall canoe, an image, a bird made of bone, beads for necklaces and other trifles. The coaſt made no very promiſing appearance, as having neither wood nor graſs, but the rocks were of a fine bright ſtone like marble, beautified with veins of different colours.

Captain Davis was extremely pleafed with the appearance of this ftreight, which they took to be the very channel into the South Seas, in fearch whereof they came. It was therefore refolved to continue the profecution of their difcoveries; but the wind changing, they were obliged to remain at anchor; and the weather growing very foul, they on the 24th hoifted fail for England. On the 10th of September, they fell in with the land of Defolation; on the 27th they had fight of the Englifh coaft, and in a ftorm at night, were parted from the Moonfhine. However, on the 30th Captain Davis returned to Dartmouth, where he found the Moonfhine, which had arrived in that harbour two hours before.

Mr. Davis's owners were fo well fatisfied with his conduct in this voyage, that they procured him an audience of Secretary Walfingham, who not only greatly approved of the enterprize, and of the manner in which it was conducted, but recommended his completing the difcovery; to this he was alfo preffed by thofe concerned in the above undertaking, and by fome merchants of Exeter, who defired to join in the expences neceffary for a fecond expedition: and he having willingly confented, the following fquadron was fitted out: the Mermaid of 120 tons; the Sunfhine of 60 tons; the Moonfhine of 55 tons; and the North Star, a pinnace of 13 tons.

Captain Davis fet fail with the above fquadron from Dartmouth, on the 7th of May, 1586, and having coafted the fouth fide of Ireland, fteered to the north-weft, till he came into the latitude of 60°. when he divided the fquadron, and ordered the Sunfhine and the North Star, to feek a paffage northward, between Greenland and Ireland to the latitude of 80°. if not hindered by land. He left them on the 7th of June, and on the 15th difcovered land in 60°. latitude, and in 47°. weft longitude from the meridian of London. The ice lying some places ten, in others twenty, and in some fifty leagues off the shore, which obliged him to bear into the 57°. in order to get a free sea.

On the 29th, after many storms, he again discovered land in latitude 64°. and in longitude 58°. 30. when bearing in with it, he set up a pinnace, he had provided in the Mermaid, to serve as a scout in the discovery. The ships being within the sound, he sent his boats to search for shoal water, where he might come to an anchor, which in this place is very hard to find. The people of the country seeing the English, came in their canoes, with shouts and cries; when observing in the boat some of those who were there last year, they rowed up to them, and taking hold of the oars, and hanging about the boat, expressed great joy, making signs that they knew them again. Captain Davis then went on shore with others of the company, taking twenty knives with him, and they had no sooner landed than the friendly natives leaping out of their canoes, ran to them, and embraced them with many signs of a hearty welcome. There were eighteen of them, and Mr. Davis giving each of them a knife, they offered him skins in return; but making signs that they were not sold, but freely given, he dismissed them for that time.

The next day the pinnace was landed upon an island in order to be finished; and while it was setting up, the people came continually to them, there being sometimes 100 canoes at a time, bringing seal-skin, stag-skins, white hares, salmon-peal, small cod, dry copelin, with other fish, and some birds. Capt. Davis then sent one of the boats to search one part of the land, while he went to another, but first gave strict orders that no injury should be offered to any of the natives, nor any gun fired.

The men whom the Captain difpatched in the boat, paffed ten miles within the fnowy mountains, and came to a plain champaign country covered with earth and grafs, and went about ten leagues up a river, which in the narroweft place was two leagues over, but knew not how far it extended.

Mean while the Captain took what he fuppofed, another river, which though at it firft afforded a large inlet, yet proved only a deep bay, the end of which he reached in four hours, when leaving the boat well manned, he went with the reft of the company three or four miles into the country, but found nothing, nor faw any thing but fnipes, ravens, and fmall birds, fuch as larks and linnets.

On the 3d of July, Capt. Davis manned his boat, and attended by 50 canoes, entered another found, to which the people invited him by figns, and he confented, in hopes of finding their place of refidence. At laft they made figns that he fhould go into a warm place to fleep, upon this he went on fhore.

Thefe people are of good ftature, and are well proportioned. They have broad faces, fmall eyes, wide mouths, and large lips; but their hands and feet are fmall and flender. They are very fubject to bleed at the nofe, and therefore ftop their nofes with deers hair. One of them kindled a fire after the following manner; he took a piece of board in which was a hole half through, and having fmeared the end of a round ftick, like a bed-ftaff, with train-oil, put it into the hole, and then turning it round with a piece of leather, fomething in the manner of our turners, by the violence of the motion, foon produced fire, upon which he laid an heap of turfs, and then with many words and ftrange geftures, put feveral things into the flames, which the Englifh fuppofed to be intended as a facrifice. They then defired the Captain to go into the smoke, which he desiring them to do, and they refusing, he thrust one of them into it, and then commanded his men to tread out the fire, and spurn it into the sea, to shew their contempt for this sorcery.

They eat their meat raw; and live mostly upon fish, which they catch with nets made of whale fins. They probably make war on their neighbours on the continent: for many of them were much wounded, and let the English know by their signs, that they received them upon the main land.

But though these people behaved with great simplicity, they appeared extremely addicted to theiving, particularly of iron, for which they had a very great esteem, for they cut away the Moonshine's boat from her stern, and also the cables and cloth which lay to air, stole the oars, a caliver, a spear, a sword, and several other things, which so exasperated the sailors, that they desired the captain to dissolve this new friendship, upon which he ordered a caliver to be shot among them, and immediately after a falcon, when they were so frightened with the noise, that they instantly fled. However, about ten hours after, they returned, making signs of peace, and this being granted, they brought seal-skins and salmon-peal; but on their seeing iron could not forbear stealing again; which the captain perceiving, commanded that they should not be treated with severity, and that his own people should be more careful in keeping what was under their charge.

On the 17th of July the captain went on shore in his new pinnace, and with most part of the company walked to the top of a high mountain, with the hopes of taking a view from thence of the country; but the number and heights of the mountains bounded their prospect in such a manner, that they could see but a small distance; they therefore returned to their pinnace, where they observed a water-spout, which at that time was considered as a very strange and astonishing sight.

On the 19th they returned to their ships, where the sailors complained heavily of the people, who had not only stolen an anchor, and cut one of the cables, but had thrown stones at them. However, the next day the captain went on shore, and treated the natives with much civility, which removing their apprehensions, they at his return followed him in their canoes. He then gave them some bracelets, and seven or eight of them going on board, were used kindly, and afterwards suffered to depart; and yet the sun had no sooner set, than taking their slings, they threw stones into the Sunshine, and knocked down the boatswain. Upon this the English pursued them in their boats, and even fired upon them; but they rowed so swiftly, that it was impossible to overtake them. However, a few days after five of them came to make a new truce, among whom was the ringleader of these disturbances, who came crying Iliaout, and striking his breast, offered a pair of gloves to sell, upon which a knife was offered for them, when two of them coming up, the English dismissed one of them, and kept the other prisoner. They then pointed to him and his fellows for their anchor, which having got, they made signs to him that he should be set at liberty, but about an hour after the wind coming fair, they set sail, and took him away with them. One of his companions followed the ship in his canoe, talked with him, and seemed to lament his condition; but the English using him well, and saying Iliaout, that is, We mean no harm, he in a short time became a pleasant companion. Capt. Davis then gave him a new suit of frize of the English fashion, with which he seemed highly pleased. He soon trimmed up his darts, and all his fishing tools, was very ready at making oakum, and willingly set his hand to the rope.

On the 17th, being in the latitude of 63° 8, they imagined they faw a very high land, which had feveral bays and capes, and therefore fent out their pinnace to difcover it; but on her return, they were affured that it was no more than a prodigious mafs of ice. This they coafted till the 30th, when the air grew fo foggy, and the fea fo peftered with ice, that all hopes of proceeding were banifhed.

In this extremity the men beginning to grow fick and feeble, and to lofe all hopes of fuccefs, earneftly entreated the captain to preferve his own and their lives, by returning to England: but though he commiferated their condition, he refolved to profecute the difcovery; yet he altered his courfe, and on the firft of Auguft difcovered land, without either fnow or ice, in the latitude of 66°. 33. and in 76. longitude from London.

On the 2d of Auguft, they anchored in a very good road, where they graved and re-victualled the Moonfhine. They here found it very hot, and were much troubled with mufketoes. The people of the country having caught a feal, tied bladders to him, and fent him to the Englifh with the flood, fo that he came right up with the fhip, and this the captain took as a friendly prefent. On the 5th Capt. Davis walked up to the top of a hill, and obferving three canoes under a rock, went to them, and found in them fkins, darts, &c. but without taking any thing, he left in every boat a filk point, a leaden bullet, and a pin.

The next day the natives came to them without fear, and bartered with them for fkins. Mean while the Indian kept clofe, and by figns let them know, that he was very defirous of having another companion.

On the 11th Capt. Davis departed, leaving the Mermaid at anchor, whofe crew finding many occafions of difcontent, were unwilling to proceed. Two days after, failing weft fifty leagues, they discovered land in 66°. 19. and the next day stood to the south. On the 18th, they discovered a promontory to the north-west, and having no land on the south were in great hopes of a passage. They then coasted an island towards the south from 67 to 57°. and on the 28th distrusting the weather, sailed ten leagues into a fine harbour, two leagues broad, with woods on both sides. Here they continued till the 1st of September, in which time they had two very great storms. The captain and some persons with him went six miles into the country, and found the woods consisted of firs, pines, elders, yews, and birch-trees. In this excursion they saw a black bear, and plenty of birds, as pheasants and partridges, wild-geese, blackbirds, jays, thrushes, and other small birds.

They now coasted the shore with fair weather, and on the south anchored in a good road among many islands. Eight leagues to the north of this place, they had hopes of a passage from observing a prodigious sea, rolling between the two lands from the west, and they had a great desire to enter this sea; but the wind was directly against them.

On the 6th they sent five young men on shore to another island to fetch some fish, which they had left there covered all night. But the natives who had concealed themselves in the woods, suddenly assaulted the men, which being perceived from the ship, those on board let slip their cable, bore in to the shore, and twice discharged a double musket upon them, at the noise whereof they fled, after their having killed two of the men with their arrows, and wounded two more; the other narrowly escaped by swimming with an arrow shot through his arm.

Having that night a most dreadful storm, that lasted till the 10th, they unrigged their ship, and intended to cut down their masts; and as the cable of their sheet anchor broke, they expected to have been driven on fhore, and murdered by the natives; but having afterwards a fair fea, they recovered their anchor, and new moored their fhip, when they were fully fenfible of their great deliverance, two ftrands of their cable being broken.

On the 11th, the wind coming fair at weft-north-weft, they fteered directly for England, where they arrived in the beginning of October. The Sunfhine had returned a few days before them. She had been at Iceland, and from thence to Greenland, afterwards to Eftoitland, and thence to the Land of Defolation, where fhe traded with the people, and ftaid in the country twenty days. But they had loft the pinnace called the North Star, in a ftorm, and never heard of her more.

Capt. Davis was afterwards fent on another voyage to make difcoveries, with three fhips, two of which were to be employed in fifhing, while the other endeavoured to find out a paffage to the South Seas, and in this voyage he reached the latitude of 73°. north, where he found the fea all open, and the ftreight forty leagues broad, whence he concluded, that the paffage was moft certain, and the execution eafy, in which he was miftaken.

We fhall now mention an attempt made for fixing a fettlement farther to the fouth than any we have yet obtained.

CHAPTER VI.

Sir Walter Raleigh fails with a fmall fquadron in order to difcover Guiana: Arrives at the ifland of Trinidad, where he burns the town of St. Jofeph, and fets five Indian kings at liberty. Proceeding towards Guiana, he enters the mouth of the river with a detachment of 100 men in boats: rejoins his fhips, and after burning feveral Spanifh towns, returns to England. A concife account of his fending feveral other fhips to Guiana.

SIR Walter Raleigh had feen with regret the plantation of Virginia abandoned, and well knew that the want of immediate profit was the caufe, he refolved therefore to ftrike out the means of fettling a new colony in another part of America, that fhould be free from this inconvenience, and transfer the richeft products of that country to the Englifh, if they had but courage and conduct enough to fetch them. In order to this, he enquired with the greateft diligence into the ftate of Guiana. He fought from books and papers all the affiftance that could be had of that kind; and drew from perfonal informations, which were more in his power, than perhaps they ever were in any other man's, all the notices they were capable of giving. But he drew the greateft lights from his own profound knowledge and extenfive experience.

In order to proceed cautioufly in an affair of fuch importance, he fent before him one Capt. Whiddon, to take a view of the coaft, that he might be perfectly informed of the ftate things were then in, and become more able to take the proper meafures for overcoming thofe difficulties, which a man of lefs fagacity would have deemed infuperable. This gentleman performed his bufineſs effectually, though he met with ſome obſtructions from the force, and much greater inconveniencies from the frauds of the Spaniards, who were at that time endeavouring to ſecure to themſelves this valuable country, particularly Don Antonio de Berreo, with whom Capt. Whiddon had ſome dealings, got eight of his men into his hands, whom he uſed with great barbarity.

When Sir Walter's project was ripe for execution, he was aſſiſted by the Lord Admiral Howard, and Sir Robert Cecil; and five ſhips were fitted out for this expedition. Sir Walter, however, left Plymouth on the 6th of February, 1595, with only one bark beſides the veſſel in which he himſelf ſailed, and on the 22d of March arrived at the iſland of Trinidad, where he ſpent a conſiderable time in viewing that iſland, in examining all its ports and havens, and even every little creek, with the greateſt care and exactneſs.

Here was a Spaniſh ſettlement, and a new city called St. Joſeph, governed by the above Don Antonio de Berreo, a man of courage and reſolution, but very unfit to proſecute diſcoveries. On this governor Sir Walter reſolved to be revenged, for his treatment of Capt. Whiddon's people, by making himſelf maſter of the place, which he knew would gain him the friendſhip, and ſecure the obedience of the Indians, who were moſt cruelly oppreſſed by the Spaniards.

He accordingly ſent Capt. Calfield to attack the main guard with ſixty men, and following with forty more, reduced the town of St. Joſeph without much trouble. He then ſet the inhabitants at liberty, and in particular many Indian captives, among whom were five caciques, who were linked together in one chain, and confined in a place where they were almoſt ſtarved with hunger. Theſe unhappy princes had ſuffered the ſevereſt torments, for they had been baſted with the ſcalding fat of bacon, and endured a variety of other cruelties. He kept the governor and his Spaniards prisoners, and afterwards, at the request of the Indians, burnt the place: but in other respects behaved towards his prisoners, and particularly towards the governor, with such civility, that he drew from him a faithful account of all his adventures in attempting the conquest of Guiana.

The same day arrived to Sir Walter's assistance, Capt. Giffard, in the Lion's-Whelp, and Capt. Keymis, in a galego, with several gentlemen and soldiers, and some useful supplies. But before Sir Walter would proceed on his discoveries, he summoned an assembly of the Indian chiefs of the island, who were enemies to the Spaniards, and told them by an Indian interpreter, whom he had brought out of England, that he was the servant of a virgin queen, who was the most powerful cacique in the north, and had more caciques under her command than there were trees in that island. That she was an enemy to the Castilians, on account of their tyranny and oppression, and having freed all the coasts of the northern world from their servitude, had sent him to free them also: and to defend the country of Guiana from their future invasions. He then shewed them the queen's picture, which they greatly admired. By these and other speeches of the same kind, both here and on the borders of Guiana, he made the people familiarly acquainted with the name and virtues of the queen, and at the same time strongly engaged them in his interest.

Sir Walter now prepared to proceed towards Guiana, though Berreo used many arguments to dissuade him from engaging in that enterprize. He told him, that he must venture to pass many dangerous shallows in small boats, without being able to carry provisions sufficient to last him half the way; that he must not expect the least succour from the natives of the countries through which he paffed, who would not admit of a parley; but would burn their towns, and retire to their fortreffes: that they had been enjoined by their chiefs not to barter gold, nor to hold any communication with chriftians, as the only means to preferve them from deftruction: befides, that the way was long, winter was approaching, and the rivers beginning to fwell.

Notwithftanding thefe remonftrances, Sir Walter directed his Vice-Admiral Captain Giffard, and Captain Calfield, to fteer into the mouth of the river Capuri, and at the higheft flood to pafs over the fhoal; but this they found impracticable, the water falling before they could accomplifh it. He then fent the mafter of the Lion's Whelp to try another branch called Amana, in order to know if either of the fmall veffels could enter; but he met with no better fuccefs. Sir Walter now caufed his carpenter to cut down an old galego boat, and to fit her with banks for oars, in fuch a manner as to draw but five feet water.

In this veffel he embarked with fixty of his people, and was followed by the fhallop and boat of the Lion's Whelp, carrying twenty; Captain Calfield's fhallop carrying ten, and a barge of his own, ten more; having in all 100 men well armed, with provifions for a month. Their accommodations were extremely bad, being expofed to the weather, and obliged to endure the burning heat of the fun and ftorms of rain, to lie upon the hard boards, to bear the difagreeable fmell of the wet cloaths of many people crouded together, and the dreffing of their food, which moftly confifted of ftale fifh, fo that no prifon could be more loathfome and unhealthy.

At firft fetting out they had twenty miles of an high fea to crofs in their crazy boats, and were driven by the wind into the bottom of the bay of

Gauanipa, inhabited by a barbarous nation who ufed poifoned arrows. From thence they entered one of the rivers, and after four days, got above the force of the tide; but they were there bewildered by fuch a confluence of ftreams, that they were whirled about by different currents and eddies, fo that after toiling a long time, they were brought back to the place they had been ftriving to avoid, or from which they fet out, paffing between iflands and ftreights, fo overfhadowed with trees, that their fight was bounded by the breadth of the river, and the length of the avenue, while the gloominefs of the profpect added horror to the loathfomenefs of the places in which they were confined.

At length on the 22d of May, they entered a river, and not knowing any other name for it, called it the Red Crofs River: here they put into a creek which led to a town at a fmall diftance, where their Indian pilot going on fhore, was fet upon by his countrymen, who hunted him with dogs. In return, Sir Walter feized an old man who was paffing that way, and threatened to cut off his head if he did not procure his pilot's liberty; but the pilot by his agility foon efcaped them, and fwam to Sir Walter's barge; they, however, kept the old man, whom they ufed with the utmoft kindnefs, in hopes of obtaining many ufeful informations from a native who had been long acquainted with thofe parts; and indeed he was of great ufe in guiding through the intricacies of the rivers, though he himfelf was often in the utmoft perplexity which river to take.

The people who inhabit the country at the mouth of this great river, were called Tivetivas, and were a bold and hardy race of people, who knew the value of liberty, and had the courage to defend it. During the fummer they live in houfes, built on the ground: but in the wet or winter months, dwell in huts built upon trees, as is very common both on this coaſt, and even in the Eaſt-Indies, where the countries are ſubject to be overflowed.

Some time after, Sir Walter's barge ran a ground with ſuch force, that they deſpaired of getting her off, ſo that the diſcovery ſeemed at a ſtand; however, four days after, they again ſet her on float, and ſtriking into the Amana, one of the nobleſt branches of the Oronoko, the men with incredible fatigue continued their voyage, and being now within 5° of the line, Sir Walter endeavoured to keep up their ſpirits by directing his pilots to give them hopes, that their labours would ſoon have an end.

At length the old Indian perceiving that their proviſions were exhauſted, and that they muſt periſh without an immediate ſupply, told them, that if they would venture up a river on the right hand, he would bring them to a town where they might be ſure of refreſhments, and be able to return before night. Sir Walter took him at his word; but he amuſed them all day and the greateſt part of the night, without their ſeeing any town, ſo that a leſs prudent commander might have puniſhed him for impoſing upon them. However, about one of the next morning they reached this long expected town, and obtained the ſupplies of which they ſtood in ſuch need. In this hungry and hazardous voyage, which was fourſcore miles up the river, they obſerved many fiſhes of a ſurprizing ſize, and abundance of alligators, one of which devoured a young negro who attended Sir Walter, and who leaped into the water to refreſh himſelf by ſwimming.

Soon after, being again in want of proviſions, they took two canoes laden with excellent bread, belonging to the Indians called Arwaycas, who run them on ſhore, and took refuge in the woods:

when Sir Walter purſuing them, in hopes of obtaining ſome intelligence, found, as his men were creeping through the buſhes, a refiner's baſket, in which were quick-ſilver, ſaltpetre, and other things, uſed in refining of metals, together with ſome gold duſt, that had been refined from the ore.

Sir Walter then landed more of his men, and offered 500l. to any of his ſoldiers who ſhould take one of the Spaniards: but this they were unable to perform, they, however, diſcovered the Arwaycas concealed in the woods, who had ſerved as pilots to the Spaniſh adventurers, and who informed him, that they had been accompanied by two other canoes, laden with gold ore, which had eſcaped. One of theſe people he kept for his own pilot, and from him learned, where, when, and how the Spaniards worked for gold. Having here ſufficiently refreſhed his companions; they appeared as well ſatisfied as their commander, and promiſed to follow him to the end of the world.

On the 15th day from their leaving their ſhips, Sir Walter and his men entered the great river Oronoko, and obtained a true account of the nations inhabiting its banks; they then ſteered by the mountain Aio and a large iſland, and on the 5th day after their entering the above river, came to an anchor at Morequito, in the province of Aromaia, 300 miles within land.

He here ſent a meſſenger to the king of Aromaia, who, the next morning, came on foot from his houſe, and returned the ſame evening, though he was 110 years of age, and his journey was twenty-eight miles. This old monarch had a large train of attendants of both ſexes, who brought great plenty of fleſh, fiſh, and ſeveral ſorts of fruits. The old king having refreſhed himſelf a-while in a tent, which Sir Walter had cauſed to be pitched for him, they entered by means of the interpreter, into a difcourfe on the murder of Morequito, his predeceffor, and the other barbarities of the Spaniards. Sir Walter then told him the defign of his coming thither, and expatiated on the virtues of his queen, whofe greateft ambition, he obferved, was to relieve diftreffed nations, and humble the pride of the Spaniards, which were her only motives for fending him to Guiana.

The old man liftened to him with great attention, and on his afking him many queftions relating to the ftrength, polity, alliances, and government of Guiana, with the readieft way of entering into the heart of the country, the king replied in fo clear and fenfible a manner, that Sir Walter could not help being furprized at finding a perfon of fuch judgment and good fenfe, who had received none of the advantages of education. Some of the king's attendants made Sir Walter a prefent of a fmall but curious kind of parroquito, and of an animal then fcarcely known, called the armadilla, whofe head, body, and tail are covered with hard and beautiful fcales. The form of the head is like that of a hog, the feet refemble hands, and the tail is near four inches thick at the root, tapering to the end.

After the king's departure, Sir Walter failed weftward to the river Caroli, becaufe it led to the ftrongeft nations of all the frontiers, who were enemies to the Epuremei, the fubjects of the Inca or Emperor of Guiana and Manoa. Long before he came to it, he heard the roaring occafioned by the falls of this river; but on his entering it, in order to proceed forty miles up to the Cafiagotos, he found the ftream fo rapid, that he could not advance with his eight oared barge above a ftone's throw in an hour. He therefore encamped on the banks, and fent an Indian to acquaint the Lords of Canuri, who dwelt in that province, of his arrival.

Upon this meſſage, one of the princes named Wanuretona, attended by a numerous train of followers, came to viſit him, bringing great plenty of refreſhments: from him he learned that a nation called the Carolians, were enemies both to the Spaniards and Epuremei, and that there were mighty nations at the head of that river, and were of the ſame diſpoſition.

Upon this intelligence, he diſpatched a party of between thirty and forty men up the ſide of the river, while he himſelf, with a few officers, and half a dozen men armed with muſquets, marched to take a view of the cataracts of the river Caroli.

From the top of the firſt hills that commanded a view of the river, they beheld a prodigious cataract, beneath which, the water divided into three ſtreams, and ran with amazing rapidity upwards of twenty miles; for ſo far they imagined they were able to take in the proſpect. In this courſe no leſs than ten or a dozen more appeared in view, each as high above the other as a church ſteeple, whence the water ruſhed down with ſuch violence, that the vapours ariſing from the rebound, were like the thick ſmoke hanging over well-inhabited cities; but on their nearer approach, where they could better diſcern and diſtinguiſh, the effects reſembled heavy ſhowers of rain; while the prodigious roaring of theſe torrents, at leaſt equalled the noiſe of thunder.

Sir Walter Raleigh obſerves, that he never ſaw a more beautiful country, nor more delightful proſpects: The valleys were interſperſed with hills, and the waters winding through them in various branches; the plains free from brambles, were covered with fine graſs; the ſoil was an hard ſand, fit for either walking or carriage; the deer croſſing every path; and towards evening the birds ſinging on every tree a thouſand different notes; while on the banks of the rivers, were cranes,

herons, white crimſon, and carnation; the air was
refreſhed with gentle eaſtern breezes, and every
ſtone they ſtooped to take up, ſeemed to be intermixed with gold or ſilver. Sir Walter afterwards
ſhewing ſome of theſe ſtones to a Spaniard of the
Caraccas, was told they were the mother of gold,
and though of ſmall value themſelves, were a proof
of there being mines at no great diſtance.

There were now many reaſons which rendered
their ſtay improper. The rains were ſo heavy,
and the floods poured ſo ſuddenly from the hills,
that they were ſometimes before night up to the
neck in water, upon the very ſpots of ground
over which in the morning they had marched dry-
ſhod. The men had worn their clothes above a
month without a change, or being in any other
manner refreſhed, but by the rains which frequently waſhed them ten times a day on the owners
backs. They had beſides no inſtruments with them
to open mines, and if they advanced farther, were
to act againſt a numerous civilized, and warlike
people. Theſe and many other inconveniences,
made them reſolve to make the beſt of their way
back to the ſhips, from which they had now been
abſent above a month, and had in that ſpace proceeded about 400 miles from the ſea coaſt.

They therefore embarked in their boats, and
though the wind was againſt them, arrived in a
day's time at the port of Morequito; for gliding
down the ſtream, they went without labour little
leſs than 100 miles a day. Sir Walter on his
coming to an anchor, was very deſirous of having
another conference with the old king, who ſoon
arrived with a numerous train, loaded with preſents, when Sir Walter having taken him into his
tent, enquired the beſt way to the richeſt parts of
Guiana. The old cacique intimated to him, that
he ought not to think of penetrating to Manoa,
the capital; for neither the ſeaſon of the year, nor

the small number of his men, were proper for the enterprize: That in the plains of Magureguarai, the first civilized town of Guiana, 300 Spaniards had been lately slain; as they had invaded it, without having made any friends among those nations, who were ready to join in any attempts against the kingdom of Guiana, and therefore advised Sir Walter not to invade the strong parts of Guiana, without obtaining the assistance of those nations, who were their enemies. The king also informed him, that he believed he might, with his present force, seize on the town of Magureguarai, where all the gold plates were made that were dispersed through the neighbouring nations, and which was but four days journey from thence, and offered to assist him with his subjects, provided fifty Englishmen were left behind for his guard; but Sir Walter declining the expedition, the king begged him to leave his territories as soon as possible, left the Epuremei should learn that he had given him any assistance, or the Spaniards should return and insult him; they having once before taken him prisoner, and led him seventeen days in chains, till he had paid 100 plates of gold for his ransom. But if Sir Walter would promise to return early the next year, he would engage all the neighbouring nations to assist him against the Epuremei, who had plundered them of their wives, and assured him, they would gladly renew the war to recover them; for the old king complained grievously, that the Epuremei possessed from 50 to 100 women each, while he and his principal subjects had but three or four wives a-piece.

Sir Walter, while he stayed here, obtained many images and plates of gold, not so much for the value, as to shew them as samples; and to prevent these people from entertaining a notion, that he came for gold, he gave among them more twenty shilling pieces of the queen's coin, than they were worth. He alſo took with him ſome of the ſpar and ore, to juſtify his report of the riches of the country; and as the higheſt teſtimony of his having obtained the confidence of the natives, the old king ſent over his own ſon Cayworaco into England, where he was afterwards baptized, with much ceremony, by the name of Gualtero.

On the other hand, Sir Walter at their own requeſt left behind him two of his company, an excellent draughtſman who undertook to deſcribe, as he did, all the country very exactly, and a boy who waited upon Sir Walter, and who was to learn the languages of the Indian nations, which he did to great perfection; but was unfortunately devoured by a wild beaſt.

After this a cacique whoſe name was Putoma, and another called Warapana, offered to conduct him to a gold mine, which they accordingly performed, but the weather being extremely bad, Sir Walter reſolved to return as expeditiouſly as poſſible to his ſhips; but in his paſſage was overtaken by a violent ſtorm, and had like to have been loſt among the ſhoals, being obliged to quit his galley, and take to his boat, with which he ventured out upon a very boiſterous ſea; however, he was the next day ſo happy as to reach Curiapa in the iſland of Trinidad, where his ſhips lay at anchor, and where he was ſoon joined by his galley.

In all this tedious and ſurpriſing expedition, in which they were alike expoſed to the ſeverity of the weather, and to the attempts of their enemies, abſolutely wanting moſt of the conveniences, and frequently the neceſſaries of life, he loſt not a ſingle man, except the negro devoured by the alligator. And yet took a conſiderable quantity of gold ore, which he brought to England, and proving extremely rich, turned to a very good account.

In his return home he burnt the town of Cumana, becauſe the Spaniards refuſed to ſupply him with provifions, and two other Spanifh towns underwent the fame fate, after which he returned fafe to England, where he was received with great acclamations of joy.

Capt. Keymis who was one of the adventurers, wrote a latin poem on this expedition, and Mr. George Chapman compofed an heroic poem of 200 lines on the fame fubject, in which he beftows the greateft encomiums on the prudence and integrity of Sir Walter, who alfo publifhed an account of this expedition, written by himfelf.

Notwithftanding the great fuccefs of this voyage, and the high probability of eafily forming a fettlement in this rich country, Sir Walter's enemies, jealous of his great abilities, endeavoured by the moft invidious infinuations to difcourage all attempts againft Guiana, by throwing the moft groundlefs afperfions on his veracity. Thefe he eafily anfwered, and immediately fitted out two veflels under the command of Capt. Keymis, who left England in the latter end of January following, in order to cherifh the friendfhip he had contracted with the Indians, rather than to purfue any acts of hoftility. This gentleman, on his arrival at the port of Morequito, received intelligence of the death of the old king, and that the draughtfman who had been left behind had been carried into captivity by the Spaniards, who had made a fettlement at the mouth of the river Caroli, in the paflage to the mines, whence Sir Walter had taken ore the preceding year.

Capt. Keymis, therefore, after having had conferences with feveral of the natives, who were loud in the praifes of Sir Walter Raleigh, and expreffed their inclination to fupport any meafures fet on foot by his countrymen, returned to England, and arrived at Portland in the latter end of June, having been only five months upon the voyage.

Sir Walter foon after fitted out an handfome pinnace, and having provided her with all neceffaries for trade and difcovery, fhe fet fail from Weymouth the following December, under the command of Capt. Leonard Berry, who about the beginning of March fell in with the river Wiapoco on the coaft of Guiana, where beginning to be in want of provifions, and finding no inhabitants, he fteered to a town called Armatto, at which place he was plentifully fupplied, and treated with great hofpitality by the natives, who freely traded with the Englifh; Capt. Berry then invited a neighbouring cacique named Ritimo, on board his fhip, who accepted the invitation, and was entertained in a very magnificent manner.

The inhabitants of the neighbouring towns being now convinced that this was an Englifh veffel, flocked to the fea-fhore from all quarters, bringing plenty of provifions and tobacco, and appearing perfectly fatisfied with what was given them in exchange. Thefe eagerly folicited the Englifh to come and drive the Spaniards out of their territories.

This gentleman afterwards failed up feveral rivers, and having procured all the intelligence poffible, quitted the coaft of Guiana, and arrived at Plymouth on the 28th of June, 1597.

CHAPTER VII.

Capt. Leigh forms a fettlement at Guiana, but foon after dying, and his people falling fick, they return to England, &c. Capt. Harcourt's voyage to Guiana, where he leaves a fettlement, and returns to England.

THOUGH Sir Walter was at that time prevented from making any farther difcoveries of this rich country, by the death of the queen, and his own long imprifonment, yet other attempts were made. In the year 1604, Capt. Charles Leigh being affifted by his brother Sir Olive, made a voyage to Guiana, at their mutual expence, in a bark of about fifty tons, with forty-fix men and boys on board, and on the 22d of May entered the river Wiapoco, in 8°. 30'. north latitude, intending to fix at the town of the fame name on the coaft of Guiana.

The captain was received very kindly by the inhabitants, who confented to allow him, for the prefent, a fpace of ground and fome houfes, in confideration of which, he was to affift them againft their inveterate enemies the Caribbees. This agreement was made by means of two of the natives of Guiana, who had been in England, and could fpeak fome Englifh, and for the better fecurity of the Indians performing their promifes, five of them, among whom were two confiderable perfons, were to be fent to England.

The firft fettlement made by the Englifh, was on a part of the mountain that lies on the weft fide of the entrance of a river, to which they gave the name of mount Howard. Captain Leigh might here have lived a quiet life, and been of great ufe to his country, had not his men been difcontented and mutinous. However, the next year he fent his fhip to England for a frefh fupply of fuch things as he wanted, keeping with him 35 of his men and boys, to fettle his fmall village, and by this means fet his colony upon a better footing than it had hitherto been. They had fome trade with the natives, as well round their fettlement, as farther up the river, by which they obtained wax, fine white feathers, tobacco, parrots, monkeys, green and black, cotton-yarn, and wool; fweet gums, red pepper, with feveral forts of wood, roots, and berries, partly for medicine, and partly for dying: but the flux and other diftempers, carried off a confiderable number of the company, and at length the captain himfelf being feized with it, alfo died. By this unhappy ftroke the whole undertaking was ruined, and every one fhifting for himfelf returned to England, very much to the regret of the Indians; fome of them in a French fhip, and others in two Dutch veffels.

In the mean time, Sir Olive Leigh, refolving to fupport his brother in the eftablifhment of his government at Guiana, before he had an account of his fuccefs, fitted out another fhip under Captain Catalin, and Captain St. John, to carry him a frefh fupply of men and neceffaries. This fhip fet fail in April, 1605; but by contrary winds and currents, and the unfkilfulnefs of the mafter, was carried fo far to the leeward, that the men defpaired of ever recovering their intended port, and therefore put in firft at Barbadoes, and afterwards at the ifland of St. Lucia, defigning to return from thence to England: but examining their ftores of provifions, and finding that they were far from being fufficient to fupply fo large a company for fo long a voyage, Capt. St. John, with fixty-feven of the paffengers, refolved rather to ftay and take their lot upon that ifland, than to run the hazard of being ftarved at fea.

The Englifh foon made an acquaintance with the Indians, who in exchange for trifles furnifhed them with roots, fruit, and fome fowls: and they had every night an opportunity of taking, with very little trouble, the moft delicate turtle upon the fands, fo that they were in no want of food. Five or fix days they lived in huts of their own building, without making any excurfions into the country; but the captain one day feeing fome pieces of metal upon the arms of fome of the Indians, and being informed by a refiner in his company, that they were at leaft three parts gold, he enquired of the Indians from whence they had them; upon which they pointed to a very high mountain in the north-weſt part of the iſland.

Upon this Capt. St. John, with ſome of the chief of his men, went in queſt of this golden mountain, the reſt being appointed to keep guard at home, with the aſſurance of their returning in a week's time. When they were gone the others expected that the Indians would bring them proviſions as uſual, but they heard nothing of them for three days together.

It ſeems the Indians had obſerved the captain's departure, and following him, cut him off with his whole company: which they had no ſooner done, than they reſolved to ſerve thoſe who ſtaid behind in the ſame manner. For this purpoſe they got one Augramart, a man of reſolution, and captain of the iſland of St. Vincent, to head them in this enterprize. However, to cover their deſign they carried it fair, and frequently viſited the Engliſh, till one day Augramart having dined with them, perſuaded the Engliſh to go with him to his quarters, where he promiſed to furniſh them with whatever proviſions they wanted.

Upon this invitation, a gentleman ſet out with ſeventeen of his men; but the Indians, inſtead of conducting them to their quarters, led them into an ambuſcade, where they were ſurrounded by about 500 of the natives, who diſcharged their arrows at them on all ſides, till the Engliſh, after exerting themſelves as much as was in their power, were all of them ſlain but one, who made his eſcape from this bloody ſlaughter, and was forced to hide himſelf in a wood, whence ſwimming over a lake, with much difficulty he returned home, juſt time enough to alarm his companions; for it was not long before the Indians appeared before their houſes; but the Engliſh diſcharging ſome ſmall pieces of ordnance, they quickly marched off: however, in two or three days they returned, to the number of 13 or 1400, and after having attacked a little fort and houſes for ſeven days together with ſmall ſucceſs, reſolved to burn them by throwing in fire with their arrows, which in a ſhort time reduced the habitations of the Engliſh to a heap of aſhes. They continued, however, to defend themſelves in ſo brave a manner, that the Indians finding that they could not accompliſh their deſign againſt this handful of men, at laſt abandoned the enterprize.

After their departure, ſome of the neighbouring Indians were prevailed upon to furniſh them with an old pitiful boat for ſome hatchets, knives and beads. This the Engliſh fitted up as well as they could, and nineteen of them, the miſerable remains of ſixty-eight, ventured out to ſea in her, without chart or compaſs, and with only four or five gallons of water, with a few plantains and potatoes, about twenty biſcuits, and a little rice. What was ſtill worſe, they had not one mariner among them, and this little boat was ſo overladen, that her gunnel lay almoſt even with the water.

When they had been ten days at ſea, during which four of the men were obliged by turns to continue ſcooping out the water, they, when all hopes began to fail them, diſcovered land; but on their going on ſhore, found to their unſpeakable diſappointment, that it was an uninhabited iſland which afforded no manner of ſuſtenance. In this miſerable ſtate they had no other remedy, but to ſend five of the men to the continent to ſeek relief. Theſe, after many difficulties reached the main land, and went to an Indian town called Tocoyo, from whence, after being abſent fifteen days, they brought ſuccour to their miſerable companions, who were now reduced to thirteen. By the help of this ſupply they got to a Spaniſh town, called Coro, where they were treated with great humanity, and where two more of them died. Three of them went from thence to Carthagena, and were followed thither by two more, where they procured a paſſage to Spain ; but what became of the reſt does not any where appear.

Notwithſtanding ſuch a ſeries of misfortunes as had attended the attempts made for eſtabliſhing this ſettlement, Robert Harcourt, Eſq. cauſed a ſquadron of three veſſels, commanded by himſelf, to be fitted out; the Roſe, a ſhip of eighty tons ; the Patience of thirty-ſix tons, and the Lilly ſhallop of nine tons burden, which ſailed from Dartmouth on the 29th of March, 1609, and arrived in the bay of Wiapoco on the 17th of May.

It was not long before ſeveral canoes of Indians came to ſee who they were, and finding they were Engliſh, came on board without the leaſt fear or ceremony. Theſe people were of the town called Caripo, on the eaſt ſide of the hill, at the mouth of Wiapoco river. Their king or chief, who had been many years in England, was then with Mr. Harcourt, and another of his countrymen came paſſenger with him, though he had not diſcovered his quality till the joy of his ſubjects at the ſight of him made him known. Among the Indians who came firſt on board, was one who ſpoke the Engliſh tongue perfectly well, and was known to ſome of the ſailors, he having ſerved Sir John Gilbert in England many years ; and the Indian who accompanied the king or chief, having been fourteen years in England, theſe two were of ſingular ſervice to the adventurers.

The firſt ceremonies being paſt, Mr. Harcourt informed them, that he was come to ſettle a colony there, and to take poſſeſſion of the country for the king of England, by virtue of their grant of it to Capt. Leigh, and by ſome of their countrymen before, to Sir Walter Raleigh, aſſuring them at the ſame time, that his majeſty intended no unjuſt uſurpation over them ; but would only be their friend and protector, and secure them from the insolence of the Caribbees. After some debate, the Indians consented to their living among them, but expressed some diffidence in their performing their promises, as Sir Walter had been so long without accomplishing his.

This affair being concluded, they all went on shore, where they met with the best reception the Indians could give them, and were dispersed up and down the town, on the side of a hill, while the ships rode at anchor at the foot of it. The great rains, which confined them near a month, being over, the captain endeavoured to discover the golden mountains, which had been the spurs to this undertaking; but his guide, who had promised great things, failed in the performance of them: for when he came to the spot no gold was to be found: and yet all the English were fully satisfied that the country afforded gold, as well from the assurances given them by the natives, who shewed them some images, which upon an essay appeared to contain at least one third gold, as from their observing great quantities of the white spar in which gold is contained; but they had reason to believe these mines were too far up in the higher parts of Guiana, and were perhaps too strongly guarded for them, to hope that they should be able to reach them; and besides, they had neither time nor power to search in a proper manner for finding these mines.

This disappointment was near occasioning a mutiny among those who came with no other view but to amass wealth. But the captain with great prudence prevented its running to such a length, and to keep them employed, not only went himself up the river of Wiapoco upon discovery; but sent his brother with some others, on the same errand to the river Arraway, and the country bordering upon it, which reaches to the river so the Amazons. He alfo went and took poffeffion of the mountain Gomoribo, the utmoft point of land to the northward in the Wiapoco. This he did according to cuftom, by the ceremony of twig and turf, in the prefence both of his own people and the Indians.

The attempt of the captain's brother, in making the difcovery of the river Arrawary, was attended with great difficulties and hazards; for the length they ran by fea to this river was near 100 leagues, through terrible breaks of flats and fhoals. They went alfo fifty leagues up the river, and all this was done with only flat bottomed canoes, fomething longer than the common Thames wherries, but not fo broad. The Indians they met with in this river, plainly difcovered that they had never feen any Europeans before. It was long ere they could be brought to any fort of trade or converfation with them, though they had other Indians in their company, but at laft the fight of their toys induced them to purchafe them with provifions. But the want of thefe, however, at laft obliged them to return to Wiapoco; they neverthelefs took poffeffion of the country in form, as Mr. Harcourt had done of Gomoribo.

Some time after Mr. Harcourt returned to England, leaving behind him fifty or fixty of his men, over whom he appointed his brother commander in chief, and joined Captain Harvey as his affiftant. In his way homewards, he made feveral difcoveries upon the coaft, and in fome of the rivers, and after his return to England, obtained by the favour of Prince Henry, a patent for all the coaft of Guiana and the river of the Amazons; but being foon involved in many troubles, he was unable to fupply his colony. However, his brother kept poffeffion of that part of the country, wherein he was fettled during three years, in all which time he loft but fix of his people.

CHAPTER VIII.

Sir Walter Raleigh's laſt voyage to Guiana, with an account of what took place till his return to England, when he was called down to his former ſentence, and beheaded.

AT length Sir Walter Raleigh, after ſuffering a very long impriſonment in the tower of London, on the pretence of a plot, for which he had been condemned to die, procured his liberty, and though he had been twelve years in priſon, obtained a commiſſion to execute his laſt expedition to Guiana. In order to do this, he turned the beſt part of his fortune into money, which he employed in fitting out ſhips for this expedition, and prevailed on many of his beſt friends to do ſo too. Several of theſe embarked with him, and among them his eldeſt ſon. This fleet conſiſted of ſeven ſail of different ſizes, with which Sir Walter left Plymouth harbour in July 1612, and before he had paſſed the coaſt of England, he was joined by as many more, ſo that his whole fleet conſiſted of fourteen ſhips. However, he waited for theſe laſt ſome time, and it had been better if he had left them behind; for they proved a burden to him, and ſome of them deſerted the expedition.

Soon after he obtained this reinforcement, he met with a ſtorm, which obliged him to put into Cork, from whence he ſailed on the 19th of Auguſt, and on the 6th of September arrived off the iſland of Lancerota, when he ſent to deſire leave of the governor to purchaſe proviſions; but though that gentleman at firſt promiſed him a meeting, he deferred giving it him, and at length refuſed to have any dealings with Sir Walter, under the pretence, that the inhabitants were so much afraid of him, that he dared not, and therefore desired him to draw off such of his men as were landed upon the island. But though he complied with this request, they fell upon his men in their retreat, and slew one of them. Of this outrage, Sir Walter complained to the governor of the Canaries, who, instead of sending him an answer, sallied out upon his men as they were marching, in order to draw water in a desert part of the island; and had not young Raleigh and some other officers, behaved with great bravery on this occasion, they would all have been slain. But Sir Walter was so careful of giving no offence to the court of Spain, that he did not return these acts of hostility.

Hence he steered to Gomera, where the Spaniards also resolved to oppose the landing of the English. They lined the beach and standing close to the water, saluted them very roughly, but were soon dispersed by the ship guns. After this treatment, Sir Walter sent a messenger on shore to let the governor know, that he had no hostile intention; that he only wanted a few necessaries, for which he would pay very honourably, and that if any of his men should attempt the least fraud or riot, he would hang them in the market-place: and so well did he keep his word, that the governor wrote a letter for him to deliver to Count Gondamor, the Spanish Ambassador at the Court of London, wherein he acknowledged Sir Walter's polite behaviour, and gave him the character he justly merited. Many civilities passed between Sir Walter and the governor's lady, who was of English extraction, she being related by the mother's side to the Staffords. This lady sent him sugar, fruits and other useful presents, for which, in return, he complimented her with a beautiful picture of Mary Magdalen, a ruff finely wrought, and some extracts of amber and rose-water, which were highly valued in the island.

After Sir Walter's leaving the Canaries, his ship's companies grew very sickly, and before he reached the island of Trinidad, he lost many of his men, and was himself dangerously ill. In this weak and low condition, he arrived off Wiapoco, where he hoped to have been assisted by Leonard, an Indian who had lived with him three or four years in England; but finding that he was removed so far up into the country, that there was no procuring him, he stood away for Caliana on the coast of Guinea, at the first discovery called Port Howard, where the Cacique had been also his servant, and had lived with him two years in the Tower of London, under the name of Harry. There he arrived in a day or two, having passed by an island remarkable for its being covered with a multitude of birds, from whence he sent to the Cacique, his late Indian servant, who, with other Caciques, came and brought him great plenty of cassavi bread, plantains, roasted mullets, pistachios, and pine-apples.

In this place he landed his sick men, and had tents pitched on shore, by which means, both he and his people recovered strength daily, from the benefits they received by the land air, and the refreshments they obtained. He here also set up his barges and shallops, which he had brought in pieces from England; cleansed his ships; fixed up a forge; made such iron works as were wanted; and took in a fresh supply of water.

Thus the English were employed about three weeks on shore, and in the river. During this time, Sir Walter was very much caressed by the Indians, with whom he had been formerly acquainted, and by the other natives of the place, who daily furnished him with the best provisions the country afforded; offered him their obedience, and even propofed to make him their Sovereign, on condition, that he would abide and fettle among them; fo high was the gratitude they ftill felt for his former behaviour. Thefe propofals, he mentioned in his difpatches to England with the greateft modefty and unconcern.

On the 4th of December they left this river, and the next day came to an ifland, where Sir Walter's fhip ran on the fhoals, and was with difficulty got off.

Sir Walter ftill continuing ill, it was refolved, that he fhould ftay with five of the fhips at Punto de Gallo, in the ifland of Trinidad, while the reft, commanded by Capt. Keymis, young Raleigh, Sir Walter's fon, and a few other gentlemen, with five or fix companies of foot, fhould proceed up the river Oronoko, with a month's provifions, in fearch of the mine, the men being ordered to encamp, till the depth and breadth of the mine was difcovered. Sir Walter at the fame time defired, that if they found the Spaniards very ftrong, they would be careful of landing, as a repulfe from them, would reflect difhonour on the nation; and he concluded with obferving, that if they did not find the mine well worth their pains of working, they need only bring a fmall quantity of the ore, to convince the King, that it was not a mere fiction of his invention.

With thefe inftructions the five fhips fet forward on the 10th of December, and foon reached a new Spanifh town, called St. Thomas, upon the main channel of the Oronoko, where Antonio Berreo, who was taken by Raleigh in the ifland of Trinidad, had planted a fettlement. This town confifted of about 14 houfes flightly built, with a chapel, a convent of Francifcans, and a garrifon. Keymis and the reft now thought themfelves obliged, through fear of leaving the enemy between them and the boats, to deviate from their inftructions, by which they had been enjoined firſt, to take a ſmall party to make trial of the mine, under ſhelter of their own camp, and then to deal with the town as they ſhould ſee cauſe. It was reſolved, to go on ſhore in one body, between the mine and the town; but unhappily landing by night nearer the town than they ſuſpected, and intending to reſt themſelves by the river ſide till morning, they were attacked by the Spaniſh troops, who had been apprized of their coming. This charge was ſo unexpected, that the common ſoldiers were ſtruck with ſuch conſternation, that had not they been animated by their Commanders, they had been all cut to pieces, but ſoon rallying by the example of theſe brave men, they made ſuch a vigorous defence that the Spaniards were put to flight. However, in the heat of the purſuit, the Engliſh found themſelves at the Spaniſh town, before they knew where they were. Here the battle was renewed, they being aſſaulted by the Governor himſelf, Don Diego Palameca, and four or five Captains, at the head of their companies, againſt whom Capt. Walter Raleigh, a brave and ſprightly young man of 23 years of age, ruſhed forwards at the head of a company of pikes, without waiting for the muſketeers, and having killed one of the Spaniſh captains, was mortally wounded by another: but preſſing ſtill on with his ſword, upon Erinetta, probably the Captain who had ſhot him, that Spaniard knocked him down with the but-end of his muſket, upon which the brave youth, crying, Lord have mercy upon me, and proſper your enterprize, expired. But at the ſame inſtant, young Raleigh's Serjeant, thruſt the Spaniſh Commander through with his halbert. Two other of the Commanders were alſo ſlain, and at length the Governor himſelf, fainting under his wounds, was trampled to death, on which his men diſperſed; ſome of them taking ſhelter in the houſes about the market place, from whence they killed and wounded the Englifh at pleafure; who finding it not eafy to diflodge them, fet fire to the houfes, and drove them into the woods and mountains, whence the Spaniards ftill continued to alarm them.

Capt. Keymis now leaving a garrifon in the place, refolved to make an attempt upon the mines, fome of which were not far diftant; but the Spaniards who had fled, having taken poffeffion of the paffes that led to them, Capt. Keymis found all approach to them very difficult, particularly with refpect to the mine he had in his eye, for the river was fo low, that in moft places he could not approach the banks that were near it by a mile, and where he found an afcent, he received a volley of mufket fhot from the woods, which killed two of the rowers, and wounded fix more of his men, among whom was Capt. Amhurft.

Capt. Keymis finding the attempt very hazardous, the paffage being full of thick and impaffable woods, and thinking that the Englifh who were left on fhore at the Spanifh town, would not be able to defend it, efpecially if the enemy fhould be recruited, he gave over the enterprize, and returned to St. Thomas's, where the Englifh plundered the town, and carried away the moft valuable part of the treafure: and the enemy not daring to appear, in order to ranfom the reft, they fet fire to that part which was ftill unconfumed.

Sir Walter, upon the news of his fon's death, and the ill fuccefs of this expedition, which had difappointed him in his hopes, feverely reprimanded Capt. Keymis, and exclaimed, that he had undone him; obferving, that if he had only brought 100 weight of the ore, though with the lofs of 100 men, it would not only have given the king fatisfaction, and have preferved his reputation, but have afforded the nation encouragement to have returned the next year with a greater force, and to have held the country for his majefty, to whom it belonged.

Upon this, Keymis retired in difcontent to his cabbin, and foon after a piftol going off, Sir Walter called out to know the occafion, when Capt. Keymis anfwered, that it was nothing but a piftol he had let off, on account of its being long charged: but in about an hour after, his boy found him lying dead, weltering in blood, with a piftol and long knife lying near him, and upon examination it appeared, that he had endeavoured firft to fhoot himfelf, but the bullet being fmall, had only cracked one of his ribs, fo that effectually to put an end to his life, he had thruft the knife through his left pap.

Sir Walter now called a council of his officers, who were of opinion, that they ought to retire to Newfoundland, in order to refit and take in refrefhments; but many of his men mutinying on the way, he fent them home directly to England.

On his arrival at Newfoundland, great difturbances arofe on board his own fhip, which being unable to quell, he joined with the ftronger party, who, againft his own inclinations, declared for returning to England.

Sir Walter Raleigh arrived at Plymouth about the end of July, when he found the king had publifhed a proclamation, requiring him and his people to appear before the privy-council, for having burnt the town of St. Thomas. He was foon after arrefted, and on his being brought to London, was committed prifoner to his own houfe, but endeavouring to efcape from thence to a veffel which waited for him at Gravefend, he was feized near Greenwich, carried to the Tower, and on the 28th of October, 1618, brought from thence to the court of king's-bench, where the record of his former fentence being examined, he was ordered to the gate-houfe, and the next morning beheaded in Old Palace-yard, aged fixty-fix.

Upon this great occafion he behaved like a brave man and a Chriftian. He made a nervous and eloquent fpeech in juftification of his conduct, and then feeling the edge of the axe, faid with a fmile, " It is a fharp medicine, but a found cure for all " woes." After which his head was ftruck off at two blows.

All Europe were aftonifhed at the injuftice and cruelty of this proceeding; but Gondamor, the Spanifh Ambaffador, thirfted for his blood, on account of his having been the fcourge of Spain, during the reign of Queen Elizabeth, and King James durft not refufe him the life of a man, who as a foldier, a fcholar, and a ftatefman, was the greateft ornament to his country. That meanfpirited prince, to his eternal infamy, foon after ordered Cottington, one of the refidents of Spain, to inform the Spanifh court how able a man Sir Walter Raleigh was, and yet to give them content he had not fpared him, though by preferving him he would have given great fatisfaction to his fubjects, and had at his command upon all occafions, as ufeful a man as ferved any prince in Chriftendom.

CHAPTER IX.

The voyages of Capt. Gofnold, Capt. Pringe, Capt. Gilbert, and Capt. Weymouth, to the countries then called Virginia.

IN the year 1602, the Virginia company fitted out a veffel for that country, under the command of Capt. Bartholomew Gofnold, who failed from Falmouth on the 26th of March, with only thirty-two perfons on board, and on the 11th of May arrived among the iflands, which form the north fide of Maffachufett's Bay in New-England, where finding no conveniencies for forming a fettlement, he entered what is now called Plymouth Bay, and afterwards went on fhore in a fmall but uninhabited ifle, which he called Elizabeth's Ifland, and on another, which he named Martha's Vineyard. Here fome of his company fowed Englifh corn, and faw it come up very kindly. On Elizabeth's Ifland he erected a fort for his own fecurity, that he might trade from thence with the neighbouring Indians, to whom the Europeans feemed to be no ftrangers. For the commander of the firft body that came for the fake of trade, after the figns of peace being given on both fides, made a long fpeech, and then boldly came on board the fhip; but what was moft extraordinary, he was dreffed in a waiftcoat, a hat, breeches, fhoes and ftockings, but his attendants had only deerfkins about their fhoulders, and feal-fkins about their waifts. Their hair was very long, and tied up with a knot behind, and though they were painted all over, the natural fwarthinefs of their complexions was eafily difcovered.

On the north-weft fide of Elizabeth's Ifland, the captain found a lake of frefh water, about a league in circumference, very near the fea, and in the middle of it was a fmall ifland, which contained about an acre, and this they pitched upon as the moft commodious place for building the above fort. In this lake they found an infinite number of turtle, with feveral forts of fifh and fowl, whence thofe who propofed to fettle there, had the agreeble profpect of being in no want of provifions. On their vifiting the continent near Elizabeth's Ifland, they found the country extremely delightful, and abounding in meadows, brooks and rivers. They had alfo fome communication with the Indians of the main land, for they traded with them for European commodities, and gave in exchange for knives and toys, beavers, martins, otters, foxes and rabbits, together with seals and deer-skins.

The affairs of the plantation might have gone on very prosperously had all the planters been unanimous, but they were solely intent upon their private interests, and upon making a profitable voyage. The captain having in vain endeavoured to persuade some of them to stay in the fort, took in a large cargo of sassafras, cedar, furs, &c. and leaving the island on the 18th of June, arrived at Plymouth on the 23d of July following.

At the time of the queen's decease, a design was on foot for prosecuting the discoveries and trade to North-America, in which were concerned several of the gentlemen and merchants of Bristol, among whom was the Rev. Mr. Hackluit, prebendary of the cathedral of that city, who was chosen to apply in behalf of himself and the rest of the persons concerned, to Sir Walter Raleigh, who was still considered as the proprietor of Virginia, in order to procure his licence for that trade, and upon his application, Sir Walter not only granted him a licence under his hand and seal, but generously made over to them all the profits that should arise from the voyage.

Being thus empowered, they raised the joint stock of 1000l. and fitted out two small vessels, the Speedwell of fifty tons burden, commanded by Matthew Pringe, with thirty men and boys, and the Discoverer, a bark of twenty-six tons, commanded by William Brown, who had under him a mate and eleven men and boys. They were victualled for eight months, and had a large cargo on board of the goods thought most proper for that country.

These vessels sailed from Bristol on the 20th of March 1603, but were obliged by contrary winds, to put into Milford-Haven, where they continued till the 20th of April following, when they proceeded on their voyage, and without any remarkable accident arrived on the coaſt of North-America, in the latitude of 43°. whence they ſailed ſouth-weſt, in ſearch of that part of the country, which had been viſited by Captain Goſnold.

They at length found in the latitude of 41°. and ſome few minutes, a very convenient bay, to which they gave the name of Whitſon's Bay, in honour of Mr. John Whitſon, who was then Mayor of Briſtol. Here they landed and cut a good quantity of ſaſſafras, which they carried on board; but firſt to prevent their being ſurprized in the woods by the natives, while they were at work, they erected a ſmall fort or redoubt, in which they left their effects under a guard of about four or five men.

Forty or fifty, and ſometimes an hundred of the Indians, frequently came in a company to trade with the Engliſh, with whom they eat and drank, and were very merry, and once on their obſerving an Engliſh lad playing upon a guitar, they got round about him, and taking hold of each other's hands, danced twenty or thirty in a ring, after the American manner. The ſeamen obſerving, that the natives were more afraid of two maſtiffs they had with them than of twenty men, whenever they wanted to get rid of their company, had the brutality to let looſe one of the maſtiffs, at which the natives ran ſhrieking into the woods. This ill treatment, and the erecting a fortification in the country, probably made the Indians look upon the Engliſh as their enemies: for ſoon after a party of them came and ſurrounded the fort, when moſt of the Engliſh were abſent, and would probably have taken it, if Captain Pringe had not fired two guns, which alarmed the workmen in the woods, who immediately returned to its relief.

The Indians indeed pretended that they had no hoſtile intentions, but the Engliſh did not care to truſt them afterwards, and the day before they embarked, the natives came in great numbers and ſet fire to the woods where they had cut their ſaſſafras, which was probably to let the Engliſh know, that they would preſerve nothing in their country, that could invite ſuch gueſts to viſit them again.

About the middle of June, they had completed the freight of their bark, and having ſent her to England, made all the diſpatch they could in loading their own veſſel with a valuable cargo of ſkins and furs, which they had before procured of the Indians, in exchange for the commodities they had brought with them.

Theſe Indians much reſembled thoſe mentioned by Captain Goſnold, and among the other curioſities the Engliſh found in the country, they took one of the boats uſed by the inhabitants, made of the bark of a birch-tree, ſewed together with twigs, the ſeams of which were covered with roſin or turpentine, and though this boat was ſeventeen feet long, four broad, and capable of carrying nine perſons, it did not weigh ſixty pounds. Thoſe boats were rowed with oars reſembling our baker's peels, by the help of which they went at a great rate.

Capt. Pringe having quitted the coaſt of Virginia on the 9th of Auguſt, ſailed to England, and on the 2d of October entered King's Road, where he had the ſatisfaction of finding, that the bark was ſafely arrived a fortnight before.

In the ſame year, another attempt was made upon the ſame account by Capt. Bartholomew Gilbert, who had been the year before at Virginia with Capt. Goſnold. This gentleman ſailed from Plymouth on the 10th of May, in the Elizabeth, a bark of fifty tons burden, and in his paſſage touched at St. Lucia, Dominica, and Nevis, where he traded, and at the laſt of theſe places cut about twenty tons of lignum vitæ.

On the 3d of July he ſailed from thence for the coaſt of Virginia, and in particular for Cheſapeak Bay, where he was very deſirous of obtaining ſome intelligence of the manners and diſpoſitions of the people.

He arrived on the 25th near the mouth of that harbour; but the wind blew ſo hard, and the ſea ran ſo high, that he could not enter it, and therefore, after beating about two or three days, was obliged to ſteer more to the eaſtward.

On the 29th, being not far from the ſhore, the captain with four of his beſt men landed in their boat, and being provided with arms, proceeded ſome way up the country; but in their march being attacked and overpowered by the inhabitants, they were all killed; and it was not without ſome difficulty that the boat, with two young men who were left in her, returned to the ſhip with this melancholy news.

There being now in all but eleven men and boys in the ſhip, they were afraid to venture the loſs of any more of their ſmall company; and their proviſions growing ſhort, Henry Shute the maſter, who had taken the command, reſolved, though they were in extreme want of wood and water, to return homewards, which they did, and arrived ſafely in the river of Thames about the end of September.

The buſineſs of ſettling and planting the northern continent of America being now laid open by the attainder of Sir Walter Raleigh, on the ridiculous pretence of a very improbable plot, and thoſe who had been concerned in the laſt voyages, not only giving a favourable account of the country, but obtaining very conſiderable profits, ſeveral perſons of diſtinction were determined to promote thefe difcoveries; and in particular Henry Wriothefly earl of Southampton, and Thomas Lord Arundel of Wardour, refolved to fit out a fhip for that expedition.

This veffel, which was called the Archangel, and was commanded by Capt. George Weymouth, failed from Dartmouth on the 31ft of March, 1605, and met with nothing of confequence, till they imagined that they were near the coaft of Virginia, when the winds carrying them to the northward into the latitude of 41°. 30'. and their wood and water beginning to grow fhort, they became very defirous of feeing land, which their charts gave them reafon to expect. They therefore bore directly in with it; but found none in a run of almoft fifty leagues. However, after much expedition, they obtained fight of an ifland that was very woody along the fhore. It abounded in fruit, and vaft numbers of fowls; the fea afforded plenty of fifh, while large ftreams of frefh water ran down the cliffs.

This was the eaftern part of what is now called Long Ifland; from thence they could difcern a great many other iflands, and the main land ftretching from the weft-fouth-weft to the eaft-north-eaft; they vifited feveral of the iflands near the continent, and found them very full of timber, and fruit-trees of various forts.

Among thefe iflands they met with an harbour in which fhips of any burden might lie defended from all winds, from fix to ten fathom water, and this they called Pentecoft harbour, from its being difcovered about Whitfuntide. The fir-trees, which grew in great numbers on the iflands, yielded excellent turpentine, and many of the fhells they found about the rocks, afforded fmall pearls.

While they lay here, the natives from the continent came to trade with them for fkins and furs, in exchange for knives, beads, and fuch trifles, very readily giving the value of ten or twelve pounds in their goods, for such English hard-ware as was not worth above five shillings.

Their bows, arrows and canoes, were like those of the other Indians on the coast. The heads of their tobacco pipes were sometimes made of clay, and sometimes were only the claw of a lobster; but they were all sufficient to hold as much as ten or twelve of ours.

The most extraordinary discovery made in this voyage, was that of a river, which was esteemed by those who found it, the most beautiful in America. They sailed several leagues up it with their ship, and found it of a considerable breadth for forty miles together, it being in most places a mile broad, in some three quarters, but never less than half a mile. It flows sixteen or eighteen feet, and is six or ten fathom deep at low water. On both sides there are at a small distance from each other, many fine coves, some of which are able to contain above 100 sail, where the ground is soft ooze with a tough clay underneath for anchorage. Nature has also formed several convenient places like docks, in which ships of all burdens might be graved and careened. The neighbouring land treads along on both sides in a smooth line, and instead of rocks and cliffs, is bordered with grass, and tall trees of different sorts.

After they had remained here about six weeks, and during all that time carried on a very profitable trade with the natives, they thought of returning to England; for which they set sail on the 16th of June, and arrived that day month in sight of the Land's End.

CHAPTER X.

Patents granted by King James I. for erecting two Virginia Companies. The London Company fit out a fquadron under the command of Capt. Newport, who fettles a colony in a Peninfula in Pouhatan, or James's river, and calls the place James's town. A defcription of the climate, foil, beafts, birds, fifhes, trees, and plants of Virginia; particularly of Maize or Indian Corn, and the manner of cultivating Tobacco.

THE above profperous voyage inducing many perfons of rank and fortune to wifh this trade thoroughly eftablifhed, they applied to the crown, for fuch legal authorities as were neceffary, and two companies were formed for fettling this large tract of land, which was at this time divided into north and fouth Virginia. One of thefe companies confifted of the adventurers of the city of London, who were defirous of fixing a plantation between 34, 41°. of north latitude, and the other of thofe of the cities of Briftol, Exeter, and the town of Plymouth, who wanted to fettle in between 38 and 45°. Each of thefe companies obtained letters patents in which it was provided, that the above refpective colonies, fhould not plant within 103 miles of each other. That they fhould poffefs an hundred miles of the country to the weftward within the land; fifty miles either way along the coaft, from the feat of their firft fettlement, and all the iflands oppofite to the coaft for the fpace of 100 miles at fea. They were empowered to dig mines in and beyond their refpective limits, to the weftward, paying the crown a fifth of all the gold and copper ore, they fhould obtain; they were likewife empowered to feize all the fhips that should trade within their respective limits; and even to coin money, and raise forces for their defence.

These two companies no sooner received this extensive authority from the crown, than they began in earnest to provide for making settlements within the bounds, proscribed by their respective grants. With this view, the London company fitted out three vessels, one of 100 tons, another of 40, and a pinnace of 20; on board of which were 110 landmen, and every thing necessary for settling a colony. The command of this small squadron, was given to capt. Christopher Newport, but the orders relating to the government of the colony, and the name of the council who were to be intrusted with the administration of it when settled, were delivered to them in a box sealed up, which was not to be opened till they were on shore.

This squadron sailed from London on the 20th of December, 1606, took in water and other necessaries at the Canaries, and proceeded to the Caribbee Islands, where they arrived on the 23d of February, and staid among them, but chiefly at the island of Nevis, about five weeks. On the 3d of April they sailed for Virginia, and on the 26th of the same month, landed at the southern Cape of Chesapeak Bay, where they built a fort, which they called Cape and Fort Henry, and to the northern Cape gave the name of Cape Charles, in honour of the two princes; but the river Powhatan, they called James's River, in honour of the king.

This river they completely searched, before they would come to any resolution about forming a settlement, and then, by unanimous consent, they pitched upon a peninsula, about fifty miles up the river, which, besides the goodness of the soil, was esteemed most capable of being made a place of trade and security, two thirds of it being surrounded by the main river, which all along affords good anchorage; and the other third by a small river, able to receive veſſels of 100 tons burden, till it comes within thirty yards of the great river, where it generally overflows in ſpring tides; on which account, this peninſula obtained the name of an Iſland, and both the town and river received their name from king James. The whole iſland thus incloſed, contains about 2000 acres, beſides many thouſands of very good marſh-lands, with as fine paſturage as any in the country. The narrow paſſage rendered this place very ſecure from being attacked by the enemy, and to add to its ſtrength, they here built caſtles and a fort. This was the firſt Engliſh plantatation that ſucceeded.

The firſt buſineſs the colony entered upon after their landing, was opening their orders, when they found that ſeven gentlemen were appointed their council, one of whom was Captain Smith, on whoſe ſkill and experience, the company in England ſeemed to rely, more than upon any of the reſt; but the other gentlemen had ſuch a diſlike to him, that they had confined him priſoner ever ſince they left England, and now excluded him from the council; but afterwards the planters themſelves, after they had by their perpetual jars almoſt ruined the company's affairs, were obliged, not only to admit him into the council, but in a manner to reſign the adminiſtration into his hands.

The ſhips having ſtaid five or ſix weeks before the intended new town, Captain Newport departed with them for England, leaving upwards of 100 men ſettled in the above form of government: but the ſhips were no ſooner gone, than the ſame feuds and diſorders broke out again with freſh violence. However, in the midſt of theſe feuds, they fell to planting, ſowing, building and fortifying. They alſo carried on a very advantageous trade with the natives, of which they might have had much greater profit, and have managed it more to the fatisfaction of the Indians, if they had been under any rule, and not at liberty to outbid one another. Thus they not only leſſened their own profit, but created jealouſies and difturbances among the Indians, by letting one have a better bargain than another, by which means thoſe who had been hardeſt dealt with, thought themſelves cheated and abuſed, whence they conceived an averſion to the Engliſh in general, and even made it a national quarrel. This feems to have been the original cauſe of moſt of the vexations the Engliſh received from the Indians: However, the former ſubſiſted chiefly by the help of their proviſions, till the return of the ſhips.

But now an object drew their eyes and thoughts not only from trade, but from taking the neceſſary care of their preſervation: They found in the iſthmus of the peninſula on which James's Town was built, a ſpring of water that flowed from a ſmall bank, and waſhed down with it a yellow ſort of duſt-iſinglaſs, which lay ſhining at the bottom, and filled their minds with an inſatiable deſire of riches; for taking this to be gold, they were ſo ſtupid as to neglect both the neceſſary defence of their lives from the attacks of the Indians, and the ſupport of their bodies by procuring proviſions; abſolutely relying upon the power of gold; thinking that where this was in plenty, nothing elſe could be wanting; and thus infatuated with the hopes of obtaining mountains of wealth, they deſpiſed the mines of Peru and Mexico, in compariſon of their own ineſtimable ſtream. They, however, foon grew in ſome meaſure ſenſible of their error; for by their negligence, they were reduced to great ſcarcity of proviſions, and the little they had was loſt by the burning of the town, while all hands were employed about this imaginary treaſure, ſo that they were obliged to live upon fruit, crabs, and muscles, without having a day's provision before hand. By this neglect many of them also became a prey to the Indians, while the rest not daring to venture abroad, were forced to be contented with what they could get.

They were in this miserable condition when a ship arrived the next year, freighted with men and provisions for the supply of the plantation, and as they neither thought nor spoke of any thing but gold, they put on board this vessel all the yellow sand they had gathered, with the skins and furs, for which they had bartered with the Indians, and then sent her away. Soon after another ship arrived, filled with supplies, when they also stowed her with this imaginary gold-dust, and filled her up with cedar and clap-board.

However, being at length persuaded that they might apply themselves to other labours more necessary than collecting yellow sand, which if ever so valuable, would be always in their power, if they did but take care to fortify themselves effectually, they began to do this in earnest, and by the good management of Capt. Smith, made several discoveries in James River and Chesapeak Bay, and in the year 1608, they first gathered Indian corn of their own planting. But unhappily Capt. Smith going to make discoveries up the country, was attacked by 300 of the Indians, under the command of one of their chiefs, who slew all his men, and taking him prisoner, carried him to Powhatan, their principal sovereign, who would have put him to death had it not been for the intercession of his daughter Pacahunta: however, Capt. Smith being afterwards released, returned to James Town, when the president of the council resigning his office, he was unanimously desired to accept of it.

While Capt. Smith was employed in making the above difcoveries, things ran again into confufion in James Town; and feveral uneafy people taking advantage of his abfence, attempted to defert the fettlement, and to run away with a fmall veffel that was left to attend it; for Capt. Smith was the only man among them who could manage difcoveries with fuccefs, or keep the people in any order; they, however, now made two other fettlements, one at Nanfamona in James River, above thirty miles below James Town, and the other at Powhatan, fix miles below the falls of the river, which laft was bought of Powhatan for a certain quantity of copper; each fettlement confifting of 120 men; and foon after they made a fourth fettlement near the mouth of James River.

Two thirds of the adventurers coming over with a view of having every thing provided to their hands, were fubfifted by the labour of the other induftrious third, till Capt. Smith compelled them all to take a fhare in the work, which being done, a fufficient quantity of ground was foon planted to fubfift the colony in plenty, when by moderate exercife and good food, they were not only reftored to health, but became in a very flourifhing condition; and being now no longer under the neceffity of procuring food from the Indians by violence, they lived and traded together very amicably, and Powhatan fuffered them to make feveral other fettlements in the country.

But when their affairs were in this profperous fituation, the arrival of fix or feven fhips from England, with a large fupply of ammunition and provifions, and between 3 and 400 planters, threw the whole colony into confufion, which being made known to the company in England, they obtained a new patent from King James, which empowered them to appoint a governor, and they prevailed on the Lord Delawar to accept of this office. Whereupon that nobleman made Sir Thomas Gates, Sir George Summers, and Capt. Newport his deputies, till his arrival, and thefe gentlemen fet fail from England with nine fhips and 500 men, in May 1609.

Thefe three deputies being embarked in one fhip, were unfortunately caft away on the Bermudas iflands, which were then uninhabited; but they and all the crew efcaped on fhore, where they found plenty of provifions, and took poffeffion of thofe iflands for the crown of England, fince which time they have been called the Summer Iflands, from Sir George Summers.

In the mean time the reft of the fleet arrived fafe in Chefapeak Bay, where Capt. Smith was ftill the prefident, but both the old and new planters declared, that they were not obliged to obey him, as another commiffion had been granted, which had fuperfeded his. Capt. Smith however, kept them in fome order while he remained among them: but having the misfortune to be accidentally wounded by the explofion of fome gunpowder, it was found abfolutely neceffary for him to return to England with the veffels that failed foon after. But he was no fooner on board than every thing fell into the utmoft confufion; all bufinefs was neglected, and the people living profufely upon what was contained in the magazines, were quickly reduced to want, which no fooner happened, than they rambled about without order through the country, plundering the natives of their provifions, while they attacking them in their own defence, cut off great numbers of them.

They were in this fituation when the deputy governors arrived in two floops, which they had built in the Bermudas, and thofe gentlemen had the mortification to fee that the vices of thefe men, together with ficknefs and famine, had reduced them from upwards of 400 to lefs than eighty. Sir

Thomas Gates and Sir George Summers endeavoured all in their power to remove their uneafinefs, and to reduce them once more to order; but it was all in vain, for the people fhewed their empty warehoufes, their ruined fettlements, and the number of their fick, obliged them to confent to their embarking for England, as the only means of faving thofe who were left.

But juft as they were failing out of Chefapeak Bay, they were met by a fhip in which was their new governor, the Lord Delawar, who obliged them to go back to James Town, in order to repair their houfes and forts, and they had no fooner returned on fhore, than his lordfhip fet before them, in a free and plain difcourfe, the folly and madnefs of their proceedings; reproving them for their divifions, idlenefs, and ill conduct, which had occafioned their misfortunes; advifing them to reform, or he fhould be compelled to draw the fword of juftice, and cut off the delinquents; declaring, however, that he had much rather draw his own fword in their defence, telling them for their encouragement, that he had brought them fuch plenty of provifions, that there would be no danger of wanting for the future, if they were not wanting to themfelves. He then proceeded to conftitute a council, and afterwards to furnifh the people with flefh, for though there were no lefs than 5 or 600 hogs in the plantation, when Capt. Smith went to England, there was not at this time one left alive, for they had been either eaten by the colony, or deftroyed by the Indians, who had likewife driven all the deer and other game out of the country, and the Englifh were fo ill provided with nets, that though there was plenty of fifh in the rivers, they knew not how to take them.

The company had fent over a fupply of cloathing, bifcuit, flour, beer and other liquors, but taking it for granted, that there were hogs, venifon, fowl and fish enough in the country, had sent no cattle. Upon which sir George Summers was dispatched to Bermudas to bring over live hogs from thence, for he had found plenty of them in that island, when he was cast away upon it. The governor also employed some in fishing, but the nets and tackle were so bad, that they had no success; he endeavoured to settle a correspondence with Powhatan, and other of the Indian chiefs, in order to purchase flesh of them for English goods, and in some of these negotiations he succeeded, particularly with the king of Patomack, one of the most powerful of the Indian chiefs. But though Powhatan had already promised to acknowledge the king of England for his sovereign, and had on that account received presents of considerable value he was so exasperated at the English, that he would return no other answer, than that he desired them to depart the country, or confine themselves within the limits of James Town-Island, and not continue ranging through his dominions, with a view, as he supposed, of subduing them; threatning to give orders for their being cut off, if ever they went beyond their limits. He also commanded the messengers sent by his lordship, not to see his face again, unless they brought him a coach and six horses; for he had been informed by some Indians who had been in England, that all persons of distinction rode in those vehicles.

The lord Delawar, exasperated at this answer, had an Indian taken prisoner, whose right hand he caused to be cut off, and in this condition he sent him to Powhatan, with orders to tell him, that he would send him all his subject in that manner, and burn all the corn in the country, which was then ripe, if he did not for the future forbear all acts of hostility. This instance of barbarity had its effect, and the colony lived for some time in peace and plenty, making frefh difcoveries, and forming new alliances with the Indian princes.

Mean while Sir Thomas Gates was fent to England to give an account of the ftate of the colony; when the fhips being freighted home with cedar, black walnut, and iron ore, thefe returns appeared fo inconfiderable, that the company were in fome fufpence, whether they fhould not fend for the lord Delawar and the colony home; but Sir Thomas Gates told them, that if they would fend over men who knew how to make pitch and tar, and plant flax and hemp, they might furnifh England with all kind of naval ftores. That as the country abounded in mulberry trees, they might eafily fet up a manufactory of filk; that the foil was exceeding fertile, producing corn, grafs, grapes, and a variety of other fruits: that European cattle and corn multiplied prodigioufly, and that their colony would never want fifh and fowl, was it provided with boats, nets and engines, which would enable the Englifh to fupport themfelves.

This reprefentation made the patentees refolve to proceed with alacrity in improving this plantation, in which refolution they were confirmed by the lord Delawar, who having left the honourable Mr. Percy as his deputy, returned to England for the recovery of his health.

While the lord Delawar was in England, his deputy brought about a peaceable correfpondence with the natives, which at laft advanced fo far, that feveral intermarriages took place, and among thefe, the Indian princefs Pacahunta, who had faved Capt. Smith's life, efpoufed Mr. John Rolf, an Englifh gentleman, whofe pofterity ftill enjoy the lands defcended to them from this lady.

CHAPTER XI.

The tranfactions of the firft colony in New-England with the Indians, and the furprizing increafe of the fettlements. The fituation and climate of New-England.

IN the laft chapter we have given an hiftory of the fettlements made by the London or South-Virginia company, and are now to mention the proceedings of the weftern or Plymouth company, as they are ftiled by the writers of that age. They were for fome years contented with trading with the natives of North-Virginia for furs, and with fifhing upon that coaft; but at length two fhips being employed in this fifhery in the year 1614, commanded by Capt. John Smith, and Capt. Thomas Hunt, the former went on fhore, took a particular view of the country of the Maffachufets, and had fome fkirmifhes with the natives. After which, he ordered Hunt to difpofe of his fifh in Spain, and then return to England; but Hunt, bafely propofing to make a market of the natives, as well as of their fifh, treacheroufly enticed 27 of the Indians on board his fhip, and then fetting fail with them to Malaga, fold them to the Spaniards for flaves, at the rate of 20l. a man, keeping only an Indian called Squanto, who was afterwards of great fervice to the Englifh.

This outrage was fo refented by the Indians, that for the prefent all commerce between them became impracticable; and though capt. Dormer was fent to New-England, in the year 1619, with Squanto for his interpreter, in order to conclude a peace with the natives, and to fettle a colony near Maffachufets-Bay, the Indians refufed to be reconciled, and attacking the Englifh, Dormer was wounded, upon which he left Squanto on fhore, and proceeded to Virginia.

The patentees were at laft fo affected by thefe difcouragements, as to give up all thoughts of making a fettlement. However other adventurers carried on a trade to New-England, that turned to a very good account; and it is probable that this commerce might have been carried on for feveral years in the fame manner, without any thoughts of planting, had it not been for a congregation of Brownifts, or Independants, who being perfecuted in England, had retired to Holland, and formed themfelves into a church, under Mr. John Robinfon, their minifter, and foon after projected the defign of feeking an eftablifhment in the new world. In order to this, they, by means of Sir Robert Nanton, obtained the confent of king James I. for fettling in America; and afterwards, by means of their agents in England, contracted with fome merchants for a fettlement on the bank of Hudfon's river.

Thefe merchants were proprietors of the country, and agreed to a contract, which bore hard upon thofe who were to be the firft fettlers. Mr. Robinfon's congregation, however, fold their eftates, and made a common bank for a fund to carry on this undertaking. They then hired a fhip of 180 tons, which they freighted with proper goods and merchandize, and the whole company, confifting of about 120 perfons, coming to England, embarked on board this veffel at Southampton.

This fhip failed from Plymouth, on the 6th of September 1621, and fell in with Cape Cod on the 9th of November, a very improper time of the year for beginning to build and plant. Here they refrefhed themfelves for about half a day, and then tacked about to the fouthward for Hudfon's River; but Jones, the mafter of the fhip, having been bribed by the Dutch, who intended to take poffeffion of thefe parts themfelves, as they did fome time after, inftead of putting out to fea, entangled them among dangerous fhoals and breakers, where meeting with a ftorm, the fhip was driven back again to the cape, on which they put into the harbour, and refolved to attempt a fettlement there; but Cape Cod not being within the limits of the land for which they had obtained a grant, they affociated themfelves into a body politic, by a formal inftrument, wherein having declared themfelves the fubjects of the crown of England, they folemnly engaged fubmiffion to the laws that fhould from time to time be made for the good of the country.

Having chofen a very commodious place for building a town, with a very agreeable country about it, they refolved not to trouble their friends about obtaining any farther licence, but to rifk their fortunes where Providence had caft them, and in confequence of this refolution went hard to work, in building a town, in 42°. north latitude, which they named Plymouth. The planters who agreed to ftay in this place, were about 100, including women and children, and of thefe there were only nineteen families; but fuch were the fatigues endured by this infant colony during the firft winter, that fifty perfons out of the hundred died within the fpace of two months, and had the Indians attacked them they had probably all perifhed.

They, however, faw none of the natives, till the middle of March, when Samofet, one of their fagamores or captains, came and told them that his people would be glad to trade with them. The next day, coming to them again with other Indians, he informed the Englifh that Maffaffoiet, their great fachem, had his refidence three days march to the northward, and intended them a vifit. Accordingly Maffaffoiet arrived on the 22d of March, with a retinue of ſixty people, and being received by Captain Standiſh, at the head of a file of muſqueteers, was conducted to a kind of throne, prepared in one of the houſes. He was of a large ſtature, was middle-aged, had a grave countenance and was ſparing in his ſpeech. His face was painted red, and both his head and face were ſmeared over with oil. He had a deer-ſkin mantle; his breeches and ſtockings which were of a piece, were of the ſame materials, and his arms were covered with wild cats-ſkins. His knife hung by a ſtring at his breaſt, and his tobacco-pouch behind. His principal attendants were dreſſed in the ſame garb, and there appeared no marks of diſtinction between this prince and his ſubjects, unleſs it were a chain of fiſh-bones which Maſſaſſoiet wore about his neck. This chief had not been long ſeated when Mr. Carver, the governor came in with a guard of muſqueteers, whereupon Maſſaſſoiet roſe up and kiſſed him, after which they both ſat down, and an entertainment was provided by the Engliſh, of which, no part appeared more acceptable than the brandy, the ſachem himſelf drinking very plentifully of it.

In Maſſaſſoiet's retinue was Squanto, who had been carried to England by Hunt, and brought back again into the country. This Indian had, it ſeems, a very great affection for the Engliſh, among whom he had lived ſeveral years, and from his favourable repreſentation of the colony, the ſachem was induced to make them this friendly viſit. At this firſt meeting he entered into an offenſive and defenſive alliance with the Engliſh, acknowledged King James for his ſovereign, and as an evidence of his ſincerity, granted part of his country to the planters and their heirs for ever: for the ſachem being informed by Squanto of the great power of the Engliſh, both by ſea and land, promiſed himſelf their aſſiſtance againſt his enemies the Naraganſet Indians, while the Engliſh ſtood in no leſs need of his friendſhip, to eſtabliſh themſelves in this country. This alliance being therefore founded upon the mutual intereſts of the contracting parties, was inviolably maintained for many years.

The treaty being concluded, Maſſaſſoiet returned to his capital, leaving Squanto with the colony, who was extremely ſerviceable to them, not only as an interpreter, but by inſtructing them how to plant and manage their Indian corn, in piloting them along the coaſt, and ſupplying them with fiſh, fowl, and veniſon. The Engliſh however ſtill remained ſickly, and ſeveral of them died, among whom was Mr. Carver, their governor, and the ſeamen were ſo ill that they were not in a condition to ſet ſail till May, when the ſhip returned to England, to give their friends an account of the ſituation of the colony.

When the ſhip was gone to England, the colony made choice of Mr. Bradford for their governor, who enjoyed that poſt for many years, and ſaw the plantation thoroughly eſtabliſhed, though in his time there aroſe great feuds and jealouſies, on account of differences about religion.

The colony remained without a charter till in the year 1624, they ſent a perſon to England, who procured one that enabled the planters to elect a governor, council, and magiſtrates, and to make laws, provided they were not contrary to thoſe of England, or encroached on the prerogatives of the crown. Thus this colony became firmly eſtabliſhed without any aſſiſtance from the North-Virginia company.

We are now to ſpeak of that, which though later in point of time, is now become in every reſpect the moſt conſiderable; for in the year 1625, Mr. White, miniſter of Dorcheſter, obſerving the ſucceſs of the Plymouth colony, projected a new settlement in Maſſachuſett's Bay, and while ſome of his friends went over to make choice of a proper ſettlement, procured a grant from the North-Virginia, or New-England company, for himſelf and his friends, of all that part of New-England that lies between the great river Merimack and Charles River, at the bottom of Maſſachuſett's Bay, and of all the lands, &c. three miles north of Merimack River, and three miles ſouth of Charles River, and in length between theſe rivers, from the Atlantic Ocean to the South-Sea.

This new colony, which ſettled the town called Salem, was ſupported with the ſame ſpirit and vigour as the former, and ſoon after obtained a patent from King Charles I. whereby they were incorporated, by the name of the governor and company of the Maſſachuſett's Bay, in New-England, and were empowered to make laws for the good of the plantation, not repugnant to thoſe of England, and liberty of conſcience being granted to all who would ſettle there, great numbers went over, and in a little time two new ſettlements were made, the one ſtyled Charles-Town, on the north ſide of Charles River, and the other Dorcheſter, at the bottom of Maſſachuſett's Bay. Soon after part of the inhabitants of Charles-Town paſſing over to the oppoſite ſhore, erected Boſton, which is now the capital of New-England.

As new planters arrived every year, the colony ſoon became over-ſtocked, and diviſions breaking out among them, Mr. Roger Williams, paſtor of a church of Browniſts, ſettled without this government, and called this his plantation, Providence, which was afterwards united to the government of Rhode-Iſland.

At length the Pequen Indians beginning to grow very troubleſome, it was confidered that a town and fort on Connecticut River would make a good frontier on that ſide. Agents were therefore fent to view the country, who made fuch an advantageous report of the fertility of the foil, and the largenefs of the river, as induced many of the planters in feveral of the towns to entertain thoughts of removing thither, they being already ftraitened for room where they were.

Upon this Mr. Hooper, minifter of Newtown, put himfelf at the head of about 100 of thefe new adventurers, who fet out in the month of July, and travelling on foot with their children and baggage, about nine or ten miles a day, arrived at the banks of the river, where they began a town, which they called Hartford. After thefe came another draught, who built a little town which they called Windfor; a third detachment built Weathersfield; and a fourth Springfield.

The towns thus built being from fifty to fixty miles up this river, a fhip freighted with provifions for thefe planters at the Maffachufett's colony, came fo late in the year that its mouth was frozen up fixty miles from fome of thefe plantations, upon which many of the new adventurers travelled back in the depth of winter, and others who attempted it were frozen to death. However, thofe who had courage to ftay till the fpring, carried on their fettlements with fuch fuccefs, that they were not only in a capacity of fubfifting, but of making head againft their enemies. They had a fort of commiffion from the government of the Maffachufetts Bay; but finding they had extended their plantations beyond the limits of that colony, they entered into a voluntary affociation, to obey the laws that fhould be made by proper perfons for the common good, and then chofe a governor.

In this fituation the colony of Connecticut continued, till they obtained a charter from King Charles the II. authorizing them to elect their own Governor, Council and Magiftrates, to form a political affociation like that of England, and to enact such laws as should be thought most advantageous to the colony, provided they were not opposite to the laws of the mother country.

Great numbers of people still removing to New-England, and the old colonies being overstocked, there was an absolute necessity of forming new plantations, and in 1637, Theophilus Eaton, Esq; and the Reverend Mr. Davenport, finding there was not room at the Massachusetts Bay, and being informed of a larger bay to the south-west of Connecticut River, purchased of the natives all the land between that river and New-York or Hudson's River. thither they removed, and having seated themselves in the bay, over against Long-Island, built New-Haven, from whence that colony, province and government were so denominated. They also built Guilford, Stamford Milford and Brainford; then going over to Long-Island, formed several settlements there, and erected churches in all places where they settled. But being without the limits of the Massachusetts jurisdiction, they had no charter, and no other title to the lands than what they purchased from the natives. The men who settled in this country were generally London merchants, who first applied themselves to trade, in which they followed the example of their governor, Mr. Eaton; but they met with so many losses and discouragements, that they resolved to remove to Maryland or to Ireland; but at last applying themselves to husbandry; they had surprising success, and therefore laid aside all thoughts of removing.

While the south-west parts of New-England were thus filling with inhabitants, the north-east were not neglected; for as the English frequented the coast for the benefit of fishing and the fur-trade, this put some of them on attempting a settlement between the rivers Merimack and Sagadahock, which succeeded so well, that in a few years two counties were laid out, New-Hampſhire and Main, and ſeveral towns built, as, Dover, Hampton, Wells, Kittery, &c. Theſe planters and traders being alſo ſettled without the limits of the Maſſachuſetts colony, voluntarily formed themſelves into a body politic, after the example of the Connecticut colony. Thus they continued till being wearied out with feuds and diviſions, they petitioned the General Court of the Maſſachuſetts colony, to be brought within their juriſdiction; yet in 1684, they made an abſolute reſignation of their charter, and the government remained in the hands of the crown until the late revolution.

In ſhort, in the ſpace of about 20 years, New-England had above forty towns, and the people were in a happy and thriving condition.

CHAPTER XII.

The firſt ſettlement of the Bermudas or Summer-Iſlands. An account of five perſons who failed from thence in a boat to Ireland. A deſcription of thoſe iſlands, and of the plants and animals found in them.

THE Bermudas iſlands were diſcovered by John Bermudas, a Spaniard, after which they were frequently touched at by his countrymen, in their paſſage to the Weſt-Indies; but were unknown to us till the year 1593, when one Henry May was ſhipwrecked upon them in a French veſſel: but they became much more famous by Sir George Summers and Sir Thomas Gates ſuffering the like misfortune in their paſſage to Virginia in 1609, of which we have before given an account, as well as of Sir George's being ſent thither a ſecond time to fetch hogs, when he died upon the iſland, at above fixty years of age; but though Sir George directed his men to return to Virginia with black hogs for the relief of that colony, they having ftored their fhip with provifions, fet fail for England, and arrived at White-church, in Dorfetfhire, with Sir George Summers's corpfe on board, leaving only the heart and bowels at Bermudas, where twelve years after, Capt. Butler built a handfome monument over them.

Thefe men gave fuch an account of the country to the Virginia company, that 120 perfons of the fame fociety obtained a charter from King James, and became the proprietors of thefe iflands, whofe name was changed to Summer's Iflands, from the above gentleman, and are by our mariners called the Summer-Iflands, a name they well deferve from their pleafantnefs and fertility.

When Sir George Summers firft left thefe iflands, two of his men who had committed fome crime for which they would have been put to death, ftayed behind, and were there at his return. They lived in St. George's ifland, where they fupported themfelves on the productions of the place, and built a hut. Thefe two men, whofe names were Chriftopher Carter, and Edward Waters, alfo ftaid behind Sir George's fecond company, and even perfuaded Edward Chard to remain with them; and now Carter, Waters, and Chard, were the fole lords of the country; but they foon fell out among themfelves, and Chard and Waters were going to fight, when Carter, though he hated them both, yet not liking to be alone, prevented it, by threatening to declare againft the man who ftruck firft. At laft, neceffity made them good friends, and they joined together in making difcoveries, in one of which expeditions they found a large piece of ambergris among the rocks, that weighed eighty pounds, befides other fmaller pieces. This treafure made them almoft mad, they grew giddy with the thoughts of it, and that they might have an opportunity of making ufe of it, refolved on the moft defperate attempt that men could run upon; which was, to build a boat after the beft manner they could, and to fail to Virginia or Newfoundland, juft as the wind happened to blow: but before they could put their project in execution, they were prevented by the arrival of a fhip from England; for Capt. Matthew Summers, Sir George's brother, had promifed to come to them, or fend a veffel to their relief. This fhip was the Plough, with fixty perfons on board, fent by the New Bermudas company, to make a fettlement, of which Mr. Moore was governor. That gentleman pitched upon a plain in St. George's ifland, and there built a cabbin of palmetto leaves, large enough for his wife and family; and the reft of the adventurers following his example, it grew in time into a town of confiderable bignefs. This is now St. George's Town, one of the ftrongeft and beft built in the American colonies; for all the houfes are of cedar, and all the forts are of hewn ftone. Moore proved an excellent governor; and in the year 1614 difappointed the Spaniards in a defign they had formed of conquering thefe iflands.

This governor was fucceeded by Capt. Daniel Tucker, who having a better education, and more experience, eftablifhed a regular form of government, traced out plantations, and obliged every man to build uniformly in the town, and to plant regularly in the country; by which means the iflands were much improved, and the exportations to England increafed. He alfo eftablifhed a tolerable militia, and placed the iflands in fuch a pofture of defence, as put it out of the power of any of their enemies to hurt them.

The feverity of Capt. Tucker's government gave fuch difguft to fome licentious perfons, that five of them executed as defperate a defign to efcape, as

Waters and his companions had propofed. They knew the governor would not give them leave to go off, and therefore hearing that Capt. Tucker had a great defire to go a fifhing out at fea, but was afraid of doing it, becaufe feveral fifhing boats had been driven off by the weather; they propofed to built a boat of two or three tons, with a deck, and fo fitted that fhe fhould live in all weathers. The governor confented to this, they began to build in a private place, under the pretence of its being convenient for getting timber and launching the boat. Thefe perfons were, Mr. James Barker, a gentleman; Richard Saunders, who contrived the defign; William Goodwin, a fhip carpenter, who undertook to build the boat, and Henry Puet, a common failor, who promifed to navigate it.

They finifhed the boat fooner than was expected, and the governor fending for it in order to go on board a fhip that was ready to fail for England, the men, on coming to the place, could neither find the boat nor the builders, and all that they could hear of them was, that the boat being finifhed the night before, thofe who built it went off to fea, in order to try how it would fail; but at laft they found, by fome letters they had left behind them, that they were gone for England.

Thefe men had on fome pretence or other borrowed a compafs-dial from a neighbour; and then going on board the fhip bound for England, exchanged fuch things as they could fpare for provifions, and one of them at parting told the mariners, that though they were forbidden to go with them, yet they hoped to be in England before them; at which the mafter of the fhip laughed, and away thefe fearlefs adventurers failed, with a fair wind and weather, that lafted twenty one days. They then met with a ftorm which lafted forty-eight hours, and drove them a little out of their courfe to the weftward; but the wind coming fair again, and continuing ten days, they went on cheerfully. In that time they met with a French privateer, and went on board to beg some relief; but instead of assistance, the French plundered them of all the little they had, took away even their instrument of navigation, and then cruelly turned them adrift. In this miserable condition they sailed on, growing every day weaker and weaker. Their provisions were almost spent, their fire-wood quite gone, not a drop of fresh water left, nor food for above a day, when at last, in the very hour when they expected to perish, they to their unspeakable joy, made land, which proved to be Ireland, where going on shore in the county of Cork, they were nobly entertained by the earl of Thomond, to whom they related their voyage, which had lasted forty-two days.

In the year 1619, Capt. Tucker resigned to Capt. Butler, who arrived with four good ships, in which he brought 500 passengers, and there being as many English before on the island, the colony began to make a considerable figure.

These islands lie in 32°. 30'. north latitude, and in 35°. west longitude, at a vast distance from either continent, since the nearest land, which is cape Hattaras in Carolina, lies at least 250 leagues to the west of them. They lie very contiguous to each other, in the form of a shepherd's crook, but authors differ greatly as to their number, some asserting there are but 300 of them, while others affirm there are more than 500. However, scarce an eighth part of them are inhabited, and all but St. George's, St. David's, and Cooper's isles, have only a few houses scattered up and down. There are none of them of any considerable bigness, the main or greatest island, which is called St. George's is only about 16 miles in length, and not a league over in the broadest place. But it is fortified by nature all round, with rocks every way extending themſeves a great way into the ſea. To its natural ſtrength, eſpecially to the eaſtward, where it is moſt expoſed, the inhabitants have added that of forts, batteries, parapets and lines, ſo well diſpoſed, that they command the ſeveral channels, and inlets into the ſea. There are no more than two places where ſhipping can ſafely enter, and the rocks lie ſo thick, that without a good pilot from the ſhore, a veſſel of ten tons could not find the way into theſe harbours, which being once known, the biggeſt ſhips in the world may enter. But they are ſo well fortified, that if an enemy ſhould attempt either of them, he might be eaſily kept out. Indeed all theſe iſlands are ſo environed with rocks, that they ſeem to threaten all the ſhips that venture on the coaſt with preſent deſtruction; and ſo many have been wrecked upon them, that the Spaniards gave them the name of Los Diabolos, or the Devil's Iſlands.

The air of theſe iſlands has been always thought extremely ſalubrious, and the appearance of every thing very delightful and charming, whence people have been accuſtomed to remove thither from the other colonies, in order to recover their broken conſtitutions. The heat in ſummer is very ſupportable, and with reſpect to winter they have really none; ſome even go ſo far as to affirm, that there is but one ſeaſon, and that a perpetual ſpring, in which the trees never loſe their verdure; for though the leaves at one time of the year fall off, others bud out at the ſame time. But notwithſtanding the fineneſs of the climate, theſe iſlands are ſubject to ſtorms of thunder and lightning.

There grow here all the plants found in the Weſt-Indies, and all kind of trees, herbs, roots and flowers, brought from Europe thrive to perfection. Maize, or Indian corn, which is the principal ſupport of the people, is twice reaped; for what they ſow in March, they reap in July; in a fortnight after they fow again, and reap in December. Laurel, olive, mulberry and date trees, are very common, as are alfo palmettos, which are a kind of palm-tree, and are extremely ufeful, for the leaves being eight or ten feet long and near as broad, they cover their houfes with them inftead of thatch or tiles. Thefe trees produce a very lufcious fruit, in fhape, fize and colour refembling a damfon. Their forefts alfo abound with a variety of odoriferous woods, fome black, fome yellow, and fome of a red colour. The berries of thefe trees have the ftyptic quality of a floe, and are much ufed by the Englifh to cure the flux, which they frequently get by eating the lufcious palmberries too greedily.

But amongft a multitude of fhrubs and trees, peculiar to thefe iflands, and equally valuable for their timber and fruit, there are two, which though found in other parts of the world, have a peculiar excellence here; the firft is their orange tree, whofe fruit in point of fize, fcent and flavour, far exceeds thofe either in the Weft or Eaft-Indies: the fecond is their cedar, which is firmer and more durable than any of its kind we are acquainted with, and anfwers in every refpect to oak timber. It is therefore ufed in fhip-building, and the beft floops, brigantines and other fmall veffels, both for fervice and failing in ufe throughout the Weft-Indies, are built at the Bermudas. They have alfo a very fingular plant called the Summer-Ifland redwood, the berry of which is as red as the prickle-pear, and alfo gives the fame kind of tincture: out of this berry come firft worms, thefe afterwards turn into flies, fomething bigger than the cochineal fly, and have a medicinal virtue much exceeding it. They have alfo a plant called the poifon weed, that grows much in the fame manner as our ivy, but this is the only noxious thing in any of thefe iflands.

As for animals, there were none in the Bermudas, but hogs, infects and birds, when Sir George Summers was fhipwrecked there; thefe hogs he found by fending out two or three of his own to feed, which rambling home, a huge wild-boar followed them, and being killed was found excellent meat. The hogs they afterwards killed were all black, whence it is concluded that the Spaniards left them there to breed, becaufe they were of the fame kind with thofe they carried to the continent of America.

Thefe iflands abound in more fowl, and in a greater variety than are to be found in any part of America. There are fwans, moor-hens, teal, fnipe, ducks, widgeons, herons, bitterns, offpreys, baldcoots, cormorants, and hawks of all forts; bats and owls are alfo very common, and there are multitudes of fmall birds, as wood-peckers, fparrows, &c. The Englifh at their firft coming, found a fort of fowl called cowkoes, that breed in the holes of the rocks and in burrows like rabbits. They were extremely numerous, and fo gentle that they were taken by hand; but they are now almoft deftroyed. This bird is of the fize of a feamew. There is alfo the tropic bird, and the pemlico.

They have as great plenty of fifh as of fowl, and fo many forts that authors have not yet found out names for them, and in particular, they have great numbers of turtle, which are as good and as large, as any in the world.

CHAPTER XIII.

Hudſon's and Burton's voyages for the diſcovery of a north-weſt paſſage.

WHILE theſe diſcoveries were making, the merchants of England again attempted to find a new paſſage to the Indies, by the north-eaſt and north-weſt, and in particular fitted out Mr. Henry Hudſon in 1607, who undertook to ſail directly north, which he did to the height of 81°. 30. where he found the weather in July pretty warm. He propoſed to have paſſed round the great tract of country called by the Danes, Groenland; afterwards to fall into Davis's Streights, and then to return home; but being diſappointed in this, he undertook two voyages for the diſcovery of a north-eaſt paſſage, with no better ſucceſs. At laſt he reſolved to make an attempt towards the north-weſt, and ſet ſail on this voyage in April 1610. He now proceeded to the mouth of Davis's Streights, then ſteered directly weſt, and afterwards ſailed through thoſe ſtreights that now bear his name, till he doubled Cape Worſenham, after which he ſailed down the weſt coaſt of New-Britain, to the very bottom of the bay, where he made choice of a place to winter in, that was almoſt as far ſouth as any part of Great-Britain, in hopes of performing ſomething very conſiderable the next ſpring. However, the hardſhips the men endured while they wintered in this place, were exceeding great. The cold was ſo extreme, that it lamed moſt of the company; but during the firſt three months, they ſaw ſuch flights of white partridges that they killed above 100 dozen, befides other fowl.

At the approach of fpring, the partridges left them, and were fucceeded by fwans, geefe, ducks and teal; but thefe were hard to catch. They flew from the fouth to the north, and whenever a northerly wind arofe, ftaid till the wind ferved them.

At the approach of fummer, the fowls difappeared, and the men were obliged by hunger to fearch the woods, hills and vallies, for any thing that might ferve for food. The frogs, though in their engendering time, when they were as loathfome as toads, were not fpared, and they alfo fed on the mofs that grew on the ground. As foon as the ice began to break, one of the natives came to the fhip, and fold them fome furs and fkins, for knives and hatchets; and when the found began to be clear of the ice, fo that the boat could move from place to place, feveral of the men were fent to catch fifh, in which they had indifferent fuccefs, though not enough to fupply the wants of the fhip's company. At length, fome of the men refolving to get the little provifions that were left to themfelves, barbaroufly contrived to turn Captain Hudfon, the carpenter and all the fick men, out of the fhip, and to make the beft of their way for England. This they performed by forcing Captain Hudfon and eight more into the fhallop without provifions, though moft of them were taken fick out of bed, and after that time they were never heard of more. The leaders of this mutiny, did not efcape much better; for being obliged to land frequently on the defert coaft to obtain fubfiftence, moft of them were killed by the inhabitants, and the few who remained, returned to England in a miferable condition.

Upon the imperfect account of Hudfon's Bay, received from Pricket, one of thefe men, feveral perfons who had already been engaged in expeditions for the difcovery of a north-weft paffage, began to hope that they had now a fairer profpect than ever of bringing it to bear, and therefore applying to Henry, Prince of Wales, who was then the great patron of learning, his highnefs refolved to fend one Captain Button, his own fervant, and a man of great abilities, courage and experience; and accordingly he failed in the year 1611, on this expedition; paffed Hudfon's Streights, and then leaving Hudfon's Bay to the fouth, failed above 200 leagues to the north-weft, through a fea above eighty fathoms deep, and difcovered a great continent, called by him New Wales. He wintered at Port Nelfon, in 57°. 10'. north latitude, where the men fuffered greatly by the cold, and many of them died, though he kept three fires in the fhip all the winter, and had great plenty of white partridges and other fowl, befides deer, bears and foxes. The next fummer he carefully fearched all the bay, from him called Button's Bay, back almoft to Digg's Ifland, and difcovered the great ifland called Cary's Swan's Neft.

Upon his return from this voyage, he received the honour of knighthood, and great expectations were raifed from his difcoveries, which would certainly have been farther profecuted, if Prince Henry had not died foon after.

CHAPTER XIV.

An account of the fettlement and produce of Barbadoes.

WE are now brought by the order of time to the fettlement of Barbadoes, an ifland that may be efteemed the beft peopled, and beft cultivated, not only in America, but in the whole known world. It is not eafy to determine by whom this fmall ifland was difcovered; but it is moft probable that it was firft feen by the Portuguefe. However, the firft Englifhmen who landed there, are faid to have been fome of Sir William Curteen's feamen, that were cruifing in thofe feas, in the latter end of the reign of king James I. and they at their return to England, reporting that the foil was fruitful, fome adventurers went thither in order to plant it; but the ifland being covered with wood, and there being fcarce any other animals upon it than hogs, it was a long time before it anfwered their expectations.

In the firft year of the reign of Charles I. the property of this ifland was granted by that prince to James, earl of Carlifle, of whom feveral adventurers purchafing fhares, tranfported themfelves thither, and began with planting tobacco, which not fucceeding, they proceeded to try cotton and indigo, which yielded confiderable profit. But little fugar was made in the ifland till the year 1647, when colonel Modiford, colonel Walrond, colonel Drax, and feveral other cavaliers, not chufing to ftay in England after the king's death, converted their eftates into money, and tranfported themfelves to Barbadoes, with fuch machines and implements as were proper for carrying on fugar-works, and had fuch fuccefs, that in a few years colonel Drax is faid to have acquired an eftate of 7 or 8000l. per annum. The adventurers fixed their principal fettlement on the great bay, in the fouth-weft part of the ifland, and gave it the name of Carlifle-Bay, in honour of the proprietor, which it ftill retains.

Afterwards the ifland was divided into four circuits, and eleven parifhes, each parifh fending two reprefentatives to the general affembly; and fo prodigious was the encreafe of the inhabitants,

that in the year 1650, they amounted to between
30 and 40,000 white perfons, befides the negroes,
who were much more numerous, and frequently
plotted the deftruction of their mafters; but their
plots were conftantly difcovered, and the moft
terrible punifhments inflicted on the ringleaders;
however, the cruelties fuffered by thofe who thus
endeavoured to recover their liberty, did but increafe the difaffection of the reft, and laid the
foundation of frefh confpiracies: notwithftanding
which, no colony of fo fmall an extent, ever arrived within the fpace of twenty or thirty years,
to fuch riches and grandeur. The parliament
thought this ifland of fuch confequence, that in
1651, they fent thither a ftrong fquadron of men
of war, under the command of Sir George Afcue,
who compelled Lord Willoughby, the governor to
furrender the ifland, upon condition that the
royalifts fhould remain in the poffeffion of their
eftates and liberties, and Mr. Searl was appointed
governor,

In the Dutch war the colony was prohibited from
trading with the Hollanders, who till this time
had conftantly furnifhed the ifland with negroes,
and taught the barbarians to plant and manage
their fugars to the beft advantage, moft of which
they took off their hands, in order to fupply themfelves and the reft of Europe; and the barbarians
were compelled by the parliament to bring all
their fugars directly to England: this ftep was alfo
taken by the miniftry after the reftauration of king
Charles II. and this was the foundation of the act
of navigation, which requires all the Britifh colonies to bring their fugars and tobacco to England,
and prohibited their trading with foreigners in
thefe and fome other articles.

The vaft fuccefs of this firft fugar-colony promot-
ed the fettlement of the others; and as the fugar
plantations increafed, more hands were required to

carry on the work than could at that time be spared from home. This gave birth to the Guinea trade, for supplying those colonies with negroe slaves; and as the planters flourished and increased, so did their demands for all sorts of British manufactures, and such of the necessaries of life as could not be produced in that climate, which also opened new sources of trade for the British merchants. In short, the act of navigation, by obliging all the sugar to be brought to Great-Britain, soon made London the chief mart in Europe for sugar, and there being annually more imported than was necessary for home consumption, the merchants exported the surplus to foreign markets, and by underselling the Portuguese, they in time beat them out of almost all their sugar trade to the northward of Cape Finisterre.

In the year 1668, king Charles II. purchased the property of this island of the lord Kinowl, heir to the earl of Carlisle, and appointed the lord Willoughby of Parham, governor; upon which the colony granted a duty of four and a half per cent. for the support of the civil government, and for maintaining the forces and fortifications of the island, which duty is said to amount to 10,000l. a year.

The island of Barbadoes is situated in the Atlantic Ocean, in 13° north latitude, and 59° west longitude. It is of a triangular from, and where broadest, about 25 miles from north to south, and only 15 from east to west. It is, for the most part, a plain, level country, with some small hills of an easy ascent, and though it was covered with woods when the English first settled there, they have been all cut down to make way for plantations of sugar-canes, which at present take up almost the whole island, for their very corn, flesh, and fish, are for the most part imported.

There is scarce an harbour in the island; the best is that of Bridge-Town, in Carlisle-Bay, which lies open to the westward, but is secure from the north-east. This is here the constant trade-wind, and blows all night and all day, except when they have their tornadoes and hurricans, which usually happen in the three summer months, and blow from every quarter. At such times the ships in the bay are in the utmost danger of being wrecked on shore, if they cannot get out to sea, and therefore they seldom attempt to ride out those storms.

The coast is defended on the east from the invasion of an enemy, by rocks and shoals; and on the west, where it is most exposed to a descent, breast-works and redoubts are erected for its security. There is scarce a stream in the island that deserves the name of a river, though there are two on the east side, to which they have given the names of Scotland River and Joseph's River. However, they have good water in their wells almost all over the island, and do not dig very deep for it: they have also large ponds and reservoirs, where they preserve rainwater. The weather is generally fine and serene, and their rains, as in other parts of the torrid zone, fall chiefly when the sun is vertical, and after these are the proper seasons for planting.

Their heats are not so excessive as in the same latitude on the east side the continent of America; the air being constantly refreshed by the trade-wind in the day-time, which increases as the sun advances, and abates as the sun declines; but there being no mountains on the island, the trade-wind is not interrupted.

The only town of any consequence in the island is that of Bridge-Town, or St. Michael's, in Carlisle Bay, which was formerly encompassed with a morass that rendered it unhealthy; but this has been in a great measure drained. However, the low situation of the town renders it still subject to inundations. It is said to contain 1000 or 1200 houses built with brick and stone; and there are commodious wharfs and keys for loading and unloading of goods. The chief produce of this island, as has been already intimated, is sugar; of the melasses or dregs of which, they make great quantities of rum; they have also some cotton, indigo, and pimento. They have scarce any forest-trees left; but their fruits are oranges, limes, citrons, pomegranates, pine-apples, guavas, plantains, cocoa-nuts, Indian figs, prickle-pears, melons, and almost all manner of roots and garden-stuff, but very few flowers.

Their horses they import from New England, &c. and they have a slight breed of their own. They have also some asses, cows, and sheep; but the last do not thrive here: however, they have a great number of hogs. They have good poultry, and sea-fish, but no fresh water fish, and all manner of provisions are so dear, that there is no dining at an ordinary under a crown a head. Fresh meat is indeed a rarity, and chiefly the food of people of condition: the rest are glad of salt pork, beef and fish, imported from the United States; from whence also come their wheat, flour, Indian corn, beans, peas, &c. They make bread also of the cassavi root, and the negroes feed on yams, potatoes, and other roots and fruits. The gentry chiefly drink Maderia wine, and wine and water, and great quantities of rum punch are drank by the vulgar. They have also strong beer imported from Old and New England, and liquors made of maize and fruit.

CHAPTER V.

A concise account of the settlement of St. Christopher's, Nevis, Montserrat, Barbuda, Anguilla, and Antigua, and of the produce of those islands.

WE shall next speak of the island of St. Christopher's, which was called by the Indians, Liamuega, and was discovered by Cristopher Columbus, in his first voyage to America. He gave it the name of St. Christopher's from the figure of its mountains, there being in the upper part of the island a very high mountain, bearing on its summit another of a smaller size, as St. Christopher is painted like a giant carrying our Saviour on his back. It is situated in 17° north latitude, and is about seventy-three miles in circumferrence. Sir T. Warner, an English adventurer, and Monsieur Desnambue, a French gentleman, who commanded for the French in America, arrived at St. Christopher's on the same day, and both took possession of the island in the names of their respective masters. It was then inhabited by the Caribbees, and the Spaniards used to put in there, in their West-India voyages, to take fresh water. These last were on such good terms with the Caribbees that they sometimes left their sick there, of whom the natives took great care.

The above gentlemen left some of their men in the island, and returned to their respective countries for recruits, when their masters approved of their conduct, sent them back in 1626, with supplies of men and provisions, and with commisions to be governors of the new settlements. Monsieur Desnambue arrived there about the month of January, 1627, with about 300 people, after a long and sickly voyage. The English colony had as many men, and Sir Thomas had proceeded a good way in his settlement before Monsieur Desnambue's arrival. The two governors therefore, to prevent any differences among the people about the limits of their respective territories, on the 13th of May, 1627, set boundaries to their several divisions, with this particular proviso, that fishing and hunting should be equally free to the inhabitants of both nations; that the salt-ponds, and most valuable timber should be in common, together with the mines and havens; and a league offensive and defensive was concluded between them against all enemies; after which they proceeded with great harmony.

However, the English receiving supplies of men and provisions from London, throve better than the French; and not only became strong enough to keep what they had, but to spare men for settling plantations at Nevis, of which Sir Thomas Warner took possession, and left a settlement there in the year 1628.

Mean while the Spaniards being alarmed at the progress of the English and French in the Caribbee Islands, thought the safety of their own plantations required their preventing those nations from settling in their neighbourhood, and therefore in the following year, sent Don Frederic de Toledo with a fleet of twenty-four ships and fifteen frigates to dispossess the English and French of the island of St. Christopher's. Don Frederic seized some English ships near the isle of Nevis, and then anchored in the road of Marigot, under the cannon of a fort called the Basse Terre, where Monsieur Rossey commanded. Neither the French nor the English forts were in a condition to oppose such an enemy. Rossey, therefore, after a small opposition, abandoned the Basse Terre, and retreated to Cabes Terre, another fort, commanded by Monfieur Defnambue in perfon: but they could not prevail on their men either to defend themfelves there, or to retire to the forefts and mountains, where a few men might have refifted a thoufand, and nothing could content them but embarking, and leaving the place, which Monfieur Defnambue was obliged to comply with. Mean while the Englifh being in great confternation, on their hearing the news of Defnambue's being gone with his colony, fome endeavoured to efcape by fea; others fled to the mountains, and all who were left, fent deputies to treat with the Spaniards.

Don Frederic having them now in his power, commanded all on the ifland to depart immediately, on the pain of being put to the fword, and to forward their going fent them the Englifh fhips he had taken at Nevis; but as there was not room in thefe fhips to carry off all the people with their families, he confented that thofe who could not embark, fhould ftay till they could be removed.

Don Frederick having made thefe regulations, weighed anchor, taking with him 600 of the Englifh, who were fitteft for his fervice. But he was no fooner gone, than the Englifh who were left refolved to go on with the fettlement; when the French who were got no farther than Antigua and Montferrat, fent a fhip for intelligence to St. Chriftopher's, and being informed that the Spaniards were gone, and the Englifh bufy in rebuilding and planting, they rejoiced at this happy and unexpected turn, and failing back to St. Chriftopher's, refumed the poffeffion of their former habitations.

The Englifh now continued carrying on their colony till they were able to fpare more men for fettlements at Burbuda, Montferrat and Antigua, which were peopled and planted by Sir Thomas Warner. At the fame time the Dutch made themfelves mafters of St. Euftatia, and the French took poffeffion of fome other iflands. Monfieur Defnambue died about the the year 1637, and Sir Thomas Warner did not long furvive him; but before this laft gentleman's death, the colony was fo increafed, that the Englifh in the ifland amounted to between 12 and 13,000.

The chief employment of the firft planters, was cultivating tobacco, by which they gained a competent livelihood; but afterwards, the quantity lowering the price, they in feveral places applied themfelves to the planting of fugar, ginger, indigo, and cotton, and in a little time became a rich and flourifhing people; both the French and Englifh living cordially together.

Though St. Chriftopher's is the largeft of all the Caribbee iflands, the middle part of it being extremely mountainous, it is thought there are not above 24,000 acres of land fit for fugar in the whole ifland, and yet it annually produces about 10,000 hogfheads of that valuable commodity.

It has been already obferved that Sir Thomas Warner fettled Nevis or Mevis about the year 1628, and notwithftanding the Englifh had been difpoffeffed by the Spaniards, as has been already related, the inhabitants of that ifland in twenty years amounted to at leaft 4000 people, and they continued increafing in the fame manner, for a confiderable time, having no enemy to ftruggle with, but the hurricanes, which generally vifited them once a year.

When Sir William Stapleton was governor of thefe iflands, he ufually made this the place of his refidence, and moft of the affairs of government were tranfacted here; for each of the Lee-ward iflands has a particular lieutenant-governor, council, and affembly, while the general government centers in the captain-general.

In the reign of King James the II. Nevis supplied the others with almost all their wines and negroes, and was computed to contain above 10,000 persons besides the negroes, who amounted to above 20,000. What prodigious improvement must then have been made of this little island, which is not more than twenty miles in circumference, to render it capable of maintaining above 30,000 men, women and children! Its annual produce is about 6000 hogsheads of sugar.

The island of Montserrat so called by the Spaniards, from its resembling a mountain in Catalonia of the same name, famous for a chapel dedicated to the Blessed Virgin, is situated in 17°. north latitude, and is about three leagues in length, and almost as much in breadth, so that it seems to be round. It was discovered by Columbus, at the same time with St. Christopher's, but no settlement was made upon it, till Sir Thomas Warner procured a small colony to settle there, in 1632.

This island at first flourished more than Antigua; but since the lord Willoughby's time, the latter has got and kept the start of it. Sixteen years after its being first inhabited, there were 700 men in the island, and the rolls of the militia amounted to 360.

The climate, soil, animals, trade and productions of Montserrat, are the same with those of the other Caribbee islands. This, however, is fuller of mountains, which are covered with cedars and other trees, that afford a most delightful prospect from the sea. The vallies are fruitful, and better supplied with fresh water than those of Antigua; and it is computed, that at present there are in this island about 4500 white people, and about 12,000 negroes. As Montserrat is less than any other of the Caribbee islands, it annually produces only 2500 and sometimes 3000 hogsheads of sugar.

The ifland of Barbuda, which was planted by Sir Thomas Warner as early as Montferrat, is fituated in 17°. 30'. north latitude, and is about fif.een miles long. The firft colony was fo often difturbed by the Caribbees, that the people were frequently forced to defert their plantations; for they hardly paffed a year in which they did not make one or two incurfions, and that generally in the night, for they durft not attack them by day; fo that the Englifh grew weary of dwelling in a place where they were fo much expofed to the fury of the natives; and therefore deferted the ifland: but the Caribbees diminifhing daily in number, and the Europeans in the other iflands increafing, the Englifh again poffeffed themfelves of Barbuda; in a few years the inhabitants amounted to 500, and they are now increafed to about 1200 perfons. The proprietor choofes the governor, and has the fame privileges as the other lords-proprietors in their feveral jurifdictions in America. The inhabitants apply themfelves chiefly to the breeding of cattle, for which there is always a good market in the fugar-iflands.

The next plantation is that of Anguilla or Snake-Ifland, fo called from its figure; it being long, narrow and winding almoft about. It is near St. Martin's, from whence it may be feen, and lies in 18°. 12'. north latitude. The country is extremely level, and there is not a mountain in it; however, it is very woody. In the broadeft part of it there is a pond, about which the Englifh fettled in the year 1650, and applied themfelves to the planting of corn and the breeding of tame cattle. They were afterwards joined by fome people from Barbadoes and other of the Englifh Caribbee-iflands, who incorporating with the reft, learned their manners, and though they are faid to amount to about 150 families or 900 fouls, yet they have neither minifter or magiftrate among them. They apply themselves to farming, in which they have had very good success, and live like the old patriarchs, every man being a kind of sovereign in his own family.

Antigua or Antego, is the last of these islands settled by the English. Sir Thomas Warner attempted to form a settlement there, but without success. However, Francis Lord Willoughby, who was governor of Barbadoes, obtained a grant of the island of Antigua, in 1663, from King Charles II. and planted a colony in it about three years after. It is situated in 16°. 11'. north latitude, and in 63°. west longitude from London. It is of a circular form, about twenty miles diameter, and near sixty in circumference. The climate is far from being agreeable, since it is hotter than in Barbadoes, and very subject to hurricanes. The soil too is sandy, and great part of the land is overgrown with wood. The greatest disadvantage is, there being but few springs, and not so much as a single brook in the whole island; so that the people depend chiefly upon rain water, for which they are sometimes distressed; yet notwithstanding these inconveniences, it is a very considerable and a very thriving plantation.

Antigua is divided into five parishes, four of which are towns, as St. John's-Town to the northward, which is the capital of the island, and consists of about 200 houses; and Falmouth, Parham and Bridge-Town, to the southward. The other parish is St. Peter's.

Besides St. John's harbour, which is the most commodious, there are other very good ones, as Five-Island Harbour, so called from five little islands to the westward of the isle of Carlisle-bay; English Harbour, at the bottom of which is Falmouth Town, defended by Charles fort; next to it is Willoughby Bay; on the east shore Green Bay; of which is Green-Island; next to this is Nonsuch

Harbour, which is a spacious bay. There are also several little islands, particularly to the northward. The forts are in pretty good repair; Monk's Hill fort is mounted with thirty pieces of ordnance; the other fort erected at St. John's Harbour, is mounted with fourteen; and there are seven other batteries for the defence of so many landing-places.

CHAPTER XVI.
Maryland planted by Leonard Calvert, Esq.

MARYLAND was esteemed a part of Virginia, till the year 1632, when king Charles I. made a grant of all the country not then planted, on the north of Potowmac River, to Cecilius Calvert, Lord Baltimore, and his heirs, and this part of the country was afterwards called Maryland, in honour of Henrietta-Maria, the Queen Consort. The Lord Baltimore sent his brother, Leonard Calvert, Esq; with some Roman Catholic gentlemen, and other adventurers, to the number of 200, to take possession of the country, who sailing from England on the 23d of November, 1633, arrived at Point Comfort, in Chesapeak bay, on the 24th of February following, where being supplied with provisions by the English of Virginia, they continued their voyage northward to the river Potowmac, which was appointed the boundary between Virginia and Maryland.

The adventurers sailed up this river, and landing at several places on the northern shore, informed the inhabitants, that they were come to trade and settle among them; but though the natives did not seem to desire their company, no acts of hostility were committed on either side, and the English returning down the river Potowmac again, chose a place near the mouth of a river which falls into it, and which they called St. George's River, and there settled their first colony. They afterwards advanced to an Indian town called Yeamaco, the capital of the country, and at a conference with the Weorance, or sovereign of the place, to whom they made considerable presents, the Weorance consented, that the English should dwell in one part of the town, and his own people in the other till after harvest, and that being over, they should resign the whole to the English, and retire farther into the country, which they accordingly did. It was also agreed on both sides, that if any wrong was done by either party, the nation offending should make full satisfaction. The reason why the Yeamaco Indians were so ready to enter into a treaty with the English, and to yield them a part of their country, was the hopes of obtaining their protection and assistance against their northern neighbours, the Susquahannah Indians, with whom they were then at war.

The English having thus obtained the possession of the town, gave it the name of St. Mary's, and immediately applied themselves with great diligence in cultivating the ground, and raising Indian corn, while the natives went every day into the woods to hunt for game, bringing venison and turkeys to the English colony in great plenty, for which they received knives, tools and toys. Thus both nations lived in the greatest friendship, doing mutaul good offices to each other, till some of the English in Virginia, envying the happiness of this thriving colony, wickedly suggested to the Indians, that these strangers were not really English, as they pretended, but Spaniards, and would enslave them, as they had done many of their countrymen.

The Indians being so credulous as to believe this report, grew jealous of Mr. Calvert, and made preparations for attacking the colony, which the English perceiving, stood upon their guard, and erected a fort for their security, on which they planted several pieces of ordnance, at the firing whereof, the natives were so terrified, that they abandoned their country, and left the English in full possession of it, who continually receiving supplies, and reinforcements from England, soon became a flourishing people, many Catholic families of quality and fortune transporting themselves thither, to avoid the penal laws made against them in England; and no country in America can boast of having had fewer disturbances on account of religion.

CHAPTER XVII.

An account of the conquest of Jamaica. A descripition of that island and its productions, particularly the Cacao, or Chocolate-Nut, Pimento, or Jamaica Pepper, the wild Cinnamon-Tree, and the manner in which Indigo is cultivated and prepared.

OLIVER CROMWELL being sensible of the advantages the Spaniards obtained from their provinces in America, formed a project for taking from them the fine island of Hispaniola, and, for that purpose sent a considerable squadron of men of war commanded by general Penn, with a fleet of transports under general Venables, with which they sailed from Portsmouth, and arrived at Barbadoes on the 15th of January, 1654. They afterwards sailed to Hispaniola, where being repulsed with loss, it was resolved to try what could be done against the island of Jamaica.

Venables attacks and takes Jamaica.

The fleet and troops being arrived at this laſt iſland, general Venables iſſued orders, that if any man attempted to run away, the next man to him ſhould put him to death, and that if he failed to do it, he ſhould be liable to be tried for his life. The troops were no ſooner landed than they advanced towards the fort, which they made themſelves maſters of with little loſs, and the next morning when the ſun aroſe, began to march towards the Savannah near the town, when ſome Spaniards coming forwards deſired to treat; but this that general refuſed, unleſs they would ſend his men a conſtant ſupply of proviſions, of which they were in great want, and to this the Spaniards conſented, and actually performed their promiſe. After which the following articles were at laſt agreed upon. That all the forts, arms, ammunition, and neceſſaries of war: that all the ſhipping in the harbours of the iſland; and all wares, merchandize, &c. ſhould be delivered up to general Venables, for the uſe of the Protector and the Commonwealth of England. That all the inhabitants of the iſland, except ſome that were particularly named, ſhould have their lives granted. That thoſe who choſe it, ſhould have leave to ſtay, and the others to be tranſported to New-Spain, or ſome other of his Catholic Majeſty's dominions in America, together with their apparel, books and papers. That the commiſion-officers alone at their departure ſhould be permitted to wear their rapiers and poynards, and that the artificers and meaner ſort of the people, ſhould be permitted to remain in the iſland, and to enjoy their goods, provided they conformed to the laws that ſhould be eſtabliſhed.

Thus the fine iſland of Jamacia was ſubdued, and though the Spaniards continued to lurk about ſome parts of it for ſeveral years afterwards, and once made a bold attempt to recover the place, yet colonel Doyly forced them to withdraw, and so effectually reduced the whole island, that at the restoration the Spaniards yielded it to the crown of Great Britain to which it has belonged ever since; and is the noblest possession they have in those parts.

Jamaica is situated in between 17 and 18° north latitude, and between 76 and 79° west longitude. It is 140 miles in length, and in the middle about 60 in breadth, growing less towards each end. It is about twenty leagues east of Hispaniola, and as many south of Cuba, and is upwards of 150 leagues to the north-ward of Porto Bello and Carthagena. The whole island is one continued ridge of hills, which run from east to west through the middle of it, and are generally called the Blue Mountains; and on each side there are other hills much lower. The mountainous part is very steep and furrowed on the north and south sides of the highest hills, by very deep channels, made by violent rains, which almost every day fall on the mountains. and first wearing a small channel for their passage and afterwards carrying all before them, make their channels extremely deep. All the high lands are covered with woods, in which there is very good timber, though the soil is there extremely barren, and they are obliged to shoot their fibrous roots into the crannies of the rocks. Most of the savannahs, or plains fit for pasture and cleared of wood, are like our meadow land, and lie near the south side of the island, where a person may ride many miles without meeting with the least ascent; some of these plains are within land encircled with hills. These savannahs are very green and pleasant after rain, but after a long drought look yellow and parched.

The chief ports in the island are Port Royal, which is a fine capacious harbour; Old Harbour, which lies seven or eight miles west of St. Jago;

Port Morant at the east end, and Point Negril, at the west end of the island; besides which there are several others on the south and north sides. But it is dangerous approaching the coast without a pilot, on account of the coral rocks with which it is almost surrounded.

There are near 100 rivers in Jamacia, but none of them navigable; for rising in the mountains in the middle of the island, they precipitate themselves down the rocks to the north and south, falling into the sea before they have ran many miles, and frequently carry down with them, large trees and great pieces of rock, and it is very common to have cataracts among the mountains fifty or sixty feet high: Yet in dry years water is very scarce in the savannahs distant from rivers, so that many cattle die with driving to water. and it is remarkable that some rivers in the mountains rise above and sink under ground in many places, and in particular the Rio d'Oro falls and rises two or three times. Some of the springs and rivers petrify their channels and stop their course by a cement, which unites the gravel and sand in their bottoms. There are several hot springs, and also many salt springs which form salt lagunas, or great ponds, particularly Riottoa-Pond, which receives a great deal of water by a river, and yet has no visible rivulet or discharge running from it; and in these and other ponds formed by the sea water, great plenty of salt is made by the heat of the sun exhaling the moisture.

This island being 7°. within the tropic, has the trade wind continually there, which is on the south side of the island, and is called the sea breeze. It comes about eight o'clock in the morning, and increases till twelve in the day, and then as the sun grows lower it decreases till there is none at four in the afternoon. The land breeze begins about eight in the evening, blowing four leagues into the fea: it continues increafing till twelve at night, and decreafes again till four. Thus as the land wind blows at night and the fea breeze in the day time, no fhips can come into port except in the day, nor go out but at break of day or very foon after.

This ifland is fo very fubject to earthquakes, that the inhabitants expect one every year; fome of thefe have been extremely dreadful, particularly in the year 1692, when the town of Port Royal was almoft fwallowed up. Thunder is heard almoft every day in the mountains, with the rains there; froft and fnow, however, are never feen in this hot climate, but hail is fometimes very large.

The dews are here fo great within land, that in a morning the water drops from the leaves of the trees, as if it had rained; and a man riding in the night, will find his cloaths and hair very wet in a fhort time; but there are feldom any fogs in the plains or fandy places near the fea. The rains are violent, and the drops very large. Generally fpeaking, the great rainy feafons are in May and October, when they begin at the new or full moon, and continue day and night for a fortnight, fo that Sir Hans Sloane obferves, that all the level places are laid fome inches under water. The month of January is alfo expected a rainy feafon; but this is neither fo conftant nor fo violent as the two others.

As to the produce of the ifland, it has all the tropical fruits, as plantains, cocoas, pine apples, cacao or the chocolate nut, pimento, cotton trees, woods for dying, mahogany, and manchineel wood: ginger, and feveral medicinal drugs and gums. As this ifland produces more of the cacao or chocolate nuts than any Englifh plantation, we fhall here give a particular account of them.

The cacao nuts grow on a tree, in green, red and yellow pods, every pod having in it three, four or five kernels, about the bigness and shape of chesnuts, which are separated from each other by a substance like the pulp of a roasted apple, that is moderately sharp and sweet, from which these kernels or nuts are taken when ripe and cured by drying. The body of a cacao-tree is commonly four inches in diameter, five feet in height, and about twelve to the top of the tree. These trees are vey different, for some shoot up in two or three bodies, and others only in one; their leaves, unless in very young trees, are many of them dead, and most of them discoloured; a bearing tree generally yields from two to eight pounds of nuts a year, growing out of the body or great limbs and boughs; and at the same place there are both blossoms, young and ripe fruit. These trees are always planted under the shade. Some set them under plantain trees, and some in the woods. The nuts are cured by their being cut down when ripe, and laid to sweat three or four days in the pods, which is done by throwing them on heaps; after this the pods are cut; the nuts taken out and put into a trough covered with plantain leaves, where they sweat again about sixteen or twenty days; they are then put to dry three or four weeks in the sun, and then become of a dark reddish colour.

Pimento is another of the natural productions of Jamaica, from whence it is called Jamaica pepper, that being the chief place where it is found. The pimento tree is generally very tall and spreading, with a trunk as thick as a man's thigh: it rises strait above 30 feet high, and is covered with an extraordinary smooth bark of a grey colour: it then spreads into branches, which have leaves resembling those of a bay-tree, and when bruised are very odoriferous. The ends of the twig are branched into bunches of flowers, which falling off, are succeeded by bunches of berries crowned with four small leaves: these berries are at first small and greenifh, but when ripe they are bigger than juniper berries; they are then black, fmooth and fhining, and contain a fmall green aromatic pulp, with two large feeds feparated by a membrane.

This tree grows on all the hilly parts of the ifland of Jamaica, but chiefly on the north fide; it is generally left ftanding when other trees are felled, and is fometimes planted where it never grew before, on account of the great profit arifing from the fruit, which is annually exported in great quantities into Europe. The Pimento tree flowers in June, July and Auguft, fooner or later according to the fituation, and different feafon for rains, and after it flowers, the fruit foon ripens, but in clear open grounds, it is fooner ripe than in thick woods.

There is no great difficulty in curing or preferving this fruit: this is for the moft part done by the negroes, who climb the trees, and pull off the twigs with the unripe green fruit, after which they carefully feparate the fruit from the twigs and leaves, and expofe it to the fun for many days, from its rifing to its fetting; fpreading the berries thin on cloths, turning them frequently, and carefully avoiding the dews. By this means they become a little wrinkled, and from a green, change to a brown colour, when they are fit for the market; being of different fizes, but commonly of the bignefs of black pepper, and refembling in fmell and tafte a mixture of fpices, from whence it is called Allfpice. The more fragrant and fmaller they are, they are accounted the better. That great phyfician Sir Hans Sloane obferves, that this is defervedly reckoned the beft, moft temperate, mild and innocent of all fpices.

The wild cinnamon, or more properly canella alba tree, alfo grows in this ifland. Its trunk is about the bignefs of that of the Pimento-tree, and rifes 20 or 30 feet high, having many branches and twigs hanging downwards, and forming a very beautiful top. The bark confifts of two parts; the outward bark is as thin as a fhilling, of a whitifh afh or grey colour, with fome white fpots here and there upon it, and feveral fhallow furrows of a darker colour, running varioufly through it. The inward bark is as thick as a crown piece, fmooth, and of a whiter colour than the outward; it has a much more biting and aromatic tafte, fomewhat like that of cloves. The leaves fhoot out near the ends of the twigs without any order, ftanding on foot ftalks, each of them two inches in length, and one in breadth. They are of a yellowifh green colour, and are fmooth and fhining without any incifure about their edges. The ends of the twigs are branched into bunches of fcarlet or purple flowers, which falling off, are fucceeded by clufters of roughifh green berries, of the fize of a large pea, that contain a pale, green, thin pulp, and four black fhining feeds of an irregular figure.

All the parts of this tree, when frefh, are very hot and aromatic; but in the inward bark of the tree is what is chiefly in ufe both in the Englifh plantations in the Weft-Indies, and in Europe, and it is eafily cured by only cutting off the bark and letting it dry in the fhade, The ordinary fort of people, in the Weft-Indies, ufe it inftead of all other fpices, it being thought very good to confume the immoderate humidity of the ftomach, to help digeftion, and expel wind. Rum lofes its difagreeable fmell if mixed with this bark. The tree grows in the favannah woods, and is found on each fide the road between Paffage-Fort, and the town of St. Jago de la Vega.

As great quantities of indigo have been produced in Jamaica, we fhall here give a particular account of the manner in which it is cultivated and prepared. It thrives beft in fandy ground. The feed from whence it is raifed, is yellow, round, and fomewhat lefs than a tare. The foil is made light by hoeing; then trenches are dug like thofe our gardeners prepare for peafe, into which the feed is put about March: it grows ripe in eight weeks time, and frefh broken ground will fpring up about three feet high, but in others to no more than eighteen inches. The ftalk is full of leaves of a deep green colour, and will, from the firft fowing, yield many crops in one year. When it is ripe it is cut, and fteeped in fats twenty four hours, after which it is cleared from the firft water, and put into proper cifterns, where, when it has been carefully beaten, it fettles in about eighteen hours. In thefe cifterns are feveral taps, which let the clear water run out, and the thick is put into bags of about three feet long, made commonly of ofnaburgs, which being hung up, all the liquid part drops away; and when it will drop no longer, what remains is put into wooden boxes about three feet long, fourteen inches wide, and one and a half deep; thefe boxes are placed in the fun till the indigo is very hot, and then taken in till the extreme heat is over; and this is repeated till it is fufficiently dried.

In land that proves proper for indigo, the labour of one hand, will in a year's time produce between eighty and a hundred weight, if no accidents happen; for indigo, as well as other commodities in thofe parts is fubject to many; the moft common are blafting and worms, by which it is frequently deftroyed.

CHAPTER XVIII.

The manner in which Carolina was settled by the English, after the attempts made by the Spanish and French. The climate and soil of Carolina. An account of the settlement of New-York.

CAROLINA is a part of that extensive country in north-America, which was formerly comprehended under the name of Florida. It was first discovered by Sebastian Cabot, and afterwards received the name of Florida from Juan Ponce de Leon.

The Spaniards endeavoured several times to make settlements in this country; but after many unfortunate and expensive expeditions, being entirely discouraged, abandoned it for several years. At length the French, perceiving that this large tract of land was neglected by the Spaniards, admiral Coligny sent John Ribaut, who formed a settlement here in the reign of Charles IX, and having built a fort, called it Charles-Fort, giving the name of Port-Royal to the harbour.

However, the civil war raging in France, Ribaut's soldiers mutinied for want of supplies; for though the natives were very kind to them out of hatred to the Spaniards, they could not furnish them with many of the necessaries they wanted; Ribaut, therefore, having made some discoveries in the east part of Florida, returned to France; but in his passage the men were reduced to such extremity, that they killed and eat one of the crew, and would probably have done so by others, had they not providentially met with an English ship, which supplied them with some provisions. Two years after, a peace being concluded in France between the papists and protestants, admiral Coligny procured more ships to be sent; and some time after Ribaut followed with other vessels and a supply of men and provisions.

The French now began to conceive great hopes of this plantation, when a ſquadron of Spaniſh ſhips drove the French out of the fort, baſely killed Ribaut and 600 men, after having given them quarter, and obliged the few whom they ſuffered to remain alive, to return to France.

The French king was the leſs moved with this outrage committed on his ſubjects, on account of their being proteſtants: however Peter Melanda, who had diſlodged the French, ſo provoked the Indians by his cruelty and injuſtice, that they only waited for an opportunity to be revenged, which happened ſoon after: for Capt. de Gorgues, a French gentleman, at his own expence, fitted out three ſtout ſhips, and ſailing to Carolina with 280 men, was aſſiſted by the Indians, and having taken Fort Charles put all the Spaniards he found therein to the ſword. They had built two other forts which he eaſily reduced, ſerved the garriſon in the ſame manner, and then demoliſhed the fortifications. It does not appear that monſ. de Gorgues made any ſettlement here, or that the Spaniards endeavoured to recover the country, which from the year 1567 lay deſerted by all European nations, till the reign of Charles II. king of England.

In 1622, ſeveral Engliſh families flying from the maſſacres committed by the Indians in Virginia and New-England, were driven upon thoſe coaſts, and ſettled in the province of Malica, near the head of the river May, whare they became a kind of miſſionaries among the Malicans and Apalachites, and in the year 1653, Mr. Brigſtock, an Engliſhman went to Apalachia, where he was honourably entertained by his countrymen, who were there before. And this perſon wrote an account of this ſettlement.

Such was the ſituation of things, when after this country had been abandoned by the French for near 100 years, king Charles II. made a grant of this province in 1663, to Edward earl of Clarendon, lord high chancellor of England, George duke of Albemarle; William, lord Craven, Anthony lord Afhly, Sir George Carteret, Sir William Berkley, and Sir John Colliton; from the north-end of Luck Ifland, within 36°. of north lattitude, to the river San Matthio, which borders on the coaft of Florida, and is within 31°. of north latitude, and to the weftward as far as the fouth feas.

Thefe proprietors afterwards obtained another grant which fomewhat varied the bounds of the province, by fixing its northern frontier at Carotoch-river, in 36°. 30'. north latitude, and its fouthern frontier in 29°. within which bounds both the Carolinas, and the new province of Georgia are included.

The plan of government for this new colony was ftruck out by that great ftatefman, Anthony earl of Shaftfbury, and digefted into form by the juftly celebrated Mr. John Locke; but after it had been in the poffeffion of the proprietors or their heirs, for about fixty years, feven of them fold their fhares to the crown for 17,500l. each proprietor who had a whole fhare, having 2500l. and the quit-rents, and other incomes due to thefe proprietors, ammounting to about 9000 l. they alfo fold them to the crown for 5000 l. This furrender was confirmed by act of parliament, in the year 1728, when the remaining one eighth of the property in the poffeffion of the lord Carteret, was confirmed to him and his heirs.

This province is feated between the extremes of heat and cold; but yet the heat is more troublefome in fummer than the cold in winter, this laft feafon being very fhort, and frofty mornings frequently fucceeded by warm days. The air is for the moft part ferene and clear, both in fummer and winter; yet the inhabitants have their winter rains, and sometimes very heavy showers about midsummer, especially if the wind changes suddenly from the south-east to the north-west, when it blows exceeding cold, and brings distempers on those, who do not take care to guard against it. To those who live regularly and use any precaution, the country is generally healthful: But persons who after a hot day expose themselves to the cold breezes of the evening usually feel their effects; as do those who indulge themselves in eating great quantities of fruit, and drinking pernicious liquors to excess. The country is subject to hurricanes, as well as the Caribbee-islands, but they do not happen ever year.

The next colony in America settled by the English; was that of New-York. The coast was first viewed by Sebastian Cabot, and in the reign of queen Elizabeth, that country was considered as a part of the province of Virgina. Afterwards in the year 1608 the famous navigator Hudson, discovered the river that has since borne the name of Hudson's River, and the adjacent country, which he afterwards, without any legal authority, sold to the Dutch, who planted there. At length some English dissenters, who for the sake of religious liberty, fled to Holland, hearing the Dutch give an inviting description of the river, climate, and soil of this country, embarked in order to sail thither; but the master of the ship being bribed by the Dutch, obliged them to land farther to the northward, where they became the first planters of New England.

Two or three years before this, sir Samuel Argall had destroyed the Dutch plantations, when to prevent the like for the future, they applied to king James for his licence to stay there, to build cottages, and to plant for traffic, as well as subsistence, pretending it was only for the conveniency of their ships, touching there for fresh water and provisions, in their voyage to Brasil; but by little and little they extended their limits, built towns, fortified them, became a flourishing colony, and called the country Nova Belgia.

The Dutch colonies were in this thriving condition at the opening of the first Dutch war in king Charles the second's reign, when they were attacked by the English in 1644, by Sir Robert Carr, who was sent to take possession of this plantation. He took with him between two and 3000 men, and offering protection to such of the inhabitants as submitted, became master of the whole country without a blow. After which his majesty gave leave to such of the inhabitants as were inclined to it, to stay, and suffered the rest to depart freely with their effects. The number of the latter was but very inconsiderable in comparison of the former. Col. Nichols was left governor of the province and continued so twenty years.

CHAPTER XIX.

An account of the settlement of the East and West-Jerseys, and of the produce and trade of those provinces

THE countries now called the Jerseys, fell under the dominion of the crown of Great-Britain, by the conquest of Nova Belgia or New-York, of which they were a part. The several voyages that had been made for the planting of Virginia, rendered these coasts very well known to multitudes of English seamen, who being dispersed into different parts of the world, carried the news of these rich and pleasant countries in America, along with them wherever they went, and this inspired strangers with a strong desire of possessing what the English seemed to neglect.

The firft Europeans who fettled here were the Swedes, who had three towns in this province, Chriftina, called by the Indians Andaftaka, Elfinbourgh, and Gottembourgh. Their fettlements were chiefly on the fouth fide of the river towards Pennfylvania; oppofite to which there is a place ftill called Fort Elfinbourgh. The Swedes however made but little progrefs in their plantation, while the Dutch being always induftrious in promoting their own advantage, worked them fo far out of it, that Bergen, the northern part of New-Jerfey, was almoft entirely new planted by Hollanders. At length King Charles II. gave this tract in his grant of Nova Belgia to the Duke of York, but the Englifh made no fettlement in it till feveral years after they were in the poffeffion of that province, and had much extended their plantations.

The Duke of York having invefted this province, under the name of Nova Caneria, in John, Lord Berkley, and Sir George Carteret, they or their affignees agreed to divide it into two parts, when Eaft-Jerfey which borders on New-York, falling to Sir George, whofe family was of the ifle of Jerfey, this province took its name from thence, and Weft New-Jerfey, which borders on Pennfylvania, falling to the Lord Berkeley, it was agreed to give the name of that ifland to the whole.

This entire province containing the two Jerfeys, has the main ocean on the fouth and eaft; the river Delaware, which feparates it from Pennfylvania, on the weft; and Hudfon's River on the north. It lies between 39 and 40°. north latitude, and extends in length above 120 miles, and fixty in breadth from north to fouth. The largeft and beft inhabited part of this province is Eaft-Jerfey, which extends from Little-Egg Harbour to that part of Hudfon's River which is in 41°. north latitude, and to the fouthward and weftward was divided from West-Jersey by a line of partition, that extends in length from Egg Harbour to the south branch of Raritan River, and contains Bergen county, Essex county, and Middlesex, on the north side of the last mentioned river, and Monmouth county on the south. West-Jersey contains the same number of counties, and these are Burlington, Gloucester, Salem, and Cape-May.

These two provinces were for a considerable time, in the hands of different proprietors; but at length on the 22d of April 1702, these proprietors made an assignment of their rights to Queen Anne, and ever since that time they have constituted but one royal government, the king appointing the governor and council, and the freemen choosing the representative body of the commons. Sometimes indeed the governor of New-York is also governor of the Jerseys, but this is always by a separate commission.

The chief towns in the Jerseys, are first, Perth-Amboy, the capital of the county of Middlesex, pleasantly situated at the mouth of Raritan River, which had it been built according to the intended model, would have been one of the finest towns in North-America; but planters have not resorted to it as was expected, though it is so commodiously situated for trade, that ships of 300 tons may come up in one tide and lie before the merchants doors; but Elizabeth's-town, which is the capital of the county of Essex, and is situated to the north, flourishes much more, and may still be deemed the most considerable town in the Jerseys. The other principal towns, are Bergen, the capital of the county of the same name; Middletown, Shrewsbury, and Freehold in the county of Monmouth; Burlington or Bridlington, the capital of the county of Burlington, and of all West-Jersey. This last town is situated on an island in the Delaware, to the northward of Philadelphia in Pennsylvania, but on the oppofite fide of the river: The houfes are handfomely built of brick, and laid out into fpacious ftreets, with commodious keys and wharves, to which fhips of 2 or 300 tons may come up. It has alfo a handfome market-place, a town-houfe where the courts of juftice were formerly held, and two good bridges over the creek; the one called London-Bridge, and the other York-Bridge, and having an eafy communication with Philadelphia and the ocean, it is faid to be one of the beft towns in Weft-Jerfey, whether we confider its fituation, buildings or trade.

The foil and convenience of rivers and creeks are much the fame in both Jerfeys, except that Weft-Jerfey abounds more in the latter, from its fituation on Delawar river. As the Englifh colony behaved with fuch integrity to the Indians, as to purchafe of them the land they planted, they have had the advantage of living without moleftation, and it is computed that the inhabitants amount to about 100,000. But there are not above 200 Indians in this province.

The country produces plenty of all forts of grain, and the inhabitants, befides carrying provifions to the fugar iflands, drive a trade in furs and fkins. They alfo fhip off train oil, iron, copper, black-cattle, fifh, corn and other provifions for Portugal, Spain, and the Canaries.

CHAPTER XX.

The hiftory of the various Settlements and Revolutions in the Lucayan or Bahama iflands.

WE now come to the fettlement of the Lucayan or Bahama iflands, the firft parts of the new world difcovered by Columbus, who arrived first at Guanahani, to which he gave the name of St. Salvador, but the English changed it to that of Cat Island. The Spaniards never thought of settling there, but afterwards contented themselves with cruelly extirpating the native inhabitants, who were at that time remarkable for being the best people in all America: And thus they wantonly murdered many thousands of innocent persons, without any advantage to themselves.

As these islands lie pretty much out of the course of ships bound to the continent of America, it was long before we had any notice of them: But in 1667, Capt. William Sale being bound to Carolina, was forced by a storm among these islands, and had an opportunity of examining them carefully, particularly a large island to which he gave his own name. But being a second time driven upon it, when bound to the continent he gave it the name of Providence.

After his return to England, he let the proprietors of Carolina know the situation and circumstances of these islands; observing that in case they were settled, they might not only be of great benefit to this nation, but be a constant check on the French and Spaniards, in case of a breach with either, or both of those nations. These reasons being suggested to king Charles II. his majesty made a grant of the Bahama islands, to George duke of Albermarle, Anthony lord Ashley, John lord Berkeley, William lord Craven, Sir George Carteret, and Sir Peter Colliton.

The Bahama islands are situated to the north of Cuba, and stretch to the north-east from the south-west between 21 and 27°. of north latitude, and between 73 and 81°. of west longitude. The island of Bahama, which communicates its name to the rest, is seated in the latitude of 26°. 36. at the distance of about twenty or thirty leagues from the continent of Florida. It is about fifty miles in length, but fcarce any where fixty miles in breadth, and in many places not half fo broad. It is however very pleafant and fruitful; the foil is remarkably rich and the country every where abounds with brooks, and fprings of frefh water.

Providence Ifland, lies in the centre of fome hundreds of iflands, fome of them many miles in length, and others no bigger than fmall rocks rifing above the water; fo that it is extremely dangerous for fhips to be forced in among them by a tempeft. This ifland lies in 25°. north latitude, and is twenty-eight miles long, and eleven miles broad, at the greateft breadth. The moft confiderable profit made by the planters of Providence ifland, arofe from the misfortunes of fuch as were fhipwrecked, or from thofe who in a winter voyage to the continent of America were driven to the Bahama iflands, and put into Providence for provifions, which it is true, had little or none but what came from Carolina, however the traders in the ifland kept ftore houfes to fupply thofe who wanted, and thefe afforded great relief to unfortunate mariners.

The firft governor who was fent to Providence ifland by the proprietors was Mr. Chillingworth, who went there about the year 1672, when feveral people failed from England, and the other colonies to fettle there; but living a licentious life, they grew impatient under government, and Mr. Chillingworth, endeavouring to bring them to reafon, they affembled tumultuoufly, feized him, and fhipped him off for Jamaica, after which they lived as they thought proper.

Though fuch an unruly colony afforded but little encouragement for any man to put himfelf into their hands, yet fix or feven years after, the proprietors made Mr. Clarke, governor, whofe fate was much worfe than that of his predeceffors; for the Spaniards being at that time jealous of every new English colony towards the south, landed in Providence, destroyed all the stock which the inhabitants could not carry off, and burned their houses: but what is still more extraordinary, Mr. Trott, one of Mr. Clarke's successors, always asserted, that the Spaniards roasted Mr. Clarke on a spit, after they had killed him. It is however certain that he was killed, and that the people removing to other colonies, the island remained uninhabited till about the time of the revolution, when several persons removed thither from Europe and the continent, and a new governor was appointed by the proprietors.

About ten years after, there were in Providence and the adjacent islands, near 1000 inhabitants; some tobacco was planted; a sugar mill set up, and other improvements made, but in 1708, the Spaniards and French landed, surprized the fort, took the governor prisoner, plundered and stripped the English, burned the town of Nassau, together with the church, ruined the fort and nailed up the guns. After which they carried off the governor and about half the blacks, the rest saving themselves in the woods, but in about a month after they returned, and took most of the negroes who were left. After this second invasion the English inhabitants of the Bahamas thought it vain to stay any longer, and therefore removed, some to Carolina, some to Virginia, and some to New-England, and other places. In the mean time the proprietors appointed one Mr. Birch to go over governor, who landing in Providence and finding it a desert, he did not give himself the trouble to open his commission, but after remaining there two or three months, during which he was forced to sleep in the woods, he returned back and left the place uninhabited.

At length the Bahama islands, becoming a receptacle for Priates, and the house of lords con-

fidering that it would be of fatal confequence if
they fell into the hands of an enemy, they addreffed her Majefty Queen Anne, that the ifland of
Providence might be put in a pofture of defence:
But this advice being neglected, their lordfhips,
four years after, addreffed his late Majefty King
George the I. upon which he was pleafed to give
directions for diflodging thefe pirates; for making
fettlements, and erecting a fortification.

Captain Woodes Rogers was now appointed governor and failed for Providence in April 1718,
with a naval force for fubduing the pirates. In
the mean time col. Bennet, governor of Bermudas,
fent a floop to the ifland, ordering them to furrender, purfuant to a late proclamation. Thofe who
were then on the ifland gladly accepted the mercy
offered them, and promifed to furrender themfelves
as foon as they could get a paffage to the Englifh
colonies; adding, that they did not doubt but
their companions who were at fea would |gladly
follow their example. Accordingly, capt. Henry
Jennings, and fifteen others, immediately followed
the floop to Bermudas, and furrendered themfelves,
and capt. Laffie, capt. Nicholls, capt. Hernigold,
and capt. Burgefs, furrendered foon after, and 114
of their men. But Vane, one of the captains of
the pirates, knowing that capt. Rogers was coming
to reduce thofe robbers by proclamation, or by
force, fet fire to a French fhip of 22 guns, which
he had taken in order to burn the Rofe frigate,
which arrived at Naffau: however that frigate got
off in time by cutting her cables. But this bold
and rafh attempt could not have fecured him; for
foon after there appeared the Milford man of war
and another, on board of which was the governor,
ftanding in for the harbour, upon which Vane,
and about fifty of his men, made off in a floop.
But though the governor fent a floop with a fufficient force after them, they made their efcape.

Mr Woodes Rogers landed on the 27th of July, when he took poffeffion of the fort, and caufed his Majefty's commiffion to be read in the prefence of the officers, foldiers, and about 300 people, whom he found there at his arrival; who had been almoft daily exercifed in arms for their defence, in cafeof an attack from the Spaniards or French, and capt. Rogers brought with him him above 100 foldiers, who being added to the others were fufficient to fecure the Bahama iflands.

Mr. Rogers began to regulate the government, and to reduce it to order. He nominated fix of the adventurers who came with him to be of the council, to which he added fix out of fuch of the inhabitants as had never been pirates. As foon as the governor and council had fettled the board, about 200 of the pirates furrendered themfelves to them, had certificates of their furrender, and took the oaths of allegiance, as did voluntarily the greateft part of the inhabitants of Providence, who a few years after were computed at 1500 perfons; out of thefe were formed three companies of militia under officers of their own ifland. Thefe companies took their turn every night in the town guard at Naffau. The independant company was always upon duty in the fort, and another fort of eight guns was erected at the eaftermoft entrance into the harbour.

By thefe methods the face of affairs in this part of the world was entirely changed. The town of Naffau was rebuilt, a regular force eftablifhed, and plantations laid out. Soon after the neigbouring ifland of Eleuthera was alfo fettled, about 60 families fixing themfelves there, erected a fmall fort for their defence. The like was done in Harbour ifland, where the plantation foon grew more confiderable, and a large fort was built for the protection of the inhabitants.

At length Mr. Rogers returning to England, was succeeded in his government by Capt. Fitz Williams, and ever since this last settlment of these islands, they have been continually improving, though they advance but slowly.

CHAPTER XXI.

The history of the settlements of the Hudson's Bay company. An account of the several factories. The religion, manners and customs of the Indians, and of their plants and animals, particularly of the Beaver.

THE next corporation formed for enlarging the English commerce, was that of the Hudson's Bay company, erected by King Charles the II. upon the following occasion: Messrs. Radison and Goofelier, two Frenchmen, meeting with some Indians in the lake of Assimponals in Canada, were informed that they might go by land to the bottom of the bay, where the English had never yet been; whereupon they desired them to conduct them thither, which the Indians did; after this the two Frenchmen returned to the upper lake, the same way they came, and thence to Quebec, the capital of Canada; where they offered the principal merchants to conduct ships to Hudson's Bay, but their project was rejected; they therefore went to France in hopes of a more favourable hearing at court; but after presenting several memorials, and spending much time and money, their project was considered as chimerical, and they were answered in the same manner as at Quebec. Mean while the English Ambassador at Paris, hearing of their proposals, imagined he should do a piece of service to his country by engaging them to serve the English, who had already pretensions to the bay; he therefore persuaded them to go to London, where they met with a favourable reception, from some persons of quality, merchants and others, who employed Mr. Gillam, a person long used to the New-England trade, to perfect this discovery.

He sailed in the Nonsuch ketch, in the year 1667, into Baffin's Bay, to the height of 75°. and from thence southward to 51°. where he entered a river, to which he gave the name of Prince Rupert's River, and finding the natives disposed to a friendly commerce, he erected a small fortress, which he stiled Charles Fort. The success of this expedition was so remarkable, that the persons concerned in fitting out this vessel, upon the return of Mr. Gillam, applied to King Charles II. for a patent, who granted them one, dated the second of May, 1670.

Hudson's Bay is situated from fifty-one to sixty-four degrees north latitude, and is 600 miles in length; and the mouth of the streights, which are six leagues over, lies in about 61° north latitude. The two opposite shores are called the East-Main and West-Main: the former is also termed Labrador, and the latter New South Wales.

The company had their first fort on Rupert's River, but never had any towns there; they live within their forts in little houses and huts, in which the builders consider nothing but how to defend them from the cold and rain; they are however, not so much disturbed by the latter as by the former. In 1670, another factory was established at Fort Nelson. Mean while the company by their governors and agents, made such contracts with the captains or kings of rivers or territories, for enjoying an exclusive trade, that the Indians could not pretend that they had encroached upon them. These contracts were as firm as the Indians themselves could make them, and were confirmed by such ceremonies as they thought most sacred and obligatory.

VOL. II.   F f

In the year 1686, the company were in poffeffion of five fettlements, viz. Albany River, Haye's Ifland, Rupert's River, Fort Nelfon, and New Severn; and their trade at each of them was very confiderable. From Albany River they had generally 3500 beavers a year, and their commerce increafed fo much, that the French began to be afraid that all the Upland Indians would be drawn down to the bay. But being fenfible that they could do any thing with James II. King of England, they refolved to drive the Englifh out of all their places in the bottom of the bay. Firft they took Haye's Ifland, and then the fort on Rupert's River; after which the French company at Canada, procured a detachment of foldiers to be fent under the Chevalier de Troyes, who marched over land from Quebec, and in a time of profound peace, laid fiege to the fort at Albany River; but though the governor did all in his power to defend the place, he was obliged to furrender it in a week's time. However about feven years after, the company being affifted by the government, retook all the forts and factories of which the French had deprived them in time of peace; but they were foon after driven out of them again by the French.

In 1696 the company applied themfelves to King William, reprefenting their inability to maintain themfelves againft the French, and praying the affiftance of the crown for their fupport; upon which two men of war were fent under the command of Captain Allen, who coming into Haye's River, fummoned all the forts to furrender; when the French governor finding he could not defend them againft the Englifh, capitulated, and the French were allowed to march out with all military honours. However, in the next general war, the French renewed their attacks upon the fettlements of the Hudfon's Bay company with fuch fuccefs, that they left them only Fort Albany; but by the treaty of Utrecht, every thing was reſtored to the company again, and an equitable ſatisfaction ſtipulated for their loſſes: Since which time, their trade has greatly increaſed, ſo that it became at leaſt treble to what it was when that peace was concluded, and is ſtill in a very flouriſhing condition; they having beſides the above, York Fort, Churchill and Mooſe River factories.

As to the ſituation of the country about theſe forts: Mooſe River factory is in latitude 51°. 28. and is built near the mouth of the river, which at twelve miles diſtance from the fort, is divided into two branches, one comes from the ſouthward, and the other from the ſouth-weſt. Upon the ſouthern branch all ſorts of grain thrive, as barley, peaſe and beans do at the factory, though expoſed to all the chilling winds, that blow from the ice in the bay. Upon the ſouthern part above the falls, there grow along the river wild oats and rye, which have black huſks, though the grain is perfectly clear, and white like rice, and as it grows in the water, the Indians beat it off when ripe, into their canoes, as they paſs along the river. In the woods at the bottom of the bay, at Mooſe, Albany, and Rupert's river, are very large timber trees of all kinds; as oak, aſh, &c. as well as pines, cedars, and ſpruce, They have good graſs for making hay, and may have every where within land, all ſorts of pulſe and grain, and the ſame ſort of fruit trees, that are natural to the ſame climate in Europe; for all the ſorts they have tried, thrive very well.

The ice breaks up at Mooſe factory in the beginning of April, but higher up in the country, in March. The river is navigable for canoes a great way up among the falls; at a conſiderable diſtance there is one fall of fifty feet, but above that the river is deep, and navigable for a great way, where the climate is very good. The French have a settlement for trade near the southern branch, about 100 miles above the factory, where they sell their goods cheaper than the company, notwithstanding the difficulty and expence of carrying them so far from Canada, and give as much for a martin's skin as they do for a beaver, when we insist upon three for one; by which means the French get all the choice skins, and leave only the refuse for the company. The French have also another house pretty high up Rupert's River, by which they have gained all the trade upon the East-Main, except a little the company get at Slude River.

Though the bottom of the bay is as near the lin as London, it being in 51°. yet the air is excessively cold for nine months in the year, and the other three months very hot. However some fruits, as goose-berries, straw-berries, and dew-berries, grow about Prince Rupert's River, where the comodities for trade are guns, powder, shot, cloth, hatchets, kettles, tobacco, &c. which the English exchange with the Indians for furs, as beavers, martins, foxes, moose, and other skins.

The Indians have no beavers to the north-ward of Churchill River, on account of there being no ponds or woods, proper for those animals; but they have a great number of martins, bears, rein-deer, buffaloes, wolves, and other beasts with rich furs, the country being mostly rocky and covered with white moss. There is a great deal of small wood near the factory, but the wood improves, further up the river from the bay, where they have juniper, birch, and poplar, and still more souther-ly the timber is larger, and there is great variety of trees.

Mr. Dobbs observes, that " The company avoid
" all they can making discoveries to the north-
" ward of Churchill, or extending their trade that
" way, for fear they should discover a passage to

"the western ocean of America, and tempt, by
"that means, the rest of the English merchants
"to lay open their trade, which they know they
"have no legal right to; which, if the passage
"was found, would not only animate the rest of
"the merchants to pursue the trade through that
"passage, but also to find out the great advantages
"that might be made of the trade of the rivers
"and countries adjoining to the bay, by which
"means they would lose their beloved monopoly.
"But the prospect they have of gain to be made
"by trading with the Eskimaux Indians for whale-
"fin, whale and seal oil, and sea-horse teeth, in-
"duces them to venture a sloop annually, as far
"as 62°. 30. to Whale-Cove, where these Indians
"meet them, and truck their fins and oil with
"them."

The Indians of certain districts, bounded by particular rivers, have each of them what they call an Okimah or Captain, who is an old man, esteemed only for his prudence and experience. His authority is only what they please to give him upon particular occasions. He is their orator, when they address the English, and speaks for them in their own councils, when they assemble every spring, to settle their quarters for hunting, fowling and fishing. They have but few religious sentiments. They maintain that there are two monetoes or spirits, one who sends all good things, and the other all the bad. Their worship consists in songs and dances at their feasts, in honour of the monetoes who have favoured them; but if they are sick, or almost famished for want of provisions, they hang some little bauble, which they esteem, upon the top of a pale near the tent, to pacify the offended spirit. As they live a rambling life, they can receive no benefit from tame fowl or cattle, for they seldom stay above a fortnight at a place, unless they find plenty of game. On their removal they build their huts, and then difperfe to get game for their food, returning at night, after having killed enough to fupport them for a day. But in thefe excurfions they do not proceed above a league or two from their huts. When they find fcarcity of game they remove a league or two farther, and thus traverfe through thefe countries and bogs, fcarce mffing one day in winter and fummer, whether the weather be fair or foul, and going in the greateft ftorms of fnow. The fmaller game got by traps or fnares are generally the employment of women and children, as martins, fquirrels, ermines, &c. while the elks, or moofe-deer, ftags, bears, tygers, wild beeves, wolves, foxes, beavers, otters, corcajons, &c. are the employment of the men. But when the Indians kill any game for food, they leave it upon the fpot, and the next day fend their wives to fetch it home; directing them to the place, by breaking off branches from the trees, and laying them in the road, pointing to the place where they fhould go, and fometimes they fcatter mofs, fo that they never mifs finding it. It is obfervable that the trees all bend towards the fouth, and that the branches on that fide are larger and ftronger than thofe of the north fide, and that this is alfo the cafe with refpect to the mofs that grows upon the trees.

When they go abroad in winter to hunt and fhoot for their daily food, before they drefs, they rub themfelves all over with bear's greafe, or oil of beavers, which does not freeze. They alfo greafe the fur of their beaver coats, and then put them on. They have a kind of boots or ftockings made of beaver's fkin, well oiled with the fur inwards, and above them they have an oiled-fkin laced about their feet, which keeps out the cold and water, where there is neither ice nor fnow; and by this means they never freeze or fuffer by the cold. In fummer when they go naked, they alfo rub themfelves with oil or greafe, which keeping their fkins foft and fupple, prevents their being fcorched by expofing themfelves to the fun, and hinders their being molefted by the flies, bugs, mufketoes, or any other noxious infect. When they want to get rid of it, they go into the water and rub themfelves all over with mud or clay, then letting it dry upon them, they rub it off, but whenever they are free from the oil, the flies and mufketoes immediately attack them.

They ufe no milk from the time they are weaned, and have an averfion to cheefe, from the opinion that it is made of dead men's fat. They love pruins and raifins, and will give a beaver's fkin for twelve of them, to carry to their children; they will give the fame for a Jew's harp, or for the fmalleft print or picture, and all toys are confidered by them as jewels.

The carcajons and otters prey upon the beavers when they can take them at an advantage. The former is as big as a very large dog, and has a good fur, which in exchange is valued at a beaver and a half.

A large beaver, or caftor, is about twenty-fix inches long from the hind part of the head to the root of the tail, and is about three feet eight inches round. Its head is about feven inches long and fix broad, and its tail, which is fomewhat of an oval form and covered with fcales, is fourteen inches long and fix broad. Its ears are fhort and round; its eyes are fmall, and it has two fore teeth in each jaw about an inch long, which are extremely fharp and ftrong. Though its legs are but five inches long its feet are above fix inches in length, and its paws formed like a man's hand; but the toes of the hind feet are joined like thofe of a duck, with a membrane of a flate colour. It makes ufe of its paw in feeding as apes do, and in building its houfe.

The ancient writers of natural hiſtory are miſ-taken in aſſerting that the beavers bite off their teſticles when purſued by the huntſmen; for what the phyſicians call caſtoreum, is inguinal and glands of this animal. Beſides, the beavers are never pur-ſued in hunting; for as they ſeldom leave the ſide of the pond where they have built their kennels, upon the leaſt noiſe they dive under water, and return to their little houſes when the danger is over.

The beavers are of three colours, ſome of a red-diſh brown, others black, and others white. Thoſe of each pond are repreſented by ſeveral authors, as forming a commonwealth; as having an excellent polity and laws, and as holding frequent conſulta-tions for their mutual defence: but it is probable theſe things are greatly exaggerated: however their ſagacity is univerſally allowed to be very ex-traordinary, and the manner of building their houſes or kennels has been always a ſubject of ad-miration to the curious.

The beavers finding a rivulet that runs a-croſs a low ground, make banks that ſtop the courſe of the water, and cauſe an inundation that is ſometimes ſix miles in circumference. This bank is made with trees, which they cut down with their teeth, and then drag them along as they ſwim in the water. The trees being ranged along the bottom of the low ground, theſe animals load themſelves with graſs and earth, which they drag along upon their great tails, and throw in between the wood with ſuch art and induſtry, that it would be very diffi-cult, if not impoſſible, for man to make a ſtronger wall with ſuch materials. Their tails ſerve them, both for carts and trowels, and their teeth for axes, their paws ſupply the place of hands, and their feet ſerve inſtead of oars. In ſhort, in the ſpace of five or ſix months, about an hundred of theſe animals will make banks of 4 or 500 paces in length, of 20 in heighth, and feven or eight in thicknefs. The pond being completed, they build their houfes near the center, by making holes at the bottom of the water, for planting fix pofts, upon which each of their edifices is built in a moft curious manner, with branches of trees, herbs, and earth. Some fay they have three ftories, that they may mount up from one to the other, when the waters rife by rains or thaw; and that each beaver has an apartment to himfelf which he enters under water through a great hole in the firft floor, that has a communication with the two other rooms; but this is not true.

The chief food of the beavers is the poplar, but they alfo eat fallows, alders, and moft other trees that have not a refinous juice, feeding on the middle bark. In May when wood is not plenty, they live upon a large root, a fathom long, which grows in the marfhes, and is as thick as a man's leg, but at this time the beavers are not fo good eating as when they feed upon barks. They will cut down trees with their teeth, that are extremely thick, and when one of them obferves that the tree is ready to fall, he gives a loud cry and runs the contrary way, and is followed by the reft. They then cut off all the twigs and fmaller branches, two or three fathoms in length, and draw them to their houfes in the ponds, and having repaired their pond head, they thruft one end of thefe fticks into the clay or mud, that they may lie under water all the winter, to preferve the bark, green and tender for their winter provifions. In this manner they ferve both the fmaller and larger branches, until they come to the trunk of the tree.

The beaver, is excellent food, but the tongue and tail are the moft delicious parts. They bring forth their young in the beginning of the fummer, when the females are lean by fuckling them, the males are alfo lean all the fummer, during which they are employed in repairing their ponds and houses, and in cutting down and providing wood and branches for their winter store, but they are very fat, from November till the end of March. They breed once a year, and have from ten to fifteen at a litter, which grow up in one season; they therefore multiply very fast, whence if the Indians empty a pond, and take the whole lodge, they generally leave a pair to breed, by which it is again fully stocked in two or three years time. A good hunter among the Indians can kill 600 beavers in a season, but their canoes are so small that they can bring only 100. They therefore sometimes burn off the fur and roast the beavers like pigs.

The ounce is of the cat kind, but as large as a great dog; it preys upon all the beasts it can conquer, as does also the tyger, which is the only beast in that country that will not fly from a man. The beeves have a large bunch upon their backs, which is by far the most delicious part of them, it being juicy, rich, and as sweet as marrow, though it weighs several pounds. They are covered with exceeding good hair, almost as fine as silk, and one of their fleeces will weigh at least eight pounds.

CHAPTER XXII.

A short account of the settlement of Pennsylvania.

THE next state that was settled in America, was that of Pennsylvania, the best projected, and most flourishing of the states in North America. Admiral Penn, who in conjunction with col. Venables conquered the island of Jamaica, and was afterwards knighted, being in high credit with king Charles II. and the duke of York, had the promise of a grant of this country from that king, as a reward for his paſt ſervices, and ſome years after his death his ſon ſtrenuouſly ſolicited the promiſed grant; which, as the king owed conſiderable ſums to his father, he obtained in the year 1679, and the original patent was dated the 4th of March, 1680. Mr. Penn afterwards obtained part of Nova Belgia, or the province of New-York, which was added to the country he had acquired by the firſt grant, and both together, from his own name, he called Pennſylvania, or Penn's Country.

But before we proceed, it may be neceſſary juſt to obſerve that the Dutch were the firſt planters here, as well as at New-York, and living near the bay in the neighbourhood of that province, applied themſelves chiefly to trade. Afterwards ſome of the inhabitants of Finland ſettled near the Freſhes of Delawar, where they applied themſelves to huſbandry, and had a governor appointed them by their own ſovereign the king of Sweden. But between theſe two neighbours there happened frequent diſputes, till the Dutch growing too powerful for the Swedes, the latter ſubmitted to their ſtronger neighbours, and the Swediſh governor made a formal ſurrender of the country to the governor for the States General; after which this province continued ſubjeċt to that republic, till the Engliſh drove the Dutch out of New-York, which rendered the poſſeſſion of thoſe territories the more eaſy to Mr. Penn.

Before Mr. Penn ſent over the firſt adventurers under his patent, there were a few Engliſh in Pennſylvania, over whom he placed as Governor Colonel William Markham, his nephew, to whom both the Swedes and Dutch ſubmitted. Mr. Penn had the more earneſtly ſolicited the above grant, on account of the perſecution of the diſſenters, and particularly on his finding his friends the quakers haraffed all over England by the fpiritual courts, he himfelf being many times thrown in prifon, not only for preaching, but merely for being prefent at their affemblies: He therefore refolved to put himfelf at the head of as many as would go with him, and remove to this country, but firft fent over a body of fettlers from London, Liverpool, and Briftol, who purchafed confiderable quantities of land, at the rate of twenty pounds for a thoufand acres, and paying a fmall quit-rent. The male and female fervants were to have fifty acres when their time was out, and the owners of land thirty acres a head for fuch fervants. In order to fecure the new planters from the Indians, he appointed commiffioners to confer with them about the land and to confirm a league of peace: by thefe firft adventurers, he alfo fent a very affectionate and friendly letter to the native Indians, and the fame year went to Pennfylvania himfelf, taking with him a great number of people, who with thofe that immediately followed him, amounted to 2000 perfons.

As foon as he arrived, he took the government into his own hands, entered into a treaty of peace with the Indian kings, and inftead of taking advantage of his patent, purchafed of them the lands he had obtained by his grant. He then fettled the conftitution and laws of the country, by the confent of the inhabitants, by whom it was unanimoufly agreed, according to the fundamental conftitution of Pennfylvania, which he himfelf had drawn up and publifhed in England, that all perfons who acknowledged the exiftence of a God, fhould enjoy free liberty of confcience; and have the full enjoyment of civil liberty, and that no laws fhould be made there nor money raifed but by the confent of the inhabitants; who were alfo allowed to enact what laws they pleafed for the profperity and fecurity of the province. He eſtabliſhed courts of juſtice in every county, with proper officers, to prevent law-ſuits and contentions; and three peace-makers were choſen by every county-court in the nature of common arbitrators, to hear and put an end to all the differences that aroſe between man and man; he alſo ordained that every ſpring and autumn, an orphans court ſhould be held in each county, to inſpect and regulate the affairs of widows and orphans.

Mr. William Penn ſtaid there two years till he had ſettled every thing to his own and the people's ſatisfaction, during which he behaved in ſuch a manner to the Indians, that he inſpired them with a moſt extraordinary love and eſteem both for him and his people; ſo that they ſtill ſpeak of him with the utmoſt gratitude and affection, and whenever they would expreſs an extraordinary regard for any Engliſhman, they ſay we eſteem and love you as if you were that good man William Penn himſelf.

CHAPTER XXIII.

Some account of the motives, and the plan for ſettling the province of Georgia. The firſt colony ſent over under the direction of Mr. Oglethorpe.

BEFORE the laſt war with Spain, ſome perſons of great diſtinction obſerving, that conſiderable numbers of people in theſe kingdoms were by a variety of misfortunes rendered incapable of ſubſiſting in ſuch a way as to be uſeful to themſelves and the community, formed a deſign of ſettling that part of America which properly forms the frontier towards the Spaniards and the French, and which, though within the bounds of the province of Carolina, as defcribed in its charter, was in reality no part of it, as not being at all fettled: and for that reafon, rather a burden than an advantage to the province to which it belonged. They therefore applied to the crown for fufficient powers to fet this undertaking on foot, and meeting with all the encouragement they could defire or expect, eafily obtained a very extenfive charter. Their next care was to raife a fund fufficient for fending over a confiderable number of people, and providing them with all kinds of neceffaries, towards which they fubfcribed liberally themfelves, obtained confiderable fums by way of collection, and had alfo a grant from the parliament of 10,000 l.

In laying the plan for this frontier fettlement it was refolved, to confider each fettler in a double capacity, as a planter, and as a foldier, and to provide for them arms for their defence, as well as tools for the cultivation of the land, and to have them taught the ufe of both. It was alfo refolved, that upon the firft fettling of this colony, towns fhould be laid out, and lands allotted each of the men, for their fupport, as near thofe towns as poffible. It was agreed, that every lot of land fhould confift of 50 acres, and that it fhould be granted them in tail male as the propereft tenure for the colony in its infancy; and with refpect to any hardfhips that might arife from this tenure, they determined to remedy them occafionally, till fuch time as the condition of the colony fhould render an alteration neceffary; they alfo determined to prohibit negroes, the ufe of them being abfolutely inconfiftent with the defign of forming a frontier fettlement, and in many refpects inconvenient and dangerous.

Thefe difpofitions being made, it was refolved to fend over 114 perfons, men, women, and children, out of fuch as were in low circumftances, and by that means unable to follow any bufinefs in

England, and who if in debt had leave from their creditors to go; and of such as were recommended by the minister, church-wardens and overseers of their respective parishes, and James Oglethorpe, Esq. one of the trustees, offered to go and form the settlement at his own expence.

On the 24th of October 1732, the people were all examined whether any of them had any objections to the terms and conditions proposed, when they declared that they were fully satisfied with them, and executed articles under their hands and seals, testifying their consents thereto; but four of them desiring their daughters might inherit, as well as their sons, and that their widows dower might be considered; the trustees immediately resolved, that every person who should desire the same should have the privilege of naming a successor to the lands granted him; who in case the possessor should die without issue male, should hold the same to them and their heirs for ever; and that the widows should have their thirds as in England. This resolution was immediately communicated to all the people, who now expressed themselves fully satisfied.

The trustees then prepared a form of government, and established under their seal a court of judicature, for trying causes, as well criminal as civil, in the town of Savannah, the name given to the first town to be raised; they also appointed a bailiff, a recorder, two constables, and two tything men, out of such of the settlers as appeared most prudent and discreet.

These measures being taken, Mr. Oglethorpe set out for Gravesend on the 15th of November, 1732, and from thence sailed for Carolina, where he arrived with the colony on the 15th of January following. They were received at Charles Town, by the governor, with great kindness and civility, when Mr. Middleton, the king's pilot, was ordered to steer the ship into Port Royal, and to convey the small craft with the colony from thence to the river Savannah. On the 18th Mr. Oglethorpe went on shore upon French's Island, and left a guard upon John's, a point of that island which commands the channel, and is about half way between Beaufort and the river Savannah. Mr. Oglethorpe then went to Beaufort Town, where he was saluted with a discharge of the artillery, and had a new barrack fitted up, where the colony landed on the 20th, and were cheerfully assisted by the officers and gentlemen of the neigbourhood, From thence he went to view the Savannah river, and having pitched upon a convenient spot of ground ten miles up, the town was marked out, and the first house begun on the 9th of February, 1733.

The chief reasons that determined Mr. Oglethorpe in the choice of this place were, health, pleasure, and conveniency. Before his arrival in the country, it had the name of Yammacraw, from an Indian nation who inhabited there, under the command of their chief Tomochichi, who readily gave place to the English, and entered into a close friendship with them, which was the more agreeble, as there was no other Indian nation within 50 miles, but Mr. Oglethorpe called the town Savannah, from the name of the river.

While the town was building, Mr. Oglethorpe kept a strict discipline, none of the people were allowed to swear or get drunk; they were debarred the use of spirituous liquors, and instead of rum, had English beer. While this work was going forwards, some of the land was ploughed up, part of which was sowed with wheat. At the same time two or three gardens were sowed with pot-herbs, &c. and several fruit trees planted. The limits of the town were also pallisadoed, and every thing went forwards with the greatest regularity.

Things being in some forwardness, and every man being appointed his proper station and employment, Mr. Oglethorpe set out for Charles-Town, to solicit succours for his colony, where both the assembly and people in general contributed largely to the assistance of the new comers. Five hundred pounds of this money Mr. Oglethorpe immediately laid out in cattle, and having given directions for providing at Charles Town what his people might have occasion for, went back to Savannah.

On his return, he found that the chief men of the Lower Creek Indians were come to treat of an alliance with the new colony. These Lower Creeks are a nation that formerly consisted of ten, but are now reduced to eight tribes, that have each a different government, but are allied together and speak the same language. Their claims extended from the Savannah river, as far as St. Augustin and up Flint river, which falls into the bay of Mexico. Tomochichi and the Indians of Yammacraw, were of the same nation.

Mr. Oglethorpe received the Indians in one of the new houses. They consisted of the chiefs and war captains of the several tribes and their attendants, all of whom being seated. Oueekachumpa, a very tall old man, stood up and made a speech, which was interpreted by Mr. Wigan and Mr. Musgrove: He first claimed all the lands to the southward of the river Savannah, as belonging to the Creek Indians, and then added, that though they were but poor and ignorant, he that had given the English breath, had given them breath also, but had bestowed more wisdom on the white men. That they were all persuaded, that the great power who dwelt in heaven and all around (at which he spread out his hands and lengthened the sound of his words) had sent the English thither for the instruction of them, their wives and their children, that therefore they freely gave up to them their right to all the land they did not ufe themfelves. That this was not only his opinion, but the opinion of the eight towns of the Creeks, each of whom having confulted together had fent fome of their chief men with fkins, which was their wealth. The chief men then brought a bundle of buckfkins, and laid eight from the eight towns before Mr Oglethorpe. He then faid that thefe were the beft things they had, and that they gave them with a good heart. He thanked him for his kindnefs to Tomochichi, to whom he faid he was related, who though he had been banifhed from his nation, was a good man, and had been a great warrior, and that for his wifdom and juftice, the banifhed men had chofen him Mico or king. He concluded with faying, that he had heard the Cherokees had killed fome Englifhmen, and that if Mr. Oglethorpe would command them, they would enter with their whole force into the Cherokee country, deftroy their harveft, kill the people, and revenge the Englifh.

When he had done fpeaking, Tomochichi came in with the Yammacraw Indians, and making a low obeifance, faid, " I was a banifhed man, and " came here poor and helplefs, to look for good " land near the tombs of my anceftors, and when " you the Englifh came to this place, I feared " you would drive us away ; for we were weak " and wanted corn : But you confirmed our land " to us, and gave us food." Then the chiefs of the other nations made fpeeches, to the fame purpofe as Oueekachumpa's ; after which a treaty of alliance and commerce was agreed to, and figned by Mr. Oglethorpe and them. Which being done, a laced coat, a laced hat, and a fhirt, were given to each king : Each of the warriors had a gun and a mantle of duffils, and all their attendants had coarfe cloth for clothing and other things.

This treaty being concluded, Mr. Oglethorpe returned to England to procure the neceſſary ſupplies, and arrived there in June 1734, bringing with him Tomochichi, Mico or king of the Yammacraws, Senawki, his conſort, and Yoonakowi, his nephew; as alſo Hilliſpilli, a war captain, and Apakowtſki, Stimaletchi, Sintouchi, Hiuguthi, and Umphychi, five other Indian chiefs, with their interpreter.

Theſe Indians were lodged at the Georgia office in old Palace-yard, where they were handſomely entertained; and being ſuitably dreſſed, were introduced to the court, which was then at Kenſington. Tomochichi preſented to the king ſeveral eagles feathers, which according to their cuſtom was the moſt reſpectful gift he could offer, and then made the following ſpeech; "This day I ſee the majeſty of your face, the greatneſs of your houſe, and the number of your people. I come for the good of the whole nation called the Creeks, to renew the peace they have long ago concluded with the Engliſh. I am come over in my old days, though I cannot live to reap any advantage to myſelf. I am come for the good of the children of all the nations of the Upper and Lower Creeks, that they may be inſtructed in the knowledge of the Engliſh. Theſe are the feathers of the eagle, the ſwifteſt of all birds, who fly round our nations. Theſe feathers are in our land a ſign of peace, and we have brought them over to leave with you, O great king, as a ſign of everlaſting peace. O great king, whatſoever words you ſhall ſay unto me, I will tell them faithfully to all the kings of the Creek nations." In anſwer to this ſpeech his majeſty aſſured him, that all thoſe nations ſhould have his protection, and ſincere regard.

Theſe Indians afterwards took a tour through the nation, and during their ſtay in England gave the most evident marks of good sense, and of a sincere inclination to carry on a friendly correspondence between their own nation and ours. They in particular desired the trustees, that the weights, measures, prices, and qualities of goods to be purchased by them with their deer-skins might be settled. That nobody might be allowed to trade with them without a licence from the trustees, that if they were injured they might know where to complain, and that there might be but one store-house in each Indian town, for supplying them with the goods they might want to purchase, and that in each, the traders should be obliged to supply them at the fixed prices. Alleging that the traders had often in an arbitrary manner raised the price of goods, and defrauded them in their weights and measures; which had frequently created animosities between the English and Indians, that had ended in wars, prejudicial to both nations.

In compliance with this request, the trustees procured several acts of parliament; one for maintaining peace with these Indians; another to prevent the importation and use of spirituous liquors into the province of Georgia; and another to prevent the introduction of negroes into that province.

Things being thus settled, two embarkations were made the same year, chiefly of Saltburghers, who with others that went before, built and settled a town, called Ebenezer, upon the river Savannah. The succeeding year, the colony of South Carolina, sending over a memorial relating to their danger from the French and Spaniards, the parliament granted the trustees an extraordinary supply of 26,000l. and very considerable benefactions were made both in England and Carolina, on which account great numbers of people were sent, who consisted mostly of persecuted

German proteſtants, and others from the north of Scotland.

In January 1735, ſome highlanders arrived in Georgia and were ſettled on the Alatamaha river, about ſixteen miles diſtant from the iſland of St. Simon which is at its mouth. They ſoon raiſed convenient huts, till their houſes could be built, and the town at their deſire was called Darien, which name that diſtrict ſtill remains, though they afterwards changed the name of the town to that of New Inverneſs.

On the 6th of February following arrived the great embarkation, conſiſting of 470 perſons, under the direction of Mr. Oglethorpe, and was ſettled upon the iſland of St. Simon, The Creek Indians came down upon this occaſion, and in conſequence of their claiming a right to the country, were treated with, when they agreed that the Engliſh ſhould poſſeſs that and all the adjacent iſlands; which neceſſary ſtep being taken, the town of Frederica was laid out, and the people ſet to work in building of houſes.

The iſland of St. Simon is conveniently ſituated at the mouth of the Alatamaha, a very fine river; it is about forty miles in extent; has a rich and fruitful ſoil, and is full of oak and hickery trees, intermixed with meadows.

As ſoon as this ſettlement was made, care was taken for its ſecurity, on account of its being the ſouthern barrier. A regular fortreſs ſtrengthened with four baſtions, and a ſpur work was erected at Frederica, towards the river, and ſeveral pieces of cannon mounted upon it: A ſtrong battery was alſo raiſed, for the protection of Jekyll ſound, where ten or twelve forty gun ſhips may ſafely ride. Another fort was built on the ſouth-weſt part of Cumberland iſland, where ſeveral pieces of cannon are pointed towards the river, ſo as to command all the ſloops and ſmall craft navigating that paſſage; within the palliſade which ſurrounds the fort, are fine ſprings of water, and a good timber houſe, with large and convenient magazines under it, for ammunition and proviſions.

But while ſuch care was taken of the ſouth frontier, the northern part of the colony was not neglected: Orders were given for erecting a fort at Auguſta, a place ſituated on the river Savannah, where the traders with the Indians from South Carolina and Georgia reſort, and where there are large warehouſes furniſhed with ſuch goods as are wanted by the Indians. The deer ſkins taken in exchange are ſent 230 miles down the river, to the town of Savannah, in boats that carry each about 9000 weight. A horſe road was alſo made from thence to the town of Savannah, and to the dwellings of the Cherokee Indians. By theſe precautions the trade of both colonies with theſe Indians was facilitated, and the country on that ſide, ſecured from any farther attempts of an enemy.

The ſettlements now became ſo conſiderable as not only to draw the attention but to excite the jealouſy of the Spaniards, who would have been glad to have overpowered and driven out their neighbours, but the Indians being ſtrongly attached to the Engliſh, the governor of St. Auguſtin, upon mature deliberation, found it more expedient to enter into a negociation, and to endeavour to conclude an amicable agreement with the Engliſh ſettlements, and Mr. Oglethorpe concluded a treaty with him, upon very ſafe and advantageous terms; in which it was mutually agreed, that neither the Indians ſubject to the king of Spain ſhould attack the ſubjects of Great-Britain, nor the Creeks commit hoſtilities againſt the ſubjects of his Catholic majeſty. That Mr. Oglethorpe ſhould draw off the garriſon and artillery from the iſland of St George, provided that none of his Catholic majeſty's ſubjects ſhould inhabit it, and that no prejudice should thence arise to the right of his Britannic majesty to that island. That the subjects of neither crown should molest each other, and the differences that might arise concerning the limits of their respective governments, and the dominion of the two crowns should remain undecided till the determination of the respective courts. But it seems the governor of St. Augustin was not in the secret of his court, for the Spanish ministry laid claim to Georgia, as being within the dominion of Spain, and began to transport troops into Spanish Florida from the island of Cuba, and other parts of their dominions. They disapproved of the treaty concluded by the governor of St. Augustin, and made open preparations, in order to attack the settlements of Georgia.

These preparations soon came to the knowledge of the lieutenant-governor of South-Carolina, who sending a memorial to his Majesty, he was pleased to order a regiment of 600 effective men to be raised and sent for the protection of Georgia; and as a farther encouragement to these soldiers, the trustees gave each of them an allotment of five acres of land to cultivate for their own use and benefit, and it was resolved that each soldier, who after being seven years in the service, should be desirous of quitting it, should have his regular discharge and be entitled to a grant of twenty acres.

In the beginning of the year 1737, the parliament considering the great expences the trustees had been at in making roads, building fortifications and sending presents to the Indians, granted them 20,000l. more for the farther settling and securing the settlement; on which the trustees made another embarkation, chiefly of persecuted German protestants; and in consequence of so considerable an augmentation of people, all the towns laid out in Georgia, received great supplies, and the utmost care was taken to put the fortifications into the best pofture of defence, that their circumftances would allow.

On the arrival of the regiment of which Mr. Oglethorpe was appointed colonel, he diftributed them in the propereft manner for the fervice of the fettlements; but ftill kept up the fame difcipline and took as much care to form and regulate the inhabitants with refpect to military affairs as ever. He alfo provided different corps for different fervices; fome for ranging the woods; and others for fudden expeditions; he likewife provided veffels for fcouring the fea coafts and for gaining intelligence.

The truftees by their letters and inftructions to the magiftrates, had conftantly exhorted and encouraged the people to cultivate their lands; but in 1738, finding that there were many who ftill continued in idlenefs, and were a burden to them, they gave orders for ftriking off the ftore, all who having had time to cultivate their lands, neglected this important duty, and at length a part of the people fent over a memorial to the truftees complaining of the want of a fee fimple in their lands, and of not being permitted the ufe of negroes. But thofe who were fettled on the frontier and were confequently moft expofed to the Spaniards, having by their induftry improved their plantations, fo as to draw from them a comfortable fubfiftence, fent over a contrary memorial, wherein they reprefented the difadvantages and dangers that would arife from the permiffion of negroes.

At this very time they had intelligence, that a confpiracy was formed by the negroes in South-Carolina, to rife and forcibly make their way out of the province, in order to put themfelves under the protection of the Spaniards, who had proclaimed freedom to all who fhould run to them from their owners. As there was great reafon to believe that this rifing was to be univerfal, and as the negroes were computed at 40,000, while the white inhabitants did not exceed 5000, the whole province was upon its guard. However, several negroes who were employed in Periaguas carried them off, and took the benefit of the proclamation by going to St. Auguſtine, upon which the government of South-Carolina, ſent a ſolemn deputation to demand their ſlaves; but though this was a time of profound peace, the governor of St. Auguſtine peremptorily refuſed to deliver them up, and even declared that he had orders to receive and protect all who ſhould come to him. Upon theſe repreſentations the truſtees ſent an anſwer, in which they poſitively refuſed to ſuffer the ſettlements to have the uſe of ſlaves.

The truſtees had the greateſt reaſon for acting in this manner; ſince among the perſons to whom grants were made in order to their ſettling at their own expence, ſome never went over to take them up or to ſettle at all; others were gentlemen of Carolina, who neglected the proſecution of their grants, and never ſo much as deſired to have their lands laid out; and ſeveral had quitted the laborious life of planters to reſide more at their eaſe at Savannah, where, by the exerciſe of their ſeveral trades and profeſſions, they brought many people in debt; beſides horſe races and other diverſions were ſet on foot, and ſuch a ſpirit of idleneſs began to prevail, as eaſily accounted for their eagerneſs in deſiring to have the uſe of negroes, and plainly ſhewed with what fatal conſequences it muſt have been attended, if the truſtees had nor remained firm to their firſt reſolutions, and had not given ſuch an anſwer as ſhewed they were reſolved to preſerve that ſpirit in the colony, upon which it was ſettled. However, to make the people as eaſy and contented as they could, they enlarged their grants on failure of iſſue male, and made a certain proviſion for the widows of the grantees.

In the mean time the French growing very uneafy at the fettlement of Georgia and their intercourfe with the Indians, began to make ufe of every method in order to raife jealoufies between them and the Creeks, which was no fooner known, than it greatly alarmed not only the people fettled in Georgia, but the whole province of Carolina, from a juft fenfe of the danger to which they fhould be expofed, if the French either by their artifices or prefents, fhould draw over the Creek Indians to their party. Upon this, Mr. Oglethorpe thought it neceffary to enter into a clofer alliance with that nation, and to take a journey to the Coweta town, though at the diftance of no lefs than 500 miles from Frederica, where he then was, and through a country very little known and very difficult for Europeans to travel. He however provided himfelf with horfes and prefents, and after a painful and fatiguing journey reached that place in fafety, where he was received by the Indians with all imaginable marks of friendfhip and refpect, and had an opportunity of conferring, not only with the chiefs of all the tribes of that nation, but alfo with the deputies of the Choctaws and Chickefaws, who lie between the Englifh and French fettlements, and who had fent their deputies thither with that view.

His coming to the Coweta town diffipated all the fears, and extinguifhed all the jealoufies of the Indians. They told him at the firft conference that it had been infinuated to them, that he was coming into that country to deprive them of their lands, and that they had been affured he was actually preparing to invade them, but that by the entire confidence he placed in them, by coming without a body of regular troops, he convinced them that thefe were all falfhoods and calumnies, and that inftead of injuring them by the fettlement he was making, it would prove a new fecurity to to them as well as to the Englifh, and put it out of the power of their common enemies to hurt them; and in fhort they readily concluded a new, more full and explicit treaty with him. Thus the defigns of the French were unravelled, and the Creek nation became more clofely connected with the Englifh.

The land of Carolina lies low near the fea, and is covered with wood, but begins to rife into hills, at twenty-five miles diftance, and at length terminates in mountains, which running in a line from north to fouth along the back of Virginia, and Carolina, end in the province of Georgia, about 200 miles from the Bay of Apalachia, in the gulph of Mexico. As there is a level country from the foot of thefe mountains to that fea, it was the more neceffary to fortify the banks of the river Savannah and Alatamaha, in order to prevent the incurfions of the Spaniards and French by land. The Savannah is navigable 300 miles for boats, and 600 for canoes. A range of iflands runs parallel to the coaft of Georgia, and defends it from the fury of the ocean; and as both the continent and iflands are well wooded, the channels between them are extremely pleafant. There are alfo fandbanks, that extend upwards of feventy miles from the coaft of Georgia, the water fhoaling gradually, till within fix miles of the land, where the fhallownefs of the banks bars all farther paffage, except in the channels that lie between the bars. Thefe were fuppofed a fufficient defence againft the fleets of the French and Spaniards, till the latter found means to pafs the channels, in the year 1742, and to attack the ifland of St. Simon, which had been loft with the town of Frederica, if general Oglethorpe had not by his excellent conduct, defeated their defigns.

CHAPTER XXIV.

An account of Novia Scotia from its firſt diſcovery to its complete ſettlement in 1749.

WE are now brought by the order of time to the ſettlement of Nova Scotia or Acadia. This country was in the reign of queen Elizabeth, conſidered as a part of Virginia, and as ſuch was included in the charter of the weſtern company eſtabliſhed by king James I.

In the year 1618, Sir Samuel Argall, governor of Virginia, made a cruiſing voyage along the coaſt northwards, as far as Cape-Cod in New England, when the Indians informing him that ſome white men, like himſelf, were come to inhabit to the northward of them, he being ſenſible that all the country, as far as it had been diſcovered by Cabot, belonged to the Virginia company his employers, ſailed thither, and found a ſettlement, with a French ſhip riding before it. This veſſel having but one deck, Sir Samuel ſoon drove the men from it with his ſmall arms, and having taken the ſhip, landed his men, marched to the fort, and ſummoned it to ſurrender. The French aſked time to conſider of it; but this being denied, they got privately away, and fled into the woods; upon which the Engliſh entered the place, and having lodged there that night, the French came the next day, and ſurrendered themſelves to Sir Samuel, cancelling the patents that had been granted for their ſettlement by the French king. Sir Samuel now permitted thoſe who choſe it, to ſtay and take a paſſage to Europe in the fiſhing veſſels, which then frequented the coaſt, and the reſt, who were willing to join the Engliſh, he took with him to Virginia.

Sir Samuel being then informed, that the French had another fettlement at a place they called Port Royal, fituated on a bay on the fouth-weft coaft of Acadia, failed thither without delay, and obliged them alfo to furrender ; when refolving that they fhould quit the country, he made thofe who did not care to return home, to remove to the river St. Laurence, where Quebec, now the capital of Canada, has fince been built.

In the year 1621, Sir William Alexander, afterwards created the earl of Sterling, applied to king James I. for a grant of the country to the north of New-England: when it was fuggefted to that king that the tract of country on the continent of North-America, belonging to the crown, being very large, and not likely to be planted by the Englifh in any reafonable time, it would be a very wife and prudent meafure, to grant, under the great feal of Scotland, a part of it to his fubjects of that kingdom, upon a fuppofition that it would be more beneficial to them, and more for the intereft of his kingdoms, if they went over and fettled there, than if, as they frequently did, they removed to Poland, Sweden, and Ruffia, where there were at that time many thoufands of Scots families.

Thefe reafons appeared of fuch weight to king James, that he readily granted a patent to Sir William, and the next year that gentleman, and fome others who were concerned with him, fent a fhip with paffengers to plant and fettle there.

At that time Newfoundland was well known, on account of the fifhery, and the fhip being late in her voyage put in and wintered there. In 1623, they failed from thence, and made the cape at the north fhore of the ifland of Cape-Breton, and coafting till they came to Cape-Sable in Acadia, they found three good harbours, and went afhore at one of them, which they called St. Luke's

Bay. They there found a large river, that had eight fathoms water at ebb, and having failed up it, the ſhip returned to England, and the proprietors publiſhed an account of the country, which they deſcribed as a kind of a paradiſe; Sir William Alexander himſelf wrote and publiſhed a book on this ſubject, and king James, in order to facilitate this plantation, erected a new order called the knights of Nova-Scotia.

Thus, that country, called by the French, Acadia, obtained the name of Nova-Scotia, or New-Scotland, from its being intended to be ſettled by the Scots; but the ſcheme of that ſettlement was unhappily turned into a job, and by that means defeated. Afterwards another grant was made of the northern part of the country to Sir David Kirk, from whom the French king bought it, or at leaſt agreed to give him 5000l. for it. Though it is evident this proprietor had no more right to diſpoſe of the property of the crown in that country, than a nobleman in England has to diſpoſe of his eſtate to the French king, yet this is an evident proof that the French acknowledged the right by which that proprietor held it, and held ſo juſt an opinion of puſillanimity of king James, as to be in no apprehenſions of his vindicating the unalienible rights of the nation.

Oliver Cromwell, however, ſent major Sedgwick to diſlodge the French from Port-Royal, which he did, and though he afterwards conſented that a French proprietor ſhould enjoy the country, yet it was upon condition that he ſhould purchaſe it of the earl of Sterling, which he afterwards did, and then ſold it to Sir Thomas Temple, who was both proprietor and governor at the reſtoration: after which the French ſettled there again, and continued in the quiet poſſeſſion of the country till the year 1690, when they were diſpoſſeſſed by Sir William Phipps, governor of New-England; but it was afterwards given up again to the French, by king William III. at the treaty of Ryfwick.

In all thefe changes the ifland of Cape-Breton followed the fate of Nova-Scotia, and both continued in the hands of the French till the year 1710, when governor Nicholfon made himfelf mafter of Port-Royal, which was then become a place of great confequence, as it gave the French an opportunity of diftreffing the trade, to fuch a degree, that it was properly ftiled the Dunkirk of America. The taking of this place was therefore confidered as an important fervice, and queen Anne, to fhew that fhe would never part with it, gave it her own name, and called it Annapolis-Royal. Upon col. Nicholfon's return to England, fhe made him governor of Nova-Scotia and of Annapolis-Royal, and commander of all her majefty's forces there, and in Newfoundland.

Things were in this fituation, when the treaty of Utrecht was concluded, by which the right to Nova-Scotia, or Acadia, with all its ancient boundaries, the city of Port-Royal, now called Annapolis, and every thing in thofe parts that depend on lands and iflands, together with the dominion, property, and poffeffion, of the faid iflands and lands, fhall be for ever vefted in the crown of Great-Britain: to which the French king added, the exclufion of the fubjects of France from fifhing on the coaft of Nova-Scotia, and within 30 leagues, beginning from Cape Sable, and ftretching along to the fouthweft.

This colony was however much neglected for many years; for though Nova-Scotia had been fo long delivered up to the Englifh, yet there was fcarce any fettlement there, except at Annapolis Royal, and Canfo, while the French had a number of little towns and villages, fcattered along the coaft, and on the banks of the rivers; but the Englifh commander at Annapolis, was in fome degree acknowledged as goverror. The country was then divided into ten or twelve diſtricts, and each diſtrict annually choſe a deputy to be approved by the commander and council at Annapolis; this deputy was a ſort of agent for his countrymen the deſcendants of the French in that diſtrict, and reported the ſtate of it from time to time; but in what manner is not difficult to determine. There was no civil power; the French miſſionaries who were not only appointed by the biſhop of Quebec, but abſolutely under his direction in their ſeveral diſtricts and villages, acted as the ſole magiſtrates, or juſtices of the peace; yet all complaints might, if the parties thought proper, be brought before the commander and the council at Annapolis, which was very rarely done.

In this wretched ſituation were theſe two ſettlements in the beginning of the war before the laſt, ſurrounded by diſguiſed enemies, continually encroaching, and whoſe numbers daily encreaſed. At length theſe deſcendants of the French, though profeſſedly the ſubjects of Great Britain, joined with that nation, deſtroyed Canſo, and, laid ſiege to Annapolis, but without ſucceſs, ſo that at the concluſion of the peace in the beginning of 1749, there were no other Engliſh in Nova Scotia, beſides the garriſon of Annapolis, and the inhabitants who lived within a few miles round that place.

However, the peace was no ſooner concluded, than the earl of Halifax projected the complete ſettlement of Nova-Scotia by the Engliſh, and animated with the warmeſt zeal for the honour and intereſt of his country, reſolved to uſe his utmoſt endeavours to carry it in the moſt effectual manner into execution. He with the other lords commiſſioners of trade and plantations, having gained his majeſty's approbation, they in March 1749, publiſhed propoſals, offering proper encouragement to ſuch of the officers and private men, as after the late conclusion of the peace, had been dismissed his majesty's land and sea-service, and were willing to accept of grants, in order to settle in Nova-Scotia. Fifty acres of land in fee simple were offered to every private soldier or seamen, free from the payment of any quit-rents and taxes, for the term of ten years, and at the expiration of that time they were to pay only one shilling a year for every 50 acres. But this was not all, every private soldier or seamen, who had a family, was to have ten acres for every person of which his family consisted, including women and children; and farther grants were to be made to them on the like conditions, in proportion as their families encreased, or to their abilities for cultivating the land.

Eighty acres were offered on the same conditions, to every officer in the land-service under the rank of ensign, and that of lieutenant in the sea-service, and to those who had families, 15 acres more for every person of which their families consisted.

On the same conditions 200 acres were to be granted to every ensign, 300 to every lieutenant, 400 to every captain, and 600 to every officer above the rank of captain, in the land service. Every lieutenant in the sea-service was to have 400 acres, and every captain 600; while such of the above officers who had families, were offered a further grant of 30 acres, over and above their respective quotas for every person belonging to them. The same conditions that were proposed to private soldiers and sailors, were also offered to carpenters, shipwrights, smiths, masons, joiners, brickmakers, bricklayers, and all other artificers necessary in building and husbandry.

In short, all who were willing to accept these proposals, were to be subsisted with their families, not only during their passage, but for 12 months after their arrival at Nova-Scotia, and to be furnished with arms and ammunition as far as should be thought necessary for their defence; with a proper quantity of materials and utensils for husbandry, clearing and cultivating their lands, erecting houses, carrying on the fishery, and such other purposes as might be found proper for their support.

These generous proposals had all the success that could be desired; and about the beginning of May most of the transports set sail from Portsmouth, with above 3000 families, and soon after others followed from Liverpool and Ireland. This embarkation, which was the largest ever made on such an occasion, was doing at once what in other settlements had not been done under a long course of years. This great number of settlers arrived safe at Chebucto harbour on the 28th of July, after a pleasant passage of between five and six weeks; losing few or none in the voyage, which was in a great measure owing to the ventilators, fixed in the transports; a happy invention, then but lately discovered.

On the arrival of this numerous body, they found the Sphinx of 20 guns, which had entered the harbour a few days before, with col. Cornwallis, their governor on board. His excellency had been informed of the arrival of the French at Cape Breton, which had been just restored to that nation, he therefore sent for the English garrison from Louisburgh, and they soon after entered the harbour, with the regiments of Hopson and Warburton, on board other transports; the officers bringing with them all their furniture, several milch cows, and other stock, with military stores, and ammunition of all sorts. About the same time there also arrived a company of rangers from Annapolis, and encamped near the new settlers, in order to give them assistance and protection.

The next care of the governor, was to pitch upon a proper spot for the first settlement, and as the peninsula appeared preferable, both on account of its commodious situation, and the fertility of the soil, the able-bodied men on board each ship were employed in clearing ground in order to build a town at the south point, at the entrance of Sandwich River; but many objections being soon found against that place, another spot was chosen by the governor, at about the distance of a mile and a half from it on the side of Chebucto Harbour, and on the declivity of a rising ground that commands the whole peninsula, and would shelter the town when built from the north-west winds. The beach they found was a fine gravel, convenient for small boats, the anchorage was every where good for large ships within gun-shot of the town, and small but navigable rivers of fresh and wholesome waters flowed round about it. Here then they made a second and more successful attempt, and indeed it would not have been easy to have chosen a more happy situation, they therefore cleared the ground in as expeditious a manner as possible, and having erected a large wooden house for the governor, with proper storehouses, the ground was laid out so as to form a number of strait and beautiful streets, crossing each other at equal distances, upon a most excellent plan, said to have been formed by the earl of Halifax; the work went on briskly; the people of New-England brought several ships laden with planks, door-cases, doors, window frames and other parts of houses; and the people being employed in ships companies, this created an emulation that rendered their labours remarkably successful, so that in about three years time, this town which was named Halifax from that noble lord, to whom this settlement owed its beginning, was finished, and every family had a good house of their own, of which the master was the landlord. Within the same space of time were also erected a church and wharves, the town was pallisadoed and other fortifications erected; some land was also cleared for agriculture and already planted, notwithstanding the opposition they met with from the French and their tools the Indians. To explain this circumstance it is necessary to observe, that in the beginning of the settlement and soon after the landing of the English, 100 black cattle and some sheep were brought them by land from a French settlement at Minas, a town about thirty miles from the bottom of Bedford Bay; and French deputies also coming to make their submissions, it was proposed to cut a road thither, those deputies promising to contribute fifty men towards carrying on that work. The English also received the promise of friendship and assistance from the Indians, their chiefs waiting upon the governor for that purpose. But these submissions and these promises were soon broken by the perfidy of the French court, which disapproved of these proceedings, and resolved to harrass the English before their town was built and their fortifications erected. Instructions were therefore sent from France, to be communicated to the descendants of the French in Nova-Scotia, and immediately the scene was changed; the French engaged the Indians to use their utmost endeavours to prevent the new colony from proceeding; and the year in which peace was proclaimed and Cape-Breton restored was not expired, when the town began to be frequently attacked in the night, and the English in a country, which in the strongest terms had been secured by treaty to the British crown, could not stir into the adjoining woods without the danger of being shot, scalped, or taken prisoners. The English however prosecuted the settlement with indefatigable industry, and the town as has been already mentioned, was soon happily finished.

But it was impoffible to clear the woods and plough lands without feparating into fmall parties, and this was rendered extremely dangerous: for though the French and Indians durft not attack any confiderable body of the Englifh, yet they frequently fell upon fmall parties; and though they had been often repulfed, they always returned whenever they could find an opportunity of doing it to advantage. Complaint of this open war in a time of peace, was now made to the court of France, when his moft chriftian majefty propofed that commiffaries fhould be appointed to fettle the bounds of Nova Scotia; but thofe of the French endeavouring by all the arts of fophiftry, to prove that Nova-Scotia ceded to the Englifh by the treaty of Utrecht, was no more than the peninfula of that country, the Britifh commiffaries juftified their claim to the whole, by memorials filled with the ftrongeft and moft evident proofs; and the moft trifling anfwers being returned to thefe, Admiral Bofcawen was fent to feize the French fhips in North-America, that England might once more have fomething to reftore to France, as an inducement to that powerful nation to adhere to her treaties; but this expedient was in vain; France appeared evidently to have concerted the means of conquering all the Britifh dominions on the continent of America, and therefore war was entered into to prevent it. During which the town of Halifax became firmly eftablifhed, and that being the principal rendezvous for their men of war, which naturally caufes a quick circulation of money, the inhabitants were foon in a very profperous fituation.

Nova-Scotia is fituated in between 41°. 30. and 49°. 30'. north latitude, and between 60 and 66°. of weft longitude, and is bounded by the bay of St. Laurence on the north-eaft; by the river of St. Laurence on the north-weft; by New-England on the south-west, and by the Bay of Fundy, and the Atlantic Ocean on the east. According to these limits it contains about 420 miles in length, and 380 in breadth. The south-eastern part is a large peninsula, extending from the north-east to the south-west, and joined to the main land by an isthmus a little above the gulph of Canso Though the weather is very sharp in winter, yet the air especially about the town of Halifax is remarkably clear, so that the severest frosts are frequently accompanied with a fine azure sky and sunshine: but though the cold in winter is very severe, the summer is hotter than in England. The coast has the advantage of many bays, harbours and creeks, and the land is enriched by many rivers, some of which are navigated for a long course by the native Indians. The harbour of Chebucto, upon which is situated the metropolis, may justly be esteemed one of the finest in the world, and has extraordinary advantages for a fishery. The entrance into it is from the south, with a large island of an irregular form, lying on the north-east side named Cornwallis Island, from the first governor of Halifax. Betwixt this island and the opposite shore on the south-west, is a channel deep enough for the largest ships. This island, as well as a smaller one that lies higher up the harbour, named George-Island, is very commodiously situated for a fishery, and has conveniences of all sorts proper for drying and curing the fish.

About two miles higher up the harbour is a creek on the south-west side, with a small harbour at its entrance. This creek, which was called by the first settlers of Halifax, Sandwich River, is at the mouth about as wide and deep as the Thames at London Bridge, and is salt water for about four or five miles up when it terminates where a small fresh water rivulet falls into it from the north. From the mouth of Sandwich River to the opposite fide of the harbour is about two miles, with good anchoring ground for the largeft fhips in any part of it, and a fine watering place on the north-eaft fide: the land on both fides is exceeding high, and in general very rich and fertile, but covered with wood.

About four or five miles north of the above river is a narrow entrance of half a mile into Bedford Bay, which is about 12 miles in circumference, and has feveral creeks at the bottom of it, abounding with the fineft falmon in the greateft plenty: there are alfo feveral iflands in it; and a great quantity of pines, fit for mafts, grow on the weftern fide of it. This bay, with the harbour, and Sandwich river divide the peninfula from the main land.

Upon the oppofite fhore are feveral large rivers, among which that of St. John is the moft confiderable. It is ten leagues diftant from the gut of Annapolis, and has a very long courfe. There are prodigious falls of water near its mouth no lefs than thirty fathoms deep, occafioned by the great head of water above, and the channel here being pent up between two fteep mountains. By this river, and the affiftance of fome land carriage, there is a communication with the river of St. Laurence; the French had therefore erected a fort upon it, which was taken by the Englifh in the beginning of the late war.

The woods abound with game, efpecially partridges, wild ducks, wild geefe, woodcocks, herons, pigeons, &c. among the beafts are moft of the forts found in New-England. The trees are oak, fir, fpruce, birch, &c. and the fruit growing wild, are goofberries, rafberries, ftrawberries, &c.

THE
Discoveries and Settlements
OF THE
FRENCH IN AMERICA.

CHAPTER I.

An account of the voyages made to America, by John Verazzano under the reign of Francis I. The first establishment of the French on the banks of the river St. Laurence, and the difficulties they found in fixing a colony in those parts.

THE French have published some accounts of their visiting North America, at the close of the 15th and the beginning of the 16th centuries, but these accounts, which are very uncertain, can at most only prove, that some French seamen and pilots were then employed in the Newfoundland fishery, and had some small knowledge of the adjacent continent.

However in 1523, Francis I. began to think of forming settlements on the coasts of America, and with this view sent John Verazzano a Florentine with one ship, on board of which were fifty men with provisions for eight months; but he returned to Dieppe in July 1524, and we have no account that he made any discoveries.

He however sailed again on the same design towards the latter end of the following year, and arrived on some part of the coast of North-America, but where is not certain. He was however so timerous, that he did not care to venture within any of the bays or ports; but wanting water, and lying in a road near the shore, persuaded one of the mariners to swim to it, and by means of some presents, with which he furnished him, endeavour to procure what he wanted from the natives, who came down in crowds, upon the strand to gaze at the ship.

The poor mariner on his landing and getting a nearer view of the Indians was so extremely amazed and terrified at their uncouth appearance, that throwing his presents upon the ground, he ran as fast as he could and cast himself again into the sea, in order to swim to the ship; but the waves threw him back upon the shore with such force, that he lay breathless upon the sands, and would probably have been drowned if the natives had not hastened to his relief, and taking him up, carried him in their arms to a place at some distance, where with great humanity, they took all the pains they could to bring him to himself. But when he recovered his senses a little, and saw none about him but Indians, he set up such a cry as made the woods ring, at which the natives hoping to pacify him, cried as loud or louder than he, which terrified him still more. At last they made a great fire, before which they undressed him, greatly admiring the whiteness of his skin, and the hair on several parts of his body. The poor fellow concluding that they were going to eat or to burn him, trembled extremely, while those on board seeing every thing that was done, were very much frightened, and every moment expected to see him sacrificed: however by degrees they were all convinced that these dreadful Indians had not the least intention to hurt him; for after drying his cloaths, they suffered him to put them on again, and having given him something to eat, conducted him, at his own desire, to the sea side, and then retiring to some distance looked on till he swam safely on board the ship, and then quietly departed;

upon which Verazzano returned to France, and reported nothing but this ſtory, and that it happened in the latitude of 50°.

The next year however, he engaged in a third voyage, wherein he was loſt ; but from his expeditions, which were carried on thirty years later than thoſe of the Cabots, the French have no great reaſon to boaſt of their ſucceſs.

It was ſome years before the French thought of fitting out any more ſhips for diſcovery, but at length James Cartier an experienced pilot of St. Maloes ventured on another expedition, and ſailed from that port on the 20th of April 1534, with two ſhips of 60 tons each, and 120 men, and arriving on the coaſt of Newfoundland, on the 10th of May, found the country covered with ice and ſnow ; this induced him to ſail to the ſouthward, and entering a bay which bears the name of Spaniſh Harbour, he liked both the country and the people, and boldly went on ſhore.

It is reported that the Spaniards had long before viſited this coaſt, and ſome authorities are brought to prove it, but finding neither gold nor ſilver, they haſtily returned on board, crying in Spaniſh Aca Nada! or there is nothing here. Theſe words being remembered by the Indians, they no ſooner ſaw the French land than they cried Aca Nada! Aca Nada! which the latter took for the name of the country, and it has ever ſince been called Canada : ſtrange as this derivation is, it is mentioned by the beſt French authors.

Cartier afterwards ſailed along great part of the coaſt which borders upon the gulf of St. Laurence and the iſlands ſituated in it, and then returned to France.

The next year he was ſent again with three large ſhips to make a ſettlement, and entering the gulph on the feaſt of St. Laurence, gave it that name, which was afterwards extended to the river, though in the firſt voyage, he had called it the river of Canada ; he now ſailed up as high as the fall of St. Louis, giving ſuch names to the iſlands and rivers, as he thought proper. But though he at firſt was much pleaſed with the country, yet twenty-five of the people dying with the ſcurvy, he began to conſider it was a very unwholeſome climate. At laſt he himſelf was attacked with this dreadful diſtemper, upon which he applied to the inhabitants as well as he could, to learn whether they had any cure for it, and they taught him to make an infuſion of the leaves and bark of the white thorn tree, by which means all who were ſick were ſpeedily recovered ; and as ſoon as the ſeaſon of the year would permit, he returned to France without making any ſettlement.

Three or four years after the project for ſettling this country was again revived, and Francis de la Roque lord of Roberval, undertaking this affair, king Francis I. granted him letters patent in 1540, and gave him abundance of titles, as viceroy and lieutenant general of Canada, Hockelaga, Sagueny, Newfoundland, Belle Iſle, Cape-Breton, Labrador, &c. allowing him the ſame power and authority in thoſe places, that he had himſelf, which was very eaſily done, as there was not a Frenchman, or a cottage in any one of thoſe places. De la Roque, however being a man of family and fortune, reſolved to purſue this expedition, and therefore prevailed upon James Cartier by large promiſes, to undertake another voyage to the coaſt of Canada, in quality of his pilot ; and this gentleman in two or three voyages, formed ſome ſettlements which were the firſt made by the French in America, but theſe were afterwards abandoned.

The navigation of the river St. Laurence fell from time to time into different hands, and ſeveral voyages were made thither to very little purpoſe. However about the year 1608, the French, after having settled and abandoned several places, founded the city of Quebec, and some time after bestowed the name of New France upon that country, under which name they not only included Acadia and other coasts that had long been discovered by the English, but set up crosses and the French arms, to shew that they had taken possession of them. But though the English colonies were then but thinly inhabited, they boldly asserted their prior rights to those places, demolished their crosses, drove away the French wherever they found them within their limits, and forced them to confine their views to the gulph and river St. Laurence; where the French, with much difficulty raised three or four settlements in the space of twenty years, of which Quebec was, and still continues the capital.

In 1629 Sir David Kirk with the English under his command, considering Canada as within the limits of the British dominions, attacked Quebec and made himself master of all the French settlements, and when this news was carried to France, Canada was considered of such little consequence, that it was long debated whether they should demand the restitution of it, though they had already established a company for managing that commerce; but it was at last resolved that it should be demanded, and it was accordingly restored by the treaty of 1632. From that time they pursued their discoveries and settlements in those parts, for several reigns without molestation; but those settlements were attended with great difficulties and a vast expence, and company after company was set up to promote a trade to them, without obtaining any great advantage; for before the French had made any regular settlements, the country was so far from being agreeable to the constitution of the people, that of the numbers sent thither, a great part perished by the hardships they endured, many took the firſt opportunity of returning, and afterwards gave ſuch a dreadful account of the colony they had left, as diſcouraged others from going thither; but the greateſt obſtacle the colony met with, was their continual wars with the natives, of which they have given us very large accounts.

The French kept poſſeſſion of this country till the 13th of September, 1759, when Quebec was ſurrendered to the generals Monkton and Townſhend, who commanded the Britiſh troops that had been deſtined for the expedition againſt it the preceding ſpring, under the command of general Wolfe, and on the 8th of September, 1760, all Canada was given up to the Engliſh by the capitulation ſigned at Montreal, by Monſ. de Vandreueil the French governor, and general Amherſt, and has ſince been confirmed to the Britiſh crown by the late treaty of peace concluded at Fontainbleau. Quebec, the metropolis, which is near the centre of the province, is ſituated in the 46th degree 55 minutes north latitude, and in 69 degrees 48 min. weſt longitude, and is bounded on the north-eaſt by the gulph of St. Laurence, and St. John's river; on the north-weſt by wild uninhabited lands; on the ſouth-weſt by the ſame; and ſoutherly by New-York, New-England, and Nova-Scotia; extending about 500 miles from the north-eaſt to the ſouth-weſt, and upwards of 200 miles in breadth.

Though the northern parts of Canada are ſituated in the temperate zone, yet the air is exceſſive ſharp, and their winter, which ſets in about the middle of November, and laſts till the middle of May, is ſo exceſſively ſevere, that their largeſt rivers and lakes are frozen over, and the country is generally covered with diſagreeable fogs: but notwithſtanding theſe inconveniences, the French boaſt very much of the fertility of Canada, and indeed where it is cultivated, as it is to the south, it yields Indian and other sorts of corn, peafe, beans, and great plenty of moſt kinds of herbs and vegetables. The trees and fruits are much the fame as in New-England, and the fame may be faid with refpect to animals; fo that with a reafonable degree of labour people may fubfift there tolerably well, and as they are not burdened with taxes, they live much at their eafe.

The produce of Canada confifts of furs, efpecially caftors, and in feveral kinds of fkins, which they purchafe from the natives; and there are exported from thence fome forts of drugs, planks, pipe ftaves, &c.

The greateſt part of the commerce of the country is carried on in light canoes made of bark, and proper for navigating their lakes and rivers, which are encumbered with rocks and interrupted with water-falls, that render them unfit for other veffels. In winter they make ufe of fledges, drawn either by horfes or dogs; and as thefe are proper for pafling over vaft tracts of fnow and ice, they enable them to continue their commerce with the Indians all the winter.

The city of Quebec is fituated upon the great river of St Laurence, at the diftance of about 100 leagues from its mouth. It is very large and ftrong, for befides a fortrefs, or kind of citadel in which the governor refides, the whole extent of the place is covered by a regular fortification, with feveral redoubts well furnifhed with artillery. The principal buildings in this city are the cathedral, the epifcopal palace, the Jefuits college, and feveral other religious houfes But if it be confidered that this is not only the capital, but almoſt the only town in New-France, it is not at all furprizing that thefe edifices are very magnificent; and that befides thefe it contains upwards of 15,000 well-built dwelling-houfes. The town of Montreal is ftrong by its fituation, is furrounded with a wall and a dry ditch, and is faid by fome authors to have as many inhabitants as Quebec. The Indians come thither in boats to fell their fkins, for the fake of which Montreal was built, and is now nearly as large and populous as Quebec.

As the manner in which the trade was carried on by the French is pretty fingular, we fhall here give it our readers: when the Indians in alliance with the French came thither to trade, their chief firft demanded audience of their governor general, and if he was not there, of the governor of Montreal, to whom he was with great ceremony admitted. This audience was generally given in a great fquare in the middle of the town; where a chair of ftate was placed for the governor, and the chiefs of the feveral Indian nations, took their places round him, with their pipes in their mouths. After a due filence, the eldeft chief of the Indians laid down his pipe, ftood up, and addreffed himfelf to the governor: he told him, that his brethren were come to vifit him, and to renew their ancient league and friendfhip with his nation: that having nothing in view but the care and advantage of the French, they had brought down with them good quantities of fkins and furs, being fenfible that the French could not obtain fo many, or fo good, if they did not bring them down to their fettlements; that they were fenfible how much they were efteemed in France, and knew that what they were to take in exchange, were but paltry things and of little value; but that their good friends the French might not be without furs they were content to deal with them; and therefore hoped, that in order to enable them to bring a greater plenty of them the next year, as well as to fall upon their enemies, they would let them have guns, powder, and ball, upon reafonable terms. At the clofe of this fpeech he laid a ftring of beads, and a bundle of skins at the governor's feet, and defired leave to fecure them a free and fair trade, and to protect them from robbers. Then he retired to his place, and took up his pipe again. The governor now affured them of his protection, and made them a prefent in return. The next day the trade began, and was foon over; by which the French gained very confiderably; but they were not allowed to fell either wine or brandy to the Indians, becaufe they were extremely apt to drink to excefs, and were then furious and mad, and at fuch times if they did any mifchief to one another, or to the French, they could fcarce be brought to give any fatisfaction; for they affirmed, it was the liquor, and not the man, that did the mifchief; and that it was unjuft to punifh a perfon for what he did when out of his fenfes. The other fettlements are fcattered at a great diftance from each other, along the banks of the rivers and lakes, between which a communication is kept up, by water, and by land carriage, where the cataracts render failing in the rivers impracticable, without immediate deftruction. The firft of thefe lakes of any confequence is Ontario, which is 180 leagues in circumference, and between 20 and 25 fathoms in depth. It receives feveral rivers, befides that of St. Laurence, and its coafts are pretty even and level. From this lake to that of Huron, there is a communication by means of the river Tanaouate, and by the affiftance of a land carriage of fix or eight leagues to the river of Toronto, and there is alfo a paffage from it to that of Erie up the river Niagara, though a dreadful cataract renders it neceffary to make part of the way by land. The lake of Erie with thofe of Ontario and Huron form a triangular peninfula. The lake of Erie which lies to the fouth, is called by the French by the name of Conti; it is 230 leagues in circumference, and every where affords the moft delightful profpects, its banks being adorned with oaks, elms, chefnut, walnut apple and plumb trees; and with vines that bear their fine clufters up to the very top. The ground is extremely level, and vaft quantities of deer and turkeys are to be found in the woods.

Before we take leave of this lake, it will be proper to give a particular defcription of the fall of Niagara. The whole ftream of this river runs with prodigious rapidity on its approaching a very deep precipice, whence it falls with a more terrible noife than that of thunder; being interrupted in its defcent by an ifland which runs along the middle, it rufhes from thence into the bed of the river at the bottom, where it raifes a mift which rifes as high as the clouds, and may be feen at fifteen miles diftance, when in fine weather it forms a moft beautiful rainbow. The rapidity of this river above the defcent is fo great for near two leagues, that it violently hurries down the wild beafts that endeavour to pafs it in order to feed on the other fide, cafting them down above 150 feet. At the bottom of the cataract, the waters boil and foam in a furprizing manner, and ftill continue their courfe with great impetuofity, while the banks are fo prodigioufly high, that a fpectator can fcarcely look on the water below without trembling. The lake of Huron, which has a communication with that of Erie, is about 400 leagues in circumference, and among feveral iflands has one called Manitoualan, which is about twenty leagues long and ten broad. On the north-weft of this lake is the bay of Toronto, which is above twenty leagues long and fifteen broad at its mouth. This bay receives a river that fprings from a little lake of the fame name, and forms feveral cataracts. From the above fmall lake is a paffage by land to the river of Tanaoute, which falls into Lake Frontiniac.

On the north-weft of the lake of Huron is a channel that has a communication with the Illenois lake, which is alfo of confiderable extent.

The Superior or Upper Lake, has alfo a communication with that of Huron by a channel, that on the north-weft extends to Huron lake, and this Upper Lake is computed to be 500 leagues in circumference, including the windings of the creeks and little gulphs. All thefe large lakes abound in fifh, and are expofed to ftorms and tempefts. This laft has fome pretty large iflands, that abound with elks and wild affes.

CHAPTER II.

A defcription of Ifle Royal or Cape Breton.

THIS ifland was very early difcovered by the Englifh, and was always reckoned a part of Nova-Scotia, for that very charter which conftituted that extenfive country a diftinct province, included Cape Breton in exprefs terms. This was never difputed till after the treaty of Utrecht; though the French had fettled there as well as in Nova-Scotia; but by that treaty the French confented to deliver it up to the Englifh; yet notwithftanding Queen Anne ordered the Duke of Queenfbury, her Ambaffador at the court of France, to declare that fhe looked upon that ifland as a part of the ancient territory of Nova-Scotia, the French were fuffered to keep poffeffion of it, and as they reaped great advantage from its fituation, both with refpect to the trade of Canada and the large fifheries carried on at this ifland, they foon erected fortifications at a very large expence, and the greateft encouragement was given to thofe who would fettle there. However in 1745 it was taken by the New-England men, with very little affiftance from Great-Britain; but was given up by the treaty of Aix-la Chapelle.

That peace was no fooner concluded than the French diftreffing the new colony at Halifax in Nova-Scotia, and attempting to hem in all the colonies on the continent by a chain of forts, the late war broke out, and Louifburgh, the capital, with the ifland of Cape-Breton, was taken by the Englifh, who landed in the fight of a numerous army, though oppofed by a chain of batteries; and after fcaling rocks that were thought inacceffible, drove the French from the coaft, and afterwards obliged the garrifon of Louifburgh to furrender prifoners of war : this conqueft was made on the 26th of July, 1758, by general Amherft, commander of 1100 land forces; with the train of artillery; and by admiral Bofcawen, with 23 fhips of war befides frigates; and a few days after, a part of the fleet made themfelves mafters of the ifland of St. John.

The ifland of Cape-Breton, or Ifle Royal, is fituated in between 45 and 47°. of north latitude, and forms with the ifland of Newfoundland, from whence it is diftant only about fifteen leagues, the entrance of the gulph of St. Laurence; the ftreight which feparates Cape Breton from Nova Scotia is about five leagues in length, one in breadth, and is called the paffage of Fronfac. The length of the ifland from the north-eaft to the fouth-weft is not quite fifty leagues. It is of a very irregular figure, and in fuch a manner cut through by lakes and rivers, that its two principal parts are held together, only by an ifthmus of about 800 paces in breadth; this neck of land feparates the bottom of Port Touloufe from feveral lakes, which are called Labrador. The lakes empty themfelves into the fea to the eaft, by two channels formed by the iflands of Verderronne and la Boularderie.

All its ports open to the east, turning a little to the south, and are within the space of 55 leagues, beginning at Port Dauphin and continuing to Port Touloufe, which is almost at the entrance of the passage of Fronsac. In all other parts it is difficult to find anchorage for small vessels in little creeks or among the islands. The northern coasts are very high and almost innaceffible, and it is difficult to land on the western coast, till you come to the passage of Fronsac, near which, as has been already observed, is Port Touloufe, formerly known by the name of St. Peter. This port is between a kind of gulph called little St. Peter's, and the island St. Peter opposite the islands Madame or Maurepas. From thence proceeding towards the south-east is the bay of Gaborie at twenty leagues distance from St. Peter's island. This bay is a league broad, between islands and rocks, and is two leagues deep, but it is not safe to come near the islands. The harbour of Louisburgh, formerly called English Harbour, is not above a league from the above bay, and is perhaps one of the finest in America. It is near four leagues in circumference, and has every where six or seven fathoms water. The entrance is not above 200 fathoms wide, and lies between two small islands. The town of Louisburgh is situated on the south-west side, and is pretty strongly fortified with as much regularity as the situation will admit. It has a good rampart, with irregular bastions, a dry ditch, a covert way, with an excellent glacis, and before two of the curtains is a ravelin, with a bridge to the sally-ports; but the chief strength of the place consists in the thickness of the walls, and the impassable morasses which extend from the foot of the glacis to a considerable distance. When Louisburgh was taken from the French on the 26th of June, 1758, it was defended by 231 pieces of cannon. At that time the town consisted of only several narrow lanes, and had hardly a tolerable house in it, except the governor's and intendant's, which were built with stone and brick, without the least elegance ; the best buildings in the place were the magazines, a convent, and an hospital ; and few of the other houses were much better than boarded cottages one story high.

The sea round the island is subject to violent storms of wind, with snow and sleet, and such fogs that it is frequently impossible to see the length of a ship. But what is still more extraordinary, these fogs will in the space of one frosty night case over the rigging of ships with such thick ice, as to render them impossible to be worked till it is beaten off: the quantity beat off from only one of the English ships employed in the last conquest of this island, was computed to amount to six or eight tons weight ; yet this amazing quantity was all congealed on the night of the 5th of May, when warmer weather might have been expected. All these circumstances shew the advantages of an island filled with such a number of excellent ports situated in such a tempestuous sea.

The climate of the island is pretty much the same with that of Quebec, but mists and fogs are more frequent. A great part of the land is but very indifferent, it however produce oaks of a prodigious size, pines for masts, and all sorts of timber fit for carpenters work. The most common sorts are, besides those already mentioned, cedar, oak, ash, maple, aspin, wild cherry, beech, and plane tree. It produce some sorts of fruits, particularly apples, with pulse, herbs, and roots. They have wheat and all other kinds of grain, with some hemp and flax as good as any in Canada.

It is observable that the mountains may be cultivated up to the tops; that the good soil always inclines towards the south, and that the island is covered from the north and north-west winds by the mountains of Nova-Scotia, that border upon the river St. Laurence. Thefe mountains abound with coal, and there is alfo plafter here in great abundance.

There are here great numbers of fowls, and particularly partridges, almoft as large as pheafants, which they refemble in their feathers.

The ifland was full of deer, and had vaft numbers of moofe-deer, but they are now fcarce; there are here alfo animals brought from Europe, as horfes, horned cattle, hogs, fheep, goats and poultry. All the lakes, rivers and bays abound with excellent fifh in the greateft plenty, and what is got by hunting, fhooting, and fifhing, is fufficient to maintain the inhabitants a good part of the year. It is faid that there is no part of the world where more cod fifh is caught, nor fuch good conveniency for drying it; and the fifhery of the fea-pike, porpoifes, &c. is carried on with great eafe.

CHAPTER. III.

An account of the fettlement made by the French in the Leeward Iflands, and their proceedings, in them.

WE have already given an account of the fettlement of the ifland of St. Chriftopher by the Englifh and the French, who lived in the greateft harmony together; of the French flying from that ifland, upon the landing of the Spaniards; and of the Englifh being driven from their fettlements, as well as of the return both of the Englifh and French.

Mr. Defnambue the French governor, obferving that the Englifh colony had made themfelves mafters of feveral of the adjacent iflands, refolved to fend fome of the principal perfons in his colony to

France to procure fupplies, chiefly with a view of fettling the ifland of Guadaloupe. Among thofe fent over, was one Mr. Olive, a bold enterprizing man, who had nothing in view but his own intereft, and having fome notice of the governor's defign, he refolved to fupplant him. For that purpofe he entered into a treaty with one Mr. Du-Pleffis, and fome other merchants of Dieppe; who forming a company for the fupport of the fcheme he had laid, thefe two were fent over governors with joint authority to the ifland of Guadaloupe; where they arrived with about 500 men, on the 8th of June 1635.

However, thefe governors, in the very beginning of their enterprize, committed two miftakes; they fettled on the wrong fide of the ifland, where the foil was very bad, and quarrelled with the natives, before the colony was well able to fubfift without them. The bad confequences with which thefe errors were attended, foon broke the heart of Mr. Du Pleffis; when Mr. Olive being left fole governor, his haughtinefs and pride had certainly brought the colony to ruin, if he had not fallen blind. Upon this, the company fent over Mr. Aubert, a very difcreet and prudent gentleman, who in a few years time, put the affairs of this colony into order, and fo effectually eftablifhed it, that the Inhabitants have fubfifted very happily ever fince. But notwithftanding Mr. Defnambue's having the misfortune to fee Guadaloupe thus taken out of his hands; yet before his death he had the pleafure of fettling the ifland of Martinico, of which he by that means became proprietor, and of leaving it to his family by his laft will.

In the mean time, cardinal Richelieu, being raifed to the miniftry, thought proper to fend over a perfon of diftinction, to take upon himfelf the government of the whole ifland; and accordingly made choice of Mr. De Poincy, a knight of Malta, whom he fent with the title of governor and lieutenant general of the iflands in America.

This gentleman embarked at Dieppe on the 15th of January 1639, and after a fhort paffage arrived at Martinico, from whence he went to Guadaloupe, and afterwards to St. Chriftopher's. He was very fevere in the execution of his authority againſt thofe who were for haftily making eftates at the public expence, but was extremely kind to the induftrious part of the inhabitants, who were willing to let their private fortunes depend on the flourifhing ftate of the colonies. He caufed churches to be built in all thefe iflands, took care to have the priefts well maintained, but would have no monafteries or monks. He eftablifhed an excellent form of juftice, granted commiffions to privateers, and hanged up pirates with very little ceremony. His concern for the public good was fo apparent, that he became in a manner abfolute; and the people being fenfible that he had nothing in view but their intereft, obeyed his orders with the utmoft alacrity. In fhort, he changed the whole face of affairs in that part of the world, fettled defert iflands, and though he made hundreds of people rich and happy, contented himfelf with the pleafure of doing it, without making any fortune of his own.

However, during the difturbances that arofe in France after the death of cardinal Richelieu, the colony funk by the ill management of the company; and in the year 1651, the chevalier De Poincy purchafed the iflands of St. Chriftopher, St. Bartholemew, St. Martin, and Santa Cruz for the order of Malta; and in the fame manner other iflands were difpofed of to fuch as would give any thing for them; which foon brought the affairs of the French in that part of the world into a very ftrange fituation. When the Dutch, taking notice of the condition things were in, eftablifhed magazines at Flushing and Middleburgh for West-India commodities, and annually employed in the trade of the French islands upwards of 100 ships.

This continued till about the year 1664, when a new company being set up in France, they, with the assistance of the government, purchased back from the nights of Malta and the other proprietors, the rights they had acquired; and having put an end to the Dutch trade, brought the commerce of the colonies once more into their own channel. But after possessing their grant ten years, they began to oppress the people, in such a manner that the ministry thought proper to interpose, and in 1680 every thing was settled so as to render the diligent and industrious secure of reaping the fruits of their labours.

After this general veiw of the manner in which the French islands were settled, we shall proceed to a very concise account of the islands themselves.

Martinico is situated in 14°. 30'. north latitude and in 61°. west longitude. It is about thirteen leagues in length and seven in breadth. From the inland parts which are mountainous, fall numerous rivulets, which after watering the country, flow into the sea. It has several bays well fortified; the chief of which is the great bay of Port-Royal, the capital of the island, and the bay of St. Pierre, a large town about seven leagues from it, to the north-west. This island was inhabited by Indians when the French first attempted a settlement, in the year 1635, and many battles were fought between them and the natives with various success; but at last the French overpowered, and cruelly extirpated the ancient inhabitants. The governor of the Caribbee islands resides there, and it is the seat of the sovereign council, whose jurisdiction extends not only throughout the Antilles, but over the French fettlements in St. Domingo and Tortuga.

This ifland was on the 19th of January 1759, attacked by a fquadron of ten men of war befides frigates, &c. under the command of Commodore Moore, and a body of land forces, commanded by General Hopfon; but after obtaining fome advantages, the troops and failors re-embarked and failed to Guadaloupe. It was however, taken by the Englifh on the 13th of February 1762.

Guadaloupe the largeft of the Caribbee iflands, is fituated in 16°. north latitude and 61°. weft longitude, about thirty leagues from Martinico. It is remarkable for the height of its clifts and mountains. It is about fifteen leagues in length and twelve in breadth, divided into two parts by a fmall arm of the fea or narrow paffage, through which no fhip can venture, and the inhabitants crofs over in a ferry from one part to the other. The country to the weft is called Baffe Terre, where ftands the metropolis of the fame name, and where the citadel and chief ftrength of the ifland lies; the part to the eaft is called Grande Terre. The French began to fettle this ifland about the year 1632, but being unacquainted with the nature of the foil, they were in danger of ftarving, and afterwards the planters were almoft ruined by their divifions; but fince the beginning of the prefent century, the inhabitants have flourifhed fo much, that they make more fugar than any of the Britifh iflands except Jamaica. The foil is rich, and efpecially at Grande Terre fo fertile, that the canes are cut fix times without replanting. The far greateft part of what are called Martinico fugars, are the real produce of Guadaloupe, the inhabitants of which are obliged to fend them to Martinico, before they could be tranfported to France. On this account the French fortified it with feveral forts and redoubts, which were in so good a condition in 1702, when Admiral Bembo made a descent upon it with a considerable body of land forces, that he did not think proper to attack them, but was satisfied with destroying many of their plantations and open villages.

We have already observed that in 1759, a fleet of ten men of war besides frigates and bomb-ketches, under the command of Commodore Moore, with a body of land forces commanded by General Hopson, after making an unsuccessful attack on Martinico, sailed for Guadaloupe. This squadron began to bombard the town and citadel of Basse Terre on the 23d of January; the officers and sailors behaved with the utmost intrepidity, and notwithstanding many batteries erected on the shore, the houses and churches were that night every where in flames, and the powder of the magazines blown about the enemies ears. The next day the English landed, and found both the town and citadel abandoned, but the island was far from being taken. The French with their armed negroes threw up intrenchments on the mountains, and bravely resolved to defend themselves as long as possible. Soon after General Hopson dying, the command devolved on Major General Barrington. The English were harrassed by perpetual alarms and fatigued with constant duty; they however, gained one pass after another, and still advanced alert in the hour of caution, and invincible whenever they attacked. They frequently suffered from concealed fires out of the woods, and from lurking parties of armed negroes, that could not be discovered. At length the French Governor finding all resistance in vain, sent a flag of truce; and the articles of capitulation, by which Guadaloupe was surrendered to the English, were signed on the first of May 1759.

Within the same month Marigalante, four little islands called the Santos, Deseada, and Petit Terre also surrendered to the English. Marigalante is about twenty leagues in length and about fifteen in breadth, and is situated in 16°. north latitude, a little to the south-west of Guadaloupe. The French began to send colonies thither about the year 1647, and after having several wars, expelled the natives, and remained in the peaceable possession of this island, till May 19, 1759.

Granada is twenty-five leagues in circumference and has several good bays and harbours, some of which are fortified. It is situated in 11°. 51'. north latitude, about thirty leagues south-west of Barbadoes, and about the same distance north of Andalusia.

The smaller Caribbee Islands belonging to the French, are St. Bartholomew's, which is about ten leagues north of St. Christopher's, and was taken in the year 1689, by the English under the command of Sir Timothy Thornhill; but restored to the French at the peace of Ryswick. By the late peace in 1763, Martinico, Guadaloupe, Marigalante, St. Bartholomew, and Deseada, were restored to France; but Granada, and some small islands near it, called the Granadillas, or Granadines, were ceded to Great-Britain.

As sugar is the staple commodity of these islands, it is proper to give a short account of the quantities raised in them. In Martinico it is computed, that the inhabitants make one year with another, 10,000 hogsheads of about 600 weight each: In Guadaloupe are made about 40,000 hogsheads, and in the other islands about 1000 hogsheads altogether. These islands also draw a considerable profit from cacao or the chocolate nut, and from ginger, cassia, and pimento, which is what is called Jamaica pepper or all-spice, of which they export considerable quantities. The inhabitants also send home rocou for the use of dyers, and a variety of medicinal gums, and wet sweetmeats of several kinds. These islands likewise produce several sorts of valuable woods used in dying, in-laying, and cabinet-work; as rose-wood, which when wrought and polished, has a very beautiful appearance, as well as a fine smell. The Indian wood is also of the same nature, and the iron-wood, so called from its excessive hardness, is preferable either to cedar or cypress. They have great quantities of Brasil wood, brasiletto, fustic or yellow wood, and green ebony, which is used both by the cabinet makers and dyers. To these commodities may be added, tortoise-shell and raw hides.

But though these islands produce so many rich and valuable commodities, yet they stand in need of very large supplies of various kinds of necessaries, without which they could not possibly subsist, such as horses and cattle of all kinds; dry fish, corn, roots, and all sorts of lumber, of which they receive considerable quantities from North America. Mr. Savary observes, that the goods exported from France to these islands, annually, amounted to about four millions of livres, or near 200,000l. sterling; for which they brought home nearly double the value in West-India commodities.

CHAPTER IV.

The manner in which the French first formed settlements in the islands of Tortuga and Hispaniola or St. Domingo, &c.

WE shall now proceed to the island of St. Domingo, which was discovered by Columbus in his first voyage in 1492, and called by him Hispaniola; but he afterwards building a city to which he gave the name of St. Domingo, in honour of his father Dominic, the name was first extended to that quarter, and at length the whole iſland was called St. Domingo; by which it is as well known as by that of Hiſpaniola. Though this iſland is reckoned only 400 leagues in circumference, yet if all the creeks, bays and inlets be meaſured, it will be found to amount to at leaſt 600. It is at preſent the moſt fruitful, and much the pleaſanteſt iſland in the Weſt-Indies; for the foreſts are of vaſt extent, and the trees are taller and larger, the fruit more beautiful and better taſted than in the other iſlands: the ſavannahs or meadows are alſo vaſtly extenſive, and contain innumerable herds of black cattle that belong to the country, as alſo wild horſes and wild hogs produced from thoſe animals brought over by the Spaniards. Scarce is there any place in the world better watered, by ſmall brooks and navigable rivers, all of which are full of fiſh; add to this, that there were at firſt found great quantities of gold, ſilver, and copper, which have failed ſince the deſtruction of the natives. This with many other reaſons concured at length to induce many of the Spaniards to leave the iſland, particularly the ſeverity of the government; for the ſovereign council of the Indies being eſtabliſhed at St. Domingo, the inhabitants were kept within ſtricter bounds than in other places: the immenſe riches gained by their countrymen, induced numbers to forſake this iſland, in hopes of coming in for a ſhare of thoſe treaſures: the great demands for people to maintain the Spaniſh conqueſts on the continent; their cruelly deſtroying the Indians, which rendered them unable without fatigue to cultivate their lands; for as yet the uſe of negroes had not reached the Spaniſh ſettlements; and the deſcents of the Engliſh and French on the weſtern part of the iſland; theſe ſeveral circumſtances by degrees induced the Spaniards to abandon all the country between Monte Chriſto and Cape Mongou.

The manner in which the French settled themselves being very singular, we shall give it our readers. The Buccaneers who were originally no more than hunters, fixed themselves upon the coast of Hispaniola, to enjoy the advantage of killing black cattle, and selling their skins. These having built some villages, erected several fortifications for their defence, while others laid out plantations, in which they raised tobacco and other valuable commodities Mean while the privateers furnished by commissions from the French governor of Petit Guaves, to cruize upon the Spaniards, with persons on board of all nations, frequently entered the ports, in order to careen and victual their ships; and these three sorts of people became extremely useful to each other; for while the hunters and other settlers furnished provisions and hides in vast quantities, the privateers brought in prizes of great value, and spent their money freely, and by enriching, increased the number of the Inhabitants; so that in a short time, the French extended their settlements all along the south-west coast of St. Domingo. In the mean time Tortuga became thorougly planted, and the tobacco raised there being very good, was most esteemed. With respect to this last island, it is to be obseved, that the Buccaneers had formed a settlement there, which had been destroyed by the Spaniards with inexorable cruelty in the year 1638. However the Buccaneers returned, and were re-settled by the English under Capt. Willis, by whose courage and conduct they were soon in no fear of being disturbed by the Spaniards. But they did not continue long in this situation, for Mr. De Poincy sending thither Mr. Vasseur, to secure that small island for the French, the Buccaneers of that nation, settled in the island, joined him, and Capt. Willis was obliged to abandon the place, with the troops under his command; but though this put the French in possession, they were for many years harassed by the Spaniards, who more than once drove them out of the island; but being constantly supported from their own islands, and joined by the adventurers of all nations, they not only effectually fixed themselves there, but made the above settlements at St. Domingo, and in 20 years time became so strong that the Spaniards were glad to live upon good terms with them.

But to proceed; both the Spaniards and the English complained loudly of the conduct of the French governors, under colour of whose commissions, the Buccaneers committed great disorders, and in time of peace, took ships of all nations; but the French gave good words, promised redress, and suffered the governors to go on after their own manner, as they found it drew numbers of people to their settlements, and was likely to secure them the western part of St. Domingo: They however did not gain a legal possession of that part of Hispaniola, till the year 1697, when the Spaniards yielded to them one half of the island by the treaty of Ryswick, by which the boundaries were fixed by a line drawn across the country from north to south; so that the French enjoy all the western half of St. Domingo.

For many years the principal trade of this island consisted in tobacco, in which it is said there have been employed from 60 to 100 ships; but upon the establishment of an exclusive farm of this commodity in France, the trade began to decline, and at last sunk to nothing. They then fell to planting of sugar, and though they at first met with some difficulties, yet in a short time it became the staple commodity of the island. This is said to be the best sugar made in the West-Indies, and generally sells for three or four shillings a hundred more than the sugar brought from any of their other islands; which has occasioned a surprising progress in the cultivation of that valuable commodity. The principal place the French possess on the north side of the island is Cape Francois, which is happily situated and has a very good port. The town is large and well peopled, and is supposed to contain 4000 white, and as many negroe inhabitants. On the west side, they have the town and port Leogane, which is the seat of the government, besides which they have several other considerable towns and good ports. The number of people are computed at 30,000 whites, and 100,000 mulattoes.

Sugar had been so greatly cultivated by the French, that in the year 1726 they had 200 sugar works in the island, which were computed to yield one with another 400 hogsheads of sugar every year, each hogshead containing about 500 weight; so that it appears from this computation, that the sugar of this island is annually worth near 200,000l. and the French indigo brought from thence, is said to produce near half as much. They also raise cacaos, ginger and cotton; coffee grows there very well, and some maintain that cinnamon, clove, and nutmeg trees, might be raised there; but the great profit the inhabitants at present make of their sugar and indigo prevents their attempting new improvements.

On the south side of the French part of St. Domingo is Avache, a little island at about twelve leagues distance from the continent. It is only about eight leagues in compass, but it has a very good soil, and two or three tolerable ports, one of which is capable of receiving ships of 300 tons. It lies very conveniently for carrying on a trade with the Spanish colonies on the continent of America.

Cayenne, an island situated in 5° north latitude and in 53° west longitude, was settled by the French, in the year 1625. It lies close to the continent of Guiana, from whence it is only separated by the rivers Ovia on the eaſt, and the Cayenne on the weſt, from which laſt it takes its name. It is 18 or 20 leagues in circumference, and is about ſeven leagues long and three broad. As it ſtands high on the coaſt, it at a diſtance ſeems part of the continent. It has three principal capes, thoſe of Fort St. Lewis, Seperon, and Matiuri, and its banks are moſtly covered with man-groves, which grow in ſalt water, and from the roots other trees riſe up without end, ſo cloſe and interwoven with each other, that, in ſome parts of the iſland, a man may walk ſeveral miles on them without touching the ground. In ſeveral parts there is much meadow and paſture ground, but the reſt is low and marſhy, eſpecially in the middle, ſo as to be almoſt impaſſable.

The iſland is rendered uncomfortable by the long rainy ſeaſon which happens every year; by the ſcorching cloſe air, both by day and night, and by the vapours exhaled from the ſwampy grounds, which occaſion many diſorders. The inhabitants are alſo continually tormented with gnats, flies, worms, ants, bugs and other vermin, which altogether render the place very diſagreeable. The ſoil produces plenty of ſugar canes, which, though ſmall and ſhort-jointed, yield very plentifully. It alſo abounds in ananas, or pine-apples, oranges, lemons, figs, papaias, ebony, and violet wood, and alſo in indigo and cotton, as well as in ſeveral ſorts of American and European grain. The principal four-footed animals for food are, hogs, wild boars, deer, and hares; for large cattle can ſcarce live there. The fowl are, carion turkeys, cocks and hens, flamingos, which are an exceeding tall bird, and appear in flocks like wild geeſe; large wild ducks with red tufts on their heads; pigeons, ring-doves, wood-cocks, ortolans, nightingales, parrots, paroquets, and other birds; but the inhabitants chiefly ſubſiſt on turtle. Among the reptiles there are lizards, camelions, and ferpents of a monſtrous fize, fome of which are faid to be above 25 feet long. There are alfo many fmall ones.

The principal town is alfo called Cayenne, and ſtands on the weſt part of the iſland in an advantageous fituation, nature and art having equally contributed to forify it. The fortifications are an irregular hexagon, and confiſt of a dry ditch, and a rampart with feveral batteries mounted with cannon, within which ſtands above 200 houſes, formed into two ſtreets. On the north eaſt part of the town, the jeſuits have a little chapel that ſtands in an open place, and has before it a grove of lemon trees. On a a pretty ſteep eminence is the fort of St. Lewis de Caperoux on the fea fide, mounted with 42 iron guns, and commonly defended by four companies of regular troops. The weakeſt places of the iſland are alfo defended by batteries.

The next town in the iſland is Armire, which is about three leagues diſtant to the eaſt-ward, but is fmall and thinly peopled: the jeſuits have however a chapel there. Theſe are the moſt remarkable towns in the iſland.

The poorer fort, befides turtle, eat the fleſh of the manatee or fea-cow, which is brought ready falted from the river of the Amazons, whither feveral of the principal inhabitants fends barks, to buy it of the Indians for beads, knives, linen, toys, and iron tools. The men in theſe barks take falt with them, and on their entering the river of the Amazons, the Indians employed in the manatee fiſhery go on board, and having taken the falt, run up the river in canoes, to catch the manatees, which they cut in pieces, and having faited them, return to their barks.

The trade carried on with France, chiefly confiſts in proviſions, as falt-meat, flour, wine, brandy, linen, stuffs, shoes, and other wearing apparel, tools, and small wares; in return for which they export sugar, dying-woods, and for the most part the same kind of commodities as the leeward islands. The number of whites exclusive of the soldiers, are said to amount to about 1500, and the whole number of people, including the soldiers and slaves, is said to be about 3000.

CHAPTER V.

Mr. De la Salle attempts to discover the great river Mississipi, and is murdered by his own soldiers; its being afterwards settled by M. d'Ibberville, and the affair turned into a bubble, &c.

Some of the French had already proceeded from the rivers and lakes of Canada, to the river Mississipi, when Mr. Robert Cavaler de la Salle, conceived the design of finding out a passage from the gulph of Mexico to the South-Sea, by means of the river Mississipi; for though this great river does not run that way, he was in hopes that by sailing up it, he should discover one that did. In pursuance of this plan he laid his proposals before the French king; when his project being approved, he was supplied with four vessels, a man of war of 56 guns, a large fly-boat, a small frigate, and a ketch. This squadron was commanded by Mr. Beaujeau, who was victualled for a year, and Mr. de la Salle had under his command 150 landmen, who were to settle in the country, and twelve gentlemen volunteers; it being proposed to plant a colony and build a good fort in the gulph of Mexico, which was to serve both as a magazine, and as a place of retreat, in case of misfortunes either by sea or land.

With this fquadron Mr. de la Salle failed from Rochelle on the 5th of Auguft 1684, and paffing by Martinico and Guadaloupe, took in frefh provifions and water, with feveral volunteers. The ketch being feparated by a ftorm, was taken by the Spaniards, but the other three veffels arrived about the middle of February 1685, in the bay of Spirito Santo, and at about the diftance of ten leagues found a large bay, which Mr. de la Salle miftook for the right arm of the Miffiffippi, and called it St. Lewis. Having founded this bay, he found it deep but narrow, and therefore exprefsly forbid the captain of the fly-boat's attempting to enter it, without his having on board the pilot of the frigate, who was an experienced mariner, and to unlade his guns into the pinnace; but the captain neglecting thefe orders, ran the fly-boat upon the fands, where fhe ftuck faft.

Mr. de la Salle was at this time on fhore, and being in pain for the fafety of the veffel, was going on board in order to fave her, when he was prevented by the appearance of about 120 of the natives advancing to attack him. He immediately put his men in a pofture of defence, but the noife alone of his drums put the Indians to flight. Mr. de la Salle then following them, prefented the calumet of peace, which they accepted, and went along with him to his camp; where having entertained them, he fent them back with fome prefents. With this treatment they were fo well pleafed, that the next day they returned his civility, by bringing provifions and concluding an alliance with him, which might have proved of great advantage, had it not been interrupted by an accident. For as they were unlading the fly-boat in order to endeavour to get her off the fands, a pack of blankets fell into the fea, and was driven on fhore by the waves. This being found by the Indians, Mr. de la Salle fent to demand it in a very civil manner; but they shewing some reluctance at parting with it, the officer rashly threatened to kill them, unless they restored it immediately. At this they were both frightened and incensed, and resolving to be revenged for the affront, assembled in the night in order to attack the camp. The centinel being asleep, they advanced as near as they pleased, and discharging their arrows, killed four officers, and wounded two of the gentlemen volunteers; upon which the French running to their arms fired upon them and put them to flight, though none of them were wounded; but the next day they killed two of Mr. de la Salle's men, whom they found asleep.

In the mean time the fly-boat was unloaded, but was too far sunk to be got off. At length Mr. Beaujeau seeing all the goods and merchandize landed, and the fort almost finished, sailed for France, and Mr. de la Salle having left 100 men under the command of Mr. de Moranger his nephew, marched with the remainder, who amounted to fifty persons, into the country in order to the discover the Mississippi.

In the mean time, a new fort was built in a very advantageous post, defended by twelve pieces of cannon, and the old fort destroyed; but the Indians still killing the French, whenever they got them in their power, and Mr. de la Salle, seeing no method of concluding an alliance with them, resolved to make war upon them in order to oblige them to come to an accommodation. He therefore set out again from the fort on the 13th of October, with 60 stout men, armed with pieces of wood on their breasts to defend them from the arrows of the Indians. He had not advanced far, before he found them encamped, and after several skirmishes, in which he killed and wounded a great number of them, he returned with many prisoners. He then found that though he had ordered the captain of the frigate to fuffer none of his men to land, yet pleafed with the delightful appearance of the country, he had gone on fhore with fix of his beft men, in a canoe, in which leaving their arms, they went into a meadow, where falling afleep, they were killed by the Indians, who broke the canoe in pieces, and this accident had put the whole colony into great confternation.

However, at length, Mr. de la Salle fet out again with 20 men, in order to difcover the mouth of the river Miffiffippi: continual rains now rendered the ways very bad; but at length finding what he imagined to be that river, he fortified a poft on its bank, and leaving part of his men, returned to the fort, delighted with his difcovery. He had there the mortification to find that the frigate, the only veffel he had left, and in which he intended to fail to St. Domingo for frefh fupplies, had, by the negligence of the pilot, run a-ground, and was dafhed to pieces, by which all his men were drowned, except the Sieur Chefdeville, the captain, and four failors, and all the goods, provifions and tools loft.

Their affairs being thus ruined, they had no other way to return to Europe than by that of Canada. Mr. de la Salle therefore refolved to undertake that dangerous journey with 20 men, and an Indian called Nicana, who had formerly attended him into France, and had given him the greateft proofs of his affection. Mr. Cavalier, Mr. de Moranger, and father Anaftafius, alfo defired to be of the company. They took with them powder and fhot, a quantity of glafs beads, and two kettles for boiling their meat, and then fet out in order to find the Illenois river.

Having marched for three days to the north-eaft, they entered a fine champaign country, and were met by feveral men on horfeback, with boots, fpurs and faddles, which fhewed they had fome communication with the Spaniards. They then marched two days over vast meadows, where they saw such numbers of wild cows, that the smallest herds consisted of about 400. Ten of these cattle they killed, and stopping to rest themselves for two days dressed their meat, that it might serve them for the remainder of their journey. Mr. de la Salle here altered his course, and marched directly to the eastward. One day Nicana the Indian crying out that he was bit by a rattle-snake, and was a dead man, they immediately gave him some Orvietan, and having scarified the wound, applied to it the salt of vipers, by which he was recovered; but this accident made him stop for several days.

At length passing through a delightful country, they came to the settlements of the Cenis, one of the largest and most populous nations in America. These extended twenty leagues in length, and all that space was intersperfed with hamlets. Among these people they found several things which they must have obtained from the Spaniards, as pieces of eight, silver spoons, clothes and horses, particularly a bull from the Pope, exempting the Spaniards of New-Mexico, from fasting in summer; horses were so common among them that they exchanged one for an axe, and from these people they learned that the Spaniards resided at the distance of six days journey.

Having staid several days among the Cenis, they continued their march through the country of the Nailonis, where Mr. de la Salle, and Mr. Moranger his nephew, being seized with a violent fever, they were obliged to stay two months; which disappointed all their measures. Though they had not advanced above 150 leagues in a direct line, their powder was almost spent, some of the men had deserted to the Indians, and others were ready to follow them; which Mr. de la Salle considering, resolved to return back to Fort Lewis, and this resolution being approved by the whole body, they marched back to their camp, where they arrived on the 17th of October 1686, and were received with the greatest joy by their companions.

Mr. de la Salle having staid two months at the fort, during which he caused new entrenchments to be made, and took all possible precautions for the security of the colony, set out again with 20 men, his brother, his two nephews, father Anastasius, and the Sieur Joutel, with a resolution not to return till he had found the Illenois river. He began his march on the 11th of January 1687, and having crossed several rivers that were much swelled with rains, came into a fine hunting country where he and his company staid several days to refresh themselves. He there sent out Mr. de Moranger his nephew, his valet, and seven or eight men to a place where Nicana, the faithful Indian, had laid up a stock of beef, in order to get it smoked and dryed, that they might carry it along with them to prevent their being obliged to retard their journey by frequently hunting for provisions; but Mr. de Moranger, the valet, and Nicana, never returned, they being murdered by some of the Frenchmen, who had plotted their destruction.

Mr. de la Salle being at two leagues distance from the place where these murders were committed, was surprized at his nephew's not returning, and apprehending his being seized by the Indians, desired father Anastasius to go with him in search of his nephew, taking two Indians along with them. When they had got about two leagues, they observed some of the French by the waterside, and going up to them, enquired for Mr. de Moranger, on which they pointed to the place where he lay; and two of the villains lying hid in the grass, one of them shot Mr. de la Salle through the head. Thus died this gentleman, who was diſtinguiſhed by his bravery and conduct, and deſerved a much better fate.

Father Anaſtaſius having performed the laſt offices for this unhappy gentleman, went in ſearch of Mr. Cavalier, Mr. de la Salle's brother, whom he found in a hut, and was ſoon after followed by the murderers, who rudely entered, and having ſeized all they could find, were ſoon after joined by the reſt of thoſe who had engaged in the conſpiracy. It was agreed to ſave the lives of theſe gentlemen on account of their being eccleſiaſtics, and to proceed to the nation of the Cenis. The murderer of Mr. de la Salle was choſen their leader, but ſoon after a conteſt ariſing between him, and one Hans, a German, the party divided, and Hans taking his opportunity, ſhot the murderer to the heart.

Upon their arrival among the Cenis, they found them ready to march againſt their enemies; upon which Hans and ſeveral others joined them, while the reſt ſtaid in the country: but they were no ſooner gone than father Anaſtaſius, the Sieur Joutel, and ſome others having procured horſes and two Indians for their guides, ſet out and proceeding to the north-eaſt, on the 5th of September, reached the mouth of the river Illenois, diſtant 100 leagues from Fort Crevecoeur, to which they proceeded, and were received at the fort with the greateſt reſpect by the commander; whence being conducted to Quebec, they ſailed for France on the 20th of Auguſt 1688.

About ſeven years after, Mr. d'Ibberville, who had already performed great things, undertook to execute what Mr. de la Salle had promiſed, and being encouraged by the court, carried over a number of people to the mouth of the Miſſiſſippi, where he founded the firſt colony the French ever had on that river. He provided the men with every thing neceſſary for their ſubſiſtence, and having erected a ſtrong fort for their protection againſt the Indians, returned to France, in order to obtain ſupplies. The king being extremely pleaſed with his ſucceſs, promiſed him all the aſſiſtance he could deſire, and he was ſoon in a condition to put to ſea again. His ſecond voyage was as fortunate as the firſt; but he fell ſick, and died as he was preparing for the third, which might have proved of fatal conſequence to the colony, had it not been for the generoſity and public ſpirit of a private gentleman, who having received from the government authority to act, undertook to ſupport it at his own expence.

In the grant of Louiſiana made to Mr. Crouzat by Lewis XIV. in the year 1712, it is ſaid to be bounded by the river and lake of Illenois on the north; by New Mexico on the weſt; by the gulph of Mexico on the ſouth; and by Carolina on the eaſt; though indeed the weſt part of this country belongs to the Spaniards, and the eaſt to the Engliſh, and by patents the latter have obtained from the crown, are empowered to extend the plantations of Carolina as far to the weſtward as they think proper.

Mr Crouzat's grant did not ſubſiſt long; for there being a neceſſity of having ſome plauſible pretence for changing the face of public affairs in France, the ſettlement of this country was thought the moſt convenient, and all imaginable pains were taken to repreſent it as a paradiſe, and a place from whence inexhauſtible treaſures might be drawn, provided due encouragement could be obtained from the government. For this purpoſe it was neceſſary to erect a new company, to make way for which Mr. Crouzat was prevailed upon to reſign his grant. Hence aroſe the noiſe that was made about the Miſſiſſipi, and the romantic ſtories of the fertility of the banks of that great river, and the incredible wealth that would flow from thence. This bubble ſhook the credit of France, and made way for the bubbles formed for the south sea company in England.

The Miſſiſſippi, or river St. Lewis, as it is sometimes called, is said by the French to rise in the north-west part of Canada, taking its course to the south-east, but in 45°. turns almost due south, and in that direction continues its course till it falls into the gulph of Mexico in 30°. north latitude, and 95°. of west longitude. It is swelled into a very large deep river by the streams of four or five considerable rivers that fall into it, both from the east and west; and some French authors maintain, that it has a gentle stream and is navigable for large vessels, almost up to its source; but other French writers as well as some English seamen, affirm, that it has a very rapid stream, that in several parts it has cataracts which obstruct its navigation, and that there are such shoals at its mouth, that large ships cannot approach it. In short this river is full of islands, which being filled with trees, look like groves rising out of the water, and afford a very agreeable prospect. And on its banks are woods, meadows, and hills.

The soil in the neighbourhood of the Miſſiſſippi is extremely various, being in some places barren, and in others extraordinary fruitful, and naturally abounds with the same plants and animals as Georgia, Carolina and Virginia. Much noise has been made about the silver mines in this country, and the probability of finding those of gold; but some persons who have been sent from France to make trial of the mines, reported that they are far from being valuable, and that it would be very difficult, if not impracticable, to work them. The principal produce of this country exported to Europe are furs, raw hides, and tobacco.

The French divided this extensive country into nine provinces, in each of which they had some small posts; but the only place they possessed of any confequence was New-Orleans, feated in a very fruitful part of the country, about 120 miles from the mouth of the Miffiffippi, where the inhabitants raife corn enough for their own fubfiftence, and a fmall quantity of tobacco. The number of people fettled in this extenfive country is computed by fome French authors to amount to 12,000.

Since the laft peace, the French refigned this country, to which they had given the name of Louifiana, to the Spaniards.

THE
Discoveries and Settlements
OF THE
DUTCH IN AMERICA.

CHAPTER I.

The manner in which Surinam was taken by the Dutch. The commodities brought from thence, with a description of the country, and manners of the Indian inhabitants.

THE most considerable of the Dutch settlements on the continent is that of Surinam, which they took from the English. We have already given an account of the expeditions of Sir Walter Raleigh, and other persons to Guiana, and it must here be observed, that after the restoration, the Lord Willoughby, who was governor of Barbadoes, obtained a grant of this country from King Charles II. and actually made a considerable settlement on the river of Surinam, which they might have possessed much longer than they did, had it not been for their own indiscretion. About that time the coast of Guiana was possessed by three European nations, from Cape Orange almost to the river Oroonoko. The English had a small colony and redoubt on the river Moronny, but their chief settlement was at Surinam river, which was so deep that ships of 300 tons might run 20 leagues up. The French had the island of Cayenne, and the rivers of Ovia, Corrou, and Sinemary, which last is about 53 leagues eaſt of Surinam; and the Dutch were ſettled about the river Aproague, while the Zealanders poſſeſſed the river Berbiche, and had repulſed the Engliſh, who had attacked them there, witth conſiderable loſs. When the firſt Dutch war broke out, in which the French took part with the Republic, both thoſe nations deſired a neutrality in thoſe parts, but the Engliſh would not conſent to it.

In the year 1666, the ſtates of Zealand being provoked at the Engliſh having invaded and taken from them all the lands they poſſeſſed in America, except about the river Berbiche, ſent Commodore Creiſſen with four ſhips of war and 300 men, to attack Surinam. He ſailed from Zealand the latter end of January, arrived at Cayenne in March, and from thence ſteered for Surinam. He ſailed three leagues up the river under Engliſh colours, to the fort of Paramorbo, without being taken for an enemy: when being diſcovered for want of ſignals, the fort began to fire on his ſhips, which he anſwered with broadſides from all the veſſels, and immediately landed his forces. The Engliſh who had lived for a long time in profound ſecurity, found themſelves too weak to make a defence on the land ſide, and the ſettlements being diſperſed along the river for thirty leagues up, the fort could receive no ſuccours but by water, where the Zealanders were maſters. The Engliſh therefore capitulated, that all the inhabitants of the river Surinam and Kamomioque, who ſhould take an oath of fidelity to the ſtates of Zealand, ſhould enjoy the peaceable poſſeſſion of their eſtates. But the houſes, &c. belonging to the lord Willoughby, and to thoſe who abſented themſelves, were to be forfeited; that all foreigners who had no eſtates ſhould remain priſoners of war, and all the Engliſh deliver up their arms.

This capitulation being executed, Commodore Creiffen put the moſt valuable part of the plunder on board a fly boat, took the priſoners on board a man of war, then after cauſing the fort to be repaired and put in a poſture of defence, left it in the poſſeſſion of the Sieur de Rome, and then ſailed for the iſlands. Afterwards when the peace was concluded at Breda, it was agreed that the Dutch ſhould keep Surinam ; and in return, the Engliſh ſhould keep the poſſeſſion of New-York, which was then called the New Netherlands.

While this ſettlement of Surinam was in the poſſeſſion of the Engliſh, they made but very little advantage of it, however, it was attended with very ſmall expence, as they were upon very good terms with the natives, with whom the Dutch were and ſtill are upon ſo bad a footing, that they are obliged to keep up a ſtrong fort ſecured by a good garriſon ; and if any Dutchmen venture out of the limits of their ſettlements, the Indians are ſure to give them no quarter.

The commodities raiſed by the Dutch at Surinam, are ſugar, indigo, ginger, tobacco, and cotton, for the cultivation of which, they have negroes from their colonies in Africa, where a part of their goods is alſo taken off.

Beſides this ſettlement, they have Boron, Berbiche, and Approwack, ſituated at a ſmall diſtance from each other, which for the moſt part raiſe the ſame commodities as at Surinam. At Berbiche however, beſides an extraordinary quantity of cotton, they prepare a rich dye called orlane, from an herb of the ſame name ; and being there upon good terms with the Indians, trade with them for proviſions, hides, and other kinds of merchandize.

Surrinam, the capital of theſe ſettlements, is ſituated in 6°. 30'. north latitude, and in 56°. weſt longitude from London. The country is in many parts thinly peopled, eſpecially the low lands, which are often overflowed by the rivers; but the upper hilly countries are very populous. The foil is well watered; the air cooler than towards the coaft, and the hills rich in mines of feveral forts. All kinds of grain grow there all the year round, (except wheat) coming up in a fhort time, and with little or no diftinction of feafons; for there being no winter, the trees are always green and full of leaves, bloffoms, and fruit, which is very plentiful and good. Though this country lies within the torrid zone, the climate is pretty temperate, and the air wholefome; the heats being generally allayed by a frefh eafterly wind, which reigns in the day during the greateft part of the year; and at night the land breezes prevail, but do not reach above two or three leagues out at fea. The waters are alfo excellent, and are found by experience to keep fweet during the longeft voyages. On the fea coafts, which are generally low, are many large iflands fit for feeding of cattle.

Among the fruits of this country, are the bread fruit, tamarinds, papayas, accajou apples, and many other tropical fruits.

The papaya is produced on a tall flender tree or fhrub with large leaves, fomewhat refembling thofe of the vine; the tree is hollow and grows fifteen feet high in one year. The fruit is thick and round, and in tafte has fome refemblance to a cucumber.

The accajou apple is long, thick, and of an orange red; it has a fharp tafte and is commonly eaten baked. At the end of the fruit is a green nut, much in fhape of a little fheep's kidney, the kernel has the tafte of a filbert, the fhell is oily, and on the fkin being touched with this oil, it is ftained black, fo as not to rub off in a long time.

This country alfo produces vanillas, tobacco, pete and rocou, Indian wheat, mandioka, cotton, indigo, and feveral other ufeful plants, among which cotton is moſt cultivated by the Indians, whoſe women ſpin it as fine as they pleaſe in order to adorn themſelves.

The vanilla is a weed that creeps up trees in the ſame manner as ivy, the leaves are of a bright green, long, thick, and pointed at the end; when it has been ſeven years ſet in the ground, it begins to bear a kind of huſks full of an oily matter, and a ſeed ſmaller than that of a poppy, which is uſed in Europe in perfuming chocolate, liquors, and tobacco.

This country likewiſe produces ſeveral kinds of phyſical gums, woods, and roots, as alſo various ſorts of woods for dying, and making of cabinet work, and, in particular, ſeveral different kinds of ebony.

Here are incredible numbers of monkeys of various kinds, among which is one called by the Indians Sapajous, a little yellowiſh ape with large eyes, a white face, and black chin. They are of a low ſtature, and very lively and diverting, but ſo tender, that it is with great difficulty they can be taken over alive to Europe. The woods alſo abound with ſmall tygers, deer, hogs, porcupines, camelions, monſtrous ſerpents, and many other animals and reptiles.

Tame and wild fowl are alſo very plentiful, and with theſe they ſupply the European ſettlements, on the ſea coaſt. They conſiſt of parrots, toncans, flamingos, large wild ducks, with red feathers on their heads, and ſeveral other birds chiefly remarkable for their feathers.

The ſea, near the coaſt, abounds with fiſh, the moſt common is the cat-fiſh, which is yellow and very large, mullets, thornbacks, lamentines and turtle.

The natives are of a reddiſh complexion, of a low ſtature, and of a robuſt ſtrong conſtitution. They have long black and lank hair, and have no other covering than a little cotton wool, which hangs from their waist down to their legs, except several folds of cotton cloth, wherewith they cover their arms and faces, and a sort of crown of feathers of various colours, which they wear on their heads by way of ornament. They also bore a hole between their nostrils, and hang to it a small piece of money, or a large green stone, or rather crystal, brought from the river of the Amazon, and on this stone they set a great value. They also cut off their beards and dye their faces with rocou.

The women are generally shorter than the men, but though they appear of a red complexion, they are tolerably handsome, for their eyes are usually blue, and their features well formed. They fasten to their waists a piece of cloth about six inches square, of the same sort as that worn by the men on their arms and faces, and woven in stripes of several colours.

These Indians generally live to above 100 years of age. They are endued with good sense, and are judicious, ingenious, patient and skilful in fishing and hunting. They spend the greatest part of their time in these exercises, and spare no pains in procuring provisions. They are more inclined to peace than war, but will engage in the latter, either upon a just quarrel or for the sake of revenge. Their wars are seldom concluded till they have made forty or fifty of their enemies prisoners, whom they either kill, or sell to the Europeans on the coast, for slaves. This barbarity seems rather the effect of an ancient custom, than proceeding from their natural dispositions; for when the Europeans represent to them, that by the laws of God, men are forbid to kill an enemy whom they have taken prisoner, they make no reply; and some of the Asoquas have appeared full of indignation, on being told, that some of the Galibis insinuated to the Europeans, that they would be roasted by them, if they should travel through their country. They are generally great eaters. Their common food is cakes made of the mandiaca root, baked on the embers, as also Indian wheat, fish, and fruit. They do not drink at their ordinary meals till they have done, and then only one draught; but when they assemble together for warlike enterprizes, or to admit one into their council, after they have exposed him to several trials, they make extraordinary rejoicings, which frequently hold three or four days, continuing till they have drank up all their liquors; for upon these occasions they make three or four different kinds of drink, some of which are rendered strong by fermentation.

CHAPTER. II.

An account of the island of Tobago, St. Eustatia, Saba, St. Martin, Curacao, Bonairo, and Aruba, possessed by the Dutch in the West-Indies.

In the year 1628, king Charles I. granted Tobago, Trinity island, Barbuda, and St. Bernard, to Philip, earl of Pembroke and Montgomery; but it does not appear that any settlement was made on these islands in consequence of this grant; and therefore about the year 1642, the Dutch from Flushing, sent a considerable colony to the island of Tobago where they fixed themselves very commodiously; and though they at first found the climate sickly and unhealthy, yet in proportion as they cleared the land, the air agreed with them better, and they began to extend their settlements: but while they were in this situation, the Spaniards from the island of Trinity, in conjunction with the

Indians from St. Vincent, fell upon them, murdered them to a man, and deftroyed their plantations; after which the ifland was deferted for feveral years.

About the year 1664, Mr. Adrian Lampfin, a Dutch Eaft-India director, and his brother Mr. Cornelius Lampfin, burgomafter of Flufhing, formed the defign of refettling this ifland, entirely at their own expence. Mr. Cornelius Lampfin, having obtained a licence for that purpofe of the ftates, applied to the crown of France, in order to prevent if poffible, any danger to his new colony, from the fujects of that kingdom; upon which Lewis XIV. refolving to oblige the Dutch, created Mr. Lampfin baron of Tobago, with all the privileges of a baron of France. Upon thefe encouragemens the two brothers proceeded, and by their prudent managenent, in the fpace of eleven years, rendered this wafte and defert country, the moft flourifhing for its fize of any of the leeward iflands.

This ifland, which lies in 11°. 15. north latitude, is the moft eafterly of all the iflands called the Antilles; it is about 12 leagues in length, four in breadth, and 30 in circumference. From one of the largeft ifles in the province of Zealand they called it New Walcheren, raifed a very ftrong fortrefs called Lampfinberg, and two other good forts named Beveren and Bellevifte; and, what is very furprizing, fettled at their own expence, during their adminiftration, 1200 white people in that ifland; who fucceeded in raifing all the commodities brought from the Weft-Indies, as tobacco, fugar, ginger, cotton, indigo, cacao, caffia, fuftic, rocou, ananas, citrons, oranges, &c. and had befides fome very valuable commodities, not to be found in the other iflands, as a great quantity of gum Copal, wild mace and nutmegs, and an excellent kind of faffafras: befides which they raifed all forts of grain and provifions, fufficient not only for their own ufe, but to export fome to the other iflands.

However in 1674, marfhal d'Eftrees, by the exprefs orders of Lewis XIV. failed with a large fleet to deftroy this very fettlement, notwithftanding its being made under his protection, and by his encouragement. The Dutch defended themfelves obftinately; but after two hard-fought battles they were defeated, being overpowered by numbers; and, to the entire ruin of the induftrious planters, and the eternal infamy of that perfidious prince, the colony was totally deftroyed.

The ifland was however reftored to the Dutch by the treaty of Nimeguen; but on the 27th of December, 1677, it was taken by the count d'Etrees, vice-admiral of France; after which Tobago was one of the four iflands, which, at the peace of Aix-la Chapelle, were declared neutral; notwithftanding which, the marquis de Caylis, governor of the French iflands, foon after began to fortify and fettle it; but the court of Great-Britain warmly remonftrating againft this violation of the peace, the French court difavowed his proceedings, ordered him home, and the fettlement to be difcontinued. In this ftate it remained till the definitive treaty of Fountainbleau in 1703, by which Tobago was ceded to Great-Britain.

In 1635, the Dutch took poffeffion of the ifland of St. Euftatia, and the ftates granted the property of it to Mr. Vanre, and fome other merchants of Flufhing, who foon fettled a colony upon it, confifting of about 600 families. But in the year 1665 the Dutch were difpoffeffed by the Englifh, and colonel Morgan was fent with 300 buccaneers to keep poffeffion of the place; however this gentlemen foon after making an attempt upon the French part of the ifland of St. Chriftopher's was killed; and the next year the Dutch and French engaging in a war againft Great-Britain, attacked and made themselves masters of this island, which was afterwards restored to the Dutch by the treaty of Breda. The French, however, took it from them in 1689, but it was restored to them again by the treaty of Ryswick; since which time they have remained in the peaceable and quiet possession of it.

St. Eustatia, is situated to the north-west of St. Christopher's in 17°. 40. north latitude. This island which is only five leagues in compass, appears to the southward like a high mountain rising out of the sea, but stretches out to the northward into a pretty good country. The number of plantations upon it, and the comfortable situation of its inhabitants do great honour to the industry of the Dutch. All the sides of the mountains are laid out into small well cultivated settlements; the houses are well built and well furnished, most of the inhabitants are in good circumstances, and have warehouses filled with European commodities, with which they furnish their neighbours at a high price, whenever they happen to be disappointed of supplies from England and France. They also raise besides some other commodities, great quantities of excellent tobacco, which comes to a good market in Holland; and yet there is not a drop of water in the island but what they are supplied with from the clouds, which they preserve so carefully in cisterns, that they are very seldom distressed. The top of the mountain is covered with a vast wood, in the middle of which, instead of the point that might be expected, as it rises in the form of a sugar loaf, there is a wide and deep cavern, which was probably once a volcano.

To the north-west of this island, lies that of Saba, in 17°. 35, north latitude. It at first sight appears to be a rock, but the Dutch governors of St. Eustatia have settled a small colony there, in a valley where they raise tobacco and other things. Both of these islands have the misfortune of not having a single port; St. Eustatia however has a good road where all the ships ride, and the Dutch have erected a pretty strong fort to command it.

We now come to the island of St. Martin, situated in 18°. 15. north lat. a little inconsiderable island, about seven leagues in length, and four in breadth, and yet inhabited by two powerful nations; though its smallness is not its only disadvantage, for the climate is far from being wholesome, and the soil cannot be very fertile, as there are no rivers, and very few springs, and even these are dried up in the hot seasons, so that the inhabitants are obliged to have recourse to their cisterns of rain water; yet as insignificant as this place may appear, it has been contended for, by the Spaniards, French, and Dutch. The French were the first European nation who attempted to settle this island; but allowing the Dutch to trade with them, they seized a favourable opportunity, surprising the French, drove them out, and then built a fort for their own security; but the Spaniards not liking their neighbourhood, drove out the Dutch in their turn and erected a strong fortress, to prevent any other nation settling upon it: however at length perceiving that the English, French, and Dutch had seized the more valuable islands, they thought it ridiculous to be any longer at the expence of keeping this, and therefore resolved to quit it. This resolution was taken in the year 1648, and was soon after executed; for having destroyed their cisterns, burned their houses, and blown up their fort, they retired to Porto Rico.

In this Spanish garrison were four Frenchmen, five Dutchmen, and a mullato, who being unwilling to go, hid themselves in a wood till the Spaniards were embarked, and then boldly sallied out to take possession of the whole island. They however soon divided, and made choice of different places to settle in, and even by a formal treaty, these ten persons agreed to divide the country, between the French and Dutch nations. The Dutch making a little canoe, sent one of their number to St. Eustatia, to inform the governor of their situation, and promised the French to send the like notice to the governor of St. Christopher's: the former being their own affair was exactly performed, but the latter concerning only their neighbours, was entirely neglected.

The governor of St. Eustatia being willing to seize this new acquisition, sent one Martin Thomas with a considerable number of planters to take possession of that part of the island, which belonged to the Dutch. After this they began to treat the French but very indifferently, who receiving no news from their countrymen began to suspect the cause, and therefore with some difficulty sent a person to St. Christopher's to inform M. de Poincy of the agreement they had made, and the hardships under which they laboured; whereupon he dispatched an officer with thirty men, to take possession for the crown of France; but the Dutch would not suffer them to land, declaring that they considered themselves as the legal possessors of that island.

The French officer no sooner returned to St. Christopher's, than M. de Poincy sent his nephew to put an end to the dispute; and this commission he performed so effectually, that the Dutch governor was glad to settle the division of the island, according to the first agreement; by which all that part of it towards Anguilla, was to belong to the French, while the other side, in which the Spanish fort before stood, remained in the possession of the Dutch; the former was indeed in every respect, the better half, only the Dutch had on their side the advantage of some salt pits. This contract was settled on the top of the highest hill in the island, which was from thence called la Montagne des Accordes, the mountain of agreement.

From this time the two nations lived together in ſtrict friendſhip; the French ſettlement however is of very little conſequence, though that of the Dutch is in a flouriſhing condition, for they have large warehouſes and carry on a conſiderable trade, particularly in tobacco. This iſland would be ſtill more conſiderable if the Dutch had a tolerable port, but they have only a road where ſhips are much expoſed, and it beſides lies too much to the leeward. In the iſland of St. Martin there is great plenty of a kind of tree, which both the Dutch and French call candle-wood, for the ſmall ſticks ſerve for candles, and at the ſame time they light the room, yield a very agreeable ſcent. We are now to proceed to their other iſlands which lie nearer the Spaniſh coaſt, and from which they receive greater advantages.

Curacao, or as it is pronounced and ſometimes written by the Dutch, Curraſſaw, is an iſland about nine or ten leagues long, and five broad, ſituated in 12°. 40'. north latitude; but though the ſoil is far from being fruitful, and the climate ſtill farther from being either agreeable or healthy, yet ſuch has been the care and induſtry of the Dutch, that they receive great advantages from this ſmall and to appearance, inconſiderable country, in which there was formerly a great quantity of cattle; but they have turned their extenſive paſtures into ſugar and tobacco plantations, ſo that the proviſions of all ſorts that are raiſed in this iſland, it is thought would ſcarce maintain its inhabitants for one day; yet theſe inhabitants are ſo far from being expoſed to want, that there is not a more plentiful or better provided place in the Weſt-Indies; every thing however, fetches a high price, but this is ſo far from being a diſadvantage, that it is the principal fource of the great wealth of the inhabitants.

The harbour of Santa Barbara is on the fouth fide of the eaft end of the ifland, but the chief harbour is about three leagues from the fouth-eaft end of the fouth fide, where the Dutch have a very good town and a ftrong fort; there is no anchoring at its entrance, but being got in it is a place of great fecurity. The Dutch town is for its fize one of the fineft in America, and it has every thing requifite to render it commodious and agreeable, as far as the climate and foil will permit. The public buildings are very neat; the port is rendered fafe as poffible, and though the entry is dangerous, yet the precautions taken by the government for the fervice of ftrangers, not only free them from all difficulties, but render them alfo in a great meafure infenfible of any hazard; by which means it is become one of the moft frequented ports in the Weft-Indies. All kinds of labour is here performed by engines, with fuch dexterity that fhips are lifted at once into the dock, where they are carefully and effectually careened; and all nations are with equal readinefs furnifhed with provifions, naval ftores, ammunition, and even artillery.

Bonaira and Aruba are alfo two iflands in the poffeffion of the Dutch, dependent upon the ifland of Curacoa. The former lies ten leagues to the eaftward of that ifland, and is about feventeen leagues in compafs. The Dutch have a deputy governor, a guard of foldiers, and a confiderable number of Indians, with a fort for the protection and fecurity of the place.

The Indians are hufbandmen, and plant yams, potatoes, maize, and Guinea corn, but they are chiefly employed about cattle, particularly in fending great quantities of goats flefh to Curacoa. There are alfo fome horfes, bulls, and cows, though they are not fo numerous as the goats;

but in all the island there are no sheep or hogs, or any other animals except those already mentioned. The south side is a plain low land, and there are several sorts of trees, but none very large. There is a small spring of water by the houses, which serves the inhabitants, notwithstanding its being brackish; however, at the west end of the island is a good spring of fresh water, and three or four Indian families live there; these springs afford all the fresh water found in the place; near the east end is a good salt pond, where Dutch sloops go for salt, which is now become a very considerable commodity there.

The island of Aruba lies seven leagues west of Curacoa; but though it is not very considerable, the inhabitants breed some cattle and a great many horses, this renders it of service to the chief colony, which it also furnishes with a great quantity of garden stuff, without which the people at Curacoa could not subsist; for, among their other methods of getting money, one is, allowing strangers to erect hospitals on shore, for their sick, wherein they consume a great many greens and roots, for which they pay a very high price, as they do for all other conveniences.

But to return to Curacoa; as this island is not above seven leagues from the Spanish coast, it is commodiously situated for carrying on a clandestine trade. This was first begun by the sale of Negroes, brought thither by the Dutch from their numerous settlements on the coast of Guinea, who were brought openly by the Spaniards, and transported 1500 at a time, in their own vessels. But since the English at Jamaica have interfered in this trade, it has sunk considerably. However the dealers at Curacoa, and their correspondents in Holland were too conversant in business to let the declension of the slave trade rob them of the benefit of this island, they therefore built vast magazines, which they ſtored with European goods ; and this not only preſerved the remainder of their ſlave trade, which was winked at by the Spaniſh governors, but the Spaniards under the pretence of buying ſlaves, run all hazards to purchaſe the European commodities they wanted, by which means vaſt ſums are annually traded for in this way.

It has been computed that in time of peace, the trade of this iſland did not produce leſs to the Dutch than five millions of florins per annum, which is about half a million ſterling.

A Danish Settlement in America.

A short description of the islands of St. Thomas and St. Croix, in the possession of the Danes.

THE only remaining islands in this part of the world, that we shall now mention, are those of St. Thomas and St. Croix, which belong to the Danes; the former is situated in 18°. north latitude, and is one of that cluster of islands called the Virgins. Though it is not above seven leagues in circumference, it is in a commodious situation, and has an excellent port of an oval form, in a manner surrounded by two promontories which defend the ships that lie within from almost all winds. In the bottom of this port is a small fortress which stands in a plain, and is a regular square with four small bastions, but it has neither outworks nor a ditch, it being only surrounded with a pallisade. On the right and left of the fort are two small eminences which in other countries would be called bluffs; but though they seem designed for batteries that would command the whole harbour, no such use is made of them. The king of Denmark has here a governor and a garrison; notwithstanding which, there is a large factory on the island belonging to the Brandenburghers, the subjects of the king of Prussia.

The neighbourhood of the Spanish island of Porto Rico is only at seventeen leagues distance, and secures the inhabitants from the danger of wanting provifions, to which they would otherwife be expofed; for though the foil is tolerably good and every foot of it cultivated, yet it would not produce fufficient for the maintenance of the inhabitants, who are very numerous.

The town of St. Thomas confifts of one long ftreet, at the end of which is the Danifh magazine, a large magnificent and convenient building. The Brandenburgh factory is alfo very confiderable, and the perfons belonging to it are chiefly French refugees, who fled thither when the proteftants were expelled from the French iflands. The chief produce of their plantations is fugar, which is very fine grained, but made in fmall quantities; yet the Danifh governor, who is ufually a man of fome rank, lives in a manner fuitable to his character, and generally acquires a good fortune in that ftation. The director of the Danifh trade alfo becomes rich in a few years, and the inhabitants in general are in very eafy circumftances.

To this ifland the Spaniards are continually fending large veffels to purchafe flaves. This is the chief fupport of the Danifh and Brandenburgh commerce, as thefe flaves are drawn from their fettlements upon the coaft of Africa, which, if they had not this trade, would have long ago become ufelefs, and confequently deferted. The Spaniards alfo buy here, as well as at Curacoa, all forts of European goods, of which there is always a vaft ftock in the magazine, belonging chiefly to the Dutch. There is likewife a great refort of Englifh, Dutch, and French veffels to this port, where they can always depend upon the fale of fuperfluous, and the purchafe of neceffary commodities. But though a prodigious deal of bufinefs is tranfacted in time of peace, in time of war it is vaftly increafed, for being a neutral port, the privateers of all nations refort thither to fell their prizes.

St. Croix is feated about five leagues eaft of St. Thomas's, and about thirty weft of St. Chriftopher's, in 18°. north latitude and in 65°. weft longitude. It is about ten or twelve leagues in length, but not above three broad. The air is very unhealthy but the foil is eafily cultivated; very fertile and produces fugar canes, citrons, oranges, lemons, pomegranates, and other fruits, and has feveral fine trees whofe wood is very beautiful, and proper for inlaying.

This ifland has had feveral mafters; but the French abandoning it in 1696, it was purchafed by his late Danifh Majefty. It was then a perfect defert, but was fettled with great expedition, many perfons from the Englifh iflands, and among them fome of great wealth, having removed thither.

THE VOYAGE

OF

SIR FRANCIS DRAKE

ROUND THE WORLD:

CONTAINING

An Account of what happened after his failing from Plymouth until his Return to England.

ADMIRAL DRAKE, who had before diftinguifhed himfelf in feveral voyages by his integrity, bravery and conduct, failed out of Plymouth Sound on the 15th of November, 1573, with the refolution to chaftife the Spaniards, for the ill treatment both he and the Englifh nation had received from that people. He had five fhips under his command; the Pelican, which he afterwards called the Hind; burthen about 100 tons; the Elizabeth of 80 tons, commanded by Captain John Winter; the Marygold, a bark of 30 tons burthen, commanded by John Thomas; the Swan, a fly-boat of 50 tons, under the command of John Chefter; and a pinnace of 15 tons, Thomas Moon commander. Thefe fhips were manned with 164 able men; furnifhed with a large ftock of provifions, and had four pinnaces on board ftowed in pieces, to be fet up as occafion required. But this fleet meeting with a violent ftorm, in which feveral of the fhips were much damaged, and the Pelican in particular, lofing her main maft, they were obliged to put back to Plymouth; where having refitted, they set sail on the 13th of December, with a favourable wind, on the 25th passed Cape Cantin in Morocco, and on the 27th arrived at the island of Mogador, eighteen leagues more to the southward, which had been appointed the place of general rendezvous in case of a separation.

Magador is situated about a mile from the main land, between which and that island, they found a very safe and convenient harbour. Here Mr. Drake ordered one of the pinnaces to be put together, and while they were thus embloyed, some of the inhabitants approached the shore, making signs of peace, and two of them ventured on board in the admiral's boat, which was sent to fetch them; one of the English being left by way of hostage till their return. These told them by signs, that the reason of their coming was to make an offer of their friendship, and that the next day they would furnish his ships with provisions; whereupon Mr. Drake returned their civility by giving them some linen cloth, shoes, and a javelin; upon which those on shore, on receiving their companions, freely released the hostage.

The next day a confiderable body of the natives appeared near the sea side: when it being imagined that they came laden with provisions, the boat was sent to receive them; but one of the men, entertaining no distrust, and hastily leaping out, as imagining himself among friends, was immediately seized, and others of the natives quitting an ambuscade, the sailors who were going to attempt to rescue their companion, were glad to recover their boat, and put off with great precipitation. The admiral being extremely exasperated at this piece of treachery, landed a body of men, and marched a confiderable way into the country to no purpose, for the Moors every where avoided him; he therefore returned to his ship, and the

Beavers, building their Hutts.

pinnace being finished in four days, they set sail from the coast of Morocco on the 30th of December.

The person who had been thus made prisoner was named John Fry. He was carried up into the country, and examined with respect to his nation, and the destination of the fleet, and having declared that they were English ships bound to the Streights under the command of admiral Drake; who to conceal his real design, had artfully caused this report to be spread, he was sent back with assurances of friendship, and some presents for the admiral; but he being gone before Fry's return, he was afterwards sent back to England in a merchant ship.

On the 17th of January, the admiral arrived at Cape Blanco, where he found a ship at anchor, with only two men left to guard her. Of this ship he made a prize, and ordering her to be taken into the harbour, staid there four days, both to lay in a stock of fresh provisions, of which he found great plenty, and to exercise the men, on shore, in order to fit them as well for the land, as the sea service. The inhabitants would have sold him some slaves, and offered him a woman with a sucking child at her breast, but Mr. Drake did not chuse to engage in this traffic. He however supplied them with fresh water, of which they were then in great want, and in return they gave him ambergrise and some precious gums.

The admiral left this harbour on the 22d of January, taking with him a Portuguese caraval, bound to the Cape de Verd Islands, for salt, and leaving behind him a small bark of his own. The master of the Portugese vessel informed the admiral that in one of the Cape de Verd Islands, called Mayo, there was a considerable quantity of dried goats, which were annually prepared for such of the king's ships as called there. At this island, on which were some Portuguese, they arrived on the 27th, but found the villages on the coast abandoned, and the wells of fresh water stopped up. A body of men commanded by capt. Winter, were ordered to march into the country to take a view of it, which they did, and found the soil extremely fertile, and producing great plenty of fruit, particularly fine cocoas, figs, and grapes of a most delicious flavour; and notwithstanding its being in the midst of winter the air was temperate and pleasant. They saw many goats and kids, but they were too swift to be easily caught, though they might have brought off many that were old, dead, and dried, that were laid in their way; from which they justly inferred, that the inhabitants had been forbid to trade with them; and this was indeed the case. They also saw large quantities of wild hens, and salt made by the heat of the sun, and at length discovered plenty of water, but at too great a distance from the ships for them to think of bringing any on board.

On the 31st of January they passed by the island of St. Jago, the vallies of which were inhabited by the Portuguese, while the mountains were possessed by the Moors. Near this island they saw two Portuguese ships under sail, and as Portugal was then annexed to the crown of Spain, he took one of them, which proved to be a good prize, laden with wine. Mr. Drake detained the pilot, but set at liberty the master and all the crew, giving them one of his own pinnaces, and restoring them their clothes, some provisions and a butt of wine. On their leaving the island, several pieces of cannon were fired at them, but without doing them any harm.

The same night they came to the island Del Fuego or the burning island, so called from the volcano on its north side. On the south side of Del Fuego they saw a very delightful island, named Brava, which produced oranges, lemons, cocoas, and innumerable vegetables, while the cooling ſtreams with which it is watered, in their progreſs to the ſea, contribute to its fertility, and improve the landſkip; but the ſea around it being unfathomable, and conſequently there being no poſſibility of anchoring, it is avoided by ſhips, and to this may be attributed its want of inhabitants, for ſome of the admiral's people travelling up into the country, met with no ſign of a human being, except a poor hermit, who fled from them, and in whoſe cell they found ſcarcely any thing beſides a crucifix, ſome images of rude workmanſhip, and and ill-contrived altar.

Having taken in a freſh ſupply of water at Brava, they quitted the Cape de Verd Iſlands, and proceeded towards the line; in their approach to which they met with very changeable weather, being ſometimes becalmed for a conſiderable time together, and at others toſſed about by tempeſts. They ſaw all the way great numbers of dolphins, bonetos, and flying fiſhes, ſome of which dropped into their ſhips; for theſe being purſued by ſharks and other fiſhes of prey, uſe their fins as wings, ſpringing up to a great height out of the water, and dropping down when their fins loſe their moiſture.

On the 17th of February they paſſed the line, and on the 5th of April ſaw land for the firſt time, after a run of fifty-four days. This proved to be the coaſt of Braſil, and they no ſooner came within ſight of the ſhore than large fires were lighted up in ſeveral parts, which were ſuppoſed to be the uſual ſacrifices made by the inhabitants on the appearance of ſhips to implore the aſſiſtance of their gods, to prevent their landing, or to put the people on their guard for fear of a foreign invaſion from ſome unknown enemy.

Two days after, they parted from the Chriſtopher, in a ſtorm of rain, thunder, and lightening, but on the 11th they came up with her at a cape, to which the admiral gave the name of Cape Joy. They here found a ſmall harbour, where the ſhips rode in great ſafety, the force of the ſea being broken by a large rock, on which they killed ſeveral ſeals; theſe they kept for food, and found them wholeſome, though they did not think them very palatable. They here alſo took in freſh water; but though the air was mild and the ſoil of the country rich and fertile, they could diſcern no other inhabitants than herds of wild deer; ſome of the ſailors however diſcovered the print of human feet in the ſand.

They now ſteered to the great river of Plate, which they entered, but finding no good harbour, they put to ſea again, and on the night of the 27th came to a bay, when Mr. Drake took his boat to go on ſhore and examine the coaſt; but was overtaken by ſo thick a fog, that he thought proper to return to his ſhip, which he could not have found without great difficulty, if captain Thomas had not ſteered in ſearch of him. He however ſome time after went on ſhore, and found plenty of water and proviſions. The inhabitants leaped and danced with all the ſigns of mirth and good humour, and were not averſe to traffic, though they would receive nothing out of any man's hand, but would have what they purchaſed laid on the ground for their examination.

The next day the fleet were joined by the Swan, which had been miſſing; and the Marygold and Chriſtopher, that had been ſent out in ſearch of a ſafer harbour, returned with the agreeable news that they had found one, and thither the whole fleet ſailed; where being arrived, the admiral ordered the Swan to be burnt as a ſuperfluous veſſel, which was done, after they had divided the provisions and iron work among the rest of the fleet. Here they found such multitudes of seals, that they killed above 200 in an hour. While they were employed on shore, the natives appeared at a distance upon a rising ground. They were strong, well proportioned, and had agreeable features; but their faces were painted. They were something wreathed about their heads, and their other covering was only the skins of beasts wrapped about their waists. They had bows of an ell long, and every one of them bore two arrows, and indeed they seemed to be not altogether destitute of military discipline, as appeared from the method observed by their commander in ordering and ranging them. Some of these people paint their bodies all over black, except their necks, which they coloured white; others paint one shoulder black, and the other white; and many of them had their legs tinged black, and adorned with white moons. This continual daubing closes up the pores, and renders these people less susceptible of cold and heat. They were at first extremely shy of coming near the English, but the admiral having caused some baubles to be tied to a pole stuck in the ground, and left for them to take when they pleased, they soon after came and removed them, leaving ostrich feathers and other toys in exchange. Upon this the admiral and some of his men came again, and approached nearer the hill, but retreated on his seeing them give signs of fear, and prepare to retire. This convincing the natives that he had no ill designs against them, they boldly advanced towards the English, and two of them, attracted by the lace on the admiral's hat, slyly came behind him, and snatching it off his head, ran away with it, and then divided the spoil, one keeping the hat, and the other the lace. To this place the admiral gave the name of Seal Bay, from the great number of those animals that frequent it.

Here is also a bird called a booby, so stupid as to stand still while it is knocked on the head, and many ostriches, the thigh of which bird is as large as the leg of a sizeable sheep; but though they cannot fly they are not easily taken; for being assisted by the fluttering of their wings, they run fast, and fling stones behind them at their pursuers with a pretty good aim.

Having left this place, they proceeded on their voyage to the southward, and on the 20th of June anchored in Fort St Julian, so called by Magellan, where the admiral accompanied by six men, going on shore with his boat to take a view of the country, was in some danger from the natives who slew the gunner, a man for whom he had a sincere regard; he however revenged his death by killing the murderer with his own hand. Here he found a gibbet which had been erected by Magellan for the execution of some of his mutinous company, who had conspired his death, and here also admiral Drake caused Mr. Doughty to be tried and hanged for the same crime against himself.

Leaving Port St. Julian on the 17th of August, they fell in with the streights of Magellan on the 20th, and the next day entering them, found the passage so intricate and winding, that the wind, though sometimes favourable, was without its changing, frequently against them; this gave them much fatigue and trouble, especially as they had many sudden squalls which rendered this passage very dangerous, for though they found several good harbours, and plenty of fresh water, yet the sea is so deep, that there is no anchoring, except in some very narrow river or between the rocks. On both sides the streights are vast ranges of mountains that rise far above the clouds, and are covered with perpetual snow, where they found the air extremely cold, and the men were benumbed with frost and snow. At the south-east part of the ſtreights are ſeveral iſlands, between which the ſea breaks in, as it does into the main entrance. It had been imagined that the current always ſet one way, but they now found from the ebb and flood that this was a miſtake, and that the water roſe five fathoms all along the coaſt. Theſe ſtreights are never narrower than one league, or broader than four. On the 24th of Auguſt they made an iſland in the ſtreights, where there were ſuch multitudes of penguins, that they killed 3000 in leſs than one day.

On the 16th of September they entered the South Sea, but the next day they were driven to the ſouthward by a ſtorm, and were obliged to anchor among ſome iſlands, where they found freſh water and excellent herbs, and not far from thence entered another bay, where they ſaw people ranging from one iſland to another, in their canoes in ſearch of proviſions, who traded with them for ſome commodities. Steering northward from hence, they on the 3d of October, found three iſlands, in one of which was an incredible number of birds.

On the 8th of October they loſt the Elizabeth commanded by captain Winter, which they imagined was forced back by a ſtorm into the ſtreights; a conjecture that proved true, though they were miſtaken in ſuppoſing her loſt, for the captain, after having taken poſſeſſion of the ſtreights and the adjacent territories, in the name of queen Elizabeth, was ſo happy as to return to England.

They now ſteered for the coaſt of Chili, and on the 29th of November caſt anchor at the iſle of Mocha, where the Admiral with ten men going on ſhore, were met by ſome of the natives, who behaved with great civility, gave them two fat ſheep and ſome potatoes in return for a few trifles, and alſo promiſed to bring them water, for which they received ſome preſents beforehand. Theſe people had been driven thither by the cruelty of the Spaniards, who had forced them to leave their habitations and retire to this island, in order to preserve their lives and liberties. The next day therefore, two of the men being sent on shore with barrels for water, the natives seeing that they had them at an advantage, and taking them for Spaniards, whom they had resolved never to spare, instantly seized them, and knocked them on the head.

The Admiral now continuing his course, met an Indian in his canoe, who mistaking his people for Spaniards, told them that there was at Valparaiso, a large ship laden for Peru. The Admiral rewarded him for his intelligence, and he readily agreed to conduct them to the place where the ship lay at anchor. Upon their coming up to this vessel, they found that she had no more men than eight Spaniards and three negroes, who supposing them friends, welcomed them by beat of drum, and invited them on board to drink some Chili wine. With this invitation they immediately complied, and driving the Spaniards under the hatches took possession, when one of the Spaniards seeing how the others were served, leaped overboard and swam to Valparaiso, upon which the inhabitants immediately quitted the town. The Admiral then having secured his new prize, in which were found to the value of 30,000 Spanish pistoles of pure gold of Baldivia, he manned her boat and his own, landed and rifled both the town and the chapel, whence he took a silver chalice, the altar cloth and two cruets, of which he made a present to his chaplain; and having also found a considerable quantity of Chili wine, he sent that on board; then he set all his prisoners on shore except one, whom he kept for his pilot, and directly steered towards Lima, the capital of Peru.

The fleet continuing their courfe, put into the haven of Coquimbo, and here fourteen men were fent on fhore to fetch water, when being difcovered by the town, the Spaniards refolved to recover the glory of their nation, by being revenged on fo daring an enemy, and therefore, ordered out a body of 300 horfe and 200 foot to attack them. The Englifh however retreated, and after fome difpute, reached their fhips with the lofs only of one man, who was fhot, and whom this formidable army beheaded, while the Indians ftuck his body full of arrows. The Admiral however, ordered a party of men the next day on fhore to bury him, to whom the Spaniards in vain difplayed a flag of truce, as if to invite them to a parley; but the Englifh believing that their fidelity was no greater than their courage, did not care to truft them, and having interred their companion returned to their fhips.

Mr. Drake then weighing anchor proceeded to a port called Tarapaxa, where landing fome of his men, they found a Spaniard afleep, with eighteen bars of filver lying by him, worth about 4000 Spanifh ducats, which they took without difturbing the Spaniard's repofe. Soon after landing again, in order to take in water, they met a Spaniard and an Indian driving eight Peruvian fheep laden with very fine filver, each of the fheep having two leathern bags on his back, in which were 100 weight of that metal, when delivering the poor animals from their burdens, they lodged the bags in the fhips, and then fuffered the Spaniard and Indian to drive away their beafts.

From hence they failed to the port of Arica, where they found three fmall barks, in which were 57 wedges of filver, each weighing about twenty pounds; the men who belonged to them, fearing no danger, were all on fhore, by which means they took no prifoners. However not being ftrong enough to attack the town, they again put to fea, and foon after fell in with a fmall bark, when finding nothing in it but linen cloth, they took a fmall part of it, and then let her go.

On the 13th of February they entered the port of Lima, where they found a fleet of twelve fhips lying at anchor, with fcarce any perfons left to guard them; the commanders and their crews being all on fhore. On their examining the cargoes of thefe fhips they found a cheft filled with rials of plate, which they took on board, with fome filks and linens; but being informed that another very rich fhip called the Cacafuego, had lately left that harbour, in order to fail to Paita, the admiral refolved to follow her; but on his arrival at Paita, found fhe had left that port and was gone to Panama; he however fell in with another, that in fome meafure atoned for his difappointment, fhe having on board 80 pounds weight of fine gold, befides a large golden crucifix adorned with emeralds, which he feized, together with fome ufeful cordage.

The admiral ftill refolving to continue the purfuit of the Cacafuego, promifed that whoever firft faw her fhould have the gold chain he himfelf wore about his neck; which fell to the fhare of Mr. John Drake, who firft defcried her at about three o'clock in the afternoon. and about fix they came up with and boarded her, after having in three fhots brought her mizen maft by the board. They found her cargo full as valuable as it had been reprefented, fhe having thirteen chefts full of rials of plate, 80 pounds weight of gold, 26 tons of filver bars, and a large quantity of jewels. Among the many rich pieces of plate were two very large filver bowls gilt, which belonged to the pilot, one of which the admiral told him he hoped he would allow him to keep by way of remembrance, to which the pilot who was one of the moft confiderable perfons on board the Spanifh fhips, readily

Admiral Drake, seizes eight Peruvian Ships, laden with Silver.

confented, and immediately prefented the other to the admiral's fteward.

Having taken this valuble treafure on board, they difmiffed the veffel, and allowed her to purfue her courfe to Panama, after having fupplied the captain and his crew with linen, and other neceffaries.

The admiral ftill continuing his courfe to the weftward, came up with a fhip laden with china ware, filks of the fame country, and linen cloth; and having taken out of it what was thought moft valuable, and among the reft a falcon of maffy gold, which had a very valuable emerald fet in its breaft, he fet the fhip and her people at liberty, keeping only the pilot to affift in navigating his own veffel.

The pilot fteered them into the harbour of Guatulco, and informed them, that there were only feventeen Spaniards in the town. Having therefore put to fhore, the admiral and fome of his people landed, entered the place, and marched directly to the public hall, where they found the court fitting, and the judge ready to pafs fentence on a number of poor negroes who were accufed of confpiring to burn the town. But the admiral's coming foon changed the fcene of affairs, for without fhewing any reverence to the authority of the court, he caufed the judges, witneffes, and prifoners, to be carried on board his own fhip, where he obliged the chief judge to write to the townfmen to keep at a diftance, and permit the Englifh to water in quiet. This being done, the town was ranfacked for plunder, but none found, except about a bufhel of rials of plate, only one of the failors purfuing a rich Spaniard, who fled from the town, took from him a gold chain, and fome jewels. Here the admiral fet on fhore his Spanifh prifoners, and an old Portuguefe pilot, whom he had brought from the Cape de Verd iflands, and then fet fail for the ifland Canno, where they anchored on the

16th of March, in a fresh water river. While they lay here they seized a Spanish vessel bound for the Philippine islands, which put in here for refreshment, and having taken a part of her cargo, discharged her.

The admiral now thinking he had in some measure taken revenge on the Spaniards, both for the wrongs his country had suffered from them, as well as from his own private injuries, began to deliberate on the best way of returning home. He reflected that to return by the streights of Magellan, the only passage that had been yet discovered, would be throwing himself into the hands of the Spaniards, who might probably wait for him there with more force than he could resist, as he had but one ship left, and that not strong, though it was very rich. All things therefore considered, he resoved to proceed to the East-Indies, by sailing to the west, and then to follow the Portuguese course, by passing the Cape of Good Hope; but being becalmed, he found it necessary to steer farther to the north, in hopes of obtaining a good wind, upon which he sailed at least 600 leagues till he came into 43°. of north latitude, where he found the air excessive cold, and on his proceeding farther, the severity of the weather became more intolerable; he therefore steered back towards the south, till he came into 38°. north latitude, where he found a very good bay, which he entered with a favourable gale.

This country, on account of its white cliffs, which are seen at a good distance at sea, he in honour of his native soil, called Nova Albion, though it has been since known by the name of California. There were several huts near the water-side, well fenced from the severity of the weather; a fire was in the middle of each, and round it the people lay upon rushes, with nothing else between them and the earth. The men were entirely naked; but the women wore a covering of bullrushes, dressed after the manner of hemp, and faftened about their waifts, with a deer-fkin flung over their fhoulders. Thefe people foon fent the admiral a prefent of fome feathers and cawls of net work, and he entertained the perfons who brought them with fuch kindnefs and liberality, that they were highly delighted. They foon after fent him another prefent, that confifted of feathers and bags of tobacco: a confiderable body of them waited upon him to deliver them, while the reft were gathered together at the top of a fmall hill, at the bottom of which the admiral had pitched fome tents; and from this eminence, one of them harangued the admiral; and having ended his fpeech, they all laid down their arms, and coming down, offered their own prefents, and civilly returned thofe the admiral had made them; while the women who remained above feemed, by their tearing their hair and howlings, to be engaged in offering facrifices, upon which the admiral ordered divine fervice to be celebrated in his tent, and thefe innocent people attended with great decency, attention, and amazement.

The news of the arrival of thefe ftrangers being fpread through the country, there came two perfons, one of whom made a long fpeech; from which, and the geftures of both, it was underftood that the king himfelf intended to pay the admiral a vifit, provided they would give fome token of his receiving a peaceful welcome. Which being readily granted, their fovereign foon after made his appearance, attended by a confiderable train. In the front came a very comely perfon, bearing a ftaff before the king, upon which hung two crowns made of net-work, artificially wrought with feathers of many colours, and three chains made of bones. The king, who immediately followed, had a very agreeable perfon, and approached with an air of dignity. He was furrounded by a guard of tall well-looking men, clothed in skins; then followed the common people, who to make the finer shew, had painted their faces with different colours, and all of them had their arms full of presents, the very children not excepted.

The admiral drew up all his men in a line of battle, and stood within the fences of his tent, ready to receive them: at some distance from him the whole train halted, and observed a profound silence, when the person who marched first with the staff, began a speech, which lasted half an hour; and that being ended, the same officer began a song, and struck up a dance, wherein he was followed by the king and his subjects, who came up singing and dancing to the fences, which the admiral had made to secure his tent from treachery; then all of them sitting down, the king is said to have made a solemn offer of his whole kingdom to the admiral; and, with the consent of his subjects, took off the crown of feathers he wore on his head, and placed it upon the admiral's, at the same time investing him with other ensigns of royalty. All which the admiral received, hoping that this surrender might one time or other add to the glory of his sovereign, and the advantage of England. But it is most probable these Indians had no such design: they seemed to consider the English as a superior order of beings; and these actions might be no more than the highest compliment they could pay them. The common people now dispersed themselves among the admiral's tents, expressing such an high admiration and love for the English, that they seemed to think them more than mortal, and even came before them with sacrifices, which they attempted to offer, with the profoundest devotion; but the English kept them back, and endeavoured by their signs to render them sensible, that there was an omnipotent Being to whom alone these honours were due.

Some time after, the admiral and his people travelled to fome diftance up into the country, which they found to be extremely full of large fat deer, that were very often near 1000 in a herd. There was alfo fuch vaft plenty of a kind of rabbits, that the whole country feemed one entire warren; but though their heads were like thofe of our rabbits, they had a bag on each fide of their jaws, in which they preferved fuch provifions as they could not immediately devour; their feet refembled thofe of a mole, and their tail was like that of a rat. Their flefh was much efteemed by the natives, and their fkins afforded clothing for the king and his principal fubjects.

The Spaniards had never been upon this fhore, and it is certain Mr. Drake had the honour of firft difcovering it. He therefore at his departure erected a pillar, and affixed to it a large plate, upon which were engraven her majefty's name and picture, her arms, and title to the country, with the day and year in which the admiral, whofe name was alfo infcribed, had arrived on that coaft.

Having taken in a frefh fupply of provifions, and a fufficient ftock of water, the admiral left Nova Albion on the 23d of July, the inhabitants appearing extremely concerned at his departure, and lighting fires on the higheft hills, as was fup-pofed to make facrifices to procure the fafety of thefe ftrangers, till the fhip was out of fight. Mean while the admiral ftretched forward to the weft-ward, for the Molucco iflands, and on the 13th of October came up with the Landrones, whence a great number of fmall veffels came off, bringing fifh, fruit, and other provifions to fell. Thefe veffels looked fmooth and fhining like burnifhed horn, and on each fide of them lay out two pieces of wood, and the infide was adorned with white fhells. The people in thefe veffels had the lower part of their ears pared round, and ftretched with the heavy pendants that hung in them. Their teeth was as black as jet, occasioned by their chewing an herb with a sort of powder, which they carried about with them for that purpose, and were esteemed of great service in preserving them. And their nails seemed designed for defensive weapons, by their suffering them to grow at least a full inch in length. These people seemed at first to deal very fairly, but soon began to steal every thing they could lay their hands on; and it was impossible to make them part with any thing on which they had once seized. This usage made the English refuse to deal with them, and hinder their going on board their ship, at which they were so exasperated, that they flung stones; but on firing a single gun, they were so intimidated, that they leaped into the water, and skulked for shelter under their vessels, till the ship was at some distance, when nimbly recovering them, they steered to the shore, but not without frequently casting their eyes behind them.

On the 18th they came to several other islands, some of which appeared to be very populous; and, continuing their course, passed by the islands of Tagulada, Zelon, and Zewarra; the first of which produces great quantities of cinnamon, and the inhabitants of most of them were friends to the Portugueze.

On the 14th of November they fell in with the Moluccas, and intending to sail to Tydore, coasted along the island of Mutyr, subject to the king of Ternate; but were prevented by meeting his viceroy, who, seeing the admiral's ship, boldly ventured on board, and advised him by signs not to prosecute his voyage to Tydore, but to sail directly for Ternate, because his master was a great enemy to the Portugueze, and would have nothing to do with him, if he was at all concerned with Tydore, or the Portugueze settled there.

This intimation induced Mr. Drake to alter his firſt reſolution, and reſolving to ſtay at Ternate, he early the next morning came to an anchor before the town, when he ſent the king a preſent of a velvet cloak; and the meſſenger was ordered to make him ſenſible, that his intentions were entirely peaceable, and that he came with no other deſign but to procure proviſions and other neceſſaries in exchange for merchandize. In anſwer to which the king let him know that he was much pleaſed with the thoughts of carrying on a friendly correſpondence with the Engliſh, who ſhould be welcome to whatever his country afforded. The author of this voyage adds, that this ſovereign profeſſed himſelf ready to lay himſelf and his kingdom at the feet of ſo glorious a princeſs as the queen of England, and to make her his ſovereign, as well as theirs; but it muſt be allowed that this monarch could have no motive for ſo high ſtrained a compliment; and that it is more natural to ſuppoſe, that this was inſerted by the author, with no other view but that of pleaſing queen Elizabeth. However, the meſſenger was received with much pomp and ceremony.

The king having a curioſity to ſee the ſhip, reſolved to pay the admiral a viſit on board, and therefore ſent four large veſſels filled with the moſt conſiderable perſons of his court. They were all dreſſed in white lawn or calico. They had a large canopy of very fine perfumed mats, ſupported by a frame made of reeds, which ſpread over their heads from one end of the veſſel to the other. They were ſurrounded by ſervants, who were alſo clothed in white, and theſe were encompaſſed by ranks of ſoldiers, on both ſides of whom were placed the rowers, in three galleries raiſed above each other. Theſe veſſels rowed by the admiral in great order, each paying him their reſpects in turn, and then acquainted him by ſigns that they were sent by the king to conduct him into a safer road. Soon after came the king himself, attended by six grave ancient persons. He seemed much pleased with the English music, and still more with the admiral's generosity, who made him and his nobles some considerable presents that were highly acceptable. He promised to return again the following day, and to send them in the mean time such provisions as they might stand in need of. In this last particular he kept his word, and they received a considerable quantity of fowls, rice, cloves, sugar, a kind of fruit called frigo and sagoe.

The next morning the king sent his brother and the viceroy on board, to excuse his not visiting the admiral, to invite him on shore, and to stay behind by way of hostage for the admiral's return. This invitation Mr. Drake declined, but however, sent some of his retinue with the king's brother, and detained only the viceroy as a pledge of their safety.

On their landing they were received by another of the king's brothers, accompanied by several of the nobles, who conducted them with great solemnity to the castle, where they found at least 1000 persons, the principal of whom were the council, which consisted of sixty very grave men. Soon after the king himself entered, guarded by twelve men armed with lances, the points inverted. A loose robe of gold tissue hung over his shoulders, several gold rings were fastened about his hair by way of ornament, and he had a chain of the same metal about his neck. He had several rings set with fine jewels on his fingers. His legs were bare, and his shoes were made of red leather, and over him was borne an umbrella richly embroidered with gold. On the right hand of the chair on which he seated himself, stood a page with a fan two feet in length and one broad, adorned with faphires and faftened to a ftaff three feet long; the page with this fan ftrove to allay the heat occafioned by the warmth of the fun, and the throng of the people. His majefty gave the Englifh gentlemen a very kind reception; and having underftood their meffage, fent one of his council to conduct them back to the fhip. The king of Ternate is a very powerful prince, he having feventy iflands under his jurifdiction. His religion as well as that of his fubjects, is Mahometanifm.

While the admiral ftaid here, he was vifited by a perfon well attended, who was of the blood royal of China, but banifhed for a term of years, on fufpicion of his being guilty of fome crimes againft the ftate; during which time he propofed to travel, in order that he might reap fome advantage from his misfortunes. He feemed to be a man of found fenfe, of a ftrong judgment and a good memory, and having probably acquired the knowledge of fome European language, proved an entertaining companion. He was highly pleafed with the admiral's behaviour, and ftrove to perfuade him to touch at China, but in vain; for having accomplifhed what induced him to undertake his voyage, his thoughts were now folely bent on returning home.

The admiral therefore having procured what he wanted at Ternate, fet fail from thence, and five days after caft anchor at a fmall uninhabited ifland to the fouthward of Celebes, where he ordered forges to be fet up, to repair the iron-work of the fhip, in which the fmiths were obliged to make ufe of charcoal, as all their feacoal was now confumed. This ifland was extremely woody, the trees were large and very lofty, ftrait and without boughs except towards the top, where the leaves fomewhat refembled thofe of the Englifh broom. Here they obferved in the night, great multitudes of shining flies no bigger than the common fly in England, which skimming up and down in the air between the trees and bushes, made them appear as if on fire: they also found bats as big as hens, and a sort of cray-fish, which live upon land and are of so extraordinary a size, that one of them is sufficient to satisfy the hunger of four persons; these burrow in the ground like rabbits.

After staying twenty-six days at this island, they weighed and again set sail; but were soon entangled among several small islands, and the wind suddenly shifting, they on the 9th of January 1579, ran upon a rock, on which they stuck fast, from eight at night till four in the afternoon of the next day. In this distress they lightened the ship, by taking out three tons of clothes, eight pieces of ordnance and some provisions, and soon after the wind chopping about happily disengaged them.

Some time after, having severely suffered by the winds and shoals, they fell in with the fertile islands of Baratene, where they found great plenty of provisions of all sorts, excellent spices, as nutmegs, long pepper and ginger, with lemons, oranges, cocoas, plaintains, cucumbers, and particularly a fruit of the size of a bayberry, which is hard but has a pleasant taste, and when boiled is soft and easy of digestion. This island also produces gold, silver, copper, and sulphur. The natives are far from being disagreeable, but their humanity and integrity render them most amiable. They are courteous to strangers, and trade with an honesty and punctuality that ought to put christians to the blush. The men have only a covering for their heads, and a piece of linen round their waist; the women have a garment which reaches from the waist to the feet, and have eight or ten bracelets on their arms, made of brass, horn, or bone, the least of which weighed two ounces each.

Weighing anchor, they left Baratene, and failed for Java Major, where they were alfo honourably entertained. The ifland was governed by five kings, who preferved a perfect good underftanding between each other. Four of whom came at once on board, and the admiral had very often the company of two or three of them at a time.

The Javans, who are a ftout and warlike people, go well armed with fwords, targets, and daggers, which they temper very fkilfully. They wear turbans on their heads, and a piece of filk from the waift downwards, which trails on the ground. Their behaviour, with refpect to their women, is very different from that of the inhabitants of the Molucco iflands, who will fcarcely fuffer them to be feen by a ftranger, while thefe run fo far into the other extreme, that they very civilly offer them as bedfellows. They are alfo extremely fociable among themfelves, for in every village they have a public houfe where they meet and bring their fhares of provifions, and joining their ftocks together, form one great feaft, for keeping up good fellowfhip among the king's fubjects. They have a peculiar way of boiling rice, which they put into an earthen pot of a conical figure, open at the greater end, and perforated all over, and this is fixed in a large earthen pot full of boiling water, and fet over the fire, when the rice fwelling and filling the holes of the pot, but a fmall quantity of the water can enter, by which means the rice is brought to a very firm confiftence; of this they make feveral agreeable difhes, by mixing it with fugar, fpices, butter, oil, or whatever elfe is moft agreeable to their palate. The venereal difeafe at this time prevailed much among the inhabitants, but inftead of falivation, they cured it by expofing the body quite naked for fome hours to the fcorching heat of the fun; by which means the noxious matter was difcharged by natural perfpiration.

The admiral having caufed the hull of the ſhip to be cleared from the barnacle ſhells ſhe had gathered in her long voyage, and her bottom new payed, weighed anchor on the 26th of March for the Cape of Good Hope, which he doubled on the 18th of June; when the few obſtructions he met with in this part of the voyage fully convinced him, that the Portugueze had grofly miſrepreſented the paſſage, and abuſed the world with falſe repreſentations of the horrors and dangers with which it is attended.

On the 22d of July, the admiral arrived at Sierra Leona, where he and the crew ſaw many elephants, and ſome trees, which hanging over the ſea were covered with oyſters, that lived and multiplied among them. With theſe, and the lemons, which were very plentiful, the crew after this long run, were much refreſhed.

After ſtaying two days, which they ſpent in wooding, watering, and taking in refreſhments, they weighed anchor, and on the 26th were off the Canaries, but being ſufficiently ſtocked with neceſſaries they continued their voyage to Plymouth, where they arrived on Monday the 26th of September 1580, and according to their own account Sunday the 25th, after having ſpent in encompaſſing the globe, two years, ten months and a few days.

No private ſubject was ever more applauded than admiral Drake for this voyage, which gave England the glory of having produced the firſt commander that ever ſailed round the world; a commander whoſe valour made the Engliſh feared, while his humanity ſhewed that they were worthy of being beloved.

THE VOYAGE

OF

SCHOVTEN AND LE MAIRE,

ROUND THE WORLD.

Giving an account of the rife and defign of this voyage, and the particulars that took place after their failing from the Texel, until their return to Holland.

THE States General of the United Provinces having granted an exclufive charter to the Eaft-India company, prohibiting all their other fubjects from carrying on any trade to the eaftward beyond the Cape of Good Hope, or to the weftward through the ftreights of Magellen, this prohibition gave great offence to many rich merchants who were defirous of making difcoveries at their own expence, and could not help thinking it a little unjuft, that the government fhould thus, againft the laws of nature, bar thofe paffages which Providence had left free. Among the reft was Mr. Le Maire, a rich merchant of Amfterdam, who earneftly defired to employ a part of that wealth he had acquired by trade, in obtaining fame as a difcoverer. With this view he made application to Mr. William Cornelifon Schovten, of Horn, a perfon in eafy circumftances, who had been three times to the Eaft-Indies, and afked his opinion, whether it might not be poffible to find another paffage into the South Seas than by the ftreights of Magellan, and whether it was not likely that the countries to the south of that passage might afford as rich commodities as either the East or West-Indies. Mr. Schovten answered that there was great reason to believe that such a passage might be discovered, and still stronger reasons to confirm what he conjectured as to the riches of the southern countries.

After many conversations upon the same subject, they at last resolved to attempt such a discovery, from a persuasion that the States General could not intend by the above exclusive charter to preclude their subjects from discovering countries on the south, by a new passage distinct from those mentioned in the charter; and it was agreed that Le Maire and his friends should advance one half towards the necessary expence of the voyage, and Schovten and his friends the other.

For this voyage such preparations were made, that every thing was ready in the space of two months, and the seamen entering into general articles to go wherever their masters and supercargoes should require; they, in consideration of so unusual a condition, were to receive extraordinary wages, and the eagerness of the sailors to engage in it, gave them an opportunity of chusing none but the most experienced mariners, on whose skill and fidelity they could depend.

These extraordinary preparations, with the secrecy that was observed, caused a great noise not only at Amsterdam, but all over Holland, where people reasoned on the intention of this voyage according to their several capacities, the common people giving them the name of the Gold-finders, while the merchants, with greater propriety, called all who contributed to it the South-Company.

Two ships were fitted out on this expedition, the largest of which was called the Unity; she was 360 tons burden, carried 19 guns, with 12 swivels, and 65 men. She had also on board a pinnace with sails, another to row, a launch for landing of men, and a small boat. William Cornelison Schovten was master and pilot, and James Le Maire, the son of the gentleman who proposed the expedition, was supercargo. The other was the Horn of only 110 tons burden, carrying eight guns, four swivels, and 22 men, commanded by John Cornelison Schovten.

On the 4th of June, 1615, they sailed out of the Texel, and on the 17th anchored in the Downs, took in fresh water at Dover, and hired an English gunner. They afterwards hired an English carpenter at Plymouth, and on the 28th sailed from that port. On the 13th of July they steered between the island Teneriff and Grand Canaria, and on the 20th in the morning fell in with Cape Verd, where they took in fresh water. On the 21st of August, they saw the high land of Sierra Leona, and the islands of Madrabomba, which lie on its south-point. They attempted to land by running to the point over the shallows of St. Ann, but finding that impracticable, steered to the above islands, which are three in number, very high, and lie in a row, half a league from Sierra Leona.

They anchored a league from one of these islands, which appeared to be full of bogs and marshes, and one entire waste, like a wilderness, scarce fit to entertain any inhabitants but wild beasts, and indeed not seeming to have any other. Going on shore on the 23d, they found a river, the mouth of which was so stopped up with sand and cliffs of rocks, that no ship could enter it; yet within the water was sufficiently deep, and broad enough for ships to turn about. Here they saw monkeys, wild oxen, a sort of birds that made a noise not unlike the barking of a dog, crocodiles and turtle, but met with no fruit except lemons.

On the 30th they arrived before a village that looks upon the road of Sierra Leona, where they anchored in eight fathoms of water. This village confifted of about eight or nine poor houfes covered with ftraw, but the Moors who dwelt in them were unwilling to come on board, without having pledges left on fhore to fecure their fafe return. However, Aris Olawfon, the fupercargo of the Horn, landed, and ftaid among them, purchafing lemons and bananas with glafs beads; and in the mean time, fome of the natives came on board. The fhips had here a good opportunity of taking in a fufficent fupply of frefh water, which pouring down in great quantities from a very high mountain, the failors had nothing to do but to place their barrels to receive it under the fall of the water. There were alfo vaft woods of lemon trees, which made that fruit fo cheap, that for a few beads and knives, they might have had ten thoufand. On the firft of September, they anchored before a fmall river, and landing got fome lemons and palmettos, took an antelope in the woods, and had good fuccefs in fifhing On the 3d, the mafter brought in a great fhoal of fifh fhaped like a fhoemaker's knife, and as many lemons as came to 150 for every man's fhare.

Early on the 4th they failed from Sierra Leona, and the next day were extremely furprized with a violent ftroke given the lower part of one of the fhips, though there was no rock for them to run upon ; but while they were amufed with this phenomenon, the fea about them began to change its colour, and looked as if fome great fountain of blood had been opened into it. The caufe of thefe events they were entirely ignorant of, till they came to Port Defire, and fet the fhip upon the ftrand to make her clean, when they found a large horn both in form and magnitude refembling an elephant's tooth, fticking faft in the bottom of the ſhip. It was a firm and ſolid body, without any cavity or ſpungy matter in the middle: it had pierced through three very ſtout planks of the ſhip, and raiſed one of her ribs, ſo that it ſtuck at leaſt half a foot deep in the planks, and about as much appeared without the hole, up to the place where it was broken off. And now the riddle was completely ſolved, this horn being the ſpoil of a fiſh that had thus rudely aſſaulted the ſhip with this piercing weapon; and after the firſt thruſt, not being able to draw it out again, had there broken it, which was attended with ſuch a plentiful effuſion of blood, that it had diſcoloured the ſea.

Having now ſailed ſo far that none on board, except the maſter, knew where they were, or whither they intended, they, upon the 25th, made known their deſign, of diſcovering a new ſouthern paſſage into the great Pacific Ocean; upon which all the ſailors ſeemed highly pleaſed, hoping to find ſome golden country, to make them amends for all their trouble and danger.

On the 7th of November keeping a ſouth courſe, they came before the haven of Port Deſire, but ſailing too far to the ſouthward, miſſed the right channel, and entered a crooked bay, where at high tide they had but four fathoms and a half water; by which means the Unity lay with her ſtern faſt a-ground, and if a briſk gale had not blown from the north-eaſt, ſhe would have been infallibly loſt. Here they found plenty of eggs among the cliffs, and the bay afforded them muſcles and ſmelts of ſixteen inches in length, whence they gave it the name of Smelt Bay; and the ſhallop being ſent to the Penguin Iſlands, returned with 150 penguins, and two ſea lions.

On the 8th they ſailed out of Smelt Bay, and entered Port Deſire, which lies in 47°. 40. ſouth latitude; but after a little more than a league's ſailing in this bay, the wind beginning to veer about, they anchored in twenty fathoms water; but the bottom being only flippery ftones, and the wind blowing hard at north-weft, their anchors could not preferve them from driving upon the fouthern fhore; fo that both the fhips were in danger of being wrecked. The Unity lay with her fides upon the cliffs, but the Horn ftuck fo that her keel was above a fathom out of the water. For fome time the north-weft wind by blowing hard upon her fide, kept her from falling over, but that fupport being gone, fhe funk down upon that fide at leaft three feet lower than her keel, and yet to the furprize of every one, the fucceeding flood which came on with ftill weather, fet her upright again, and both fhe and her companion got clear of the danger.

On the 9th, they went farther into the river, and came to King's Ifland, which they found full of black fea mews, and almoft covered with their eggs; a man without ftraining to reach might have taken between fifty and fixty nefts with his hand, in each of which were three or four eggs; fo that they were foon furnifhed with fome thoufands of them. Two days after the boat went in fearch of good water to the fouth fide of the river, but all they found was of a brackifh difagreeable tafte. They here faw oftriches, and beafts refembling harts that were extremely wild, and had remarkable long necks, and upon the hills they found great heaps of ftones, under which fome bodies of a monftrous fize had been interred, as they judged from the length of the bones they found.

Some days after, they careened the Unity upon King's Ifland, which being performed very fuccefsfully, they hauled the Horn on fhore, for the fame purpofe, placing her about 200 yards from the other fhip; but while they were bufy in cleaning both fhips, a fire of dry reeds being placed under the Horn, the flame got into that veffel, and set her on fire, and she being fifty feet from the water side, the men were unable to do any thing towards extinguishing it, by which means she was consumed. However on the 20th, at high water they launched the Unity, and the next day carried on board her every thing they had been able to save out of the Horn.

On the 13th of January, they set sail from Port Desire, and on the 24th saw land, stretching from the east to the south, with very high hills covered with ice, and soon after other land, bearing east from it, as high and rugged as the former. These lands they imagined lay near eight leagues asunder, and from there being a brisk current, that ran by them to the southward, imagined there might be a good passage between them, they therefore made up to this opening, when they saw an incredible number of penguins, and such shoals of whales, that they were forced to proceed with great caution for fear of running the ship upon them.

The next day they got up close by the east land, which upon the north side extends east south-east as far as the eye can follow it. This they called Staten Land or States Land, and to that which lay to the west, they gave the name of Maurice Land. They observed that there were good roads, and sandy bays, plenty of fish, porpoises, penguins, and some sorts of fowl, but the adjacent land seemed quite bare of trees and woods. At their entrance into this passage, having a north wind, they briskly sailed to the southward, and afterwards to the south-west, meeting with prodigious waves, that came rolling along before the wind. This, with the depth of the water, gave them full assurance that the great South Sea, was now before them, into which they had almost made their way by a passage of their own discovery. The sea mews were here larger than swans, and their wings when extended to their full length, spread about the compass of a fathom. They would come and tamely sit down upon the ship and suffer themselves to be taken with the hand, without any endeavours to fly away.

On the 29th, they had the prospect of two islands set round with cliffs lying to the west-ward, to which they gave the name of Barnevelt's Island, and taking a north-west course from thence, saw land again, which was high, and covered with snow, and ended in a sharp point, which they called Cape Horn. They now held their course to the westward, with a strong current, yet great billows rolled upon them from the west. On the 31st, they passed Cape Horn, and on the 12th of February, plainly discovered the streights of Magellan, lying to the east-ward, and being now certain of their having made a new and happy discovery, their general joy was expressed by every person on board having a cup of wine, which went three times round the company; and at the same time they gave to the new found passage the name of Streights le Maire. It is observable that all the time of their sailing through these streights, and about the southern land now first discovered, they had a settled course of bad weather, a thick and foggy air and strong currents. All which added together, made their sailing in these streights very tedious. But the joy of this discovery, the hopes of farther improvements, with the comforts of the bottle, helped to remove the sense of that tedious run, and the dangers they had entertained.

On the 28th, they resolved to sail for the islands of Juan Fernandes, in order to give those who were sick and weary proper refreshments; they saw these islands on the first of March. The road of the larger lies on the east point, and they shaped their course to the western side of it, by which means they were reduced to the inconvenience of not being able to get near enough the land to anchor. This made them difpatch their boat to found the depth, which returned with an account of there being good anchoring, and of their having feen a very lovely valley full of trees and thickets, refrefhed with ftreams of water running down from the hills, and variety of animals grazing. They brought great plenty of fifh along with them, the greateft number of which were lobfters and crabs, and obferved that they had feen a great many feals. The two following days, they repeated their attempt to anchor clofe by the land; but all their endeavours were ineffectual. The men however ftill continued fifhing, in which they had fuch fuccefs that they took almoft two tons of fifh with only hooks, in the fmall time in which fome of the company went to fetch water. At laft finding the ifland thus inacceffible, they refolved to purfue their voyage.

On the 3d of April, when they got into 15°. 12. the men from having a good ftate of health were feized with the flux, but at the fame time they faw a little low ifland at three leagues diftance, which they got up to about noon, but could find no bottom, and therefore fent out the fhallop. The men who went on fhore found no other refrefhment but fome herbs that tafted like fcurvy grafs; they obferved a very filent fort of dogs on the ifland, that could neither bark, fnarl, or make any other noife, for which reafon they called it Dog Ifland. It lies in 15° 12. and they judged it to be 925 leagues diftant from the coaft of Peru.

On the 14th, failing to the weftward they faw a large low ifland, and at fun-fet being about a league from it, an Indian canoe advanced to meet them. The men who were naked, had long black hair, and their bodies were of a reddifh colour. They made figns to the Dutch to come on fhore, and

called to them in their language, and though the
Dutch anſwered them in their own, the Spaniſh,
Moluccan, and Javan tongues, yet the Indians
could not underſtand them. When they got up
to the iſland, they ſtill found no bottom, and no
change of water, though they were within a muſket
ſhot of the ſhore. Here the Indians and they had
another unintelligible conference ; but not all the
ſigns made by the Dutch could prevail on them to
come on board, nor would the Dutch go on ſhore
to them, though they ſtill kept talking and pointing to one another. Therefore leaving theſe people
they ſteered to the ſouthward, and having made ten
leagues that night, ſailed in the morning cloſe
along by the ſhore, on which many of theſe naked
people were ſtanding, and ſeemed calling to them
to land. Soon after, one of the canoes put off towards the ſhip, but though the men would not
come near it, they ventured up to the ſhallop,
when the Dutch gave them beads and knives, and
ſeveral other things, with which they were highly
pleaſed ; and this at laſt emboldened them to come
a little nearer the ſhip, though they would not
go on board, but got back into the ſhallop. Indeed they did not ſeem to have any great reaſon for
deſiring their company, for they appeared to be
entirely void of honeſty, and were ſo fond of iron,
that they ſtole ſome nails that lay in the cabbin
window. When the Dutch gave them wine, they
drank the liquor and kept the cup, and when they
threw a rope to bring them to the ſhip, they would
neither uſe the rope nor return it. In ſhort, whatever they laid their hands on they conſidered as
their own, nor was there any way of recovering it,
without making uſe of force. Theſe people were
entirely naked, except wearing a ſmall mat round
the waiſt; and what ſeemed very ſingular, and
gave them a very odd appearance, their ſkins were

all over painted with the reprefentation of fnakes, dragons, and the like reptiles.

The Dutch being difpofed to try if any thing was to be got on the ifland, fent the fhallop with eight mufketeers, and others of the fhip's company on fhore, but they were no fooner landed, than 30 of the natives rufhed out of a wood, armed with great clubs, long ftaves, and flings, and attempted to feize the fhallop, but the mufketeers firing among them they fled. This ifland they called The ifland without Ground, from their not being able to anchor near it. It is not broad, but fomething long and full of trees, which they fuppofed to be cocoas and palmettos. It lies in $15°$. fouth latitude, and about 100 leagues from Dog ifland.

Finding that nothing was to be done here, they fteered to the weftward, and on the 16th came to another ifland at $15°$. diftance. It was very low land, with many trees growing on its fides, but they here found no food except a few herbs like thofe in Dog Ifland, with fome crabs and other fhell fifh. It however afforded them good frefh water, which they found in a pit near the fhore, and the pottage they made of the herbs gathered there, was of great fervice to thofe who were troubled with the flux. This they called Water Ifland, from its furnifhing them with a fupply of water.

On the 18th, they reached another ifland fituated to the fouth weft, at above 20 leagues diftance from Water Ifland, and the boat being fent to found the depth, found a bottom by a point of land, near which was a gentle ftream of water. Upon this the empty cafks were fent in the boat, but after the men had taken great pains in landing, they were frightened away at the fight of one of the natives; when getting into their boat there appeared five or fix more of the Indians upon the fhore, who finding they were gone off, foon returned into the woods. But though they efcaped from the natives, of whom they were under great apprehenfions, they had other very troublefome enemies, that ftuck very clofe to them, of which they brought many millions along with them out of the woods: Thefe were a fort of black flies, of which there were fuch prodigious fwarms, that the men returned covered with them from head to foot. Their hands and feet were fo befet with them, that it was impoffible to form a judgment of their complexion, and their clothes were fo entirely hidden by the multitudes of thefe infects, that they compofed a kind of living apparel. Befides, their very boat and oars were all over in the fame drefs as themfelves; fo that when they came back, the plague of flies began to rage in the fhip, and every man was employed in defending his face and eyes as well as he could; for it was difficult for any of them to open their mouths either to fpeak or eat, without taking in a mouthful of them. This dreadful perfecution lafted about three or four days, during which the men were employed in killing them with fly-flaps, which did fuch execution, that within this time their fufferings were at an end, and few of the flies left to torment them. To this place they gave the name of Fly Ifland, and by the help of a good gale left it as faft as they could.

On the 9th of May, they were in 15°. 20. fouth latitude, and gueffed they were 1510 leagues from the coaft of Peru, when they perceived a bark failing towards them, which they went to meet, and gave her a gun or two to make her ftrike; but thofe in the bark not underftanding the language of the guns, the Dutch fent their fhallop with ten mufqueteers, to take her; upon which fhe endeavoured to make her efcape, but the fhallop intercepting her, fome of her men threw themfelves and their goods overboard; but when the fhallop boarded her, thofe who were left made not the leaft refiftance, but quietly furrendered to the conquerors, who used them very kindly, dressed their wounds, saved the lives of some who had leaped into the sea, and entertained all of them in the ship. There were about twenty-three of these people, among whom were eight women and several children. They were of a reddish complexion, and had no other covering except round the waist. The men had long curled black hair, while that of the women was short, and they all appeared remarkable for their neatness and cleanliness. Their bark was of a peculiar figure and structure, it consisting only of two canoes fastened together, with several planks laid across from one canoe to the other, hanging over a good way on both sides, and being made very fast and close above. At the end of one of the canoes was a mast, with a sail made of mats. They had no compass nor charts, nor any other furniture for the sea, but a few fishing hooks, the upper part of which was stone, and the other black bone, tortoiseshell, or mother of pearl. They had no occasion for a lading of fresh water, for they quenched their thirst with the liquor of a few cocoa nuts. The Dutch sent them all back to their vessel, where the women expressed their joy by embracing their husbands, and then they sailed away to the south east.

On the 11th, they came up with a very high island, and about two leagues farther to the southward, found another which was much lower. About this time another of the same kind of barks came up to them, which had a loose canoe on board to put out upon occasion, and this vessel sailed so fast, that few Dutch ships could outstrip her. Sending their shallop to sound by one of the islands, they cast anchor at about a cannon shot from the shore, though the natives by their signs directed them to go to the other island, and sailed thither before them.

The first of these islands, which is situated in 16°. 10. is one entire mountain; it resembles the Moluccas, and being covered with cocoa trees, they gave it the name of Cocoa Island. The other is much lower, but of greater length. While they were at anchor, there came three large vessels, and nine or ten canoes with three or four men in each, some of them hanging out white flags; in which they were imitated by the Dutch. These canoes were flat at one end and sharp at the other. They were each of them hewn out of a solid piece of red wood, and were remarkable for the swiftness with which they sailed. Many of the natives on their approaching the Dutch ship, leaped into the water with their hands full of cocoas, and ubes roots, which they bartered for nails and beads, giving four or five cocoas for a nail, or a small string of beads. But this trade inducing so many of the natives to come on board that the Dutch scarcely knew how to stir in the ship, they sent the shallop to the other island in search of a more convenient station. But the shallop was scarcely out when she was surrounded by a vast number of canoes, filled with a mad sort of people armed with great clubs, who immediately boarded her and attacked the men, when firing upon these savages, they laughed without shewing the least apprehension; but one of them being shot through the breast at the next discharge, they took care for the future to keep at a greater distance. These men were lusty and well proportioned. They were excellent swimmers, yet were not only thievish, but appeared very fantastical in dressing their hair, which some wore short, and others long; some had it curled, and others platted and folded up in several fashions.

The next day they came again with their canoes laden with cocoas, bananas, ubes roots, hogs and fresh water, when there was a great contention among them who should get first to the ship, and those who were behind being shut out by those who got before them, jumped into the water with bunches of cocoas in their mouths, and diving under their canoes, climbed up the sides of the ship like so many rats, in such swarms, that they were forced to keep them off with staves; however, the Dutch bartered with them that day for 1200 cocoas. The natives were much surprised at the strength of the ship, and to try it some of them crept under it, and beat upon its bottom with stones.

Mean while the king sent the commander a present of a black hog, charging the messenger to take no reward, and soon after came himself in a large vessel, attended with 35 canoes: being come near the Dutch ship, he began to call aloud, and his example was followed by all who accompanied him, this being their manner of bidding strangers welcome. The Dutch received them with trumpets and drums, with which they were both pleased and surprised, when to shew their sense of the honour done them, they bowed and clapped their hands over their heads. The king then sent the Dutch a present, which they returned with a gift of an old hatchet, some rusty nails, glass beads, and a piece of linen cloth, which his majesty received with a low bow, and seemed much pleased with them. He was only to be distinguished from his subjects, by the reverence they shewed him, for both he and they being entirely naked, he had no ensign of dignity. He however would not be persuaded to go on board, though his son did, and was well entertained.

On the 13th at noon, the Dutch vessel was surrounded with a fleet of 23 ships and 45 canoes, in which were no less than seven or 800 men. The king himself commanded the fleet. But though they at first pretended to come only with a view of trade, and attempted by their signs to make them sail to the other island, where they would find much better accommodations, yet the Dutch fuf-pecting fome mifchief, put themfelves on their guard, and indeed not without juft caufe, for the Indians furrounding the fhip on all fides, gave a great cry, and began the attack. The king's fhip was the foremoft in the action, and rufhed with fuch force at the Dutch fhip, that the heads of two canoes, which lay before it were dafhed to pieces with the violence of the fhock, while the reft came on as well as they could, throwing a fhower of ftones; but the Dutch difcharging their mufkets, and three great guns loaded with mufket fhot and nails, all in the canoes, who lay within reach of the guns, were glad to feek for fafety, by leaping into the water, and the reft endeavoured to efcape as well as they could. From this inftance of treachery, committed by the inhabitants of the lower of the two iflands, they gave it the name of Traitors Ifland.

They fet fail the fame day, and continuing their courfe to the weftward, came on the 14th to another ifland, thirty leagues diftance from the former. This they called Hope Ifland, from the hopes they entertained of its furnifhing them with fome refrefhment; but finding no ground, they fent their fhallop to found along the fhore, which returned with the news of their being a ftony bottom at forty fathoms water, about a mufket fhot from the fhore. Hither the Indians came in ten or twelve canoes, with a fmall number of flying fifh, for which they had beads in exchange, and whatever the one gave or the other received, was conveyed by a rope let down by the ftern of the fhip. Mean while the fhallop being employed in founding at fome diftance, others of the natives offered to board her, and carry her off; but the failors gave them fo warm a reception, with their guns, pikes, and cutlaffes, that having feen two of their companions killed, they were glad to hurry away as fast as they could. This island was full of black cliffs, whose tops were covered with vegetables, and was well stocked with cocoa trees. There were several houses along the sea side, and a great village close by the strand; but finding no convenient anchoring, Mr. Schovten left it, and sailed to the south-west.

Two days after their leaving Hope Island, Mr. Schovten observed to the officers, that they were now at least 1600 leagues to the westward of the coast of Peru, and as they had not yet discovered any part of the south land they had expected, there was no probability of their now doing it. That they had sailed much farther to the westward than was first intended, and if they proceeded in the course they had hitherto pursued, they should certainly fall to the southward of New Guinea, where if they found no passage they must inevitably be lost, since it would be impossible to sail back to the eastward, on account of the easterly winds that blew continually, whence he proposed that they should sail northward, so as to reach the north of New Guinea. This proposal was immediately embraced, and it was determined to hold a north-west course.

On the 19th, they observed two islands at about eight leagues distance, which seemed to be a cannon shot from each other. On the 21st, being about a league from the land, they were visited by two canoes, and though they gave them no manner of provocation, were rudely insulted by some of the people, who began to shout, and threatened to dart their wooden assagayas at them, upon which the Dutch discharged two of their guns, and killing two of these Indians, the rest fled with the utmost haste and confusion.

On the 22d, more of the Indians came to the ship, but behaved in a very friendly and peaceable manner, bringing cocoas, ubes roots, and roasted hogs, which they exchanged for knives, beads, and nails. Thefe people were as expert in fwimming and diving as thofe of Traitors Ifland, and as well verfed in ftealing, which they always practifed whenever they had an opportunity. Their houfes, which ftood along the ftrand, were covered on the top with leaves, and had a kind of penthoufe of the fame materials, to carry off the water. Thefe edifices, which were ten or twelve feet high, and twenty-five in compafs, were furnifhed with nothing but a bed of dry herbs, an angling rod or two, and a great club ; and the houfe where the king himfelf refided, had no other furniture.

On the 24th, Mr. Schovten fent three of his principal officers to eftablifh a friendfhip with the Indians, and to ftay on fhore as hoftages in the room of fix Indians of diftinction, who went on board, and were made very welcome ; while the Dutch on fhore were treated by the king with very great refpect. He made them a prefent of four hogs, and if any of his people came near the Dutch boat to difturb them, while they were taking in water, he would drive them away himfelf, or order fome of his men to do it. For his fubjects ftood in very great awe of him, and were afraid of his being acquainted with any of their crimes : for one of them having ftole a cutlafs, and complaint being made to one of the king's officers, the thief was purfued and feverely drubbed, befides being forced to make reftitution. The officer fignified that he came off very well too ; for if the king had known it, he would certainly have loft his head.

Thefe people were extremely frightened at the noife of the guns, and whenever they were difcharged would fly with the utmoft precipitation. The king however had a defire to hear one of the great guns, and for that purpofe was feated under a canopy, with fome of his favourites about him in great order; but upon the discharge of the gun, he leaped from his seat, and began running into the woods, with all his courtiers after him, while the Dutch were unable to stop them, by all the friendly signs they could make.

On the 25th and 26th, they again went on shore to barter for hogs, but could obtain none, for the Indians had only a few of them left. The king however continued to treat them with the same kindness and respect as before, and both he and his principal attendant pulled off their caps of feathers, and placed them upon the heads of two of the company. These caps were made of white, red, and green feathers, furnished them by their parrots and doves, which last are white upon the back, and black every where else except upon the breast. Every one of the king's council had one of these doves sitting by them upon a stick.

On the 28th, they had got all their water on board, when Mr. Schovten and some of the officers went on shore with the trumpets, the music of which afforded the king great delight. Though this prince treated them with great respect, he seemed afraid of their having entertained a design of staying in his country, and let them know, that if they would go in two days time, he would give them ten hogs, and a considerable number of cocoas, yet notwithstanding his suspicions, he paid them a visit on board. His men behaved with the utmost submission to the Dutch, and with all the tokens of awe and fear, frequently kissed their feet and placed them upon their necks.

On the 30th, the king had a visit from the sovereign of the other island, who came with a train of 300 naked Indians, who had bunches of green herbs stuck round their waists, and brought, to insure his welcome, sixteen hogs. When these two princes came in sight of each other, they bowed, and muttered something to themselves;

and on their meeting, both fell with their faces flat upon the ground, and after uſing ſeveral ſtrange geſtures, walked to the ſeats prepared for them, where again muttering to themſelves, they bowed to each other, and then ſat down under a canopy. The prince of the iſland, in order to welcome the ſtranger, ſent a meſſenger to acquaint the Dutch that he wanted their muſic, which they underſtanding, came on ſhore with their drums and trumpets, with which the two kings were highly delighted. After this, preparations were made for a banquet, when a company of men came in with a good quantity of cana, an herb of which they make their drink, and each of them having taken a mouthful, they for ſome time chewed it together, and then put it into a wooden trough, poured water upon it, and having ſtirred and ſtrained it, preſented this ſtrange kind of liquor in cups to their two kings, and very civilly offered ſome of it to the Dutch, who declined taſting of it. The other part of the entertainment conſiſted of ubes roots roaſted, and hogs dreſſed after the following ſtrange manner: They had ripped up the bellies and taken out the entrails, and then putting in hot ſtones, and ſingeing off the outſide hair, they were without any further preparations fit for the king's table. Two of theſe hogs were alſo preſented to the Dutch with all the form and ceremony which they uſed to their kings, putting them firſt upon their heads, and then kneeling with much humility, they left them at their feet. They alſo gave them eleven more that were alive, for which they received a preſent of knives, old nails and beads.

Theſe people were of a dark yellow complexion, had ſtrong and well proportioned bodies, and were ſo tall that the largeſt among the Dutch was equal in ſtature only to the leaſt of them. Some of them wore their hair curled, others had it tied up in knots, and others again had it ſtanding upright like briſtles. That of the king and ſome of his courtiers was very long, hanging down below their hips, but the women were cropped cloſe, and were very diſagreeable figures; they were ſhort and ill-ſhaped, with long hanging breaſts, and both ſexes were naked from the waiſt upwards. Theſe people live upon what the earth ſpontaneouſly produces, without the labour of agriculture, or the care of attending cattle. To this place the Dutch gave the name of Horn Iſland, and to the harbour where they anchored, they gave that of Unity Bay.

On the 1ſt of June they ſet ſail, but made no land until the 21ſt, when they came up to a very low iſland, in 4°. 47. ſouth latitude, near which were ſeveral ſand banks, and three or four ſmaller iſlands very full of trees. Here they were viſited by a canoe, the people in which were blacker than thoſe they had ſeen before, and armed with bows and arrows, which were the firſt they had obſerved among the Indians of the South Seas. Theſe people told them by ſigns, that there was more land and good conveniences for ſhipping to the weſtward, where their king dwelt; upon which they again held a weſterly courſe, and the next day ſaw twelve or thirteen iſlands cloſe to each other. On the 24th they ſaw three low iſlands, lying to the ſouth-weſt, one of which was very ſmall, and the others only two miles long. Theſe they called the Green Iſlands. They were ſurrounded with cliffs, and had no convenience for anchoring.

The next day they obſerved another iſland, upon which they ſaw ſeven or eight huts, and that being St. John the Baptiſt's day, they called it St. John's Iſland. At this time they obſerved a very high land to the ſouth-weſt, which they imagined was the point of New Guinea, this they reached by noon, and finding no anchoring ſent the ſhallop to ſound, but no bottom could be diſcovered. Here two or three canoes filled with a barbarous fort of people, affaulted the fhallop with flings, but the Dutch firing upon them, they appeared greatly terrified and foon difperfed. They were of a very dark complexion, entirely naked, and fpoke a language quite different from the other. They kept fires upon the coaft all that night, and fome of them in their canoes came lurking about the fhip, which the Dutch no fooner difcovered than they ftrove to oblige them; yet they would underftand none of the figns by which they endeavoured to let them know that they were in want of provifions, but all the anfwer they made, confifted in horrible noifes and outcries.

The Unity came to an anchor that night, in a bay which had 45 fathoms water, where the country was high and green, and afforded a pleafant profpect. This bay they fuppofed to be 1840 leagues diftant from Peru

On the 26th in the morning, three canoes came up to the fhip filled with thefe favages, who were all armed with clubs, wooden fwords and flings; but though the Dutch ftill treated them kindly, and gave them feveral toys to procure their favour, or at leaft peace and freedom from any difturbance, they foon found that they were not to be conquered by kindnefs, nor taught good manners by any thing but the great guns; for they affaulted the fhip with all their force, and continued the attack until 10 or 12 of them were killed by the cannon fhot, when they leaped into the water, and began to fwim for their lives; but the Dutch purfuing them in the fhallop, knocked fome on the head, took three prifoners, and four canoes, which they broke in pieces, and ufed in the fhip for fire wood. The feverity of this treatment made the natives of the ifland more attentive to the figns made by the Dutch, who therefore brought hogs and bananas to ranfom the prifoners, giving ten hogs for one person. In this island were birds that were entirely red.

On the 28th in the evening, they again set sail, and the next day saw three high islands to the north of the former. On the 30th in the morning, several canoes of very swarthy Indians, came up to the ship, and being allowed to go on board, broke staves over the heads of the Dutch, as a sign of peace. Their canoes were neater than the others, and the people appeared more civil and modest, wearing a covering about the waist, which the others did not. They also rubbed their black hair with chalk, which made it appear as if powdered. They pretended to be so poor that instead of bringing any thing to the ship, they came to beg, and yet the three islands from whence they came afforded great plenty of cocoas.

On the 1st of July, in the morning, the Unity cast anchor between an island two miles long, and the main land of New Guinea, and was soon surrounded with 25 armed canoes, supposed to be filled with people of the same islands as those, who the day before had, in token of peace, broken their staves over their heads. Two of these fixing themselves upon two anchors fastened their girdles to them, and began to tug the ship, thinking to draw her on shore, while the rest attacked her sides with their slings and other weapons; but the Dutch firing upon them with their great guns, forced them to retire with the loss of twelve or thirteen killed, and a much greater number wounded.

After this engagement, the Dutch again set sail, and on the 4th passed by 23 other islands, some of them a league, and others not more than a cannon shot distant from each other. On the 6th they observed a very high mountain to the south-west, which they supposed to be Greemenassi in Banda; but on a nearer approach discovered three more lying to the north, at about fix or feven leagues diftance. The next day they found fome of thefe mountains to be volcanoes, for which reafon they named the ifland Vulcan's Ifle. It was well inhabited, and full of cocoas; but they had no conveniency for anchoring: the people were naked and extremely fearful of the Dutch, and their language fo very different from that of the other of the neighbouring iflands, that none of the Indians the Dutch had taken on board, could underftand them. There foon after appeared more iflands to the north and north-weft, but they fteered to a very low one to the weftward, which they reached that evening. They here obferved the water to be of feveral colours, as green, white, and yellow, which was probably occafioned by the mixture of fome rivers, for it was much fweeter than the fea-water, and full of leaves and boughs of trees, fome of which had birds and crabs upon them.

On the 8th of July, they caft anchor before an ifland in 3°, 40. fouth lat. which feemed to be an unhealthy place, and yielded nothing of any value except a little ginger. It was inhabited by Papoos, a people whofe ridiculous drefs added to their natural deformity, made them appear little fhort of monfters in human nature. There were fcarcely any of them that had not fomething odd and ftrange either in the bignefs or pofition of their limbs, which added to ftrings of hog's teeth hung about their necks, and rings faftened in their nofes, with their fhort frizzled hair, and very bad faces, rendered them perfectly difagreeable. Their houfes were entirely void of ornament, and fixed upon ftakes eight or nine feet from the ground.

The next day they anchored in a more convenient bay, near two villages belonging to thefe Indians, when fome of their canoes brought hogs and cocoas, but held up both at so dear a rate that there was no bartering with them.

Though the Dutch had sailed so long by an extensive tract of land, they were unable to determine whether it was New Guinea, or not, their charts neither agreeing one with another, nor with the land they had in prospect. On the 13th and 14th they kept sailing by the coast, and on the 14th, pursuing the same course, reached two low islands, about half a league from the main land, and in about 2°. 54. south latitude ; when seeing the country well stored with cocoas, they dispatched the boat and shallop, which were well provided for an attack, with orders to land and get some, but the Indians having observed them, prepared to receive them at their landing, and gave them the warmest reception with their bows and slings, they had ever met with, wounding at least 16 of them, and forcing them to retire, notwithstanding their being armed with muskets. However the next morning they sailed in between the two islands, and having cast anchor, landed upon the lesser island, burnt some of the Indian houses, and brought off as many cocoas as amounted to three to every man's share, when the natives finding how little able they were to defend themselves against these strangers, came to make their peace, by bringing cocoas, bananas, and ginger, and going on board the ship, the quarrel was perfectly made up, and the hearts of the Indians won, by the Dutch giving them a few beads and nails. The next day they continued bartering for cocoas, bananas, cassave, and papade, and obtained such a number of the former as amounted to 50 nuts and two bunches of bananas a man.

This island, which is the most easterly, the natives called Mosa, the other over against it Jusan, and another which was a very high one and about five or six leagues from New Guinea, they called

Arimea. These people had probably been visited by some Europeans before, for they had Spanish jars and pots among them, were not surprised like others at the firing of the great guns, nor so curious in examining the ship as those who had never seen one might be supposed to be.

On the 21st, they sailed to the north-west along the main land, and anchored among a cluster of islands, which they left on the 23d in the morning; soon after which they were overtaken by six great canoes bringing dried fish, cocoas, bananas, a small sort of fruit like prunes, and tobacco. From another island some Indians brought them provisions and china porcelain: these people, like most of the others, were extremely fond of beads and iron-work, and were remarkably distinguished from those in the last island, by the largeness of their size, and their having more of an orange-coloured complexion. Their arms were bows and arrows, and their principal ornaments were glass ear-rings of several colours, by which it appeared, that these Dutchmen were not the first Europeans they had seen.

On the 24th they steered along by a very pleasant island, to which they gave the name of Schovten, though it is distinguished in the maps by the name of Horn Island, and the west point of it they called the Cape of Good Hope. On the 26th they perceived three islands more, and on the 29th at night felt so violent a shock of an earthquake, that the men ran frightened out of their cabbins, imagining that the ship had run a-ground or bulged against a rock; but upon trial they found that the depth of water was unfathomable, and plainly saw that they were clear of all danger of rocks and shelves. On the 30th, they put into a great bay, out of which finding no opening, they returned to a northern course again. Here the ship trembled, and they had loud and horrible claps of thunder, while the ſhip would have been in danger of taking fire by the lightening, had it not been for prodigious ſhowers of rain.

On the 31ſt in the evening, they paſſed the Equator a ſecond time, and in the three following days came in ſight of ſeveral iſlands, and ſuppoſed that they reached the end of the continent of New Guinea, having ſailed 280 leagues along the coaſt.

On the 6th of Auguſt in the morning, ſeveral canoes came up to the ſhip, bringing Indian beans, rice, tobacco, and two birds of Paradiſe; when the Dutch purchaſed one of thoſe fine birds, which was white and yellow. Theſe Indians ſpoke the Ternate language, and ſome of them the Malayan and Spaniſh. They were all finely clothed about their waiſts, ſome with looſe ſilks, and others with breeches. Some of the company were Mahometans, and had ſilk turbans on their heads. They had all in general coal black hair, and many gold and ſilver rings upon their fingers. But though they bartered with the Dutch for beads and other toys, they had a much greater mind for linen cloth. Theſe people were ſo fearful and ſuſpicious, that they would not tell the Dutch the name of the country, though they imagined they were at one of the three eaſterly points of Gilolo, and that theſe were natives of Tydore, which they afterwards found to be true.

On the 6th in the morning, they weighed and ſtood to the northward, and on the 18th were ſaluted by two canoes of Ternateens, who ſhewed their peaceable diſpoſition by hanging out a white flag, and informed them that they came from the village of Soppy, where they had lately ſeen an Engliſh ſhip, and a pinnace from Amſterdam, which laid there three months for a lading of rice, and ſome of them offered to conduct them the next day into the road of Soppy, which they accordingly entered on the 19th, and bartered there for poultry, sagoe, rice, and turtle, when several of the natives coming on board, told them that an English and Dutch ship had been lately in those parts, and had procured a sufficient supply of provisions for their voyage home. This news was extremely agreeable to these people, who had spent almost their whole store, and there was a kind of public rejoicing among the whole crew, which now consisted of eighty-five men, all healthy and vigorous, who had no other apprehensions than what arose from their scantiness of provisions, and the next day they had an account that there were no less than twenty English and Dutch ships at Ternate.

On the 25th they again set sail, and on the first of September, the wind being contrary, entered into the bay, of what appeared a desert island, when some of the officers going on shore in order to view the country, endeavoured to ascend a very high mountain, but found it so very steep and rugged, that they soon abandoned the attempt. The name of this island is Moro.

On the 5th, they anchored off the coast of Gilolo, where some of the seamen going on shore unarmed to catch fish, four soldiers of Ternate suddenly rushed out of the woods, sword in hand, intending to have killed them while they were drawing up their net, but the surgeon calling out Oran Hollanda, the Indian soldiers stopped, and throwing water on their heads, which in those countries is a sign of peace, approached them in a civil manner, assuring them that the reason of their attempt was their taking them for Spaniards. At the request of the seamen, they were persuaded to go on board, where having beads and other trifles given them, they promised to bring provisions and refreshments, which they accordingly did.

On the 14th, they set sail; but the wind being slack for two or three days, they made no progrefs in their voyage. However, on the 17th, they came to an anchor before Malaya in Ternate, and captain Schovten and James Le Maire going on fhore, were entertained by the general, the governor of Amboyna, the admiral Verbaghen, and the whole council of India, and the next day fold two of their fhallops, with a great deal of what they had faved out of the Horn, which was burnt in the king's Ifland, for which they received in money 1350 rials, with part of which they purchafed two lafts of rice, a ton of vinegar, the like quantity of Spanifh wine, and about three tons of bifcuit.

On the 24th, eleven men and four boys defired leave of the captain to enter into the company's fervice, which, at the general's requeft, Mr. Schovten readily granted, and two days after, took leave of the general, who treated him with the greateft kindnefs and refpect, and accompanied him and Mr. Le Maire on board with colours flying.

On the 27th, they failed for Bantam, and on the 28th of October, anchored at Jacatra, where they found three Dutch and as many Englifh fhips in the road. But on the laft day of October, John Peterfon Koen, prefident of the Eaft-India company at Bantam, arriving in that city, he the very next day fent for the captain and both the fupercargoes, before the council of the Indies, and after very little difcourfe, required them, in virtue of his commiffion from the Eaft-India company, to deliver up the fhip and cargo immediately. The captain and fupercargoes infifted that this feizure was unlawful, fince they entered the Indies by neither of the forbidden paffages, the Cape of Good Hope or the Streights of Magellan, but by a paffage they themfelves had difcovered, which would be of great advantage to the commerce of their countrymen and to the whole trading world. But all their arguments were to no purpofe, the prefident telling them that they might feek for redrefs in Holland, This happened on Monday the firft of November, according to the reckoning of thofe who failed in the Unity, and upon Tuefday the fecond of November, according to the reckoning of their countrymen, who had failed directly from Holland. For as the Unity had failed weftward, and had with the fun fo far encompaffed the globe, they had one night, or fun fetting, lefs than their countrymen who had failed to the eaft.

Their fhip being in this manner taken from them, fome of the men entered into the Eaft-India company's fervice, and the reft were put into two fhips, that were returning to Holland; but Mr. James Le Maire, was fo fhocked at this difaftrous end of a voyage, which till that time had been fo profperous, that he died of grief and vexation, within a little more than a fortnight after the lofs of the veffel. The reft of the company had a profperous voyage to Holland, and arrived at Amfterdam on the firft of July. Their voyage round the world being performed in two years and eighteen days, which, confidering the difficulties they met with, and the nature of their courfe, muft appear extremely wonderful. But what renders it ftill more furprifing is, that they loft only four men by ficknefs in encompaffing the whole earth, and that one of thefe died of grief.

THE VOYAGE

OF

CAPTAIN WILLIAM DAMPIER,

ROUND THE WORLD.

Captain William Dampier fets fail from Virginia. An account of the many adventures from that time to his arrival in England, September 16th, 1691.

AFTER having diftinguifhed himfelf in feveral voyages, particularly in the South Seas, Mr. Dampier, while at Virginia, affociated himfelf with Capt. Cooke, with whom he had been formerly acquainted, in order to cruize on the Spaniards, and on the 23d of Auguft, fet fail from Achamack in Virginia, for the Cape de Verd iflands. In their paffage they met with a violent ftorm, which blew with prodigious fury for above a week. However they at length made the ifland of Salt, fo called from its abounding in falt ponds, and the great quantities of congealed falt found there.

The ifland of Salt, is fituated in 16°. north lat. and in 19°. 33': weft longitude from the Lizard, and is about nine leagues in length, and about two in breadth. The foil is extremely barren, without trees or grafs, and yet a few poor goats feed upon fome low fhrubs which grow near the fea-fide. There are alfo here a few wild fowl, efpecially the flamingo, a reddifh bird, refembling a heron, but much larger, frequenting ponds or marfhes, and being very shy, it is not easy to take them. They build their nests in the shallow parts of ponds or standing waters, by scraping the mud together into little hillocks, which taper up two feet above the surface of the water, where they leave a hole to lay their eggs in, which never exceed two, and these they hatch by covering them with their rumps, their long legs standing in the water, a position which nature has wisely made easy to them, since if they were to sit upon them the weight of their bodies would break them. The young ones cannot fly, but run with such swiftness that it is not easy to catch them, nor do they come to their true shape and colour, till they are ten or eleven months old. Their flesh is lean and black, though not ill tasted, but their tongues which are very large are esteemed great dainties. They generally stand in a row close together by the side of a pond; and Mr. Dampier remarks, that as their feathers are, of a reddish colour, they at a distance appear like a brick wall. Mr. Dampier and two others hiding themselves in the evening, near a place where they resorted, killed fourteen of them: the first shot being made whilst they were standing, and two others as they rose.

The inhabitants of the island amounted to no more than five or six, and yet there is a governor, but he made a most dismal figure, for he was covered with rags: However he came on board with a present of three or four lean goats, and in return captain Cooke gave him a coat. This governor also sold them about twenty bushels of salt for some old clothes, and then begging a little powder, went away extremely well satisfied. One of his followers unknown to him sold a sailor on board a piece of false ambergreafe, which was of a dark colour like sheep's dung, and was very soft, but had no smell.

From this island, they sailed to St. Nicholas, another of the Cape de Verd Islands, twenty-two leagues south-west from the former, and came to an anchor on the south side. It is of a triangular form, the longest side to the east, being thirty leagues in length, and the other two twenty leagues each. It is mountainous and barren, but about the middle, there are fruitful valleys inhabited by the Portugueze, who have good vineyards and plantations. The inhabitants are of a dark swarthy complexion, and by their dress appear in but indifferent circumstances. However the governor and thirty-four gentlemen of his company, who visited Captain Cooke, made a pretty good appearance, and were armed with swords and pistols. The governor made them a present of several gallons of a pale thick wine, which in taste resembled Madeira.

They staid here five or six days to scrub their ship's bottom, and in digging of wells for fresh water, and then sailed to Mayo, another of the Cape de Verd Islands, where they intended to have purchased some cows and goats; but one Captain Bond, a Bristol man, having a short time before, seized the governor and some other gentlemen who came on board in order to trade, and, after being paid the ransom demanded for them, villainously carried them off; the inhabitants were so justly exasperated at this instance of perfidy, that they would not permit any of Captain Cooke's men to land.

From the Cape de Verd Islands they steered to the south, directly to the Streights of Magellan, but at 10°. north, the wind blowing hard from the southward, they stood over for the Guinea coast, and in a few days came to an anchor at the mouth of Sherborough river, to the southward of Sierra Leona. On the shore a thick grove of trees concealed from their view a pretty large village, inhabited by negroes. The houses were low except one in the middle, where the captain and his crew were civilly entertained with palm wine and other refreshments, and supplied with plantains, rice, fowls, honey, and sugar-canes, at a small price.

About the middle of November, they prosecuted their voyage to the Streights of Magellan, but had hardly got out to sea, before they met with violent gusts of wind, of which there were three or four in a day, which together with calms made them advance but slowly. The wind veering at intervals to the southward, till they had proceeded one degree to the south of the line, when the wind turned to the east, and on the 28th of January 1684, they touched at the three islands of Sebald de Weers, which are extremely barren and destitute of trees, except some dildo bushes, which grow near the sea-side, and afford nothing remarkable, except vast shoals of small red lobsters, of the length of a man's finger.

As they could neither find safe anchoring nor fresh water at these islands, they proceeded towards the Streights of Magellan, and on the first of February, came in sight of the Streights of Le Maire, which they found very narrow, with highlands on both sides. But having sailed with a brisk gale, till within four miles of the mouth, were becalmed, and though they found a strong tide setting out of the Streights to the north, they were unable to distinguish whether it flowed or ebbed, the waves breaking on all sides, and tossing the ship in a surprizing manner.

On the 14th of February, they were surprized by a most violent storm, at west south-west, which lasted till the 3d of March, and on the 19th of the same month they perceived a sail to the south, which they supposed to be a Spanish merchantman bound from Baldivia to Lima, but it proved to be an English ship, commanded by Captain Eaton from London ; who being bound to the South Seas as well as they, kept company with them, through the Streights, they fupplying Mr. Eaton with bread and beef; in return for which he gave them water, of which they were in fome want.

On the 23d, they came to an anchor in twenty-five fathom water, in a bay on the fouth fide of the fertile ifland of Juan Fernandez. when a canoe was immediately fent on fhore, with a Mofkito, and two or three failors, in fearch of a Mofkito Indian, left there three years before, by Captain Watling; and notwithftanding all the fearch made after him by the Spaniards, had kept himfelf concealed in the woods ; but he now foon difcovered himfelf, for having the day before perceived an Englifh fail, he had killed three goats to feaft the crew, and now came running down from the woods to meet them.

The interview between him and the other Mofkito Indian, was extremely affecting ; and the joy he difcovered at feeing fo many of his old friends come on purpofe to bring him off, is not to be expreffed. He had built himfelf a fmall hut about half a mile from the fhore, which he had lined with goat fkins, and of thefe he had alfo made his bed ; and a piece of one of them was faftened round his waift, to fupply the want of his cloaths, which had been for fome time worn out. On his being left on fhore, he had a knife, a gun, fome powder and a fmall quantity of fhot, which being all fpent, he made a faw of his knife, and then fawed his gun-barrel into fmall pieces, and ftrengthening the iron when hot with a ftone, and rubbing it to an edge, he made harpoons, a lance and fifhing hooks, by imitating what he had remembered of the workmanfhip of the Englifh fmiths ; and indeed the Mofkito Indians make all their inftruments without either forge or anvil, and with the above inftruments he ufed to ftrike goats and fifh, from the time that his powder was spent. This man's name was Will, and the other was called Robert, for though the Moskito Indians do not distinguish themselves by any names, yet they take it as a great favour if the Europeans bestow one upon them.

After staying 14 days at the island of Juan Fernandez, they set sail on the 8th of April 1684, in company with Capt. Eaton, steering towards the line, off the mountains of Peru and Chili; but sailed no nearer the shore than 12 or 16 leagues, to prevent their being discovered by the Spaniards.

On the 3d of May, Capt. Eaton took a prize laden with timber; and on the 19th they came to an anchor off the islands of Lobos de la Mar. Having reason to believe they were discovered by the Spaniards, and that they would consequently keep all their richest ships in port, it was agreed to make a descent upon Truxillo, a populous city six miles from the port of Guanehagno; but the next day some of the men descrying two vessels to the west without the islands, and one betwixt an island and the continent, they gave them chase, Capt. Cooke's ship pursued that towards the continent, and Capt. Eaton the other two. They were soon taken and found to be laden with flour from Guanehagno to Panama, one of them had a letter from the viceroy of Lima, to the president of Panama, informing him, that having notice of some enemies lately come into those seas, he had immediately dispatched these three ships to supply his wants. They were at the same time informed by the prisoners, that the people of Truxillo were erecting a fort near the harbour of Guanehagno, upon which they resolved to lay aside the design of attacking that place, and steered with their prizes to the islands of Gallipagos, and at night came to anchor on the east side of one of the eastern most islands.

After a stay of twelve days among these islands, one of the Indian prisoners, a native of Rio Leja having given an ample account of the riches of that place, and offering his service to conduct them thither, it was resolved to take his advice, and they set sail on the 12th of June; but the fair weather and small winds led them by the beginning of June to Cape Blanco, on the continent of Mexico, so called from two white rocks, half a mile from the Cape, which are high, steep, and taper, and resemble two lofty towers. The Cape itself juts out with steep rocks to the sea; but having an easy descent on both sides from the flat on the top, which is covered with tall trees, it affords a very agreeable prospect. On the north-west side of the Cape is Caldera Bay, into which a rivulet of sweet water discharges itself through the low-lands, these are very rich and abound in lofty trees, that extend a mile to the north-east bay, where the savannas begin, and run several leagues into the country, being covered with a sweet, thick, and long grass, and beautified with small groves, which are interspersed through the plains. Deeper into the bay, the low-lands are stored with mangroves; but farther into the country, the land rises higher, and consists partly of woods and partly of hilly savannas. But in these woods the trees are much smaller than the others, and the grass of the savannas is inferior to the former.

Before they reached the above Cape, Capt. Cooke, who had been very ill ever since his departure from Juan Fernandez, died, and as in a few hours after they came to an anchor near the mouth of the above-mentioned rivulet, he was immediately carried on shore under a guard of twelve armed men, but while they were busy in digging his grave, three Spanish Indians came to them, asking several impertinent questions, which the others answered as they thought proper, and kept them in difcourfe till they found an opportunity of feizing them all, but one of them efcaped out of their hands, and the other two being carried on board, confeffed that they were fent thither as fpies from Nicoya, a fmall town at 12 or 14 leagues diftance, feated on the banks of the river of the fame name, which being a place very convenient for building and refitting of fhips, the prefident of Panama had fent advice thither of the Englifh being in thofe feas.

From thefe men they learned that the inhabitants of the country lived chiefly by tilling their grounds for corn, and feeding their cattle in the favannas or plains. That they fent their ox hides to the North Sea by the lake of Nicaragua, and alfo a red kind of wood ufed for dying, which they exchanged there for linen and woollen commodities, brought thither from Europe. They added, that at a fmall diftance was a large pen of horned cattle, where they might provide themfelves with as many cows and bulls as they wanted.

Upon this agreeable intelligence, twenty-four of the fhip's crew were immediately difpatched in two boats, and under the conduct of one of the Indians, landed at a place a league from the fhip, when hauling their boats upon the dry fand, they were conducted by their guide until they came to the pen, which was in a large favanna, two miles from the boats, where finding a great number of bulls and cows feeding, fome were for killing three of them immediately; but were oppofed by the reft, who alleged that they had better ftay all night, and in the morning kill as many as they wanted. Upon which Mr. Dampier and eleven more, thought fit to return on board, which they did without the leaft oppofition; but thofe who ftaid had foon reafon to repent their rafhnefs, for at break of day, when they were preparing to drive away as many cattle as they wanted, they found

The English coming to their Boat find it in flames, while the Spaniards at a distance mock at their distress.

themselves beset with fifty or sixty Spaniards lying in ambush among the bushes, who discharged several shot at them, they made a retreat, in expectation of getting to their boat; but when they at last came to the place where they had left it, they to their great confusion found it in flames; while the Spaniards who kept at a distance, mocked at their distress. In this perplexing situation they waded to a rock, where they were pretty sure of not being surrounded; and remained there seven or eight hours, in great danger of being swallowed up by the sea, which flowed in upon them apace. Mean while those on board every minute expected their return; but hearing nothing of them by four o'clock in the afternoon, ten men were sent in a canoe in search of them, who no sooner reached the place where they had landed before, than they found their comrades standing upon this rock, up to the middle in water, and as the tide was still coming in, they must have infallibly perished had the canoe come but an hour later, but they were now brought safe on board.

In this bay they afterwards seized two canoes. The people here have no ships or barks, and as there is scarce any fish they have no instruments for fishing. The English also provided themselves with a good quantity of lance-wood, which grows straight like the ash-tree, and being very hard and tough, they made them into scouring rods for their guns, and handles or staves for oars.

On the 19th of July, Mr. Edward Davis was appointed captain, in the room of Capt. Cooke, deceased; and the next day sailed in company with Capt. Eaton, towards Rio Leja, which is easily discovered at sea, on account of a very high burning mountain, called Volcano Vejo, which may be seen at twenty leagues distance: Being in sight of this volcano, they made towards the harbour, and then setting out their canoes, steered up to the town, and by nine o'clock in the morning discovered a house, and soon after three men going into a canoe on the inside of an island, which is a mile in length and encloses the harbour; but though these Indians made what haste they could in rowing to the continent, the English overtook them, and carried them back to the island; at the same time they observed a man on horseback on the continent, riding full speed towards the town. These men frankly confessed, that they had been placed on the island by the governor of Rio Leja, to keep watch day and night in order to give notice if they could see the English, and that the horseman was placed upon the same account upon the continent, within an hour's riding of the town. Therefore finding themselves discovered, the horseman being gone three hours before Eaton and his canoes reached the island; their design upon that town was for the present laid aside, and the men returned on board.

A consultation being now held, it was resolved to steer for the gulph of Amapalla, and Capt. Davis entering it with two canoes, in order if possible to get some prisoners and obtain intelligence, he came in the night to Mangera; and as soon as it was morning, perceiving many canoes hauled up in a bay, he landed there, and fell into a path which soon led him to the town; but the inhabitants had no sooner notice of his coming, than they all ran into the woods, except an old priest and two Indian boys, his attendants. Capt. Davis making them prisoners, brought them down to the sea-side, and obliged them to conduct him to the island of Amapalla, where being landed, he marched to a town on the top of a hill, when the inhabitants seeing them advance, would have fled into the woods, had they not been prevented by the chief magistrate's secretary, who notwithstanding his being an Indian, could read and write Spanish, and yet was an enemy to the Spaniards; this person having perfuaded them that the Englifh were friends who craved their affiftance againft their common oppreffors, they bid Davis and his men welcome, who after the firft falutations marched with them towards the church, with the prieft brought by Capt. Davis at their head.

It is obfervable that in all the Indian towns in general, the church is the only place where matters of a public nature are tranfacted. The church ferving both for their confultations and diverfions, for there are laid up their mafks, antique habits, hautboys, ftrumftrums, and other mufical inftruments. The ftrumftrum is an inftrument formed of the half of a gourd, the hollow of which is covered with a thin board, over which are laid ftrings, and it has fome refemblance to the found of a cittern. Here they meet to make merry on the night preceding any holiday or feftival, whence they dance, fing, and play with antique dreffes and geftures; but both their mufic and mirth have a melancholy air, which is not unfuitable to the yoke they groan under.

But to return to Capt Davis and his company, who intended, as foon as they were all got into the church, to prevail on the Indians to lend him their affiftance againft the Spaniards; even the prieft had promifed to contribute to this, by his good offices, and he was now upon fuch good terms with the people, that it feemed impoffible things fhould take a wrong turn. But juft as a few of the remaining Indians were entering the church, one of his men who was a little more hafty than the reft, pufhing an Indian who went flowly before him in order to make him proceed fafter, the poor man was fo frightened, that he fprang away with all poffible fpeed, and the reft taking the alarm followed him; fo that Capt. Davis and the prieft were left in the church by themfelves, and the captain being an entire ftranger to the caufe of this confufion, rafhly ordered his men to fire upon the fugitives, which entirely broke off his correspondence with these people; his best friend the secretary being killed.

In the afternoon of the same day, the ships coming to an anchor near the island of Amapalla, Capt. Davis and his men took the priest on board, who told them that since the secretary was killed, they had no other way left than to send for the cacique; which the priest having done, he came attended by six other Indians, and coming on board was received in a very friendly manner, and as they staid on board all the time the ships were in the gulph, proved extremely serviceable, both in piloting them to places where they had plenty of wood, water, and cattle, and in very cordially assisting them to the utmost of their power, and in return they were presented with some trifles, on which they set the highest value, and were fully satisfied at their departure.

The gulph of Amapalla is a large branch of the sea, which enters eight or ten leagues deep into the country; on the south side of it is Cape Caswina, and on the north-west side St. Michael's mountain, at the foot of which is a low plain a mile in length; and between these low grounds, and Point Caswina are two islands, at the distance of twelve miles from each other. The southermost, called Mangera, is high and round, two leagues in circuit, and on all sides enclosed with rocks, except to the north-east, where there is a small sandy creek. It produces very lofty trees, and has a town in the middle, in which is a handsome Spanish church. The inhabitants, who are Indians, have a few plantations of maize and plaintains. Their only tame fowls are cocks and hens, and they have no other beasts but cats and dogs. Amapalla is much larger than the other island, and has two towns that are two miles asunder, the largest of which stands on a small plain on the top of a hill, and has a handsome church. The other town has also a new church. It is observable that in most of the Indian towns under the jurisdiction of the Spaniards, the images of their saints found in their churches, are represented with an Indian complexion, and partly in their dress; while in the towns inhabited by the Spaniards, they have the complexion and dress of Spaniards.

Amapalla produces great plenty of maize, large hog plums, and a few plaintains. They have also some fowls; and no Spaniard lives there except the priest, who takes care of the two villages, and of the town in the island of Mangera. As the people have little or no money, they pay their tribute in maize, to the governor of St. Michael's town, which is seated at the foot of St. Michael's mount, and the priest has his tenths in all the produce.

In this gulph there are many other islands which are uninhabited. One that is pretty large belonging to a monastry; and four or five Indians looked after the cattle that fed there in great numbers.

On the 3d of September, capt. Davis sailed out of the gulph, through the channel betwixt Mangera and the island of Amapalla, after having set the priest on shore, and left the Cacique and his attendants in possession of one of the prizes, half full of flour. And on the 20th of the same month, came to an anchor near the island of Plata.

This island, which is situated in 1°. 10'. south latitude, is about four miles in length, and one and a half in breadth. It is pretty high, and surrounded with rocky cliffs, except in one place on the east side, where a fresh water torrent falls down from the rocks. The top is flat and plain, and produces three or four sorts of small trees unknown to Europe, that are overgrown with moss. But though in the beginning of the year it has pretty good grass, it has no land animals to feed upon it;

the vaſt number of goats which uſed to be here formerly being all deſtroyed. However, there are here many boobies and men-of-war birds, and near the ſhore are great plenty of ſmall turtle. The place for anchorage is on the eaſt ſide cloſe to the ſhore, within two cable lengths of a ſandy bay. It is ſaid to have obtained the name of La Plata, from Sir Francis Drake's bringng thither the Cacafuego, and dividing among his men the plate found in that rich prize.

After continuing one day here, they ſteered to Point St. Helena, which appears high and flat, like an iſland, it being ſurrounded with low grounds and covered on the top with thiſtles. It forms a large and good bay on the north ſide; on the ſhore of which ſtands a wretched village, alſo called St. Helena, inhabited by Indians; but the ground being ſandy and barren, they have neither trees nor graſs, corn nor fruit, except water-melons, which are here very good. They are obliged to bring their freſh water from the river Calanche, which is at four leagues diſtance, at the bottom of the bay. They live chiefly upon fiſh, and are ſupplied with maize for algatrane, a bituminous ſubſtance, ſo called by the Spaniards, which iſſues out of the earth above the high-water mark, and by long boiling becomes hard, like pitch, and anſwers the ſame purpoſes. Some of the men being ſent in the night time to take the village, landed in the morning, and took ſome priſoners, and a ſmall bark which had been ſet on fire by the inhabitants, who alleged that they had done it by ſpecial order from the viceroy.

The men returned back the ſame evening, immediately ſteered again to the iſland of Plata, where they anchored on the 26th of September, and inſtantly ſome of them were ſent to Manta, a village on the continent, ſeven or eight leagues from the iſland of Plata, and two or three leagues weſt of

Cape Loronzo, inhabited by Indians. They landed at day-break, within a mile and a half of the village; but the inhabitants being already ſtirring, took the alarm, and all of them abandoned the town, except two old women, who being taken priſoners, declared that the viceroy, upon receiving the news that a great number of the enemy were got into the South Seas, had ordered the ſhips to be burnt, the goats in the iſland of Plata to be deſtroyed, and that no more proviſions ſhould be kept there than were neceſſary for their preſent uſe.

The village of Manta is ſituated on an eaſy aſcent, and though it conſiſts only of mean and ſcattered buildings, affords a very agreeable proſpect from the ſea. It was formerly inhabited by the Spaniards, and has a very handſome church, adorned with carved work. The ſoil is here dry and ſandy, producing neither corn nor roots, but only a few ſhrubs. The inhabitants are ſupplied with neceſſaries by the ſhips from Panama and Lima, this being the firſt place at which they touch; and between the town and the ſea there is an excellent ſpring of water. At the back of the village, at ſome diſtance in the country, is a very high mountain, which riſes up into the clouds, in the form of a ſugar-loaf. Oppoſite the village, about a mile and a half from the ſhore, there is a dangerous rock, which never appears above water; but a mile within it is ſafe anchorage, at ſix, eight, or ten fathoms.

They returned the next day to the iſland of Plata, and being undetermined what courſe to take, ſtayed there till the ſecond of October, when they were joined by Captain Swan, in the Cygnet of London, a rich ſhip which was deſigned to trade on that coaſt and now come to anchor in the ſame road. But Mr. Swan being diſappointed in his hopes of trade, his men had forced him to take on board a party of buccaneers, who had travelled over the isthmus of Darien, under the command of Captain Peter Harris. There were now three of them together, for Captain Harris had a small bark given him, and the men wished for nothing so much as to meet with Captain Eaton, as they justly imagined, that with such a force they might be able to undertake an expedition of some consequence. The bark was therefore dispatched in quest of him, with a letter inviting him to share the fortune of these three adventurers, but he had lately quitted those seas, and (as it was imagined) steered for the East-Indies; a design he had long intended to put in execution. They at this time took a prize of 400 tons, laden with timber, bound from Guaiaquil to Lima, and from the people on board, they learned that the Viceroy of Peru was fitting out ten frigates against them. Though this news gave them some concern, it did not prevent their making a descent upon Paita, where 110 men landed early in the morning of the third of October, four miles south of Paita, where they took some prisoners, who were sent for a watch, and who said that the governor of Paita, with 100 men was coming to the assistance of the town; but notwithstanding this intelligence, the English attacked the fort, and took it with little opposition. Upon which the governor and inhabitants quitted the town, when the English entered it, but found that they had carried off their money, goods, and provisions. The same evening the ships came to an anchor a mile from the shore; but though the three captains offered to spare the town for 300 sacks of flour, 3000 pounds of sugar, 25 jars of wine, and 1000 jars of water; yet these moderate conditions were slighted, and therefore, after keeping possession of it six days, they set it on fire.

On the 10th of November, at night, they weighed from Paita, and taking the benefit of a land breeze, steered towards the island of Lobos de la Mare, and on the 14th touched at Lobos de la Terra, where they landed some men the following day, and the men killed a number of boobies, penguins, and seals, which were a seasonable refreshment, they having been without taking flesh of any sort for a long time. On the 19th they arrived at Lobos de la Mare, where the Moskito men on board caught a great number of turtle; and having taken on board some planks which they had got out of a prize, and formerly left there, it was resolved to attack Guaiaquil.

On the 29th, in the morning, they set sail for the bay of Guaiaquil, which is situated betwixt Cape Blanco to the south, and point Chandy to the north, and in the bottom of this bay lies a small island, called St. Clara. As they had formerly a design against the town of Guaiaquil, they left their ships at Cape Blanco, and steered with a bark and some canoes to the island of St. Clara, in the bay of Guaiaquil, and thence proceeded in two canoes to Point Arena, where the next day they took some of the fishermen of Puna, and afterwards the town. The next ebb they took a bark laden with Quito cloth, coming from Guaiaquil, the master of which told him there were three barks full of negroes coming with the next tide. Having embarked all their men in canoes, except five left on board the bark, they rowed towards Guaiaquil, but their canoes being heavy laden, the day broke when they were within two leagues of the town. Upon which they concealed themselves in an adjacent creek, sending one of the canoes to the bark which was left near Puna, with orders not to fire till the next day: but before the canoe could reach the bark with this order, the two barks filled with negroes coming out of the harbour with the evening tide, came within sight of the English bark, which fired three guns at them. The firing of these guns threw the English in the canoes into great consternation, who imagined that the townsmen had taken the alarm, whence some were for advancing immediately to the town, and others for returning to their ships; but as the ebb tide hindered them from going upwards, Captain Davis with fifty of his men resolved to march to the place by land, but the rest imagining the enterprize impracticable, remained in the creek to see the issue. When Captain Davis and his men had been gone about four hours, they were almost choaked among the mangrove woods which grow in the marshes, and returned without being able to advance far on their way to the town. It was then resolved to row up in sight of Guaiaquil, and if they found themselves discovered, to retire without making any attempt; therefore proceeding through the north-east channel, they arrived in the night within sight of the place, when at the discharge of a musket they perceived the whole town filled with lights, and as there was but one seen before, this was taken almost as an infallible sign of their being discovered; but it being alleged that these lights were used by the Spaniards in the nights before holidays, and that the next day was a festival, some of the people upbraided captain Swan and the rest with cowardice. Upon this they landed at a place two miles from the town, but it being over-run with woods, they were unable to proceed in the dark, and therefore waited till daylight. They had an Indian guide, who was led by a cord by one of Captain Davis's men, who seemed the most forward, but perhaps beginning to repent his rashness, cut the rope with which the guide was tied, and thus let him escape into the town, crying out, after he was gone, that somebody had cut the rope; so that after having searched in vain for the guide, it was unanimously resolved to desist. However they landed on the opposite bank, after day-break, where there were several horned cattle, and killed a cow, without receiving the least molestation from the town.

On the 9th of December, they returned to Puna, and in their way seized upon the two barks before mentioned, with about 1000 lusty negroes on board, out of which number they chose about sixty, and left the rest behind with the barks; though Mr. Dampier supposes, that if they had carried them all to St. Maria, on the isthmus of Darien, they might, with the assistance of the natives, and the English and French privateers that would have come to them from all parts of the West-Indies, have not only maintained themselves there in spite of all the power of Spain, but have extended their conquests to the rich gold mines of Quito.

On the 13th of December they set sail, and in three days arrived at the island of Plata, meeting in their passage the bark they had dispatched in search of Captain Eaton, and having taken in fresh water on the continent, they directed their course to Lavelia, a town in the bay of Panama. The next morning they passed in sight of Cape Passao, a round high point divided in the middle, bare towards the sea, but covered with fruit trees to the land side. Betwixt this and Cape St. Francisco, they observed abundance of small points, full of trees of several kinds, which inclose so many sandy creeks. As their design was to look into some river unfrequented by the Spaniards, in search of canoes, they endeavoured to make the river of St. Jago, on account of its nearness to the island of Gallo, in which there is much gold, and safe anchorage for ships. This river which is large and navigable, divides itself about seven leagues up in the country into two branches, which inclose an island four leagues in circumference, and runs through a very rich soil that produces all sorts of tall trees, ufually found in this climate, efpecially red and white cotton and cabbage trees, of the largeft kind.

The white cotton tree is much taller than the oak, and the trunk ftraight, without any branches, till near the top, where they are very ftrong. The bark is extremely fmooth, and the leaves, which are of the fize of thofe of a plumb-tree, are of a dark green, oval, fmooth, and jagged at the ends. Thefe fall off in April, but in a week's time are fupplied with frefh ones; and it is remarkable that the trunks are not always biggeft near the roots. Thefe trees produce filk, cotton which falls to the ground in November and December, but is not fo fubftantial as that of the cotton fhrub, but rather like the down of thiftles, whence the people in the Weft-Indies do not think it worth gathering, though in the Eaft-Indies it is ufed for ftuffing pillows. The red cotton tree is fomewhat lefs, but in other refpects refembles the former, only it produces no cotton, and its wood is hard, though both are fomewhat fpungy. They are found in fat grounds, not only on the coaft of the South-Sea, but in the Eaft and Weft-Indies.

The cabbage tree is the talleft in thefe woods, fome being 120 feet high; it has branches no where but near the top, where they fprout out to the length of twelve or fourteen feet; they are of the thicknefs of a man's arm, and are covered with long flender leaves, in fuch regular order, that at a diftance they appear only as one leaf. In the midft of the higheft branches fhoots forth the cabbage, which is a foot in length, of the thicknefs of a man's leg, as white as milk, and is very fweet and wholefome. As this tree dies after its head is gone, they cut it down after they gather the fruit. Betwixt the cabbage and the large branches fprout forth many fmall twigs, two feet long, and very clofe together; at the extremities of which grow hard round berries, of the fize of a cherry, which once a year fall from the tree, and are excellent food for the hogs. The trunk of the tree from top to bottom is full of round rings, about half a foot afunder, the bark is thin and brittle, the wood hard and black, with a white pith in the middle.

As the coaft and country of Lima has continual dry weather, fo this part of Peru is feldom without rain, which, and the thicknefs of the woods, have, in all probability, prevented the Spaniards making any confiderable difcoveries on this coaft; befides they may have been intimidated by the bravery of its inhabitants, who entertain a mortal hatred againft the Spaniards; and whoever attempts to row up the river's mouth lies expofed to their ambufcades on each fide, and they are fuch markfmen with their arrows, that they feldom mifs their aim; the chief food of thefe people is maize and plaintains.

However, Mr. Dampier, with fome others, in four canoes, ventured to row fix leagues up the river, where they difcovered two fmall huts, thatched with palmetto trees, where they found only fome fowls, a few plaintains, and a hog feemingly of European breed, which they drefled and fed upon very heartily; for the Indians feeing them approach, got into their canoes, with their wives, children, and goods, and paddled away, againft the ftream, much fafter than the Englifh could row, on account of their keeping near the banks. On the oppofite fide, they faw many other huts, at the diftance of a league; but the current being very rapid, they did not care to venture any farther up. They therefore returned the next morning to the river's mouth, in order to fail to the ifland of Gallo, where their fhips were ftationed.

Gallo is a fmall uninhabited ifland, feated in a fpacious bay three leagues from the river Tomaco, and four leagues and a half from an Indian village of the same name. It is indifferently high, well stored with timber trees, and at the north-east end is a good sandy bay, near which is a fine spring of fresh water. The river Tomaco, which is supposed to arise among the rich mountains of Quito, has its banks well peopled by the Indians, and some Spaniards, who traffic with them for gold, but is so shallow at the entrance that only barks can enter it. This river is five leagues from that of St. Jago, and leaving the latter, they sailed thither. In their way they saw an Indian house, and seized the whole family, rowed forward, and came at twelve at night to Tomaco, where they seized upon all the inhabitants, among whom was Don Diego de Pinas, a Spanish knight, who came thither to lade timber; but they found nothing in the ship that brought him but 13 jars of wine, which they took out, and then set the vessel adrift. The same day three Indians came on board in a canoe, who were straight and well limbed, but of a low stature, with black hair, long visages, and of a dark complexion, with small eyes and noses.

On the 21st of December, several of the men who had been seven or eight leagues up the river, returned with their canoes, and brought with them several ounces of gold they had found in a Spanish house, whence the people had fled.

On the 1st of January 1685, when they were going in their canoes from Tomaco towards Gallo they took a Spanish packet-boat, sent with dispatches from Panama to Lima, by which they learned that the Armada, being arrived from Spain at Porto Bello, waited for the Plate fleet from Lima, which soon made them alter their resolution of going to Lavelia, instead of which it was resolved to rendezvous among the King's or Pearl islands, by which all the ships bound to Panama from the coast of Lima must necessarily pass. Accordingly they sailed on the 7th of January, and the next day took a ſhip of 90 tons, laden with flour, and continuing their voyage, with a gentle gale from the ſouth, anchored on the 9th on the weſt ſide of Gorgona.

On the 13th they purſued their voyage to the King's iſlands, and on the 25th this ſmall ſquadron, conſiſting of two ſtout ſhips, a fire-ſhip, the prize of 90 tons, and two tenders, came into a deep well incloſed channel, at the north end of St. Paul's iſland, which is a convenient place for careening.

The King's or Pearl iſlands are pretty numerous, and are low and woody. They are ſeven leagues from the neareſt part of the continent, and twelve from Panama. But though they have obtained the name of Pearl iſlands, our author could never ſee one pearl-oyſter near them. The northernmoſt of theſe is called Pachea, or Pacheque, which is a ſmall iſland eleven or twelve leagues from Panama, and St. Paul's lies moſt to the ſouth. But the reſt, though bigger, have no particular names. Some of them are planted with rice, bananas and plaintains, by the negroes who belong to the inhabitants of Panama. Though theſe iſlands lie cloſe together, they have channels between them fit for boats, and between them and the continent is a channel of a moderate depth, ſeven or eight leagues broad.

Having cleaned their barks at St. Paul's iſland, they ſent them to cruize towards Panama, and four days after they returned with a prize laden with maize, Indian corn, a ſort of beef, and fowls. This prize came from Lavelia, a large town ſeated on the bank of a river on the north ſide of the bay of Panama. In the harbour where they careened they found abundance of oyſters, muſcles, limpets and clams, which laſt are ſhell-fiſh that ſtick ſo cloſe to the rocks, that there is no other way of getting them out, than by opening them where they grow. They alſo met with ſome pigeons and turtle doves.

Having careened the ſhips, and taken in a freſh ſupply of wood and water, they ſailed from among the iſlands on the 18th of February, and anchored in a great channel between them and the continent. The next day they cruiſed in the channel towards Panama, about which the ſhore appears very beautiful, by its being interſperſed with ſmall woods and hills. Beſides, about a league from the continent ſeveral ſmall iſlands appear in view, partly covered with trees; and on the other ſide of the channel the King's iſlands afford a delightful proſpect.

On the 18th, they anchored directly oppoſite to Old Panama, once a famous city, but the greateſt part being laid in aſhes by Sir Henry Morgan, it was never rebuilt. About four leagues from the ruins of this place ſtands New Panama, a very handſome city, in a ſpacious bay of the ſame name, into which run ſeveral long navigable rivers, ſome of which are not without gold. It has a view of many pleaſant iſlands, and the country about it affords a delightful proſpect at ſea, from the variety of the adjacent hills, vallies, groves and plains. The houſes are for the moſt part of brick, and pretty lofty, eſpecially the churches, the monaſteries, the preſident's houſe, and other public ſtructures, which, Mr. Dampier ſays, make the beſt ſhow of any buildings he ever ſaw in thoſe parts. It is encompaſſed with a high ſtone wall, on which are mounted a conſiderable number of guns, that were formerly planted on the land ſide, but now they are alſo planted towards the ſea. This city carries on a great trade, as being the ſtaple for all goods, to and from every part of Peru and Chili. Beſides, every three years when the Spaniſh galleons go to Porto Bello, the Plate fleet arrives with the king's plate, and that which belongs to the merchants at Panama, whence it is carried on mules by land to Porto Bello.

Panama is seated in a healthy air, it having the benefit of the sea-wind from ten or eleven in the morning till eight or nine o'clock at night; and the land-wind from nine, till the morning. Besides, Panama is seldom troubled with fogs, nor is the wet season, which holds from May till November, so excessive at Panama as on the other side of the bay, though it is severe enough in the months of June, July, and August, at which time the merchants of Peru, who are used to an air that is constantly serene, and without rain or fogs, cut off their hair to preserve them from fevers.

On the 20th of March, they anchored within a league of the three Perico islands, which are small and rocky, and the next day took another prize, laden with beef, hogs, fowls, and salt, from Lavelia.

On the 24th, they stood over to the island of Tobago, in the same bay, six leagues south of Panama, a small rocky and steep island, three miles in length, and two in breadth, except on the north side, where it has an easy ascent, and as the soil is good up to the middle of the mountains, it produces abundance of fruit, as plantains and bananas; and near the sea side, cocoa and mammee trees. These last are large and straight, they being sixty or seventy feet high, without knots, or even boughs, but at the top some small branches sprout out, thick and close together. The fruit, which is round, and of the size of a large quince, is covered with a rind, that is at first grey, and before it is ripe is brittle; but when at maturity grows yellow, peels with ease, and changes to the colour of a carrot. The ripe fruit smells and tastes well, and has two rough stones in the middle, of the size of a large almond.

The south-west side of Tobago is covered with trees and fire-wood, and on the north side, a clear spring of fresh water falls from the mountains into the sea, near which formerly stood a pretty town, with a handsome church; but the greatest part of it has been destroyed by the Buccaneers; and farther towards the west lies a small town, called Tobagilla.

While they were at anchor before this last town, they were in great danger of being destroyed by a pretended merchant of Panama, who, under the colour of trading privately with them, instead of bringing (in the night) his bark laden with merchandize, advanced pretty near them in a fire-ship, when some of the men, more suspicious than the rest, bid her come to an anchor; but she not doing so, they fired at her, which so terrified the men, that immediately setting her on fire, they jumped into their canoes, and the English were obliged to cut their cables to escape the danger. At the same time Capt. Swan, who lay at the distance of a mile at anchor, saw a small float, with only one man upon it, driving towards his ship, but it soon after disappeared. This he imagined to be some materials made up with combustible matter, in order to be fastened to his rudder, as it happened to Capt. Sharpe near Coquimbo; but it is supposed the fellow, thinking himself discovered, had not the courage to prosecute his enterprize. However Capt. Swan also thought fit to cut his cables, and to keep under sail all night. The above engines are said to have been contrived by Mr. Bond, who formerly deserted from them to the Spaniards, without whose assistance they could not have fitted out the fire ship; it being almost impossible to conceive the ignorance of the Spaniards in the South-Seas, especially in maritime affairs.

On the 28th in the morning, while they were busy in recovering their anchors, they discovered a whole fleet of canoes, full of men, pass between Tobagilla and the other island, who proved to be English and French privateers, that had lately crossed from the North Sea over the isthmus of

Darien. These were 280 in all, 200 of whom were French, and 80 English, which last were taken on board Capt. Davis, and the rest put into the prize they had taken, loaden with flour, under the command of a Frenchman called Capt. Gronet, who in return offered Capt. Davis and Capt. Swan, each a commission * from the governor of Petit Guaves. That governor having granted them blank commissions, Capt. Davis accepted one of them; but as Capt. Swan had received one from the Duke of York, he refused it.

Thus reinforced they sailed towards the gulph of St. Michael, in quest of Capt. Townly, who with 180 men was said to be crossing the isthmus, and the next day they came up with them among the Pearl islands; for he had taken two barks, one laden with flour and the other with sugar, with some jars of wine and brandy, part of which he readily distributed among the men belonging to Capt. Swan and Capt. Davis, because he wanted the jars, in order to fill them with water.

As it was the latter end of the dry season, and all the water on shore dried up, they now sailed to the point of Garrachina, where the natives brought them some refreshments; but meeting no fresh water there, they set sail for Porto Pinas, which obtains its name from the vast number of pines that grow there, it being pretty woody; hence it affords an agreeable prospect, the country rising from the sea side, by a gentle ascent to a considerable height. Two small rocks at the entrance of the harbour render the passage into it narrow, and

---

* About this time it was very common for this French governor to supply with commissions not only the Buccaneers, but also to give them blank ones for any others with whom they might chance to join company. But though they were in reality no more than licences to hunt, fowl, and fish on the island of Hispaniola, yet, under their sanction, the latter committed great ravages in America.

it is besides exposed to the south-west wind, on which account they did not enter the harbour, and were unable to land from the high sea near the shore. They therefore steered for Tobago, and in their way took a vessel laden with cocoas from Guaiaquil, and some time after a canoe with four Indians and a mulatto, who having been in the fire-ship that was sent to burn Capt. Davis's vessel, was immediately hanged; as if all stratagems used between enemies at war were not allowable.

While they were employed in filling of water and cutting of wood for fuel, at the island of Perico, where they had cast anchor on the 3d of April, they sent four canoes to the continent, to get some sugar in the adjacent sugar-works, to make their cocoa up into chocolate, and particularly to get some coppers, which were wanted for boiling provisions, on account of their number being so greatly encreased, and these returned with three coppers.

In the mean while Capt. Davis sent his bark to the island of Otoque, in the bay of Panama, which was inhabited only by negro slaves, who bred up a few hogs and fowls; and here the English met with a messenger sent to Panama, with an account that the Lima fleet was sailed. But though most of the letters were thrown into the sea, yet from the rest they understood that the fleet was coming under a convoy composed of all the ships of strength they had been able to assemble from Peru. Being informed that the king's ships always proceeded that way, they sailed back on the 10th, to the King's or Pearl islands, and the next day anchored at the place where they had been careened, and where they met Capt. Harris, who had brought a fresh supply of men from the river St. Maria.

On the 19th, 250 men were sent in canoes to the river Cheapo, to surprise the town of that name; the next day all the rest followed, and on the 22d they arrived at Chepelio, a pleasant island in the bay of Panama, seven leagues from the city of that name, and one from the continent. This island lies directly opposite to the river Cheapo. It is low on the north side, but rises by an easy ascent to the south. The soil is very good, and in the low grounds produces plenty of delicious fruits, as sapadilloes, avogato pears, mammee sapatos, star-apples and plaintains; and on the north side is a good anchoring place, where there is a fine spring of fresh water near the shore.

The sapadillo tree is very like a pear tree, and the fruit resembles a bergamot pear, only it is something longer. When first gathered it is hard, and the juice clammy; but on its being laid by a few days, it becomes soft and full of a thin juice. It has two or three black kernels, which resemble the seed of a pompion.

The avogato pear-tree grows as high, or rather higher, than our pear-trees in England, and has a black smooth bark, and large oval leaves; the fruit is as big as a large lemon, and is at first green; but when ripe turns yellow. The pulp is also of a yellowish colour, and as soft as butter. When they have been gathered three or four days, the rind comes off with ease. As this fruit is insipid, it is commonly eaten with lime juice and sugar, or with a roasted plaintain and salt. It has a stone as big as a horse plumb. However, this fruit being looked upon by the Spaniards as a great provocative, they have planted it in most places of the North Sea, where they inhabit.

The mammee sapota tree, has neither so tall nor so thick a trunk as the mammee of Tobago, nor is the fruit either so round or so large. The rind is smooth, and the pulp quite red, with a rough, flat, or longish stone. This is indeed a pleasant and wholesome fruit. There are some wild mammee trees, which grow tall and straight, and are therefore used for masts, but the fruit is not esteemed.

The star apple somewhat resembles our quince treee, but is much larger, and bears more abundance of broad oval leaves, that almost conceal the fruit, which is of the size of a large apple, and is esteemed very good; but Mr. Dampier acknowledges that he never tasted it.

The river of Cheapo rises in the mountains on the north, and is afterwards inclosed between them and the mountains on the south, it then turns to the west, and making a kind of semicircle, runs gently into the sea, seven leagues from Panama. But though it is very deep, and a quarter of a mile broad, yet its entrance is so choaked up with sand, that it is only navigable by barks. About six leagues from the sea side stands the city of Cheapo. On the left bank of the river is a champaign country, which affords a very pleasant view of several adjacent hills covered with woods, though the greatest part is good pasture ground. But on the south side of the river a tract of wood land extends for many leagues.

The 250 men who were sent to this place returned on the 24th, after their having taken the town, without the least opposition, but found nothing in it worth mentioning. On the 25th, being joined by Capt. Harris, they sailed for Tobago, and finding themselves now 1000 strong, it was consulted whether they should make an attempt upon Panama. But all thoughts of that expedition were laid aside, upon their being informed by the prisoners that the inhabitants had received a considerable reinforcement from Porto Bello.

On the 4th of May, they sailed again for the King's Islands, and having on the 25th taken three seamen at Panama, were informed that a strict order issued there, not to fetch any plaintains from the adjacent islands, had occasioned a great scarcity, and that they daily expected the arrival of the fleet from Lima.

On the 28th of May the fleet lay at anchor between two or three small islands on the south side of Pacheque, and consisted of ten sail, of which only two were men of war. Captain Davis's ship carrying 39 guns and 156 men, and Captain Swan's 16 guns and 140 men, the rest being provided only with small arms, amounted to 960: They had also one fire-ship. About eleven o'clock they discovered the Spanish fleet at three leagues distance; and about three in the afternoon they sailed, bearing down right before the wind upon the Spaniards, who kept close on a wind to come up with them; but night approaching, they exchanged only a few shot. As soon as it began to grow dark, the Spanish admiral put out a light at his top as a signal for the fleet to come to an anchor; in half an hour after it was taken down, but soon appeared as before; which the English supposing to be in the admiral's top, kept under sail; but the Spaniards having put this second light on the top-mast head of one of their barks, had sent her to the leeward, so that in the morning, the English fleet found that the enemy had got the weather gage of them, and were coming up with full sail, which obliged them to make a running fight of it all day, almost round the bay of Panama. Mr. Townly being hard pressed by the Spaniards, was forced to make a bold run between Pacheque, and the three adjacent small islands, Captain Harris was forced to weigh from the rest during the fight; and Captain Gronet, in the flour prize of ninety tons burthen, with 308 men, was a mile to the north of his associates when the enemy appeared, and tacking over to the main, kept himself out of the way while there was the least glimmering of danger, for which conduct some of the ships, the following day, were for displacing him; but after much dispute, it was agreed to dismiss him and his men, most of whom were French, and to suffer them to keep the ship that had been given them, with a charge to quit company immediately. Thus their long projected design vanished into smoke; but though the Spanish fleet, according to the report of some prisoners afterwards taken, consisted of twenty-four sail, besides periaguas or boats of twelve or fourteen oars each, among which were eighteen ships of good force, two fire ships, and about three thousand men on board the whole fleet, yet the English had but one man killed.

On the first of June, the fleet sailed for the island of Quibo, or Cobaya, in quest of Captain Harris, and proceeding to the northward, saw many rivers and creeks, which are not near so large as on the south side of the bay of Panama. The coast is partly hilly and partly low grounds, with very thick woods; but in the heart of the country there are fertile plains for feeding of cattle. Some of the rivers on this side afford gold, but not in such quantities as those on the other side; but there is scarce any settlement along this coast, except upon the rivers that lead to Lavelia and Nata.

On their arrival at Quibo, they found Captain Harris there before them, when it was resolved that as they had been unsuccessful in their late attempt, they should now try their fortune by land, by attacking the city of Leon, on the coast of Mexico. But as it lay a good way within the land, it was agreed to make canoes on the island of Quibo, where they were at anchor, a sufficient quantity of timber fit for that purpose being on the spot.

While these preparations were making, 150 men were sent to Puebla Nova, a town at a small distance from the continent. They took it without much difficulty, but met with nothing there.

except an empty bark. Having finiſhed all the canoes in a month's time, they ſet out for Rio Leja, which is the port for the city of Leon; and on the 9th of Auguſt, quitting their ſhips, and embarking on board their canoes, of which they had thirty-one, they were in great danger of being ſwallowed up by the waves, which ran mountains high, attended with thunder and lightening, but the ſtorm abated; yet another tornado had like to have ſent them all to the bottom: However this alſo did not laſt long, and they entered the ſouth ſide of the harbour in the night, but did not proceed farther till break of day, when they rowed deeper into the creek, which is very narrow, and the land on both ſides marſhy near the banks, and ſo full of mangrove trees, that there is no paſſing through them. Beyond theſe was a ſmall intrenchment, which they took by ſurpriſe, and having landed 470 men, left the reſt, of which number Mr. Dampier was one, to guard the canoes.

They began their march at eight o'clock in the morning, Captain Townly leading the van, which conſiſted of 100 of the briſkeſt men. Captain Swan followed him with 100 more, next came Captain Davis with 170, and Captain Knight brought up the rear. Captain Townly being advanced two miles before the reſt, was attacked, and having forced ſeventy horſe to retire at the diſtance of four miles from the city, marched forwards, and at three o'clock in the afternoon entered it without oppoſition, though he was ſoon after oppoſed by 200 Spaniſh horſe and 500 foot, firſt in a broad ſtreet, and afterwards in the great market place; but the foot ſeeing the horſe retire, followed their example, leaving the town to the mercy of the Engliſh.

Captain Swan did not enter the the town till four o'clock. Captain Davis came there about five, and Knight came not with the remainder till ſix;

but several of the men were left behind on account of their growing tired upon the road, among whom was an old grey-headed fellow, named Swan, who was eighty-four years of age, and had served in Ireland under Cromwell, and he bravely refusing to take quarter, the Spaniards shot him dead. They however took some others, among whom was Mr. Smith, who having lived a considerable time in the Canaries, spoke Spanish fluently, and being carried before the Governor, was examined as to the strength of the invaders, whom he represented to be 1500 men, 1000 in the town, and 500 in the canoes; which had such an effect upon his excellency, that notwithstanding his being at the head of upwards of 1000 men, he did not chuse to molest them. But the next day sent a flag of truce to propose a ransom for the town. But the English demanding 30,000 pieces of eight and provisions for 1000 men for four months, he refused to give it, and they accordingly set fire to the city on the 14th of August, and marched towards their canoes the next morning. However Mr. Smith was exchanged for a gentlewoman, and a Spanish gentleman was released, upon his promise of delivering 150 oxen for his ransom at Rio Leja, the place they intended to attack next.

The city of Leon stands twenty miles within the country, in a sandy plain, near a burning mountain, called the volcano of Leon. The houses are large, and built with stone, with gardens about them, but are low, and covered with tiles. It has three churches and a cathedral. The above sandy plain is surrounded with savannahs, which afford a free passage for the breezes on all sides, and render the town both pleasant and healthful. But no great commerce is carried on there, the inhabitants chiefly subsisting on their cattle and sugar-works, of which there are several between the landing place and the city; about the midway between both there is a fine fordable river, and nearer the city an Indian town. The city is alſo ſaid to have a good manufactory of hemp.

On the 16th of Auguſt, in the afternoon, they arrived in their canoes in the harbour of Rio Leja, where their ſhips were by that time come to an anchor. The creek that leads from Rio Leja is broad at its entrance, but afterwards cloſes and becomes a narrow deep channel, lined on both ſides with many cocoa trees. The Spaniards had here caſt up an intrenchment, which fronted the entrance of the creek, and was defended by 120 men, and farther down they had a boom of trees laid acroſs the creek ; ſo that had they not wanted courage to keep their poſt, they might have kept off 1000 men. But the Engliſh had no ſooner fired two of their guns, than they quitted it, and left them at liberty to cut the boom, which when the Engliſh had done, they immediately landed, and marched to Rio Leja, a fine town, ſeated in a plain a mile up a ſmall river. It has three churches, and an hoſpital with an handſome garden; they took it without oppoſition, but found nothing conſiderable, except 500 packs of flour, and ſome pitch, tar, and cordage. They alſo received the 150 oxen promiſed by the gentleman they releaſed at Leon, which, together with ſome other cattle, and the ſugar found in the country, was very acceptable. The adjacent country has indeed many ſugar works, and incloſures for cattle, and conſiderable quantities of pitch, tar and cordage, are made by the country people. Rio Leja is however ſeated in an unwholeſome air, near ſome fens and marſhes, which ſend forth a noiſome ſcent. In its neighbourhood grow melons, pine-apples, guavas, and prickly pears.

The ſhrub which bears the guava fruit has long and ſlender boughs, that have a white and ſmooth bark, and leaves reſembling the hazel. The fruit, which is like a pear, has a thin rind and many hard feeds, and when ripe is yellow, soft and well tasted. It may be eaten while green, which is the case with very few of the fruits either in the East or West-Indies, and after it is ripe, it may be baked like pears, or coddled like apples. There are however different sorts distinguished by their taste, shape, and colour, some being red, and others yellow in the inside. Before it is ripe it is an astringent, but afterwards loosening.

The prickly pear which is also common in many places in the West-Indies, grows upon a shrub five feet high, and thrives best in saltish sandy grounds near the sea shore. Each branch of this shrub has two or three round leaves of the breadth of a man's hand, not unlike house-leek, but edged with prickles of an inch long. At the extremity of the leaf grows the fruit, which is of the bigness of a large plumb, small towards the leaf, and thick at the other end, where it opens like a medlar. The fruit has also small prickles, and is at first green, but by degrees turns red. The pulp is of the same consistence as a thick syrup, with small black seeds; it is cooling, and of a pleasant taste. Our author says that he has often observed, that on eating twenty-two or more of them at a time, they will tinge the urine as red as blood, but without any ill consequence.

On the 25th, Captain Davis and Captain Swan parted, the first in order to return to the coast of Peru, and the other intending to proceed farther to the west. Upon which Mr. Dampier, desiring to satisfy his curiosity, by obtaining a more perfect knowledge of the northren parts of Mexico, left Captain Davis, and went on board Mr. Swan, who was joined by Captain Townly with his two barks, while Captain Harris and Mr. Knight followed the former.

By this time Mr. Swan's men began to be much afflicted with fevers, which were attributed to the remains of a contagious diftemper, that had lately raged at Rio Leja, Capt. Davis's men having undergone the fame fate. On the 3d of September they failed again, fteered to the weft, and met with violent tornadoes, thunder and lightning, which kept them out at fea, fo that they faw no land till the 14th, when they came in fight of the volcano of Guatimala; it appears with a double peak, like two fugar-loaves, between which the fire and fmoke is faid to break out before bad weather.

The city of Guatimala is fituated near the foot of this high mountain, eight leagues from the fouth fea, and 40 or 50 from the gulph of Matique, in the bay of Honduras, in the North Seas. It is reputed a rich city, the country about it abounding in feveral commodities, which are exported thence into Europe, efpecially the four noted dyes, indigo, otta or anatta, fylvefter and cochineal.

The land near the volcano of Guatimala is low by the fea-fide, but rifes in a grandual afcent from thence to the diftance of about ten leagues from the fhore. They obferved floating in the fea great quantities of drift wood and pumice ftones, which laft were thrown out by the mountain, and by the rains wafhed into the fea.

On the 24th, being in 14°. 30'. north latitude, Capt. Townly went on fhore with nine canoes, and 106 men, in hopes of finding the town of Teguantapeque, which was well known to be fituated fomewhere thereabouts, in order to get fome refrefhment for the fick men, both he and Capt. Swan having at leaft one half of their crews in a very weak condition; but he was obliged to return to his canoes, without being able to find it. The fhips now coafted along to the weft, in fight of a tract of high land that begins at the eaft, and after having run for ten leagues within the land to the weft, finks by an eafy defcent. On that fide next the fea they faw rich paftures, mixed with pleafant groves, but the furf which beat upon the fhore not suffering the men to land with their canoes, they were forced to continue coasting for eight or nine leagues, till Capt. Townly, seeing no prospect of landing, returned on board with his men, on the 2d of October. But being soon after resolved to try his fortune again, he ran his canoes ashore in a sandy bay, where he landed, but lost one man, and had most of his powder spoiled by the water. They were however no sooner on shore, than they found the country full of torrents and unfordable rivers. This obliged them to think of returning to their canoes, which while they were attempting, they were attacked by 200 Spaniards and Indians, whom they soon repulsed and put to flight.

Capt. Townly having again rejoined Capt. Swan, they still continued sailing to the westward; but could discover neither creek nor bay for 20 leagues farther, when they came to the island of Tangola, where there is safe anchorage, with plenty of wood and water, and from thence they coasted along till they came to Guatulco, one of the best ports in the kingdom of Mexico. On the east side of the entrance of the harbour, about the distance of a mile, is a small island near the shore, and on the west side of that entrance is a large hollow rock open at the top, from which a column of water forces its passage in the manner of a fountain, and rising to a great height even in the calmest weather, affords a good mark to seamen, bound for this port. At the bottom of this harbour, which is three miles deep, and one mile broad, there is a fine brook of fresh water, near which formerly stood a town that was sacked by Sir Francis Drake, but there are no signs of it now remaining, except the ruins of an old chapel, standing in the midst of a grove. The land is here covered with a variety of trees, which, rising in regular ridges, form a very agreeable prospect.

Capt. Swan being ill, went on shore here with all the sick, and a surgeon to attend them, while Capt. Townly marched at the head of a considerable number of men to the eastward, in search for houses and inhabitants, and about a league from Guatulco, came up with a river called Capulita, which is very deep, and has a swift current; some of his men swimming across the stream, seized two Indians, whom they supposed to be stationed there as centinels to watch their proceedings, though they were entire strangers to the Spanish tongue. One of these they carried on board a ship, and made use of the other to guide them to an Indian settlement, but they found nothing there, besides some vanelloes drying in the sun.

The vanello is a perfume sold at a pretty high price in many parts of the West-Indies, and being infused into chocolate, gives it a delicate flavour. It grows on a small kind of vine that creeps up about the trees, and at first bears a yellow flower, that produces a pod about four or five inches long, which is at first green, but when ripe becomes yellow, and has black seeds. After they are gathered they are laid in the sun, which makes them soft and of a chesnut colour. The Spaniards who purchase the vanelloes very cheap of the Indians, soak them afterwards in oil.

On the 10th of October, they sent four canoes before, to the westward, in hopes of taking some prisoners, who were acquainted with the situation of the country, and these were ordered to wait at Port Angelo. The ships at Guatulco had taken in a supply of wood and water, as well as plenty of a small kind of turtle, by which the men were greatly refreshed, they having had no fresh provisions for a considerable time. On the 22d, two of the canoes being separated from the rest, returned on board, after attempting to land at a place where they saw many cattle feeding upon a Savanna, but the sea running high, they were overset, and one man drowned, four guns lost, and the rest of their arms spoiled with the water. However, the next day 100 men landed at Port Angelo, and got plenty of salt, hogs, cocks, hens, and maize, in a house near the plain, but could carry little on board, on account of the distance of the place from the sea side.

On the 28th they continued their voyage, and at night met with the two other canoes, who had been as far as the port of Acapulco, and in their return took in a supply of fresh water, in spite of 150 Spaniards, who would have opposed them; after which they stood in a salt water bay, on the banks whereof they found a considerable quantity of dried fish, which they brought on board. The entrance of this bay is closely hemmed in with rocks on both sides, so that the passage betwixt them is not above a pistol shot over, though the bay is of considerable compass. As the ships were just off the bay, twelve men were sent in a canoe for more fish; but the Spaniards being already alarmed, posted themselves behind the rocks, and fired such a volley of shot upon the canoes at their entering the bay, that they wounded five of the men. They however rowed forward out of gun-shot where they staid two days and three nights, not daring to return the same way they came; but at last Capt. Townley, who lay near the shore, hearing the firing of guns, manned one of his canoes, and driving the Spaniards from the rocks, opened them a free passage, and they returned on board on the 21st.

On the 2d of November, they continued their course westward, until they came to a large river, two leagues to the west of the rock of Algatrofs, on the banks of which the Spaniards had cast up an entrenchment, defended by 200 soldiers. The English however landed, and with little opposition forced them to fly. They found there a considerable quantity of salt, used in salting the fish taken in the bay. They now marched three leagues into the country, and having taken a mulatto prisoner, he informed them that a stout ship was lately come to Acapulco from Lima; when Capt. Townly standing in need of a better ship than his own, proposed cutting her out of the harbour, and in spite of Capt. Swan's remonstrances on the difficulty of the enterprize, and the necessity they were under of stocking themselves with maize, and other provisions, which were to be had in great plenty where they now were, he carried his point, and the canoes were manned for the expedition; but they narrowly escaped being lost in a tornado, and the men were obliged to wait a whole day in Port Marquifs, a league to the eastward of Acapulco, where they dried their cloaths and arms, and the following night rowed softly into Acapulco harbour; but found the ship so well guarded, that quitting their enterprize, they retired greatly disappointed.

They some time after landed to the north-west of the hill of Petaplan, and 170 men marching fourteen miles into the country, came to a mean poor Indian village, which was deserted by the inhabitants, who carried off their effects, so that they found only a mulatto woman and her four small children, all of whom they brought off; but being carried on board, she declared that some mules laden with flour, and other goods designed for Acapulco, had stopped on the road to the west of that village; upon which they sailed to the harbour of Chequetan, and landing ninety-five men, with the mulatto woman for their guide, she conducted them through a pathless wood, by the side of a river into a plain, near which they found sixty mules at a farm house laden with flour, cheese, chocolate, earthen-ware, and some cows, which they killed, all which they carried off, except the earthen-ware; and foon after Captain Swan went on fhore, and killed eighteen cows without the leaft oppofition.

Having thus ftocked themfelves with as much provifions as they could conveniently ftow on board their different veffels, they difmiffed the woman and her children with a prefent of fome old clothes and other trifles, for which fhe feemed very thankful: but Captain Swan in fpite of her tears and intreaties, detained one of her boys, who was about eight years of age, had a fprightly genius, and afterwards proved a very good and ufeful boy, and the captain behaved to him like a kind mafter.

On the 21ft of November, they continued their courfe to the weftward, in hopes of difcovering a town in about 18°. 8'. north latitude; but they could find no traces of it, nor of the city of Colima, which was reported to be very rich: And though they rowed twenty leagues along the fhore, they could not meet with any place where they were able to land, or perceive the leaft fign of inhabitants. At laft they fpied a horfeman, and having with difficulty made the fhore, in hopes of taking him prifoner, they purfued him, but foon loft him in the woods; upon which, they returned on board on the 28th.

The next day, the two captains once more took to their canoes with 200 men, in order to go in fearch of a town called Salagua; and as they were rowing along the fhore, faw two horfemen on the beach, one of whom by way of derifion, drank to them out of a pocket bottle; in return for which civility they fhot his horfe; whereupon his companion fled, and two of the men ftripping themfelves, fwam on fhore, in order to fecure him; but being unarmed, they could not fucceed in their attempt, he keeping them at bay with a long knife.

On the 30th, the canoes returned on board, the fea every where running fo high, that the men could not find any fafe landing. However on the firft of December, they came in fight of the port of Salagua, which is parted by a rocky point about the middle, that gives it the appearance of two harbours. On their nearer approach, they faw a large thatched houfe, which appeared to be new, with a confiderable body of Spaniards, both horfe and foot, making a military parade, with their drums beating, and colours flying. The next morning 200 of the ftouteft of the Englifh landed; but the Spanifh foot did not ftand one charge; and the horfe foon followed them, when two of the Englifh having knocked down their riders, mounted and purfued the fugitives fo far, that they were furrounded, unhorfed, and received feveral wounds, and would have certainly been killed, if fome of the fwifteft of their companions had not come up timely to their relief. Here they found a broad ftoney road leading into the country, which was interfperfed with thick woods. This road, they were informed by two mulattoes whom they made prifoners, led to the city of Oarrah, which was four long days journey from the fea, and that the body of troops they had put to flight was fent from that city to fecure the Manilla fhip, which was to fet fome paffengers on fhore at this place.

This induced them to fail again to the weftward, towards Cape Corientes, in hopes of meeting with the above galleon; and on the 11th, coming in fight of that cape, they took their ftations in fuch a manner as they imagined would prevent their miffing her; however wanting provifions, fifty or fixty men were fent in a bark to procure fome to the weft of the cape; but returned without being able to get round it. However they left four canoes behind, manned with forty-fix men, who intended to row to the weft.

On the 18th, the ships sailed to the isles of Chametly, eighteen leagues to the east of Cape Corientes. These are five small low and woody islands, surrounded with rocks that lie in the form of an half moon, within a mile of the continent, between which, and these islands, there is safe anchorage. They are inhabited by fishermen, who are servants to some of the inhabitants of the city of Purification, which is a considerable city fourteen leagues up the country.

On the 24th the four canoes which had been left by Captain Townly's bark, returned to the ships near the cape, having got round by the help of their oars, and landed in the valley of Valderas or Val d'Iras, the valley of Flags, having met with but indifferent success. This valley lies at the bottom of a deep bay, inclosed between Cape Corientes and the Point of Pontique. It is about three leagues wide, and bounded on the land side by a green hill, which by its easy descent into the valley, affords a delightful prospect, as do the wide spread pastures stored with cattle; and the pleasant groves of guavas, orange, and lime trees; that grow here in vast numbers. At this place the canoes had landed thirty-seven men, who having advanced three miles into the country, were attacked by 150 Spaniards, horse and foot; but happily an adjacent wood afforded them a retreat, whence they fired upon the Spaniards, and having killed their leader and seventeen more horsemen, obliged them to retire; but in this skirmish the English lost four men, and had two wounded, whom they brought down to their canoes upon horses, one of which they killed and eat; for though there was plenty of horned cattle in the plain, they were afraid of venturing back for fear of meeting a fresh body of Spaniards.

On the 28th, Captain Townly, who had before sailed with sixty men to surprize an Indian village, returned on board with forty bushels of maize. They continued cruising off this cape till the first of January, when their provisions being exhausted, they steered to the valley of Valderas to provide a supply of beef. They came to anchor about a mile from the shore, and having landed 240 men, of whom fifty were constantly employed in watching the motions of the Spaniards, they killed and salted as many cows as would serve them two months, and had they not wanted salt, might have taken a much larger supply. Mean while the Spaniards often appeared in large companies, but never dared to attack them. But while they were engaged in this necessary business, the Manilla ship passed by them to the eastward, as they were afterwards informed by some prisoners whom they happened to seize. The loss of this great and valuable prize was chiefly attributed to the wilfulness of Captain Townly, in resolving to attempt taking the ship in the harbour of Acapulco, when they ought to have been providing themselves with a sufficient supply of beef and maize. They had hitherto a double design in view; first the taking of the Manilla ship, and secondly, searching after rich towns and mines near the coast, not knowing that these all lie in the inland parts of the country. But now finding themselves quite deceived in their hopes, they parted, Captain Townly failing back to the east, and Mr. Dampier in Captain Swan's ship to the west.

On the 7th of January 1686, they sailed from their station off the valley of Valderas, and on the 20th, anchored on the east side of the Chametly islands, which are different from those above-mentioned. They being a knot of six small islands in 23°. 11'. north lat. and three leagues from the continent; one or two of them have some sandy creeks, and produce a fruit called penguins, of which there are two sorts, the red and yellow. The red penguin resembles a ninepin in shape, but is no bigger than an onion. It has no stem, but grows immediately out of the ground, sixty or seventy sometimes rising upright in a cluster, encompassed with prickly leaves of a foot and a half, or two feet long. The yellow penguin grows on a stem of the thickness of a man's arm, which rises a foot from the ground, with leaves half a foot long and an inch broad. The fruit grows in clusters on the top of the stalk, it being round and of the size of an hen's egg. The rind is pretty thick, and the pulp, which has a delightful taste, is full of black seeds. Captain Swan here took 100 men with him to the north to discover the river Cullacan, supposed to lie in 4°. north latitude, with a very wealthy town upon its banks; but though they rowed above thirty leagues, they could discover no river, nor even any safe landing place. However they afterwards landed on the west side of a salt lake, seven leagues to the northward of the Chametly islands, where they found one house, in which they took seven or eight bushels of maize, and were told by an Indian prisoner they had taken, that there was generally a considerable number of black cattle in this place, which the Spaniards had driven off, but that they might probably find provisions at an Indian town, at about five leagues distance. They therefore immediately directed their course thither, but on their approaching the place, were opposed by a good body of Spaniards and Indians, but these being beaten back at the first charge, they entered the town, where they only found two or three wounded Indians, who told them that the town was called Massactan, and that five leagues from thence were two rich gold mines. They staid there till the second of February, when eighty men were ordered to a town called Rosario, on a river of the same name, whence they took ninety bushels more of maize, being at this time more valued by them than all the gold in the Indies, which was therefore neglected, though they were told that the mines were only two leagues from thence.

From Rosario the ships steered to the river St. Jago, one of the most considerable rivers on this coast, where Capt. Swan sent seventy men to look for a town, while the ships anchored at its mouth. On the east they found a large field of maize, in which they seized an Indian, who told them that four leagues farther was a town called Santa Pecaque, of which Capt. Swan being informed, he went with 140 men in eight canoes five leagues up the river, and then landing, marched through fertile plains and woods for three or four hours, and the Spaniards quitting the place at their approach, the English entered it without opposition.

Santa Pecaque is seated in a spacious plain on the side of a wood, but though it is not very large it is neatly built, and has two churches, and like most of the Spanish towns in these parts has a square market place in the middle. At five or six leagues distance from the town are silver mines, the ore of which is carried from this place on mules, twenty one leagues to Compostella, the capital of this part of Mexico. This last city is inhabited by about seventy white families, and 5 or 600 mulattoes and Indians.

As the men found here plenty of maize, sugar, salt, and salt-fish, Capt. Swan ordered one half of them to carry provisions on board, while the rest took care of the town. This they did by turns, and having seized horses, made use of them to ease them in their labour. Thus they proceeded for two days, but on the 19th of January, Capt. Swan being informed by a prisoner that 1000 armed men had lately marched from St. Jago, a rich town at three leagues distance, in order to attack him; he commanded his people to get all the horses they could, and to march in a body with all the provisions they could carry to their canoes: but they refusing to obey him till all the provisions could be carried on board, he was forced to let one half of them go on with 54 horses; these had scarcely marched a mile, before the Spaniards, who lay in ambush, attacked and killed them all upon the spot, for though Capt. Swan marched to their relief, they were all slain and stripped, but as they had probably paid pretty dear for the victory, they never attempted to engage him, by which means Capt. Swan returned on board with the rest of his men.

The day after this bloody engagement, they steered towards California, and on the 7th of February came to an anchor in Prince George's island, the middlemost of the Tres Marias. Mr. Dampier having been long sick of the dropsy, was here buried for about half an hour up to the neck in the sand, which threw him into a profuse sweat, and being afterwards wrapped up warm and put to bed in a tent, found great benefit from this extraordinary remedy. They remained careening till the 26th, but as there was no fresh water to be got here in the dry season, they sailed to a little rivulet on the continent near Corientes, where they continued a considerable time, when finding that their success in this part of the world had been hitherto very indifferent, and that there appeared no probability of its mending, Capt. Swan, Mr. Dampier, and a majority of the other men, agreed to steer their course for the East-Indies, though many on board were greatly averse to this voyage, which they thought it impossible for them to accomplish.

On the 31st of March 1686, they sailed from Cape Corientes, and after the first day, advanced very fast in their voyage, having very fair weather and a fresh trade wind; but in all this voyage, they saw neither fish nor fowl, except a large flight of boobies, which appears on their approaching the Ladrone iflands; and one on the 20th of May they difcovered land, to their great joy, as they had but three days provifions left, and the next day came to an anchor about a mile from fhore, on the weft-fide of the ifland of Guam, which Mr. Dampier computes to be 125°. 11'. or 7302 miles weft of Cape Corientes.

Capt. Swan immediately wrote a very obliging letter, which he fent with a few prefents to the governor; he in return received great plenty of hogs, cocoa-nuts, rice, bifcuit, and 50 pounds of fine Manilla tobacco, and being afterwards informed by one of the Friars, that Mindanao, one of the Philippine iflands, abounded with provifions, they left Guam on the 2d of June, and failing with a ftrong eaft wind, arrived on the 21ft on the coaft of St. John's, one of the Philippine iflands, and came to an anchor in a fmall bay on the eaft fide of Mindanao.

The Philippians are a range of large iflands extending from 5°. to 19°. north latitude, the chief of them is Luconia, which is now entirely under the dominion of the Spaniards. To the fouth of Luconia, are 12 or 14 other large iflands, befides an infinite number of fmaller ones in the poffeffion of the Spaniards; but the two fouthermoft, thofe of St. John and Mindanao are the only ones not fubject to the Spanifh jurifdiction.

The ifland of St. John lies between feven and eight degrees north latitude, about four leagues eaft of Mindanao, and is 38 leagues in length, its breadth about the middle 24 leagues, and the foil is extremely fertile.

Mindanao is next to Luconia, the largeft of all the Philippine iflands: It extending 60 leagues in length, and 40 or 50 in breadth; the foil is generally good, and the ftony hills produce many forts of trees, which are not at all known among us. The valleys are watered with brooks and rivulets, and are stored with several sorts of ever-greens, and with rice, water-melons, plaintains, bananas, guavas, nutmegs, cloves, cocoa nuts, oranges, betel nuts, durions, jackas, and particularly the tree whence sagoe is gathered, which grows wild in groves of several miles in length: this is called by the natives the Libby tree.

The Libby tree resembles the cabbage tree, but is not so tall. It has a thin hard bark, full of white pith, like that of the elder. The tree being cut down and split, the pith is taken out and beat well in a trough or mortar, and then pouring water upon it, is well stirred, and strained through a cloth, through which the water forces all the mealy substance, and leaves only an useless husk behind, which is thrown away. This, after it is well settled, they separate from the water, and form it into cakes, which when baked, are almost as good eating as bread, and on this food the natives of Mindanao live for three or four months in the year. The sagoe which is exported is dried in small bits like confits, and carried to other parts of the East-Indies. It is an excellent strengthener, and is now well known almost over all Europe.

The plaintain tree is about three feet in circumference, and grows to the height of ten or twelve feet. It springs out of a sucker, with only two leaves; but when it is a foot high, another pair of leaves sprout out, and in the same manner both the leaves increase in size and number to the very top. The fruit which is shaped like a hog's pudding, arises from the heart of the tree in cods six or seven inches long, growing in clusters. When it is arrived at maturity, it is a pure pulp without either seed or kernel, as soft and yellow as butter, and melts in the mouth like marmalade. The tree, on being cut down, is split in the middle, and left to dry in the sun, when it appears composed of threads of equal bigneſs, which are drawn out by perſons, who obtain a livelihood by that employment, and are afterwards woven into pieces of cloth of ſeven or eight yards in length. This iſland alſo produces another kind of plaintain of a leſs ſize, the fruit of which has a black ſeed, and is eſteemed a great aſtringent.

The Banana ſeems a ſmaller ſpecies of plaintain, and is more ſoft and delicate though not ſo luſcious. It is beſt eaten when raw, for it is not very agreeable when roaſted or boiled. It is ſometimes maſhed into drink, and is pleaſant enough when taken that way.

The Durion fruit is produced by a tree that reſembles the apple-tree. It is as large as a pomkin, but is not to be eaten till it is quite ripe, when the top burſting open, diffuſes a very fragrant ſmell. The pulp, which is very delicious, is as ſoft and white as cream; it is divided into cells like a walnut, and is like that covered with a thick green rind. In the heart of it, is a ſtone as big as a bean, the out-ſide of which, on being roaſted, peels off, in a thin ſhell, when the kernel in taſte reſembles a cheſnut. But this fruit will not keep above two days after its being plucked.

The Jaca-tree is a fruit of the ſame ſpecies, but yellower and fuller of ſtones or kernels, which are good when roaſted.

The Betel-nut is rounder and larger than the nutmeg, and grows upon a very high tree, which produces no leaves except near the top. This fruit is much valued, it being grateful to the ſtomach. It alſo reddens the lips, cleanſes the gums, and preſerves the teeth, though it dyes them black. It is chewed all over the eaſt, and is apt to make thoſe very giddy who are not uſed to it.

The nutmegs here are extremely large and good; and here alſo are excellent cloves, but the people do not care to propagate them, for fear of the Dutch, who monopolize the fpice trade. There are alfo many other different kinds of fruit produced here.

Though this ifland has no beafts of prey, it affords great numbers of wild and tame beafts, as horfes, cows, buffaloes, deer, goats, wild hogs, monkeys, guanoes, lizards, fnakes, and fcorpions. They have alfo centipedes, which though no thicker than a goofe quill, are five inches long, and their fting is as fatal as that of a fcorpion. Their hogs feed in prodigious herds in the woods, and are remarkable for having thick knobs growing over their eyes. There is alfo here a creature four times as large as a guanoe, which it nearly refembles; it has a forked tongue, but Mr. Dampier was unacquainted with the effects of its bite.

They have no tame fowls, befides hens and ducks, but abundance of thofe which are wild, as turtle doves, pigeons, parrots, parroquetoes, bats as large as our kites, and an infinite number of fmall birds of various kinds.

Their chief fifh are bonitos, mullets, breams, cavalies, and turtle. Here are good harbours, creeks and rivers, and in the heart of the country are mountains that afford confiderable quantities of gold.

The climate of Mindanao is not fo exceffive hot as might be expected, confidering its nearnefs to the equator; for the fea breezes cool the air by day, as the land winds do by night. From October till May the winds are eafterly, with fair weather; and from May to October they are wefterly, with rains and violent tempefts, which frequently tear up the largeft trees, lay the whole country under water, and oblige the inhabitants to go from houfe to houfe in canoes. This ftormy weather is in July and Auguft, but it abates in September, in which month they have very heavy fogs, that laft until ten or eleven o'clock in the forenoon, efpecially if it has rained the preceding night.

The people are in general much alike as to ftrength, nature, and colour. They are well limbed, have fmall heads, flat foreheads, fmall black eyes, fhort nofes, wide mouths, and black teeth and hair, though their teeth are found, and their complexions are of a bright tawny. They are of low ftature, and have fmall limbs, are ingenious and nimble, but thievifh and indolent, civil and obliging to ftrangers, but implacable when offended. The men are clothed with a turban tied once round the head, in a knot, the ends hanging down, and either laced or fringed; they wear breeches and frocks, but neither ftockings nor fhoes.

The women are fmaller featured than the men, but though they look pretty well at a diftance, they have fuch little nofes, that in fome of them fcarce any rifing can be difcerned between their eyes: They have alfo very little feet. They tie their black and long hair in a knot, hanging down behind. Their garments are a piece of cloth that ferves for a petticoat, and a loofe frock that reaches a little below the waift, the fleeves of which are longer than their arms, and fet in plaits about their wrifts, but are fo narrow that they can fcarcely get their hands through.

They have a peculiar cuftom in the city of Mindanao: as foon as any ftrangers arrive, the men come on board to invite them to their houfes, where they are fure to inquire whether any of them have a mind for a pagally, or innocent female friend. The ftrangers, in point of civility are obliged to accept the offer made them of fuch a friend, and to fhew their gratitude by a fmall prefent, in return for which, they have the liberty to eat, drink, and fleep in their friends houfe, as often as they pleafe, paying for it only a trifling gratuity. Some ftrangers are alfo allowed a female friend upon the principles of an innocent attachment, and it is not unusual, for even the wives of the sultan, and his nobles, who are here allowed to take greater liberties than those of the vulgar, to enquire of any stranger who passes by, whether he has got a pagally or comrade, and on his answering in the negative, to send him a present of tobacco and betel, as an earnest of their friendship.

The island is divided into several principalities, each governed by its own sovereign, and for the most part, the people in each speak in a different dialect, though they are all of the same religion, which is that of Mahometanism. The Kilanoones, who inhabit the inland part of the country, are masters of the gold mines, and are also rich in bees wax, both which they exchange with the Mindanaians for foreign commodities. The Salogues, who inhabit the north west end of the island, carry on a trade with Manilla, and some other of the adjacent islands. The Altoores were formerly under the same government with the Midanaians; but were separated from them, by falling to the share of the younger children of the Sultan of Mindanao, who of late has laid claim to them again. There are several other nations, but that which is the most populous and extensive is Mindanao, whence the island derives its name, the inhabitants of which being near the sea, and engaged in commerce, are pretty much civilized.

The city of Mindanao is seated near a small river on the south side of the island, and two miles from the sea. The houses are there built upon posts, eighteen or twenty feet high, having but one floor, to which there is an ascent by a ladder; but that floor is divided into several rooms. The roof is of palm leaves, and in the space under the houses, the poorer sort of the people keep their poultry, and others empty their dirt, where it lies till the land floods carry it away.

The Sultan's houſe ſtands upon 150 great poſts, and is much higher than the reſt, with a broad ſtair-caſe leading up to it. In the hall ſtand twenty pieces of cannon, placed on field carriages. The general and other great men have alſo ſome great guns in their houſes. Their Sultan has another houſe near the former, which is not more than four feet from the ground; and here he and his council ſit croſs-legged on rich carpets, when they give audience to ambaſſadors and foreign merchants; and as no chairs are uſed in the country, the floors of the houſes are in general well matted.

The food of the common people is rice, ſagoe, and ſome ſmall fiſh; but the better ſort eat buffaloes and fowls, though a great deal of rice with them. Like the other eaſtern nations, they uſe no ſpoons, but take up their victuals in their fingers. They waſh after meals, and pour all their water upon the floor near the fire ſide, when it ſinks through; and where any are ſick, they eaſe themſelves through a hole made for that purpoſe in the floor of their bed-chamber; but thoſe who are in health perform this in the river. They are extremely fond of bathing, which is a great refreſhment in theſe hot countries; and it is not uncommon for the natives to walk into the river, ſtrip themſelves there, waſh their cloaths, put them on upon the ſame ſpot, and then walk about their buſineſs.

Almoſt every one is either a carpenter, blackſmith, or goldſmith. They build good ſerviceable ſhips both for trade and pleaſure, and deal in gold, bees-wax, and tobacco, the laſt of which is better than that of Manilla.

The moſt common diſtempers are fluxes and gripings of the guts, fevers and agues, for which the country affords ſufficient medicines, that are far from being unknown to the people. They are alfo very fubject to leprofies, which after their being cured, leave large blotches upon the fkin.

Some of the inhabitants fpeak Spanifh, for the Spaniards had formerly fome footing among them; but the Malayan tongue, and that of Mindanao, are the commoneft languages. They are afraid of the Dutch and Spaniards, and have often invited the Englifh to fettle among them.

Though the Sultan is defpotic, he is very poor, notwithftanding his having the power of commanding every private fubject's purfe at his pleafure. He was between fifty and fixty years old, and befides his fultanna, had twenty-nine concubines. When he went abroad, he was carried in a litter upon four men's fhoulders, attended by a guard of eight or ten men, but he never ventured far from the city; for the country being woody, is incommodious for travelling. He however fometimes took his pleafure upon the water in a neat veffel, built for that purpofe, in which was a cabbin made of bamboo, and divided into three rooms; in one of them he frequently repofed himfelf upon a carpet, fmall pillows being laid for his head, his women attended in the fecond, and in the third, fervants waited with tobacco and betel.

His foldiers in their wars make ufe of fwords, lances, and a weapon much like a bayonet, which all perfons from the greateft to the meaneft always wear about them. They never fight any pitched battle in the field; but make fmall wooden forts defended by guns, in which they encamp and endeavour to furprize one another by fmall parties, but they never give or take quarter.

As they are Mahometans, they have their fabbath on Friday, when the Sultan goes twice to his mofque, wherein there is a great drum with only one head, which is ftruck with a large ftick, knobbed at the end with cotton, at 12, 3, 6, and 9 of the clock, by day and night, and this serves instead of a clock.

They seldom or never circumcise their children, till they are eleven or twelve years of age, which, as it is done with great solemnity, private people keep their children till some man of quality circumcises his, and so make a general circumcision. This office is performed by a Mahometan priest, who holding the foreskin, snips it off with a pair of scissars. They keep the ramadam, like the other Turks, in August, beginning at one new moon, and continuing till they see the next; during which time, they keep a very rigorous fast till the evening, when they employ an hour in prayer, and afterwards go to supper.

Their only music is that of bells without clappers, which are commonly sixteen in number, and increase in weight from three to ten pounds; these being struck with a stick, produce an uncouth noise; for the harmony that might be produced from them, is deadened by their being placed upon a table. Mr. Dampier observed a set of these, in the house of Raja Laut, the Sultan's brother, who was both chief minister and general, and his son being about to be circumcised, gave occasion to their being used for several days together, before the performance of the ceremony. There are however women who sing, and not only dance in concert to their voices, but are joined by other people, and even the Sultan's children do not disdain to dance with them.

They have a particular aversion to swine's flesh, and will not permit any one who has touched a hog, to enter their houses, for several days after; yet there are great numbers of these animals, that run wild about the island, and which they frequently desired Captain Swan's men to destroy, but would not converse with them for several days after they had been thus defiled. The following is a remarkable inſtance of their ſuperſtition in this reſpect: Raja Laut, the Sultan's brother, once deſired to have a pair of ſhoes of one of the ſailors, but being afterwards told that they were ſewed with thread pointed with hog's briſtles, he ſent them back in a great paſſion, deſiring to have another pair ſewed in ſome other manner, and his requeſt being complied with, he appeared highly ſatisfied.

As the ſeaſon of the year was far advanced, Capt. Swan imagining he ſhould be under the neceſſity of ſtaying there ſome time, reſolved to make what intereſt he could with the Sultan, and therefore ſent Mr. Moore on ſhore, with a preſent of three yards of ſcarlet cloth, and three of ſilver lace. He had an audience granted him at about nine o'clock at night, and was very graciouſly received; the Sultan diſcourſing above an hour with him in Spaniſh, and an excellent ſupper was provided for him, and thoſe who went with him before they returned on board. Captain Swan paid the Sultan a viſit the following day, and was entertained with betel and tobacco. He was alſo ſhewn a letter from the Eaſt India company to the Sultan; for they had at that time ſome notion of building a fort there. Raja Laut being at variance with the Sultan, when Captain Swan conferred with his majeſty, was not preſent; but he waited for him on his return from court, and treated him and his men very handſomely, with fowls and boiled rice. He was a man of quick underſtanding, ſpoke and wrote Spaniſh very well, and was fond of converſing with ſtrangers, by which means he was pretty well acquainted with the cuſtoms of the Europeans. He was very friendly in his advice to Captain Swan, to whom he made an offer of his houſe, and during his ſtay upon this iſland, entertained both him and his men in a very hoſpitable manner. This great man had ſeveral wives, with each of whom he lay by turns, and with the mother of his eldeſt son, two nights running. She who was queen of the night had always a particular respect shewn to her all day, and wore a striped silk handkerchief by way of distinction.

The tempestuous weather now approaching, the sailors hauled the ship up the river, 50 or 60 fishermen lending their assistance; after which they moored her in a hole dug for that purpose, wherein she was always afloat, and here many citizens came on board of her, who soon provided the men with pagallys, and Capt. Swan being generally attended at dinner with his trumpets, Raja Laut was greatly delighted with the music.

During the wet season, the city of Mindanao, which is a mile in length, and stretches along the bank of the river, was a perfect pond, and the floods frequently washed down large pieces of timber from the country, that would have endangered the vessel, had not great care been taken to prevent it. As soon as the floods began to subside, Capt. Swan hired a warehouse, in which he deposited his goods and sails, in order to careen the ship, when it was surprising to see the multitude of worms that had eaten into her bottom, during her stay in this harbour. But having new sheathed her, they steered out on the 10th of December, when they began to take in rice, and to fill their water. But the king's brother who had his views in delaying the vessel, constantly kept several of the men on shore, hunting of black cattle, under the pretence of stocking the ship with beef. However Mr. Dampier, who made one in these excursions, observes, that in ten days they met with only four cows, none of which they were able to run down.

At this time, Captain Swan had, as our author imagines, some thoughts of quitting Mindanao, in order to take in a lading of spice, in a neighbouring island, which is since fallen into the hands of the Dutch. However, moſt of his men expected that he would have continued privateering, to which he had an utter averſion, though he carefully concealed it from his people.

The day after Chriſtmas-day, Raja Laut had a hunting match, in ſearch of black cattle, in which he was accompanied by five or ſix Engliſhmen, and all his wives: but in this hunting match, they killed but three heifers. However, he and his company got drunk two or three times, with a pleaſant extract of rice.

At this time one of the Engliſh ſailors happening accidentally to find Capt. Swan's journal, in which he had taken notice of the ſlighteſt offences of every ſailor on board, and was even laviſh of invectives againſt the whole crew in general, he ſhewed it to the reſt of his comrades, who upon this, reſolved to depoſe Capt. Swan, which they accordingly did, chuſing Mr. Read, captain in his room, and Mr. Teate, maſter; and leaving him with 36 men on ſhore, ſet ſail on the 14th of January, 1687, in order to cruize before Manilla.

Our author having ſailed from Mindanao, with the greateſt part of the crew, anchored on the 3d of February, off an iſland in 9°. 15'. on the weſt ſide of the iſland of Sebo, where they took in water, and ſcrubbed their ſhip's bottom. It is about eight or ten leagues in length, and in the middle of the bay they ſaw a great number of bats of a prodigious ſize, ſome of whoſe wings when extended, reached eight feet from tip to tip, and were edged with ſharp, crooked claws, with which they clung faſt to any thing whereon they happened to lay hold. Every night they obſerved vaſt ſwarms of theſe bats take their flight towards the great iſland, and return to the ſmall one in the morning.

On the 10th of February they weighed, and coaſting along by the weſt ſide of the Philippines, paſſed by Panga, a large iſland inhabited by the Spaniards. They there ſaw many fires, ſuppoſed to be lighted to give notice of their approach; the sight of a ship on this coast being very uncommon. On the 18th, they came to an anchor at the north end of Mindora, a large island forty leagues in length; a small brook of water ran into the sea, near the place where they were at anchor; and they saw great numbers of hogs and oxen, but they were so wild, that they could catch or kill none of them. While they were here, a canoe with four Indians came from Manilla, who told them that the harbour of Manilla was seldom without twenty or thirty vessels, belonging to the Chinese, Portuguese, and Spaniards, and that if they had a mind to carry on a clandestine trade, they would deliver their letters to certain merchants who resided there.

On the 21st, they again set sail, and two days after came to the south-east end of the island of Luconia, when they took two Spanish barks, bound from Pagassanam in this island to Manilla.

The island of Luconia or Manilla, extends six or seven degrees in length, and near the middle is sixty leagues broad. It is surrounded by many small islands, especially at the north end; the chief and the nearest to it is Mindora, which gives its name to a channel that runs between that island and Luconia*. Though this island is situated in 15°. north latitude, it is esteemed to be in general extremely healthy; and the water that is found upon it, is said to be the best in the world. It is partly composed of large plains of pasture ground, and partly of mountains, which afford some gold. It produces all the fruits of the warm climates, and the savannas or plains are well stored with buffaloes, cows, sheep, goats, hogs, and a most ex-

---

* Mr. Dampier had the greatest part of this description from Mr. Coppinger, the surgeon on board, who came to this island from the coast of Coromandel. But with his description, we have incorporated that given by Mr. Walter, in his account of Commodore Anson's voyage.

cellent breed of horses, supposed to be carried thither first from Spain. The inhabitants who live in small towns are Indians, under the Spanish jurisdiction, and instructed in the Romish religion, by the Spanish priests. It is well seated for the Indian and Chinese trade; and the bay and port of Manilla, which lie on its west side, are, perhaps, the most remarkable on the whole globe, the bay being a large circular bason, near ten leagues in diameter, great part of it entirely land locked. On the east side of this bay, stands the city of Manilla, which is large and populous, and is seated at the foot of a ridge of high hills, fronting the harbour. The houses are spacious, strong, and covered with tiles, and the streets large and regular, with a market place in the middle; and it has many handsome churches and convents. The city is well watered, and is in the neighbourhood of a fruitful and plentiful country. A considerable part of the business of this place, is its trade to Acapulco.

The time of the year being too far spent to think of trade, they resolved to sail for Pulo Condore, the chief of a knot of small islands on the coast of Cambodia, and to return in May, in order to wait for the Acapulco ship. They accordingly sailed from Luconia on the 26th of February, and on the 14th of March, came to an anchor on the north side of Pulo Condore two miles from the shore.

This island is five leagues long, and is the only one among these small islands that is inhabited. It produces several sorts of trees, among which is a very tall one, three or four feet diameter, in which the inhabitants make an horizontal incision half way through, a foot from the ground, and then cutting the upper part a-slope inwardly down, till it meets with a transverse incision, a liquor distils into a hollow, made in the semicircular stump, which, when boiled, becomes good tar, and if boiled still more, acquires the consistence of pitch, for which it is used. One of these trees affords two quarts of this juice every day, for a month together, and then drying up, recovers again.

This island also produces mangoes, a fruit about the bigness of a small peach, very juicy and pleasant, and has so fragrant a scent, as to perfume the air at some distance. Of the green fruit, a very good pickle is made, by cutting it in half, and mixing it with salt, vinegar, and cloves of garlick.

Grapes grow in this island on a straight tree, the trunk is a foot in diameter, upon which the fruit are in clusters, about the body of the tree, in the same manner as the fruit of the cocoa tree. Of these, there are both red and white grapes, which nearly resemble ours, and are of a pleasant vinous taste.

This island likewise abounds in wild nutmeg trees, of the size of our walnut trees, and the fruit, like our walnuts, grows amongst the boughs. It is, however, smaller than the true nutmeg, but though it exactly resembles it, it is without either smell or taste.

Here are several sorts of fowl, as turtle doves, pigeons, wild cocks and hens, parrots and parroquetoes; and also hogs, guanoes, and lizards; and the sea affords turtles, limpets, and muscles. There are many fresh water brooks, which for ten months in the year run into the sea. The inhabitants of the island of Polu Condore, originally came from Cochin-China, and are of a middle stature, but well shaped, and of a much darker complexion than the Mindanaians. Their hair is straight and black; their eyes are of the same colour, but small, as are their noses, though they are pretty high: they have thin lips, little mouths, and white teeth: They are very civil. But though the island is conveniently situated for carrying on a trade with Japan, China, Manilla, Tonquin, and Cochin-China, yet the natives are poor, and have no other employment than gathering the juice of the tar-tree, and making turtle oil, by boiling the fat of the turtle for that purpose, which they export to Cochin-China.

They offer their women to all strangers for a trifle, a custom which is not peculiar to these islands, since it is also used at Pegu, Siam, Cochin-China, Cambodia, and other places in the East-Indies, as well as on the coast of Guinea in Africa.

They are Pagans, and our author imagines that they worship idols in the figure of an elephant and a horse, he having observed a representation of the former, in a temple on the south of the island, and an image of the latter, on the outside. This temple stood in a small village, and was a mean edifice, built of wood.

They remained at this island from the 16th of March to the 16th of April, in which time they careened the ship, and made a fresh suit of sails out of the cloth taken on board the Spanish prize. During their stay, the people supplied them with hogs, turtle, and fruit, in exchange for which they gave them rice. They afterwards went to the north side of the island, to take in fresh water. They then sailed for the bay of Siam, which they entered on the 24th of April, and afterwards steered to Pulo Ubi, where they had touched in their passage. Here they found two vessels at anchor, laden with lacquer, used in japanning: They were bound from Champa to Malacca, and had 40 brisk sociable sailors on board, armed with lances, swords and some guns.

On the 21st of May they returned to Pulo Condore, where they found a small bark at anchor, when Capt. Read sending a canoe to hail her, charged his men not to venture on board, without having firſt made friends of the people, whom he ſuſpected to be Malayans; diſregarding his orders, they boarded her without ceremony; but were ſoon obliged to retreat, being attacked with creſſets, a kind of bayonets, ſo that they were obliged to leap into the ſea, and to ſecure their eſcape by ſwimming; and it is very remarkable, that one Daniel Wallis ſwam for ſome minutes, till he was taken up, though he had never practiſed it before, nor was ever able to repeat it again. In revenge for this treatment, Capt. Read ſent two canoes filled with men well armed, to chaſtiſe the Malayans in the bark; but having firſt cut a hole in the bottom of the veſſel, they ſunk her, and then eſcaped into the woods.

On the 4th of June 1687, they weighed from Pulo Condore, intending to cruize of Manilla, but the eaſt wind continuing five or ſix days together with great violence, brought them near the coaſt of China; and on the 26th, they came to anchor on the north-eaſt end of St. John's iſland, in $22°. 30'$. north latitude.

The ſhore of this laſt iſland is for the moſt part covered with trees; the ſoil is in general fertile, and affords good paſture, and there are ſome groves ſcattered about the inland parts. Bullocks, buffaloes, goats, and China hogs abound here. Theſe laſt are all black, with ſmall heads, thick necks, very ſhort legs, and great bellies, which ſweep the ground. But though there are no wild fowl, there are plenty of tame ducks, cocks, and hens. The natives live for the moſt part by cultivating the earth, which produces rice. They are tall, ſtraight bodied men, with long viſages, and tawny complexions; they have high foreheads, ſmall eyes, aquiline noſes, black hair, and ſtraggling beards. They were formerly very proud of their hair; but when the Tartars made a conqueſt of China, they obliged them to ſhave their heads, reſerving only one lock on the crown, which they suffered to grow to a great length, generally platting it, though sometimes they let it flow loose. They never wear a covering for their head, but instead of it, use an umbrella; or if they have but a little way to go, they make use of a large fan; they wear slippers on their feet, but no stockings; and their covering is a light frock and breeches. The women of any distinction, like those on the continent of China, cannot walk far on account of the smallness of their feet, which are swathed up tight in their infancy, to prevent their growing, small feet being esteemed a great beauty. They work very well at their needles, and are curious in embroidering their shoes; but the poorer sort of women wear neither shoes nor stockings, and their feet are suffered to grow larger that they may have it in their power to earn their bread.

In the island of St. John is a small town built upon posts, in a marshy ground, but the houses are mean, low, and ill-furnished. While they were here at anchor, a Chinese junk lay near them; she was flat, both at the head and stern, had little huts on her deck three feet high, covered with palmetto leaves, and a large cabbin with an altar and a lamp burning in it. The hold was divided into several partitions, each of them so tight, that if a leak should spring in one, the goods in the next would receive no damage. Every merchant had his particular room, where he stowed his goods and sometimes lodged in it himself. These junks have only a mainmast and foremast, the former with the sail narrow aloft, like that of a sloop; and the latter has a square sail, and square yard. In fair weather they also use a topsail, which they haul down on the deck in foul weather, yard and all. The mainmasts of the largest junks, are as big as any of our third rate men of war, and not pierced, being all of one tree.

On the 3d of July, perceiving all the signs of an approaching storm, they hastily weighed anchor, and made what haste they could out to sea, with a view of having sufficient room, and at about eleven at night, the wind coming to the north-east, they had a most violent tempest, which lasted till about four in the morning, when the hopes of the men were revived, by seeing a Corpus Sanctum upon the main-mast, which they considered as a fore-runner of good weather, yet had this been upon deck, the superstitious sailors would have considered it as a sign of their destruction. The Corpus Sanctum is a small glittering meteor resembling a star, and is frequently seen dancing about a ship in hard weather.

About eleven o'clock the following day, there was a flat calm, after which, the storm returned with more violence than ever, and lasted by intervals till the 6th, when the weather proved very serene; but the men being extremely terrified by this last storm, and dreading the approaching full-moon, resolved to steer towards the Piscadores or Fisher Islands, in 23°. north latitude. These are a good number of islands that lie between the island of Pormosa, and the continent of China. Betwixt the two eastern-most is a good harbour, where they cast anchor; and on the west side of the latter is a large town, with a fort that commands the harbour, defended by a garrison of 300 Tartars. The houses are low, but neatly built. Some of the men going on shore, were carried before the governor, who being informed that they were English who intended to trade, used them in a very friendly manner, told them that he would give them assistance, but that they must not pretend to trade there, it being absolutely forbidden. He however sent a present to the captain, of a small jar of flour, some cakes of fine bread, about a dozen of pine apples, and a few water melons. The next day, an officer who made a very grand appearance, came on board with a loose coat, with breeches and boots of black silk, and a black silk cap, upon which was a plume of black and white feathers, bringing on board a present from the governor, of a very fine fat heifer, four goats, two large hogs, twenty large flat cakes of bread, two baskets of flour, two jars of sam-shu, or arrack, and fifty-five jars of hoc-shu, a strong pleasant liquor extracted from wheat, resembling mum. Captain Read, in return for these presents, sent the governor a gold chain, an English carabine, and a curious Spanish silver hilted rapier, and caused the nobleman to be saluted with three guns at his passing over the ship's side.

On the 29th of July, they left the Piscadores, and steered for some islands between Formosa and Luconia, known by no other name than the Five Isles; and on the 6th of August came to an anchor on the east side of the northern-most, in 20°. 20'. north latitude. They imagined that these islands were uninhabited; but, to their great surprise, they found three large populous towns, on the east side of this last island, all within a league of the sea. To one of these islands they gave the name of Prince of Orange island: This is about eight leagues long and two broad. To the northern-most, which is four leagues long, and a league and a half wide, Mr. Dampier gave the name of Grafton, in honour of the duke of Grafton, in whose family his wife then lived; and to a third, which lies south of Grafton island, they gave the name of Monmouth island, in honour of the duke of Monmouth. This last island is three leagues long and one broad; these were the largest of the number. One of the others they called Bashee, from a pleasant liquor of that name; and the other they termed Goat-island, from the number of goats they saw upon it.

Though Orange-island is the largest of the five, it is uninhabited on acount of its being rocky and barren, but Grafton and Monmouth islands contain many people; and there is one town in Goat-island.

The hills of these islands are rocky, but the vallies have plenty of grafs, and are well watered with fresh running streams. They produce pine-apples plantains, bananas, sugar-canes, cotton, pompions, and potatoes, and are well stored with goats and hogs.

The natives are of a dark copper colour, and are short and squat, with round faces, low foreheads, and thick eyebrows. Their eyes are of an hazle colour, and small, but much bigger than those of the Chinese; they have short noses; their lips and mouths are of a middle size; they have white teeth, and black thick lank hair, which they crop short, scarcely permitting it to cover their ears. They go always bareheaded, and the men have no other clothes but a cloth about their middle, and some of them a jacket made of a plaintain leaf, which is as rough as a bear's skin. The women have, however, a short petticoat of coarse callico, of their own making, which reaches a little below their knees. But both sexes wear ear-rings made of a pale yellow metal, resembling gold, which they dig out of the mountains. Mr. Dampier acknowledges that he did not know whether it was really that valuable metal or not; but observes, that though it looked at first of a fine colour, it afterwards fades; which made the people on board suspect it, and prevented their purchasing much of it. Their rings and other ornaments, made of this metal, the natives rub over with a paste of red earth, then throw them into a quick fire, till they are red hot, in which condition they throw them into water to cool, and then rubbing off the paste, they appear of a beautiful lustre.

Their houses are small, and scarcely five feet high, made with small posts, wattled with boughs. At one end of them they have a fire place, near which are boards, whereon they lie to sleep on the ground. They live together in small villages, built on the sides of rocky hills, three or four rows one above another. These precipices are said to be framed by nature alone into different degrees, or, as it were, deep steps or stories: upon each of which they build a row of their houses, each row being above the other, and to these rows they ascend by ladders set in the middle from one row to another, which being drawn up, there is no possibility of climbing to attack them; and to prevent their being assaulted from above, they chuse a situation where the back of the rock forms a steep precipice next the sea. There is a kind of a street to every row of houses, which runs parallel with the tops of the houses in the row beneath.

These people are very ingenious, for they understand the use of iron, work it themselves, and build very neat boats, which resemble our yawls. They have also larger vessels, managed with twelve or fourteen oars. The women manage the affairs of husbandry, while the men employ themselves in fishing. With respect to their food, they make a dish of locusts, which at certain seasons of the year come to devour their plants. These they catch in nets, and afterwards broil or bake them in an earthen pan; and this dish is not ill tasted. Their ordinary drink is water; but they have a liquor, which in taste and colour resembles English beer, and this is made of the sugar-cane, boiled and mixed with blackberries, which they afterwards put into jars, and let it work for five or six days, when it becomes a strong and pleasant liquor, and is called bashee. Their language has no affinity either with the Chinese or Malayan; but our author obferves, that bullawar, which fignifies gold among the Indians of the Philippine iflands, is the name they give to the yellow metal already mentioned.

The only arms ufed by thefe people are lances, headed with iron. They wear a kind of armour made of a buffaloe's fkin, which reaches down to the calves of their legs, and has fleeves; it is at the bottom pretty wide, but comes clofe about the fhoulders, and is as ftiff as a board. Mr. Dampier could perceive nothing like religion amongft them, or any thing like civil government; there feeming to be no man above the reft, except in his own family, for children behaved with great refpect to their parents. Yet they appeared to have fome fort of laws; for during our author's ftay there, he faw a young man buried alive, as he fuppofed for theft. Each man has but one wife, who treats him with refpect. The boys are educated to fifhing, and the girls work with their mothers in the plantations, which are in the valleys, where every perfon plants as much ground as is fufficient for the neceffities of the family. They are a civil, quiet people, both to ftrangers, and among themfelves, and though there was fometimes occafion for it, they never quarrelled with the Englifh, while they were there. They have no coin; but part with their yellow metal in grains by guefs.

When the fhip firft came to an anchor, the natives had fo little fufpicion of being injured, that above 100 boats came round the veffel, and thofe who rowed them made no fcruple of going on board; during all the time they ftayed there, they plentifully fupplied the men with hogs and goats, difpofing of a hog of fourfcore pounds weight, for two or three pounds of iron, and a good fat goat for an old iron hoop; befides a great quantity of yams, potatoes, and bashee, for old nails, spikes, and leaden bullets.

While they continued at these islands, a violent storm arose, which drove them out to sea, and they were several weeks exposed to the violence of the tempest, before they could get back to the bashee island. This last storm so discouraged the men, that they resolved to lay aside the design of cruising before Manilla, and they were now more inclined to steer to England, than to undertake any other enterprize. However, they were induced by the persuasions of Captain Read to steer for Comorin. But as the eastern monsoon was at hand, our author observes, that their nearest and best way would have been to have passed through the streights of Malacca; but Mr. Teate persuaded them to go round to the east of the Philippines, and keeping south of the spice islands, to pass into the Indian ocean about the island of Timor.

On the 3d of October they sailed from these islands to the south, and on the 16th came to an anchor between two islands that lie to the south-east of Mindanao, where they hauled their ship on shore to clean her bottom, and made for her a fore-top-mast, a fore-yard, a boltsprit, and a new pump.

While they lay here, a young prince belonging to one of the adjacent spice islands came on board, and told them that Capt. Swan and some of his men were still in the city of Mindanao, where they were highly esteemed for the great services they had performed in fighting against the Alfoores. As they were now so near him, Mr. Dampier attempted to persuade some of the men to submit to his command; but this coming to Capt. Read's knowledge, he took effectual measures to prevent it. They were however afterwards informed, that most of Mr. Swan's men got off in different ships; but that himself and the surgeon, going on board a Dutch vessel in that road, were overset by the natives, and drowned ; and that there was reafon to fufpect that this was done by Raja Laut's order, as well for the fake of fome gold the captain had in his poffeffion, and which fell into his hands at Mr. Swan's death, as in revenge for his having uttered fome few flighting expreffions againft him.

On the 2d of November. Capt. Read left thefe iflands, fteering a fouth-eaft courfe, and on the 22d, ftanding three leagues to the fouthward of the ifland of Celebes, they perceived a large proa, in which were 60 men, attended by fix fmaller ones, whom they ftrove in vain to allure on board, by fhewing them Dutch colours. On this coaft they found cockles of fo extraordinary a fize, that the meat of one of them was fufficient to ferve feven or eight people.

On the 6th of December, Mr. Read came to an anchor in an harbour on the eaft fide of the ifland of Bouton, in 4°. 54'. fouth latitude. This ifland is twenty-five leagues in length, and four in breadth. Within a league of the harbour, and half a mile from the fea, is a long town called Callafufung, feated on the top of a fmall hill, in a pleafant plain, enclofed with a wall of cocoa trees, and beyond thefe with a ftrong ftone wall. The inhabitants are not unlike the Mindanaians, though they are more cleanly. They are Mahometans, and fpeak the Malayan tongue. They are governed by a Sultan, who hearing that the fhip was Englifh, came on board attended by fome of his nobles, and three of his fons, and affured Capt. Read, that he was at liberty to trade with his fubjects for whatever he pleafed, and that he was ready to ferve him to the utmoft of his power. Mr. Read caufed him to be faluted with five guns on his coming on board, and on his returning on fhore, with the fame number. The natives readily brought fowls, eggs, potatoes, and other provifions on board; and the following day Capt. Read, by invitation, visited the sultan in his palace, which is a very neat building. He was received in a room on the ground floor, covered with mats, after his having first passed through a lane of forty naked soldiers, armed with lances; and in this apartment was entertained with cocoa nuts, betel and tobacco. The sultan some time after made him a present of a boy, each of whose jaws had two rows of teeth, and of two he-goats. Rice and potatoes were in great plenty upon this island, as were also several kinds of beautiful birds, particularly parrokeets, whose feathers are beautifully coloured, and cockadores, a bird as white as snow, with a bunch of feathers upon his head like a crown, and in other respects resembling a parrot.

They staid here till the 12th, when attempting to weigh, they broke their cable and lost their anchor, which had hooked on a rock. However, they got clear of the numerous shoals about these islands, and on the 20th passed by Ombra, which in some maps is called Pentara, where they saw thick smokes by day and large fires by night; but though there is a good town contiguous to the sea, on the north side of the island, the weather would not permit their standing in for it.

Having got clear of all the islands on the 27th, they steered for New Holland, which they fell in with on the 4th of January, 1688, in latitude 16°. 50'. south, and running along to the east twelve leagues, came to a point of land, to the east of which they anchored on the 5th.

The land is dry and sandy, and that part had no fresh water, except what was got by digging; many sorts of trees are seen growing in the country, at a distance from each other, with pretty long grass under them, among which is one that produces gum dragon, or dragon's blood; they however found no kind of fruit, nor so much as the tract of any brute beast, except one, which seemed to be the footstep of an animal like that of a large mastiff dog. There are also very few fowls or small birds, and the sea seems to be almost destitute of fish, except the manatees and turtle, of which there are great plenty.

The inhabitants appear to be destitute of all the accommodations and comforts of life, they have no houses or coverings but the heavens; no garments except a piece of the bark of a tree, tied like a girdle round the waist; no sheep or poultry; and neither boats nor iron to procure them better accommodations; their only food appears to be a small sort of fish, which is brought in with every tide, and left in stone wiers, built upon the shore for that purpose at low water.

They are tall, slender, straight, and strong limbed, with great heads, round foreheads, and large eye-brows. They have also thick limbs, wide mouths, bottle noses, black woolly hair, and a very dark complexion. They have no beards, and it is remarkable that the two fore-teeth of the upper jaw are wanting both in men and women. But whether this is a natural defect, or that they are pulled out by way of ornament, our author does not pretend to determine. There seemed to be no particular connections between the sexes, nor any such thing as marriage, for to appearance they lived in common; and Mr. Dampier could not discover whether they had either religion or government; but as neither he, nor any one on board, could understand a single word of their language, it is not improbable that he might be mistaken in several of these conjectures. Their only weapons are wooden lances, formed of a straight pole made sharp and hardened at the end, and wooden swords.

These poor people were dreadfully frightened at the appearance of the ship's crew on their coast; but their fears subsided, on finding that they had no intention to injure them. Some of the failors endeavoured to prevail with them by giving them clothes, to lend their affiftance in taking in a fupply of water; but they could find no means of making themfelves underftood; for the natives grinned at each other, examined the clothes with feeming amazement, and then laid them down on the ground.

On the 12th of March they left this coaft, in order to fteer for Cape Comorin, and on the 28th, caft anchor at a fmall woody ifland, in 10°. 30'. fouth latitude, where they watered, and caught a great number of boobies and land crabs. On the 12th of April they reached the ifland of Trieft, which is not above a mile in circumference, but fo very low, that it is quite overflowed by the tide at flood, and yet it bears great plenty of cocoa nuts, with which they ftocked themfelves, and here took a quantity of fifh; and two young alligators. This place they left on the 18th, and on the 29th took a proa at anchor, with four men on board, whom Mr. Read took prifoners, after having feized their cargo, which confifted of cocoa nuts and oil, and funk the veffel, to prevent Mr. Dampier and fome others from making their efcape.

On the 5th of May, they came to an anchor at the north-weft end of the ifland of Nicobar, the moft foutherly of a clufter of iflands, to which it gives name. The chief commodities of which are ambergrife and fruit, which are brought on board fuch fhips as come into the road, by the natives.

This ifland, which is 12 leagues in length, and three or four in breadth, is fituated in 7°. 30. north latitude. It enjoys a fertile foil, is well watered, and forms a very agreeable landfcape from the fea. The natives are tall, well limbed, and of a dark copper-colour complexion, with black eyes, well proportioned nofes, long faces, and lank black hair. The women have no eye-brows, and probably pluck off the hair with a view of rendering themselves more agreeable.

Their houses, which are raised upon posts eight feet from the ground, consist but of one room, and are neatly thatched with palmetto leaves. They have no appearance of any settled government amongst them, every person appearing upon an equal footing. They are dispersed about the island, and there are seldom found above four or five houses together. They have a few small hogs, some cocks and hens, and plaintains; but neither rice, yams, nor potatoes. They use proas, which hold twenty or thirty men, and make use of oars as we do, sitting upon benches made of spilt bamboo.

Here Capt. Read took in a fresh supply of water, and ordered the men to heel the ship, in order to clean her. While they were here, Mr. Dampier got leave of Capt. Read to go on shore, with his chest and bedding, and Mr. Hall and Mr. Ambrose being also desirous of leaving this profligate and unruly crew, came on shore with him. The place where they landed had but two houses, the master of one of which by signs invited Mr. Dampier to enter, intimating, that in the darkness of the night he might be exposed to some danger from wild beasts in the woods. Mr. Coppinger, the surgeon, was very desirous of following their example, but was prevented by force. However, the pilot they had brought from Pulo Condore, and the four men who had been taken in the proa, were also left upon the island. The above pilot being a Portuguese, and understanding the Malayan, and other Indian tongues, was an useful member of this little community.

About twelve o'clock at night Mr. Read got under sail, when those on shore laid down to sleep, which they did not dare to do before, lest he should have revoked his leave, and have difpatched fome of his men to take them on board by force; and indeed he would fcarcely have permitted them to have ftaid there, if he had imagined that they could find the means of leaving the ifland.

Early in the morning Mr. Dampier was vifited by his kind hoft, accompanied by four or five of his friends, bringing with him a large calabafh of toddy. Though the Indian was at firft furprized to fee the number of his guefts fo much encreafed, he foon appeared perfectly fatisfied, and fold them a proa for an axe, which one of them had catched up and privately brought away with him, knowing it to be a good commodity among the Indians. This proa was as large as a wherry, but they no fooner got on board her, with all their effects, but it overfet with them, and it took them up three days in drying their papers, and the other goods contained in their chefts. However, with the affiftance of fome Achin failors, they foon fet her to rights, and fitted her with a good maft and balance-logs, or out-liggers,* and then fteered for the eaft fide of the ifland, followed by the inhabitants, in eight or ten canoes; but they were frighted away by Mr. Hall, who fearing that fuch a large company would increafe the price of provifions, fired a gun over their heads, which had like to have produced very ill confequences; for the Achin men, who were their moft ufeful hands, were fo terrified that they leaped out of the canoe, and it was fome time before they could be perfuaded to believe that no harm was intended them, and it fo intimidated the inhabitants that they brought them no provifions, which they ufed to purchafe for fmall ftripes of cloth and old rags.

---

* See an accurate defcription of thefe proas, in Commodore Anfon's Voyage.

Now the inhabitants every where appeared to oppofe their landing; but in a day or two Mr. Dampier and Mr. Hall, leaping on fhore in the fight of great numbers of them, foon made peace by fhaking them by the hand, upon which they were as plentifully fupplied with provifions as ufual. Thefe confifted of mallories, the pulp of which being taken from the rind and the core, and preffed together, may be preferved fix or feven days: Some hens, and a few cocoas, with fome large cocoa-nut fhells, filled with about eight gallons of water. With only thefe fea ftores, they left Nicobar on the 15th of May, 1688, fteering directly towards Achin.

On the 18th the fky became overfpread, and a halo or bright circle encompaffing the fun, made them apprehend an approaching ftorm; and indeed the tempeft was foon fo violent, that they expected every moment to be fwallowed up by the fea. However, on the 19th in the morning, after having been dreadfully buffeted by a tempeft of wind, rain, thunder, and lightening, they to their great joy heard one of their Achin men cry Pulo-Way, which is an ifland fituated near the north-weft end of Sumatra; but about noon they difcovered that the high land they had miftaken for that ifland proved the golden mountain of Sumatra; the next day, fteering for the fhore, they came to an anchor near the mouth of a river, thirty-fix leagues to the eaft of Achin, and being half dead with the fatigues of the voyage, were conducted to a fmall fifhing town near the river, where they were kindly treated by the inhabitants, and ftaid till June; but finding that they recovered their health but flowly, they refolved to make the beft of their way to the Englifh factory at Achin; for which purpofe they were provided with a proa, that carried them thither in three days, where they were received with great hofpitality, and treated in a very friendly manner by Mr. Dennis Driscol, who was in the service of the East-Inda Company, and served as an interpreter between them and the Sabander, or chief magistrate.

Here Mr. Dampier contracted an acquaintance with Captain Bowrey, who would have persuaded him to sail with him to Persia, in quality of boatswain; but he declined accepting of this proposal, on account of the ill state of his health. However, Mr. Hall and Mr. Ambrose entered on board Mr. Bowrey's ship, and afterwards Mr. Dampier engaged with Captain Weldon, under whom he made several trading voyages, for upwards of fifteen months, and afterwards entered as a gunner to an English factory at Bencoolen; but quitted the employment five months after, from a dislike to the governor of the fort.

Upon this coast he stayed till the year 1691, and then embarked for England, on board the Defence, Captain Heath commander, when he was obliged to make his escape by creeping through one of the port-holes; for the governor had revoked his promise of allowing him to depart, but he brought off his journal and most valuable papers.

On the 25th of January, 1691, Captain Heath sailed in company with three other ships, but had not been long at sea before a fatal distemper raged on board, which was attributed to the badness of the water that was taken in at Bencoolen, during the land floods, when it is often impregnated with the tinctures of poisonous roots or herbs. Upon this occasion, Captain Heath behaved extremely well; for he not only constantly kept watch himself, but supplied the men with some of his own tamarinds; for the most effectual remedy they could discover was, mixing this fruit with the rice they eat. By this distemper they lost above thirty of their men, and had scarce so many left as were sufficient to bring them to the Cape of Good Hope: but by the assistance of a Dutch captain and his men, they came to an anchor there in the beginning of April, when they were set on shore, and supplied with beef, mutton, and other refreshments.

Here Mr. Dampier also landed with the painted prince that had been given him by one Mr. Moody, who had bought him and his mother at Mindanao, and afterwards went with Mr. Dampier to Bencoolen, when, at parting, he gave him half the share in this painted man and his mother, and left them in his custody. They were born in the island of Meangis, which, as he told our author, abounds in gold, cloves, and nutmegs. He was curiously painted on the breast, betwixt his shoulders, and on the back, but most of all on the fore part of the thighs, after the manner of flower work. This Mr. Dampier understood was performed by pricking the skin, and then rubbing into it a gum, which flows from a tree called damurer, used in some parts of the Indies instead of pitch; and he told Mr Dampier, that those of his country wore golden ear-rings and bracelets about their arms and legs, and that their food was fowl, fish and potatoes. As to his captivity, he said, that as one day he, his father and mother, were going in a canoe to one of the adjacent islands, they were taken by some of the Mindanaian fishermen, who sold them all to Raja Laut's interpreter, with whom he and his mother lived five years as slaves, and then were sold for sixty dollars to Mr. Moody. Some time afterwards Mr. Moody made Mr. Dampier a present of his other share in them; but the mother died soon after; and our author had much ado to save the son's life.

By the above sickness, Capt. Heath's ship was so thinned, that he was obliged to accept of the service of some Dutch sailors, who privately deferted to him from other ſhips, either for the ſake of profit, or of ſpeedily returning to England.

After ſtaying here ſix weeks, they left the Cape on the 23d of May; on the 20th of June they arrived at St. Helena, and ſailing from thence on the 2d of July, anchored in the Downs on the 16th of September, 1691. Mr. Dampier after his arrival in the Thames, being in want of money, ſold at firſt part of his property in the painted Prince, and by degrees all the reſt After which this Indian was carried about for a ſight, and ſhewn for money, but at laſt died of the ſmall pox at Oxford.

END OF THE SECOND VOLUME.

PRINTED BY JOHN THOMPSON.

www.ingramcontent.com/pod-product-compliance
Lightning Source LLC
Chambersburg PA
CBHW022057300426
44117CB00007B/499